W9-AWJ-597

FROMMER'S

COMPREHENSIVE TRAVEL GUIDE

Toronto

3rd Edition

by Marilyn Wood

MACMILLAN • USA

ABOUT THE AUTHOR

Marilyn Wood came to the United States from England to study journalism at Columbia University. The former editorial director of Prentice Hall Travel, she has also worked as a reporter, ranch hand, press officer and book reviewer. In addition, Marilyn is the author of *Marilyn Wood's Wonderful Weekends* and *Frommer's London from $55 a Day* and the co-author of *Frommer's Canada*.

MACMILLAN TRAVEL

A Simon & Schuster Macmillan Company
15 Columbus Circle
New York, NY 10023

Copyright © 1995 by Simon & Schuster, Inc.

All rights reserved. No part of this book may be reproduced or transmitted in any form or by any means, electronic or mechanical, including photocopying, recording, or by any information storage and retrieval system, without permission in writing from the Publisher.

Macmillan is a registered trademark of Macmillan, Inc.

ISBN 0-02-860066-5

ISSN 1047-7853

Editor: Erica Spaberg

Map Editor: Douglas Stallings

Design by Michele Laseau

Maps by Ortelius Design

SPECIAL SALES

Bulk purchases (10+ copies) of Frommer's travel guides are available to corporations at special discounts. The Special Sales Department can produce custom editions to be used as premiums and/or for sales promotion to suit individual needs. Existing editions can be produced with custom cover imprints such as corporate logos. For more information write to Special Sales, Simon & Schuster, 1230 Avenue of the Americas, New York, NY 10020.

Manufactured in the United States of America

List of Maps

Contents

What the Symbol Means

⭐ **FROMMER'S FAVORITES**—Hotels, restaurants, attractions, and entertainments you should not miss

Abbreviations in Hotel & Other Listings

The following symbols refer to the standard amenities available in all rooms:

A/C   air-conditioning
MINIBAR   refrigerator stocked with beverages and snacks
TEL   telephone
TV   television

The following abbreviations are used for credit or charge cards:

AE   American Express
CB   Carte Blanche
DC   Diners Club
DISC   Discover
ER   enRoute
EU   Eurocard
MC   MasterCard
V   Visa

Trip Planning with this Guide
USE THE FOLLOWING FEATURES:

Calendar of Events   To plan your itinerary or to see what to avoid

Easy-to-Read Maps   Walking tours, city sights, hotel and restaurant locations—all referring to or keyed to the text

Fast Facts   All the essentials at a glance: climate, currency, embassies, emergencies, information, safety, taxes, tipping, and more

Suggested Itineraries   For seeing the city and environs

What Things Cost In   To help you plan your daily budget

What's Special About Checklist   A summary of the city's highlights

OTHER SPECIAL FROMMER FEATURES

Did You Know . . . ?   Offbeat, fun facts

Family-Friendly Hotels

Family-Friendly Restaurants

Famous Torontonians   The city's greats

Impressions   What others have said

An Invitation to the Reader

In researching this book, I discovered many wonderful places—hotels, restaurants, shops, and more. I'm sure you'll find others. Please tell us about them, so we can share the information with your fellow travelers in upcoming editions. If you were disappointed with a recommendation, we'd love to know that, too. Please write to:

Marilyn Wood
Frommer's Toronto
c/o Macmillan Travel
15 Columbus Circle
New York, NY 10023

An Additional Note

Please be advised that travel information is subject to change at any time—and this is especially true of prices. We therefore suggest that you write or call ahead for confirmation when making your travel plans. The authors, editors, and publisher cannot be held responsible for the experiences of readers while traveling. Your safety is important to us, however, so we encourage you to stay alert and be aware of your surroundings. Keep a close eye on cameras, purses, and wallets, all favorite targets of thieves and pickpockets.

1

Introducing Toronto

Oɴᴄᴇ ɪᴛ ᴡᴀꜱ ʟᴀᴍᴘᴏᴏɴᴇᴅ ᴀꜱ ᴅᴜʟʟ ᴀɴᴅ ᴜɢʟʏ, ᴀ ᴄɪᴛʏ ᴡʜᴏꜱᴇ ɪɴʜᴀʙɪᴛᴀɴᴛꜱ fled to Buffalo for a good time and where the blinds were drawn on Sunday at the main department store (Eaton's) to stop anyone from the sinful practice of window-shopping. But Toronto, now with a population of over three million, has burst forth during the last three decades from its stodgy past and grabbed attention as one of the most exciting cities on the North American continent.

How did it happen? Unlike most cities, Toronto got a chance to change its image with a substantial transfusion from other cultures. Once a quiet, conservative community dominated by sedate Anglo-Saxons, who entertained either at home or in their clubs, Toronto was given a huge infusion of energy by the post–World War II influx of large numbers of Italians, Chinese, and Portuguese, as well as Germans, Jews, Hungarians, Greeks, East Indians, West Indians, and French Canadians. Now the city, a multicultural patchwork quilt, throbs with life as people flock to Harbourfront and the Ontario Science Centre, crowd aboard the ferries to the Islands in summer, gather at cafés and restaurants, shop the boutiques, attend the theater, and generally fill the city with life and movement— ad infinitum.

And somehow, although some residents would disagree, Toronto has become a model city where conservative traditions have managed to temper the often runaway impulse of developers and businesspeople to destroy the old in order to create the new. In Toronto progress has not inevitably brought in the wrecker's ball. Much has survived. When you see Holy Trinity Church and the Scadding House, one of the oldest residences in the city, standing proudly against the glass-galleried Eaton Centre, preserved because the people demanded it, you know that certain values and a great deal of thoughtful debate have gone into the making of this city.

Jane Jacobs, the urban planner, historian, and sociologist, chose to live here to watch her theories actually working on the downtown streets—where people walk to work from their restored Victorian town houses, where no developer can erect downtown commercial space without including living space, where the subway positively gleams and the streets are safe. In Toronto, old buildings are saved and converted to other uses; architects design around the contours of nature instead of just bulldozing the trees, and 200 parks invite you to ᴘʟᴇᴀꜱᴇ ᴡᴀʟᴋ ᴏɴ ᴛʜᴇ ɢʀᴀꜱꜱ. Through the efforts of residents like Jane Jacobs and others, this exciting, vibrant city has retained the traditional Canadian values of peace, order, and good government.

1   The City's Past

Dateline

■ **1615** Etienne Brûlé travels the Toronto Trail.

➤

FROM FUR TRADING POST TO MUDDY YORK   As with most cities, geography, trade, and communications are the influences that have shaped Toronto and its history. Although the city today

What's Special About Toronto

Beaches

- Wards Island and Centre Island beaches and the boardwalk and lakefront at the Beaches.

Architectural Highlights

- City Hall (1965), symbol of Toronto's rebirth.
- SkyDome (1989), the world's first stadium with a fully retractable roof.
- Underground City, five miles of interconnecting tunnels lined with 1,000 stores.
- Flatiron Building (1892), as photogenic as ever at Church and Front.
- Provincial Parliament Buildings, great Romanesque architecture in pink sandstone.

Museums

- The Royal Ontario Museum, with its Chinese and Canadiana collections.
- The Art Gallery, with the world's largest collection of Henry Moore works.
- Ontario Science Centre, with hundreds of engaging interactive exhibits that wow kids and adults alike.

Events/Festivals

- Caribana, carnival Toronto style.
- Royal Agricultural Show, a serious "state fair" plus a horse show attended by royals.

For Kids

- Ontario Science Centre, Harbourfront, Ontario Place, and Metro Zoo are the top hits.

Shopping

- The Eaton Centre, 300-plus stores in attractive glass-domed marble-and-fountain ambience.
- Bloor/Yorkville, whose designer boutiques, art galleries, and cafés make it prime shopping and strolling territory.

Streets/Neighborhoods

- Chinatown, a large bustling community with great shopping, browsing, and dining.
- Queen Street West, youthful, funky, and fun with lots of reasonably priced, sophisticated dining.

Natural Spectacles

- The Toronto Islands, a great escape from the urban landscape that's only a short ferry trip away.

Metropolitan Toronto

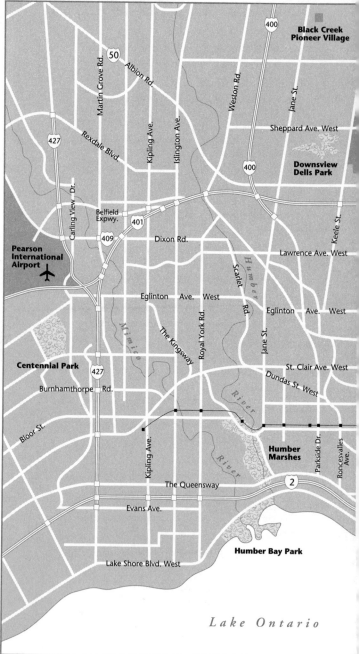

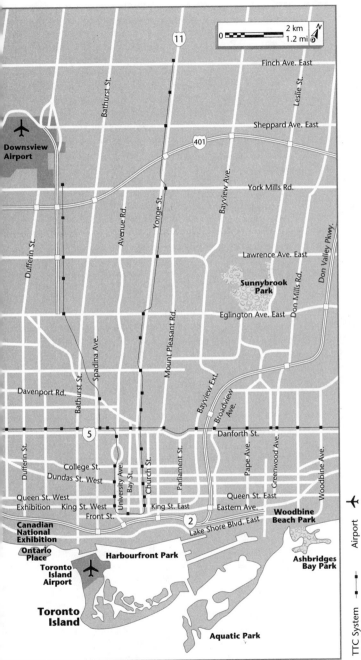

Finch Ave. East

Leslie St.

Bathurst St.

Sheppard Ave. East

Downsview Airport

401

Avenue Rd.

Yonge St.

Bayview Ave.

York Mills Rd.

Dufferin St.

Lawrence Ave. East

Sunnybrook Park

Don Mills Rd.

Don Valley Pkwy.

Eglington Ave. East

Davenport Rd.

Bathurst St.

Spadina Ave.

Mount Pleasant Rd.

Bayview Ext.

Broadview Ave.

5

Danforth St.

Dufferin St.

College St.

Dundas St. West

University Ave.

Bay St.

Church St.

Parliament St.

Pape Ave.

Greenwood Ave.

Woodbine Ave.

Queen St. West

Exhibition

King St. West

Front St.

King St. East

Queen St. East

Eastern Ave.

Woodbine Beach Park

Canadian National Exhibition

2

Lake Shore Blvd. East

Ontario Place

Toronto Island Airport

Harbourfront Park

Ashbridges Bay Park

Toronto Island

Aquatic Park

TTC System ▪▪▪▪   Airport ✈

Dateline

- **1720** France establishes post at Toronto.
- **1751** Fort Rouille built.
- **1763** Treaty of Paris effectively ends French rule in Canada.
- **1787** Lord Dorchester, British governor of Québec, purchases land from Scarborough to Etobicoke from the Mississauga tribe.
- **1791** British colony of Upper Canada formed.
- **1793** Governor of Upper Canada, Col. John Simcoe, arrives and names settlement York.
- **1796** Yonge Street laid out, a 33-mile ox-cart trail.
- **1797** Center of government transferred from Niagara to York.
- **1813** War of 1812: Americans invade, blow up Fort York, and burn Parliament buildings.
- **1820s** Immigration of Nonconformists and Irish Catholics fosters reform politics.
- **1824** William Lyon Mackenzie starts the *Colonial Advocate.*
- **1828** Erie Canal extended to Oswego on Lake Ontario.
- **1830s** Orange Order becomes

➤

possesses a downtown core, it also sprawls across a large area—a gift of geography, for there are no physical barriers to stop it. Initially, the flat broad plain rising from Lake Ontario to an inland ridge of hills (around St. Clair Avenue today) and stretching between the Don River in the east and the Humber in the west made an ideal location for a settlement.

Native Canadians had long stopped here at the entrance to the Toronto Trail—a short route between the Lower and Upper Lakes. French fur trader Etienne Brûlé was the first European to travel this trail in 1615, but it wasn't until 1720 that the first trading post, known as Fort Toronto, was established by the French to intercept the furs that were being taken across Lake Ontario to New York State by English rivals. This trading post was replaced in 1751 by Fort Rouille, which was built on the site of today's CNE grounds. When the 1763 Treaty of Paris ended the Anglo-French War after the fall of Québec, French rule in North America was effectively ended and the city's French antecedents were all but forgotten.

Only 20 miles across the lake from the U.S., Toronto has always been affected by what happens south of the border. When the American Revolution established a powerful and potentially hostile new nation, Toronto's location became strategically more important, or it certainly seemed so to John Graves Simcoe, lieutenant-governor of the newly formed province of Upper Canada, which had been established in 1791 to administer the frontiers—from Kingston and Quinte's Isle to Windsor and beyond—settled largely by Loyalists fleeing the Revolution. To Simcoe Toronto was more defensible than Fort Niagara and a natural arsenal for Lake Ontario, which also afforded easy access to Lake Huron and the interior.

The governor had already purchased a vast tract of land from the Mississauga tribe for the paltry sum of £1,700 plus such baubles as blankets, guns, rum, and tobacco. In 1793 Lieutenant-Governor

Simcoe, his wife, Elizabeth, and the Queen's Rangers arrived to build a settlement. Simcoe ordered a garrison built, renamed the settlement York, and laid it out in a 10-block rectangle around King, Front, George, Duke, and Berkeley streets. Beyond stretched a series of 100-acre lots from Queen to Bloor, which were granted to government officials to mollify their resentment about having to move to this mosquito-plagued, marshy, muddy outpost. Its muddiness was indeed prodigious, and in fact there is a story told of a fellow who saw a hat lying in the middle of a street, went to pick it up, and found the head of a live man submerged below it! In three short years a small hamlet had grown and Simcoe had laid out Yonge Street—then a 33-mile ox-cart trail—and four years later the first Parliament meeting confirmed York as the capital of Upper Canada.

FROM MUDDY YORK TO THE FAMILY COMPACT The officials were a more demanding and finicky lot than the sturdy frontier farmers, and businesses sprang up to serve them. By 1812 the population had grown to 703 and included a brewer-baker, a blacksmith, a watchmaker, a chairmaker, an apothecary, a hatter, and a tailor.

During the War of 1812, despite initial victories at Queenston and Detroit, Canada was under siege, and in April 1813, 14 ships carrying 1,700 American troops invaded York, blew up the uncompleted fort, burned the Parliament Buildings, and carried off the mace (which was not returned until 1934). The British general burned a 30-gun warship, the *Sir Isaac Brock,* which was being built, and retreated, leaving young John Strachan to negotiate the capitulation. This event did much to reinforce the town's pro-British, anti-American attitude—an attitude that persists to some extent to this day. In retaliation for the burning of Fort York, some Canadians went down and torched the American president's residence. (The Americans later whitewashed it to hide the charred wood—hence, the White House.)

Dateline

- prominent influence in politics.
- **1832–34** Cholera epidemics.
- **1834** City named Toronto: City Council replaces magistrates; William Lyon Mackenzie becomes first mayor.
- **1837** Rebellion led by former mayor William Lyon Mackenzie, sparked by bad economic times.
- **1841** Act of Union establishes the United Province of Canada, with Kingston as ruling seat; Toronto loses status as a capital.
- **1842** Streets are gas lit.
- **1843** The university, King's College, opens.
- **1844** City hall built; George Brown founds the *Globe.*
- **1840s–50s** Mass Irish immigration.
- **1849** Great fire destroys much of city; Anglican King's College converts to secular University of Toronto.
- **1851** Population 30,000 (33% Irish); Anglican Trinity College founded; St. Lawrence Hall built.
- **1852** Toronto Stock Exchange opens; Grand Trunk Railroad charted, linking

➤

Dateline

Québec-Montréal-Toronto-Guelph-Sarnia.

- **1853** St. James Cathedral completed at King and Church.
- **1858** Storm creates the Toronto Islands.
- **1861** Population 44,000; horse-powered street railway runs along Yonge to Yorkville.
- **1867** Canadian Confederation; Toronto becomes capital of new province of Ontario.
- **1868** Canada First movement begins.
- **1869** Eaton's opens.
- **1871** Population 56,000.
- **1872** Simpson's opens.
- **1876** John Ross Robertson starts *Evening Telegram,* which wields influence for next 90 years.
- **1884** Streets electrically lit.
- **1886** Provincial parliament buildings erected in Queen's Park.
- **1891** Population 181,000.
- **1893** First Stanley Cup played.
- **1896** *MacLean's* magazine started.
- **1901** Population 208,000.
- **1904** Great Fire burns much of downtown.
- **1906** First autos produced by

A conservative pro-British outlook permeated the official political oligarchy that dominated York, and this group was dubbed the Family Compact. Many of the names that visitors will see on street signs, subway stops, and maps are derived from this august group of early government officers and their families. Among them were William Jarvis, a New England Loyalist who became provincial secretary; John Beverley Robinson, son of a Virginia Loyalist, who at age 22 became attorney general and later chief justice of Upper Canada; Scottish-educated Dr. John Strachan, who rose from being a schoolmaster to an Anglican rector and the most powerful figure in York; Anglo-Irish Dr. William Warren Baldwin, doctor, lawyer, architect, judge, and parliamentarian, who laid out Spadina Avenue as a thoroughfare leading to his house of that name in the country; and the Boultons, prominent lawyers, judges, and politicians—Judge D'Arcy Boulton built a mansion, The Grange, which later became the core of the art museum and still stands today.

These men, extremely conscious of rank, were conformist, conservative, pro-British, Tory, and Anglican. Their power would be broken only later in the 19th century as a larger and more diverse population gave reformers a chance to challenge their control. But even today their influence still lingers in the corporate world where a handful of companies and individuals control 80% of the companies on the Toronto Stock Exchange.

THE EARLY 19TH CENTURY— CANAL, RAILROAD & IMMIGRATION The changes that would eventually dilute their control began in the early 19th century, especially during the 1820s, 1830s, and 1840s, when immigrants— Irish Protestants and Catholics, Scots, Presbyterians, Methodists, and other Nonconformists—poured in to settle the frontier farmlands. By 1832 York had become the largest urban community in the province, with a population of 1,600. Already well

➤

established commercially as a supply center, York was given another boost when the Erie Canal was extended to Oswego on Lake Ontario, giving it direct access to New York, and the Welland Canal was built across the Niagara Peninsula, giving it access to Lake Erie and points beyond. In 1834 the city was incorporated and York became Toronto, a city bounded by Parliament Street to the east, Bathurst to the west, the lakefront to the south, and 400 yards north of current Queen Street (then called Lot) to the north. Outside this area—stretching west to Dufferin Street, east to the Don River, and north to Bloor Street—lay the "liberties," out of which new wards would later be carved. North of Bloor, local brewer Joseph Bloor and Sheriff Jarvis were already drawing up plans for the village of Yorkville.

As more immigrants arrived, the population grew more diverse and demands for democracy and reform were voiced. Among the reformers were such leaders as Francis Collins, who launched the radical paper *Canadian Freeman* in 1825; lawyer William Draper; and, perhaps most famous of all, fiery William Lyon Mackenzie, who was elected Toronto's first mayor in 1834.

Mackenzie had started his *Colonial Advocate* to crusade against the narrow-minded Family Compact, calling for reform and challenging their power to such an extent that some of them dumped his presses into the lake. Mackenzie was undaunted and by 1837 was calling for open rebellion.

A severe depression, financial turmoil, and the failure of some banks all contributed to the 1837 Rebellion, one of the most dramatic events in the city's history. On December 5 the rebels, a scruffy bunch of about 700, gathered at Montgomery's Tavern outside the city (near modern-day Eglinton Avenue). From here, led by Mackenzie on a white mare, they marched on the city. Two days later the city's militia, called out by Sheriff Jarvis, scattered the rebels at Carlton Street. Both sides then turned and ran. Reinforcements arrived and

Dateline

Canada Cycle and Motor Company; Toronto Symphony founded.
- **1907** Bell strike broken; Royal Alexandra opens.
- **1911** Population 376,538.
- **1912** Garment workers' strike broken; Royal Ontario Museum founded.
- **1914** New Union Station built.
- **1914–18** World War 1; 70,000 Torontonians enlist. 13,000 die.
- **1920** Group of Seven exhibited.
- **1921** Population 521,893.
- **1923** Chinese Exclusion Act.
- **1930s** Depression; thousands go on relief or ride the boxcars.
- **1931** Maple Leaf Gardens built.
- **1939** Canada enters World War II; thousands of troops leave from Union Station.
- **1940–45** Toronto functions as war supplier.
- **1947** Cocktail lounges approved.
- **1950** Sunday sports allowed.
- **1951** Population 31% foreign-born.
- **1953** Metro created.
- **1960** O'Keefe Centre opens.

➤

Dateline

- 1961 Population 42% foreign-born.
- 1965 New city hall built.
- 1971 Ontario Place built.
- 1972 Harbourfront under development.
- 1974 Metro Zoo and Ontario Science Centre open.
- 1975 CN Tower opens for business.
- 1984 City's 150th anniversary.
- 1989 SkyDome opens.
- 1992 Residents of Toronto Islands win 40-year struggle to retain their homes.
- 1993 Princess of Wales Theatre and CBC Building open.

pursued the rebels and bombarded the tavern with cannon balls. Mackenzie fled to the United States and two other leaders—Lount and Matthews —were hanged. Their graves can be visited in the Necropolis cemetery.

Between 1834 and 1884 the foundations of an industrial city were laid: Water works, gas, and later electrical lighting were installed, and public transportation was organized. Many municipal facilities were built, including a city hall, the Royal Lyceum Theatre (1848) on King near Bay, the Toronto Stock Exchange (1852), St. Lawrence Hall (1851), an asylum, and a jail.

During the 1850s the building of the railroads accelerated the economic pace. By 1860 Toronto was at the center of a railroad web that linked the city north, south, east, and west. Toronto became the trading hub for the region, for imports and exports of lumber and grain. Merchant empires were founded; railroad magnates emerged; and institutions like the Bank of Toronto were established.

Despite its growth and wealth Toronto still lagged behind Montréal—its population being only half of Montréal's in 1861—but increasingly Toronto took advantage of its superior links to the south, an advantage that would eventually help it overtake its rival. Under the Confederation of 1867 the city was guaranteed another advantage when it was made the capital of the newly created Ontario, which, in effect, gave it control over the minerals and timber of the north.

As the city grew it gobbled up the countryside and so, to compensate for this loss, recreational areas were developed. In 1857 G. W. Allan donated five acres (later enlarged to 10) for the laying out of a garden. In 1860 Queen's Park was laid out. But the real gem was donated by architect John Howard in 1873 when he gave to the citizens of the west end High Park. Riverdale park and zoo were developed later in the 1890s.

During this same mid-Victorian period the growth of a more diverse population continued. In 1847 Irish famine victims flooded into Toronto, and by 1851 and 1852 the Irish-born were the largest single ethnic group in Toronto. While many of them were Ulster Irish Protestants who did not threaten the Anglo-Protestant ascendancy, these newcomers were not always welcomed—a pattern that was to be repeated whenever a new immigrant group threatened to change the shape and order of society. As the gap between the number of Anglicans and Catholics closed, sectarian tensions increased and the old-country Orange and Green conflicts flared into mob violence.

LATE & HIGH VICTORIAN TORONTO   Between 1871 and 1891 the city's population more than tripled, shooting from 56,000 to 181,000. This increasingly large urban market helped spawn two great Toronto retailers—Timothy Eaton and Robert Simpson—who both moved to Toronto from Ontario towns to open stores at Queen and Yonge streets in 1869 and 1872, respectively. Eaton developed his reputation on fixed prices, cash sales only, and promises of refunds if the customer wasn't satisfied, all unique gambits at the time. Simpson copied Eaton and also competed by providing better service, such as two telephones to take orders instead of one. Both developed into full-fledged department stores and both entered mail order, conquering the country with their catalogs.

The business of the city was business, and amassing wealth the pastime of such figures as Henry Pellatt, stockbroker and president of the Electrical Development Company and builder of Casa Loma; E. B. Osler; George Albertus Cox; and A. R. Ames. Although these men were self-made entrepreneurs, not Family Compact officials, they still formed a traditional socially conservative elite linked by money, taste, investments, and religious affiliation. And they were still British to a tee. They and the rest of the citizens celebrated the Queen's Jubilee in 1897 with gusto and gave Toronto boys a rousing send-off to fight in the Boer War in 1899. They also, like the British, had a fondness for clubs—the Albany Club for the Conservatives and the National Club for the Liberals. As in England, too, their sports clubs carried a certain cachet—notably the Royal Yacht Club, the Toronto Cricket Club, the Toronto Golf Club, and the Lawn Tennis Club.

As the city's financial power increased, many leading companies and organizations moved their headquarters to the city, and Toronto became a cultural-intellectual powerhouse. The Canadian Institute, the Ontario Society of Artists, and the Toronto Philharmonic Society were all founded in the 1870s or 1880s. On the sports front, the first Queen's Plate was run at Woodbine in 1883; the Stanley Cup competition was begun in 1893; baseball overtook cricket; and rowing was a red-hot sport, with Ned Hanlan holding the world title from 1880 to 1884.

The boom also spurred new commercial and residential construction, such as the first steel-frame building—the Board of Trade Building (1889) at Yonge and Front; George Gooderham's Romanesque-style mansion (1890) at St. George and Bloor (now the York Club); the provincial parliament buildings in Queen's Park (1886–92); and the city hall (1899) at Queen and Bay. Public transit was improved, and by 1891 people were traveling the 68 miles of horse-drawn tracks. Electric lights, telephones, and electrical streetcars also appeared in the 1890s.

FROM 1900 TO 1933   Between 1901 and 1921 the population more than doubled, climbing from 208,000 to 521,893, and the economy continued to expand, fueled by the lumber, mining, wholesale, and agricultural machinery industries, and after 1911 by hydroelectric power. Toronto began to seriously challenge Montréal. Much of the new wealth went into construction, and three marvelous buildings from this era can still be seen today: the Horticultural Building at the Exhibition Grounds (1907), the King Edward Hotel (1903), and Union Station (1914–19). Most of the earlier wooden structures had been destroyed in the Great Fire of 1904, which wiped out 14 acres of downtown.

The booming economy and its factories attracted a wave of new immigrants—mostly Italians and Jews from Russia and Eastern Europe. They were very different from the British and Irish who had come earlier. They settled in the city's emerging ethnic enclaves. By 1912 Kensington Market was well established, and the garment center and Jewish community were firmly ensconced around King and Spadina. Little Italy clustered around College and Grace. By 1911 more than 30,000 Torontonians were foreign-born, and the slow march to change the English character of the city had begun.

It was still a city of churches worthy of the name "Toronto the Good," with a population of staunch religious conservatives, who barely voted for Sunday streetcar service in 1897 and banned tobogganing on Sunday in 1912. As late as 1936, 30 men were arrested at the lakeshore resort of Sunnyside because they exposed their chests—even though the temperature was 105°F! In 1947 cocktail lounges were approved, but it wasn't until 1950 that commercialized sports could be played on Sunday.

Increased industrialization brought social problems, largely concentrated in Cabbagetown and the Ward, a large area that stretched west of Yonge and north of Queen. Here, poor people lived in crowded, wretched conditions: Housing was inadequate, health conditions were poor, and rag-picking or sweatshop labor was the only employment.

As industry grew unionism also increased, but the movement, as in the United States, failed to organize politically. Two major strikes—at Bell in 1907 and in the garment industry in 1912—were easily broken.

As the city became larger and wealthier it also became an intellectual and cultural magnet. Artists like Charles Jefferys, J. H. MacDonald, Arthur Lismer, Tom Thomson, Lawren Harris, Frederick Varley, and A. Y. Jackson, most associated with the Group of Seven, set up studios in Toronto, their first and now-famous group show opening in 1920. Toronto also became the English-language publishing center of the nation, and national magazines like *Maclean's* (started in 1896) and *Saturday Night* were launched. The art museum, the Royal Ontario Museum, the Toronto Symphony Orchestra, and the Royal Alexandra Theatre all opened before 1914.

Women advanced, too, at the turn of the century. In 1880 Emily Jennings Stowe became the first Canadian woman authorized to practice medicine. In 1886 women were admitted to the university. Clara Brett Martin was the first woman admitted to the law courts, and the women's suffragist movement gained strength, led by

Dr. Stowe, Flora McDonald Denison, and the Women's Christian Temperance Union.

During World War I, Toronto sent 70,000 men to the trenches; about 13,000 were killed. At home, the war had a great impact economically and socially: Toronto became Canada's chief aviation center; factories, shipyards, and power facilities expanded to meet the needs of war; and women entered the work force in great numbers.

After the war the city took on much more of the aspect and tone that is still recognizable today. Automobiles appeared on the streets—the Canadian Cycle and Motor Company had begun manufacturing them in 1906 (the first parking ticket was given in 1908); one or two skyscrapers appeared; and although 80% of the population still boasted British origin, ethnic enclaves were clearly defined.

The 1920s roared along, fueled by a mining boom, which saw Bay Street turned into a veritable gold-rush alley where everyone was pushing something hot. The Great Depression followed, racking up 30% unemployment in 1933. The only distraction from its bleakness was the opening of Maple Leaf Gardens in 1931, which besides being an ice hockey center also hosted large protest rallies during the Depression and later such diverse groups and personalities as the Jehovah's Witnesses, Billy Graham, the Ringling Bros. Circus, and the Metropolitan Opera.

As in the United States, hostility toward new immigrants was rife during the twenties, and it reached one of its peaks in 1923, when the Chinese Exclusion Act was passed, banning Chinese immigration. In the 1930s antagonism to the Jews intensified. Signs such as NO JEWS, NIGGERS, OR DOGS were posted occasionally at Balmy and Kew beaches, and in August 1933, the display of a swastika at Christie Pits caused a battle between Nazis and Jews.

AFTER WORLD WAR II   In 1939 Torontonians again rallied to the British cause, sending thousands to fight in Europe. At home, plants turned out fighter bombers and Bren guns, and people endured rationing—one bottle of liquor a month and ration books for sugar and other staples—while they listened to the war-front news delivered by Lorne Greene.

Already prosperous by World War II, Toronto continued to expand during the 1940s. The suburbs alone added more than 200,000 to the population between 1940 and 1953. By the 1950s the urban area had grown so large, disputes between city and suburbs were so frequent, and the need for social and other services were so great

IMPRESSIONS

Oh for a half-hour of Europe after this sanctimonious icebox.
—Wyndham Lewis, *The Letters of Wyndham Lewis*

Toronto is known as Toronto the Good, because of its alleged piety. My guess is that there's more polygamy in Toronto than Baghdad, only it's not called that in Toronto.
—Austin F. Cross, *Cross Roads* (1936)

that an effective administrative solution was needed. In 1953 the Metro Council was established, composed of equal numbers of representatives from the city and the suburbs.

Toronto became a major city in the 1950s, with Metro providing a structure for planning and growth. The Yonge subway opened, and a network of highways was constructed, linking the city to the affluent suburbs, which were populated by families who were buying cars, TVs, barbecues, refrigerators, and washing machines—all the modern conveniences associated with house-and-backyard suburbia. Don Mills, the first new town, was built between 1952 and 1962; Yorkdale Center, a mammoth shopping center, followed in 1964. Much of this growth was also fueled by the location of branch plants by American companies that were attracted to the area.

The city also began to loosen up, and while the old social elite (still traditionally educated at Upper Canada College, Ridley, and Trinity College) continued to dominate the boardrooms, politics, at least, had become more accessible and fluid. In 1954 Nathan Phillips became the first Jewish mayor, signifying how greatly the population had changed from earlier days when immigrants were primarily British, American, or French. In 1947 the Chinese Exclusion Act of 1923 was repealed, opening the door to the relatives of Toronto's then-small Chinese community. After 1950 the door swung open further. Germans and Italians were allowed to enter, adding to the communities that were already established, and then, under United Nations pressure, Poles, Ukrainians, Central European and Russian Jews, Yugoslavs, Estonians, Latvians, and other East Europeans poured in. Most arrived at Union Station, having journeyed from the ports of Halifax, Québec City, and Montréal. At the beginning of the 1950s the foreign-born were 31% of the population; by 1961 they were 42%, and the number of people claiming British descent had fallen from 73% to 59%. The 1960s were to bring an even richer mix of people—Portuguese, Greeks, West Indians, South Asians, and Chinese, Vietnamese, and Chilean refugees—changing the city's character forever.

In the sixties the focus shifted back from the suburbs to the city. People moved back downtown, renovating the handsome brick Victorians so characteristic of today's downtown. Yorkville emerged briefly as the hippie capital—the Haight-Ashbury of Canada. Gordon Lightfoot and Joni Mitchell sang in the coffeehouses, and anti-Vietnam protests took over the streets. Perhaps the failure of the experimental, alternative Rochdale College in 1968 marked the demise of that era. By the mid-1970s Yorkville had been transformed into a village of elegant boutiques and galleries and high-rent restaurants, and the funky village had moved to Queen Street West.

In the 1970s Toronto became the fastest-growing city in North America. For years the city had competed with Montréal for first-city status, and now the separatist issue and the election of the Parti Québécois in 1976 hastened Toronto's dash to the tape. It overtook Montréal as a financial/investment banking center, boasting the greatest number of corporate headquarters. Its stock market was more important, and it was also the country's prime publishing center. A dramatically different new city hall opened in 1965, symbol of the city's equally new dynamism. Toronto also began reclaiming its waterfront with the development of Harbourfront. New skyscrapers and civic buildings reflected the city's new power and wealth—the Toronto Dominion, the 72-story First Canadian Place, Royal Bank Plaza, Roy Thomson Hall, the Eaton Centre, the CN Tower—all of which transformed the old 1930s skyline into an urban landscape worthy of world attention.

Unlike the rapid building of highways and other developments completed in the 1950s, these developments were achieved with some balance and attention to the city's heritage. From the late sixties through the early eighties the citizens fought to ensure that the city's heritage was saved and that development was not allowed to continue as wildly as it had done in the fifties. The best examples of the success of this reform movement were the stopping of the proposed Spadina Expressway in 1971 and the fight against several urban renewal plans.

During the 1970s the provincial government also helped develop attractions that would polish Toronto's patina and attract visitors: Ontario Place in 1971, Harbourfront in 1972, and the Metro Zoo and the Ontario Science Centre in 1974. Government financing also supported the arts and helped turn Toronto from a city with four theaters in 1965 to one boasting 22 in 1976 and more than 40 today. And the growth continues with the 1989 opening of SkyDome—the first stadium in the world with a fully retractable roof—located right downtown.

2   Famous Torontonians

Margaret Atwood   (b. 1939) Poet, novelist, satirist, and feminist, considered the high priestess of Canadian literature (read *Survival*). One of her novels, *The Handmaid's Tale,* was made into a movie starring Robert Duvall and Faye Dunaway (1989). Her most recent bestseller was *The Robber Bride* (1993).

The Band   A Toronto quintet that rose to popularity in 1967 as Bob Dylan's original electric backing band, and later came into its

IMPRESSIONS

Returning to Toronto was like finding a Jaguar parked in front of the vicarage and the padre inside with a pitcher of vodka martinis reading Lolita.
—Article in *Maclean's*, January 1959

Toronto does not have to devote all its energies and resources to seeking remedies for yesterday's problems—slums, ghettos and unemployment. Free of these major constraints, it can be a truly future-oriented protypic city.
—Buckminster Fuller (1968)

own with hits such as "The Weight" and "The Night They Drove Old Dixie Down." The final live performance of the Band's original lineup was captured in Martin Scorsese's seminal rock film *The Last Waltz* (1978).

Drs. Frederick Banting (1891–1941) and **Charles Best** (1899–1978) Inventors of insulin at the University of Toronto in 1921.

Blue Rodeo Rock group formed in 1984 that achieved big success on the Canadian charts with the 1987 album *Outskirts*. In 1994 they released *Five Days in July.*

Jack Bush (1909–77) Member of the Painters Eleven, a group of Canadian abstract expressionists based in Toronto in the 1950s. He became internationally known for "drawing with color."

Morley Callaghan (1903–90) Novelist who met Hemingway while working on the *Toronto Daily Star* and later in Paris along with other members of the Lost Generation, a period that he recalled in *That Summer in Paris.* He contributed to the *New Yorker* and wrote many novels, including *The Loved and the Lost,* which won the Governor-General's Award.

John Candy (1950–94) A former star of "SCTV," Candy moved on to such movies as *Planes, Trains, and Automobiles, JFK,* and *Uncle Buck.* Acclaim for his particular brand of side-splitting slapstick comedy was increasing when he died prematurely at age 44.

Austin Clarke (b. 1932) Novelist born in Barbados who attended the University of Toronto. *The Meeting Point* is the first novel in his trilogy recording Caribbean life in Toronto.

Cowboy Junkies Four-person group formed in 1987 that scored American success and a big hit with their 1988 album *The Trinity Session.* More recent recordings have included *Black Eyed Man.*

Robertson Davies (b. 1913) Playwright, novelist, journalist, professor, and former Master of Massey College at the University of Toronto, famous for his *Deptford Trilogy* and for the creation of Samuel Marchbanks. His many novels often reflect a Jungian approach.

Timothy Eaton (1834–1907) Ulster immigrant turned retail magnate who transformed Canadian business in 1869 when he opened his first store, the cash-only, fixed-price Eaton's, with a mail-order service for homesteaders outside of Toronto. It is now a Canadian institution.

Marian Engel (1933–85) Novelist. Many of her novels are set in Toronto. *Bear* won the Governor-General's Award in 1976.

Glenn Gould (1932–82) Arguably the most charismatic and technically proficient pianist of all time, Gould lived largely as a recluse in Toronto after abruptly retiring from his concertizing career at the age of 32 and thereafter performing only in a recording studio. He is known for his brilliant, if controversial interpretations of Bach and Beethoven (particularly his two recordings of Bach's *Goldberg*

Variations) and such eccentricities as singly loudly to himself as he played and soaking his arms in near-scalding water before taking to the keyboard, allegedly to improve his circulation. Lesser known is his evocative trilogy of radio documentaries on solitude, for which he interviewed Newfoundlanders, Mennonites, and other Canadians who, like himself, lived apart but in harmony with their natural surroundings.

Group of Seven   Famous Canadian painters, including Tom Thomson, Lawren Harris, Arthur Lismer, A. Y. Jackson, Frederick Varley, and J. E. H. MacDonald, who were first exhibited in Toronto in 1920. They gained favor for their interpretations of the Canadian wilderness which put Canada on the map artistically well into the 1950s. However, among many artists today they are dismissed as being too mainstream and conformist.

Jane Jacobs   (b. 1916) Urban planner and sociologist, author of *The Death and Life of the Great American Cities,* who moved from New York to Toronto to observe her ideas in action.

Norman Jewison   (b. 1926) Film director. Among his films are *Fiddler on the Roof* (1971) and *Moonstruck,* for which he was nominated for an Academy Award as best director in 1987. In 1994, he directed the romantic comedy *Only You.* He grew up in the Beaches.

Paul Kane   (1810–71) Irish-born painter who lived in Toronto, famous for his landscapes and portraits of Native Canadians.

William Lyon Mackenzie   (1795–1861) Urban journalist/reformer, publisher of the *Colonial Advocate,* first city mayor, and leader of the Rebellion of 1837.

Raymond Massey   (1896–1983) Actor and member of the influential Toronto family of Massey-Ferguson fame. He played opposite Cary Grant in *Arsenic and Old Lace.*

Marshall McLuhan   (1911–80) University of Toronto professor who gave us the increasingly prescient "The medium is the message." Author of *The Mechanical Bride* (1951).

Honest Ed Mirvish   (b. 1914) A Toronto legend who rose from running the city's ultimate bargain-basement store to wealth and position. Savior of Toronto's Royal Alexandra Theatre and most recently the Old Vic in London.

Raymond Moriyama   (b. 1929) Architect who designed the Ontario Science Centre, Metro Toronto Library, and Scarborough Civic Centre.

Northern Dancer   Winner of two-thirds of the Triple Crown. He once commanded $1 million stud fees.

Michael Ondaatje   (b. 1943) Novelist and poet who was born in Ceylon but now lives in Toronto. His novels include *In the Skin of a Lion* (set in Toronto in the 1920s and 1930s) and *The English Patient* (co-winner of the Booker Prize). He has twice been given the Governor-General's Award for Literature.

Sir Henry Pellatt (1859–1939) Stockbroker and utility magnate who built Casa Loma and whose family fortunes collapsed in the 1913 crash.

Mary Pickford (1893–1979) America's silent-film sweetheart, she lived on University Avenue where Sick Children's Hospital stands today.

Rush A classic 1970s hard-rock power trio. Two of their most notable albums are *Moving Pictures* and *2112*.

Joe Shuster (1914–92) Creator of Superman, who modeled the *Daily Planet* after the *Toronto Daily Star*. He moved to Cleveland as a young man.

Jane Siberry (b. 1955) Singer-songwriter made famous by her album *The Speckless Sky* (1985).

John Strachan (1778–1867) One of the founders of Toronto, he negotiated with the invading Americans in 1813. A staunch Anglican and Anglophile, first bishop of Toronto, he dubbed Thomas Jefferson "a mischief maker."

Harold Town (b. 1924) Member of the Painters Eleven, known for his collages and "fat paint" paintings.

Wayne and Shuster (b. 1918; 1916–90) Two comics who appeared regularly on "The Ed Sullivan Show."

Neil Young (b. 1945) One-time member of the legendary 1960s group Crosby, Stills, Nash & Young, this singer-songwriter later launched a solo career with the folk-rock album *After the Goldrush* (1970) and followed up with *Harvest* (1972). Young called this album "the finest recording I ever produced," and it gave him his biggest hit, "Heart of Gold." Soon he introduced a more hard-rocking guitar style on *Rust Never Sleeps* with his band Crazy Horse. His career has enjoyed remarkable longevity; his *Lucky Thirteen* won over a new generation of fans with the single "This Note's for You" in the 1980s. His latest offering, *Sleeps with Angels* (1994), a tribute to the late Kurt Cobain of Nirvana, has won immense critical acclaim. Young was inducted into the Rock and Roll Hall of Fame in 1994.

3 Recommended Books

There are plenty of books that deal with all aspects of Canada's history and society. Canada is also blessed with several world-renowned writers of fiction.

GENERAL Anything by Pierre Berton is great reading. George Woodcock's *The Canadians* (Harvard University Press, 1979) is a lively, honest appraisal of his fellow nationals and national culture. Edmund Wilson's *O Canada: An American's Notes on Canadian Culture* (Noonday Press, 1965) provides an outsider's vision of what the culture's about. And Donald Creighton has written many books about specific issues in Canadian history as well as his *Canada's First Century* (Macmillan, 1976).

For a general sociological history of the growth of Toronto, complete with statistics and historical photographs, there's the two-volume *Toronto: An Illustrated History* (Lorimer & Company, 1985). The first volume (to 1918) is by J. M. S. Careless; the second volume (after 1918) is by James Lemon.

William Kilbourn's *Toronto Remembered* (Stoddart, 1984) is, as the subtitle states, "a celebration of the city" by the author himself and many other fine writers, all of whom provide insights into the city's life and history. It's made even livelier by the quotations and illustrations that accompany the text—a delightful read.

Other general city and provincial histories include G. P. de T. Glazebrook's *The Story of Toronto* (Toronto, 1971) and Robert Bothwell's *A Short History of Ontario* (Hurtig, 1986).

ART & ARCHITECTURE   *A Concise History of Canadian Painting* by Dennis Reid (Oxford University Press, 1988) is a well-written, well-illustrated, and informative history that has chapters on significant periods of art in Toronto, including the Group of Seven and the Painters Eleven. Entertaining and anecdotal, too.

David Burnett and Marilyn Schiff's *Contemporary Canadian Art* (Hurtig, 1983) is a well-written, concise, and liberally illustrated history of Canadian art from the 1940s to the 1980s.

Edith G. Firth's *Toronto in Art* (Fitzhenry & Whiteside, 1983) provides a pictorial history of the city as viewed by artists from the early 19th century through the 1980s. It contains more than 170 delightful illustrations.

The book on Toronto's architecture is Eric Arthur's *Toronto, No Mean City,* which, in its 1986 edition by University of Toronto Press, has been revised by Stephen Otto. Arthur conveys his great love for the city and the history of its buildings, many of which he helped to save.

Toronto Observed by William Dendy and William Kilbourn (Oxford University Press, 1986) focuses on the many architectural treasures that still stand in the city. It's a large-format volume with elegant black-and-white photographs of each of the 77 buildings and architectural groupings discussed.

For more of a walking-tour approach, complete with maps referenced to the text, there's Patricia McHugh's *Toronto Architecture* (McClelland & Stewart, 1989).

William Dendy's *Lost Toronto* (Toronto, 1978) recovers in words and pictures the great buildings that have been demolished.

Lucy Martyn's *Toronto: A Hundred Years of Grandeur—The Inside Story of Toronto's Great Homes* (Toronto, 1978) gives a glimpse into the lives of the wealthy—the era of millionaires and Toronto aristocrats. The life of one such self-made man is described in Carlie Oreskovich's *Sir Henry Pellatt: The King of Casa Loma* (McGraw-Hill Ryerson, 1982). Other titles to look for are A. S. Thompson's *Spadina: A Story of Old Toronto* (Paguarian Press, 1988) and *Jarvis Street* (Toronto, 1980).

FICTION   Many of Margaret Atwood's novels are set in Toronto, including *Life Before Man* (1980), which examines the redefinition of sexual roles that occurred in the 1960s and 1970s; *Cat's Eye* (1989), in which an artist returns to the city for an exhibition of her work and recalls her years as a child in Toronto; and *The Robber Bride* (1993), in which three Toronto friends recall in flashbacks how one woman shattered each of their lives in turn.

Austin Clarke's trilogy—*The Meeting Point* (1967), *Storm of Fortune* (1971), and *The Bigger Light* (1975)—portrays the life of a family of Caribbean immigrants in Toronto.

Marian Engel's *The Year of the Child* (1981) portrays the life of a family on one particular street in Toronto. Other novels include *Honeyman Festival* and *No Clouds of Glory*.

Several of Timothy Findley's books are also set in the city, the most recent being his Canadian bestseller, *Headhunter*.

Hugh Garner's *Cabbagetown* (1950) paints what the author described as an Anglo-Saxon slum. *The Silence on the Shore* (1962) and *The Intruders* (1978) are also set in Toronto, as are several of the mysteries he wrote.

Katherine Govier's stories, *Fables of Brunswick Avenue* (1985) for example, depict the era and social scene of Toronto's young urban professionals.

Joyce Marshal's *Lovers and Strangers* (1957) is set in Toronto in the 1940s.

2

Planning a Trip to Toronto

THIS CHAPTER IS DEVOTED TO THE WHERE, WHEN, AND HOW OF YOUR TRIP—
the advance-planning issues required to get it together and take it
on the road.

After deciding where to go, most people have two fundamental
questions: What will it cost? and How do I get there? This chapter
will answer both of these questions and also resolve other important
issues, such as when to go, what pretrip health precautions to take,
what insurance coverage is necessary, and where to obtain more information about Toronto.

1   Information, Entry Requirements & Money

Sources of Information

IN THE UNITED STATES   General information on travel in
Canada can be obtained from the following offices in the United
States:

Atlanta   Canadian Consulate General, 400 South Tower, One
CNN Center, Atlanta, GA 30303-2705 (☎ **404/577-6810**).

Boston   Canadian Consulate General, Three Copley Place, Suite
400, Boston, MA 02116 (☎ **617/262-3760**).

Buffalo   Canadian Consulate, Marine Midland Center, Suite
3000, Buffalo, NY 14203-2884 (☎ **716/852-1247**).

Chicago   Canadian Consulate General, 2 Prudential Plaza, 180
N. Stetson Ave., Chicago, IL 60601 (☎ **312/616-1860**).

Dallas   Canadian Consulate General, 750 N. St. Paul, Suite
1700, Dallas, TX 75201 (☎ **214/922-9806**).

Detroit   Canadian Consulate General, 600 Renaissance Center,
Suite 1100, Detroit, MI 48243-1798 (☎ **313/567-2340**).

Los Angeles   Canadian Consulate General, 300 S. Grand Ave.,
Suite 1000, Los Angeles, CA 90071 (☎ **213/687-7432**).

Miami   Canadian Consulate General, 200 S. Biscayne Blvd.,
Suite 1600, Miami, FL 33131 (☎ **305/372-2352**).

Minneapolis   Canadian Consulate General, 701 Fourth Ave.,
Suite 900, Minneapolis, MN 55415-1899 (☎ **612/333-4641**).

New York   Canadian Consulate General, Exxon Building, 16th
floor, 1251 Avenue of the Americas, New York, NY 10020-1175
(☎ **212/596-1600**).

San Francisco   Canadian Consulate General, 50 Fremont St.,
Suite 2100, San Francisco, CA 94105 (☎ **415/495-6021**).

Seattle   Canadian Consulate General, 412 Plaza 600, Sixth and
Stewart, Seattle, WA 98101-1286 (☎ **206/443-1777**).

Washington, D.C.   Canadian Embassy, Tourism Section, 501 Pennsylvania Ave. NW, Washington, DC 20001
(☎ **202/682-1740**).

IN CANADA   The best source for information specific to
Toronto is the **Metropolitan Toronto Convention & Visitors
Association,** Queen's Quay Terminal at Harbourfront, 207 Queen's

Quay West (P.O. Box 126), Toronto, ON, M5J 1A7 (☎ **416/ 203-2500,** or toll free **800/363-1990** from the continental U.S.). Write or call them before you leave and request the kind of information you want.

For information about Ontario, contact **Ontario Travel,** Queen's Park, Toronto, ON, M7A 2E5 (☎ **416/314-0944,** or toll free **800/ ONTARIO).**

Entry Requirements

DOCUMENTS   Every person under 19 years of age is required to produce a letter from a parent or guardian granting him or her permission to travel to Canada. The letter must state the traveler's name and the duration of the trip. It is therefore essential that teenagers carry proof of identity; otherwise their letter is useless at the border.

What Things Cost in Toronto	U.S. $
Taxi from the airport to downtown	29.60
Subway/bus from the airport to downtown	4.60
Local telephone call	.18
Double at the Four Seasons (expensive)	189.00
Double at Bond Place (moderate)	48.10
Double at Victoria University (budget)	45.90
Two-course prix-fixe lunch for one at La Bodega (moderate)*	10.40
Two-course lunch for one at Kensington (budget)*	10.00
Three-course dinner for one at Scaramouche (expensive)*	41.45
Three-course dinner for one at Grano (moderate)*	22.20
Three-course dinner for one at Jerusalem (budget)*	14.80
Pint of beer	3.50
Coca-Cola	.90
Cup of coffee	.75
Roll of ASA 100 Kodacolor film, 36 exposures	4.85
Admission to the ROM	5.20
Movie ticket	5.90
Theater ticket at the Royal Alex	25.90–67.35

*Includes tax and tip but not wine.

Note: Prices are listed here in U.S. dollars; all other prices in the book are quoted in Canadian dollars.

U.S. citizens and permanent residents of the United States require neither passports nor visas to enter Canada. You will need some proof of citizenship, such as a passport, a birth or baptismal certificate, or a voter's registration card. Permanent U.S. residents who are not U.S. citizens must have their Alien Registration Cards (Green Cards) with them.

Citizens of Australia, New Zealand, the United Kingdom, and Ireland must have valid passports. Citizens of many other countries will need visas, which must be applied for in advance at the local Canadian embassy or consulate. For detailed information, call your local Canadian consulate or embassy.

CUSTOMS   Customs regulations are generous in most respects, but they get pretty complicated when it comes to firearms, plants, meats, and pets. Fishing tackle poses no problem (provided the lures are not made of restricted materials—specific feathers, for example) but the bearer must possess a nonresident license for the province or territory where he or she plans to use it. You can bring in free of duty up to 50 cigars, 200 cigarettes, 400 grams of tobacco, and 400 tobacco sticks, providing you're at least 18 years of age. You are also allowed 40 ounces (1.14l) of liquor or wine as long as you're over the minimum drinking age of the province you're visiting (19 in Ontario).

For more detailed information about customs regulations, write to Revenue Canada, 875 Heron Rd., Ottawa, ON, K1A 0L8.

Money

Canadian money figures in dollars and cents, but with a distinct advantage for U.S. visitors, for the Canadian dollar is worth around 74¢ in U.S. money (give or take a couple of points' daily variation). So, in effect, you'll receive about 35% more the moment you change your American traveler's checks into local currency. That makes quite a difference in your budget, and since the prices of many goods are roughly on a par with those in the United States, the difference is real, not imaginary. You can bring in or take out any amount of money, but if you are importing or exporting sums of $5,000 or more, you must file a report of the transaction with U.S. Customs. Most tourist establishments in Canada will take U.S. cash, but you can often get a better rate by changing your funds at a bank.

If you do spend American money at Canadian establishments, you should understand how the conversion is calculated. Often there will be a sign at the cash register that reads "U.S. Currency 35%." This 35% is the "premium," which means that for every U.S. greenback you hand over, the cashier will consider it $1.35 in Canadian dollars. For example, for an $8 tab you need pay only $5.92 U.S.

Below is a table showing premium rates and the amount of money you're actually paying for each Canadian dollar. As you can see, if the exchange rate at a bank is 82¢ U.S. for $1 Canadian, you are entitled to a premium rate of 22%. If someone offers you 20%, you're losing money—go to a bank instead.

Major credit cards are accepted throughout Canada.

Premium Rates & U.S. Dollar Equivalents

Premium Rates	U.S. Equivalents
10%	.91
15	.87
20	.83
25	.80
30	.77
35	.74
40	.71

As we go to press the Canadian dollar is worth 74¢ U.S. Below is a table of equivalence calculated at that premium rate. Remember that this rate fluctuates from time to time and may not be the same when you travel to Toronto. Therefore the following table should be used only as a guide.

TRAVELER'S CHECKS   It used to be that before leaving home, you were well-advised to purchase traveler's checks and arrange to carry some ready cash (usually about $200). You can still purchase traveler's checks from the companies listed below but ATMs are a lot more convenient and often deliver a better exchange rate.

American Express (☎ toll free **800/221-7282** in the U.S. and Canada) is the most widely recognized traveler's check; depending on where you purchase them expect to pay between 1% and 4% commission. Checks are free to members of the American Automobile Association.

Canadian & U.S. Dollar Equivalents

Canada	U.S.	Canada	U.S.
.25	.18	15	11.10
.50	.37	20	14.80
.75	.55	25	18.50
1	.74	30	22.20
2	1.48	35	25.90
3	2.22	40	29.60
4	2.96	45	33.30
5	3.70	50	37.00
6	4.44	75	55.50
7	5.18	100	74.00
8	5.92	125	92.50
9	6.66	150	111.00
10	7.40	175	129.50

Citicorp(☎ toll free **800/645-6556** in the U.S., or **813/ 623-1709,** collect, in Canada) issues checks in U.S. dollars or British pounds.

MasterCard International (☎ toll free **800/223-9920** in the U.S.) issues checks in about a dozen currencies.

Thomas Cook (☎ toll free **800/223-7373** in the U.S.) issues checks in U.S. or Canadian dollars.

2 Timing Your Trip—Climate, Holidays & Events

Climate

As a general rule, you can say that spring runs from late March to mid-May (though occasionally there'll be snow in mid-April); summer, from mid-May to mid-September; fall, from mid-September to mid-November; and winter, from mid-November to late March. The highest recorded temperature was 105°F; the lowest, –27°F. The average date of first frost is October 29; the average date of last frost is April 20.

The blasts from Lake Ontario can sometimes be fierce, even in June. Bring a windbreaker or something similar.

Toronto's Average Temperatures (°F)

	Jan	Feb	Mar	Apr	May	June	July	Aug	Sept	Oct	Nov	Dec
High	30	31	39	53	64	75	80	79	71	59	46	34
Low	18	19	27	38	48	57	62	61	54	45	35	23

Holidays

Toronto celebrates the following holidays: New Year's Day (January 1), Good Friday and/or Easter Monday (variable; in March or April), Victoria Day (last Monday in May), Canada Day (July 1), Civic Holiday (first Monday in August), Labour Day (first Monday in September), Thanksgiving (second Monday in October), Remembrance Day (November 11), Christmas Day (December 25), and Boxing Day (December 26).

On Good Friday and Easter Monday, both schools and government offices are closed; most corporations are closed on one or the other, and some are closed on both. Only banks and government offices close on Remembrance Day (November 11).

Toronto Calendar of Events

May

- **Milk International Children's Festival.** A nine-day celebration of the arts for kids—from theater and music to dance, comedy, and storytelling. Usually starts on Mother's Day. For information call Harbourfront at **416/973-3000.**

June

★ Festival Caravan

North America's largest international festival. In it, more than 100 cultural groups take to the streets and the stages at more than 40 pavilions. The entertainment is complemented by authentic ethnic foods.
Where: Citywide. **When:** 10 days, usually 3rd and 4th weekends in June. **How:** Go, but make city hotel reservations in advance.

- **Du Maurier Ltd. Downtown Jazz.** The world's top jazz names of modern, traditional, avant-garde, African, and fusion appear in a 10-day festival. Usually the last 10 days in June. For information, call Harbourfront at **416/973-3000**.

- **Mariposa Folk Festival.** A major musical celebration of traditional folk, neofolk, R & B, and blues, featuring more than 200 top performers. Craft show, too. At Ontario Place and other venues. Usually the third weekend in June.

- **Fringe of Toronto Festival.** A 10-day theatrical event with as many as 80 performing artists/groups in performances that last no more than an hour. Shows are given on several different stages and ticket prices are low (the most expensive ticket at the time of writing is $7). Usually the last week in June and the first week in July. For information write or call the Fringe of Toronto Festival, 720 Bathurst St., Suite 303, Toronto, ON, M5S 2R4 (☎ **416/534-5919**).

July

- **Du Maurier Ltd. Open.** An important stop on the pro-tennis tour that attracts stars like Becker, Agassi, and Sanchez Vicario. Run in conjunction with a tournament in Montréal during the middle of August. In 1995, women play in Toronto; men play in Montréal. In 1996, they alternate, and so on in subsequent years. National Tennis Centre at York University. Usually 3rd to 4th weekend in July. Call **416/665-9777.**

- **Molson Indy.** At the Exhibition Place Street circuit. Usually 3rd weekend in July. Call **416/872-4639.**

★ Caribana

A West Indian calypso beat takes over the city when three-quarters of a million people dance, sway, and watch the colorful parade. Toronto's version of carnival, complete with traditional foods from the Caribbean and Latin America, ferry cruises, island picnics, concerts, and arts-and-crafts exhibits.
Where: Citywide. **When:** Last week in July and first week in August.
How: Go, but make hotel reservations in advance. Call **416/925-5435** for more information.

August

✪ Canadian National Exhibition

One of the world's largest exhibitions, featuring midway rides, display buildings, free shows, and grandstand performers. The Canadian International Air Show is an added bonus. It was first staged, by the way, in 1878. **Where:** Exhibition Place. **When:** 18 days, from mid-August to Labor Day. **How:** Contact Canadian National Exhibition, Exhibition Place, Toronto, ON, M6K 3C3 (☎ **416/393-6000**).

September

- **Toronto International Film Festival.** Second-largest film festival in the world, showing more than 250 films. 10 days in early September. For information, contact the Toronto Convention and Tourist Office or call **416/967-7371.**

October

- **Oktoberfest,** in Kitchener-Waterloo, about one hour (60 miles) from Toronto. Oct 6–14 (1995) and Oct 5–13 (1996). It features cultural events plus a pageant and parade. For information, contact Kitchener-Waterloo Oktoberfest, P.O. Box 1053, Kitchener, ON, N2G 4G1 (☎ **519/576-0571**).
- **International Festival of Authors.** A prestigious nine-day literary festival at the Harbourfront that draws some of the finest authors from all over the world to readings and other events, such as the Lives and Times presentations (biography) and on-stage interviews. Usually starts the third weekend of October. For information, call Harbourfront at **416/973-3000.**

November

✪ Royal Agricultural Winter Fair and Royal Horse Show

A major event that has been celebrated since 1922. At this show, the largest indoor agricultural and equestrian competition in the world, vegetables and fruits are on display, along with crafts, farm machinery, livestock, and more. And it's all accompanied by a horse show that is traditionally attended by a member of the British royal family.
Where: Exhibition Place. **When:** 12 days, usually second and third weekends of November. **How:** Write or call the Convention and Tourist Office for more information, or call **416/393-6400.**

3 Insurance

Before leaving home, always check with your health-insurance company to make sure that your coverage extends to Canada. If it does, fine; if it doesn't, or if the coverage is inadequate, you may want to contact an agent to purchase a short-term insurance policy that covers medical costs and emergencies during your trip.

Do the same with home-owner's insurance. Make sure that your home-insurance policy covers off-premises theft and loss wherever it occurs. Find out what procedures you need to follow to make a claim. Again, if you are not adequately covered you may want to purchase an insurance policy that will cover any loss.

Also check your auto insurance to see what it covers. And don't forget the insurance that you may have gratis from your credit-card companies.

If you have signed up for a tour or have prepaid many of your vacation expenses, you may also want to purchase insurance that covers you in the event that you have to cancel your trip for some reason.

Assess the coverage that you already have and determine any additional coverage you may need to purchase. Your best bet will probably be to purchase a comprehensive travel policy that covers all contingencies—cancellation, health, emergency assistance, and loss. These are obtainable from travel agents, or you can contact the following company directly for information: **Wallach & Company,** 107C W. Federal St., Suite 13, Middleburg, VA 22117-0480 (☎ **703/687-3166,** or toll free **800/237-6615**).

4 Tips for Travelers with Disabilities, Seniors & Students

FOR TRAVELERS WITH DISABILITIES   Toronto is a very accessible city. Curb cuts are well made and common throughout the downtown area; special parking privileges are extended to people with disabilities who have disabled plates or a special pass from the city where you're a resident that allows you to park in "No Parking" zones. The subway and trolleys are, unfortunately, not accessible, but the city operates a special service for those with disabilities, called **Wheel-Trans.** Visitors can register for this service. For information call **416/393-4111.**

For more information contact **Disabled Information on Community Services,** Community Information Centre of Metropolitan Toronto, 590 Jarvis St., Toronto, ON, M4Y 2J4 (☎ **416/392-0505,** 24 hours).

FOR SENIORS   Bring some form of photo ID, as many city attractions grant special senior discounts. Some hotels, too, will offer special discounted rates.

If you haven't already done so, think about joining the **American Association of Retired Persons (AARP),** 1909 K St. NW, Washington, DC 20049 (☎ **202/872-4700**).

Also look into the fun courses that are offered at incredibly low prices by **Elderhostel,** 75 Federal St., Boston, MA 02110 (☎ 617/426-7788).

FOR STUDENTS The key to securing discounts and other special favors is the **International Student Identity Card (ISIC),** available to any bona fide full-time high school or university student. Contact the **Council on International Educational Exchange (CIEE),** 205 E. 42nd St., New York, NY 10017 (☎ 212/661-1414). The card is available from all Council Travel offices in the United States. To find the office nearest you, call toll free **800/GETANID.**

5 Getting There

By Plane

THE MAJOR AIRLINES **Air Canada** (☎ toll free **800/ 776-3000**) operates direct flights to Toronto from Baltimore/ Washington, Boston, Chicago, Cleveland, Hartford, Houston, New York, Newark, San Francisco, Los Angeles, Miami, and Tampa. It also flies from major cities around the world and operates indirectly from other U.S. cities.

The other Canadian airline, **Canadian Airlines International** (☎ toll free **800/426-7000**), operates no direct flights into Toronto from the U.S. but does fly directly from London, Paris, Munich, Auckland, Sydney, Tokyo, Hong Kong, Rio de Janeiro, and São Paulo.

Among U.S. airlines, **USAir** (☎ toll free **800/842-5374**) operates directly into Toronto from a number of U.S. cities, notably Baltimore, Boston, Cleveland, Dayton, Philadelphia, and Rochester. **American** (☎ toll free **800/433-7300**) has daily direct flights from Chicago, Dallas, Nashville, and New York. **United** (☎ toll free **800/241-6522**) has direct flights from Chicago and San Francisco. **Northwest** (☎ toll free **800/225-2525**) flies directly from Detroit only. **Delta** (☎ toll free **800/221-1212**) flies direct from Atlanta, Cincinnati, and Syracuse.

You'll arrive at **Pearson International Airport,** 17 miles northwest of downtown, although certain flights land at the Toronto Island Airport, which will require a short ferry ride to downtown. Always confirm with the airline which airport they're using.

FARES Wherever you're traveling from, always shop the different airlines and ask for the lowest fare. Check the newspaper ads in the travel sections of the local/national newspapers, too, for special promotional fares or packages that you can take advantage of.

In general, the following are the least-expensive options. Currently the cheapest direct-flight option is the **APEX (Advance Purchase Excursion)** fare, which is usually valid from 7 to 60 days and must be purchased at least 21 days in advance. These requirements do vary, not only from airline to airline but also from one part of the world to another.

The **excursion** fare is another option. It usually requires a minimum stay of 7 days and a maximum of 60. It often allows a limited number of stopovers, at a surcharge generally ranging from $25 to $50 each. There are no advance-purchase requirements.

By Train

Amtrak's *Maple Leaf* links New York City and Toronto via Albany, Buffalo, and Niagara Falls, departing daily from Penn Station. The journey takes $11^3/_4$ hours. From Chicago, the *International* carries passengers to Toronto via Port Huron, Michigan (a $12^1/_2$-hour trip).

From Buffalo's Exchange Street Station you can also make the trip to Toronto on the Toronto/Hamilton/Buffalo Railway (THB). Connecting services are also available from other major cities along the border.

To secure the lowest round-trip fares book as far in advance as possible and try to travel midweek. Seat availability determines price levels; the earlier you book the more likely you are to secure a lower fare. Here though are a few sample one-way fares for use as guidelines only: New York to Toronto, $98 one way; from Chicago, $91. Meals are not included in these prices. Depending on when you book remember that round-trip fares could be double the fares quoted here if you leave it to the last minute or as little as $20 additional. Always ask about the availability of discounted fares, companion fares, and other special tickets. You'll arrive downtown at Union Station.

Call **Amtrak** (☎ toll free **800/USA-RAIL** or **800/872-7245** or write Amtrak, Union Station, 60 Massachusetts Ave. NE, Washington, DC 20002; ☎ **202/906-3000**), for further information.

By Bus

Greyhound/Trailways is the only bus company that crosses the border into Canada from the United States. You can travel from almost anywhere in the United States, changing buses along the way until you finally reach Toronto. The bus may be faster and cheaper than the train, and its routes may be more flexible if you want to stop along the way, but it's also more cramped, toilet facilities are meager, and meals are taken at somewhat depressing rest stops along the way.

Depending on where you are coming from you should check into Greyhound/Trailways' special unlimited-travel passes as well as into any discount fares that might be offered. It's hard to provide sample fares because the bus companies are also adopting yield management strategies so that prices change from one day to the next depending on demand.

You'll arrive at the Metro Coach Terminal downtown at 610 Bay St., near the corner of Dundas Street. Call **Greyhound/ Trailways** toll free at **800/231-2222** or your nearest local Greyhound Terminal.

By Car

Hopping across the border by car is no problem as the U.S. highway system leads directly into Canada at 13 points. Most people driving to Toronto from the United States will enter from Michigan at Detroit-Windsor via I-75 and the Ambassador Bridge or Port Huron–Sarnia via I-94 and the Bluewater Bridge; from New York via I-190 at Buffalo–Fort Erie, at Niagara Falls, N.Y.–Niagara Falls, Ont., or Niagara Falls, N.Y.–Lewiston; via I-81 crossing at Hill Island, or via Rte. 37 at Ogdensburg-Johnstown or Rooseveltown-Cornwall.

3

Getting to Know Toronto

THIS CHAPTER SETS OUT TO ANSWER ALL YOUR TRAVEL QUESTIONS, furnishing you with all the practical information you'll need during your stay in Toronto to handle any and every experience—from city layout and transportation to emergencies and women's bookstores.

1 Orientation

Arriving

BY PLANE More than 20 major airlines serve Toronto with regularly scheduled flights departing from and arriving at **Pearson International Airport,** located in the northwest corner of Metro Toronto about 30 minutes (17 miles) from downtown.

Three terminals, serviced by more than 50 airlines, cater to the traveler and offer the full services expected at international airports. The most spectacular is the new Trilium Terminal 3 (☎ **905/612-5100**) used by American, Canadian Airlines, British Airways, KLM, Lufthansa, and United, among others. This is a supermodern facility with moving walkways; a huge food court; and hundreds of stores, including North America's very first branch of Harrods.

Facilities at the airport include the exceptionally useful **Transport Canada Information Centres** in all terminals, where a staff fluent in 10 languages will answer queries about the airport, airline information, transportation services, and tourist attractions (☎ **905/676-3506**).

The most convenient way to get into the city from the airport, of course, is **by taxi,** which will cost about $40 to downtown.

Also very convenient is the **Airport Express bus** (☎ **905/ 564-6333**), which travels between the airport and downtown hotels—Harbour Castle Westin, the Royal York, L'Hôtel, the Sheraton Centre, the Holiday Inn, and the Chelsea Inn—every 20 minutes from early morning until late at night. Fare is $11.10 for adults, free for two children under 11 accompanied by an adult; additional children pay $11.10. It takes from 35 minutes to 1¼ hours depending on the traffic.

The cheapest way to go is **by bus and subway,** which will take about an hour. Buses travel between the airport and the Islington subway stop about every 30 minutes for a fare of $6.20. Buses also travel between the airport and the Yorkdale and York Mills subway stations about every 40 minutes for a fare of $6.70 to Yorkdale, $7.75

IMPRESSIONS

There is a Yankee look about the place . . . a pushing, thrusting, business-like, smart appearance.
—Charles MacKay, *Life and Liberty in America* (1857–58)

The houses and stores at Toronto are not to be compared with those of the American towns opposite. But the Englishman has built according to his means—the American according to his expectations.
—Capt. Frederick Marryat, *A Diary in America* (1839)

to York Mills. On both routes two children under 11 travel free if accompanied by an adult. For information, call **905/564-6333** from 7am to 11pm.

In addition, most first-class hotels inside and outside the downtown area run their own **hotel limousine services,** so check when you make your reservation.

If you're **driving to the airport,** take the Gardiner Expressway and Queen Elizabeth Way to Hwy. 427 North; then follow the Airport Expressway signs.

BY TRAIN   All VIA Rail passenger trains pull into the massive, classically proportioned **Union Station** on Front Street, one block west of Yonge Street, opposite the Royal York Hotel. The station has direct access to the subway, so you can easily reach any Toronto destination from here (for VIA Rail information, call **416/366-8411;** in the United States, call Amtrak toll free at **800/USA-RAIL** or **800/872-7245**).

BY BUS   Out-of-town buses arrive and depart from the **Metro Coach Terminal,** 610 Bay St. at Dundas Street, and provide fast, cheap, and efficient service to Canadian and American destinations. Voyageur Colonial, Penetang Midland Coach Lines, Can-Ar, Ontario Northlands, and Trentway Wagar (call **416/596-8423** for fare and schedule information) operate from here. So, too, does Greyhound/Trailways (☎ **416/367-8747,** or toll free **800/661-8747**).

BY CAR   From the United States you are most likely to enter Toronto via either Hwy. 401 or Hwy. 2 and the Queen Elizabeth Way if you come from the west. If you come from the east via Montréal, you'll also use Hwys. 401 and 2. Here are a few approximate driving distances in miles to Toronto: from Atlanta, 977; from Boston, 566; from Buffalo, 96; from Chicago, 534; from Cincinnati, 501; from Dallas, 1,452; from Detroit, 236; from Minneapolis, 972; and from New York, 495.

Tourist Information

For information go to or write to the **Metropolitan Toronto Convention & Visitors Association,** 207 Queens Quay West, Suite 590, in the Queens Quay Terminal at Harbourfront (P.O. Box 126), Toronto, ON, M5J 1A7 (☎ **416/203-2500**), open Monday through Friday from 9am to 5pm. Take the LRT from Union Station to the York Street stop.

More conveniently located is the drop-in **Visitor Information Centre** in the Eaton Centre, on Yonge Street at Dundas Street. It's located on "Level 1 Below" and is open year round Monday through Friday, 10am to 9pm, Saturday from 9am to 6pm, and Sunday from noon to 5pm.

The **Community Information Centre,** 590 Jarvis St., 5th floor (☎ **416/392-0505** 24 hours), specializes in social, government, and health-service information but will try to answer any question, and if they can't, they will direct you to someone who can.

City Layout

Toronto is laid out in a grid system. **Yonge** (pronounced Young) **Street** is the main north-south street, stretching from Lake Ontario in the south well beyond Highway 401 in the north; the main east-west artery is **Bloor Street,** which cuts right through the heart of downtown. Yonge Street divides western cross streets from eastern cross streets.

"Downtown" usually refers to the area stretching south from Eglinton Avenue to the lake between Spadina Avenue in the west and Jarvis Street in the east. Because this is such a large area, for the purposes of this book I have divided it into **downtown** (from the lake north to College/Carlton Street), **midtown** (College/Carlton Street north to Davenport Road), and **uptown** (north from Davenport Road). In the first area you'll find all the lakeshore attractions— Harbourfront, Ontario Place, Fort York, Exhibition Place, the Toronto Islands, plus the CN Tower, City Hall, SkyDome, Chinatown, the Art Gallery, and the Eaton Centre. Midtown includes the Royal Ontario Museum; the University of Toronto; Markham Village; and chic Yorkville, a prime area for browsing and dining al fresco. Uptown is a fast-growing residential and entertainment area for the young, hip and well-heeled.

Metropolitan Toronto is spread over 634 km² (245 square miles) and includes East York and the cities of (from west to east) Etobicoke, York, North York, and Scarborough. Some of its primary attractions exist outside the core, such as the Ontario Science Centre, the Metropolitan Zoo, and Canada's Wonderland. Be prepared to journey somewhat.

UNDERGROUND TORONTO   It is not enough to know the streets of Toronto; you also need to know the warren of subterranean walkways that enable you to go from Union Station in the south to Atrium on Bay at Dundas.

Currently, you can walk from the Queen Street subway station west to the Sheraton Centre, then south through the Richmond-Adelaide Centre, First Canadian Place, and Toronto Dominion Centre all the way (through the dramatic Royal Bank Plaza) to Union Station. En route, branches lead off to the stock exchange, Sun Life Centre, and Metro Hall. Additional walkways linking Simcoe Plaza to 200 Wellington W. and to the CBC Broadcast Centre are planned.

Other walkways exist around Bloor Street and Yonge Street and elsewhere in the city (ask for a map at the tourist information office). So if the weather's bad, you can eat, sleep, dance, shop, and go to the theater without even donning a coat.

NEIGHBORHOODS IN BRIEF   Metropolitan Toronto consists of five cities and one borough under one administrative umbrella. What follows, with a few exceptions, are in the downtown city center:

Harbourfront/Lakefront   The landfill on which the railroad yards and dock facilities were built. Now a glorious playground opening onto the lake.

Financial District   Home to the banks and the trust and insurance companies and birthplace of Toronto's first skyscrapers. From Front Street north to Queen Street, between Yonge Street and York Street.

Old Town/St. Lawrence Market   During the 19th century this was the focal point of the community. Today the market's still going strong and a stroll around the surrounding area will recapture an earlier era. East of Yonge Street between the Esplanade and Adelaide Street.

New Town/King Street West Theater District   An area of dense cultural development, it contains the Royal Alex, Roy Thomson Hall, the CBC building, the Convention Centre, and the CN Tower. From Front Street north to Queen Street and from Bay Street west to Bathurst Street.

Chinatown   As the Chinese community has grown, Chinatown has extended along Dundas Street and north along Spadina Avenue. A fascinating mixture of old and new—tiny hole-in-the-wall restaurants contrast with glitzy shopping centers built with new Hong Kong money. Dundas Street West from University Avenue to Spadina Avenue and north to College Street.

Yonge Street   Toronto's main drag. Lined with stores and restaurants of all sorts. Seedy in places, with a small section of strip and porno joints, especially around College and Dundas streets.

Queen Street Village   Youthful and funky. The old has not been entirely driven out by the new. The street offers an eclectic mix— antiques stores, secondhand bookshops, reasonably priced dining, and more. Queen Street from University Avenue to Bathurst Street and beyond.

Queen's Park and the University   Home to the Ontario Legislature and many of the colleges and buildings that make up the University of Toronto. From College Street to Bloor Street between Spadina Avenue and Queen's Park Crescent.

Cabbagetown   Once described by writer Hugh Garner as the largest Anglo-Saxon slum in North America, this area stretching east of

IMPRESSIONS

[On Toronto in 1927] Drear but pompous. . . . It looked more or less like a bit of Birmingham straightened out, drained of bawdy and homogenized—"a nest," suggested the local writer Jesse Edgar Middleton cosily, or perhaps despairingly, "of British-thinking, British-acting people."
—Jan Morris, *Travels* (1976)

The wild and rabid toryism of Toronto is, I speak seriously, appalling.
—Charles Dickens, Letter to John Forster (1842)

Underground Toronto

9465

| H | I | J | K | L | M | N | O |

Metro Toronto Coach Terminal
Atrium on Bay
Dundas Street
Dundas Station

Marriott Hotel
Eaton's
One Dundas West
Eaton Tower

Bell Trinity Square
Eaton Centre

City Hall
Cadillac Fairview Tower

City Hall Parking

Queen Station
Queen Street

Sheraton Centre Hotel
Thomson Building
520 Bay
Simpson Tower
The Hudson's Bay Company
1 Queen St. East
20 Richmond
Richmond Street

The Plaza at Sheraton Centre

Richmond Adelaide Complex
Federal Building
The Lanes
130 Adelaide W. West
Richmond Adelaide Centre
Bay Adelaide Centre
Yonge Richmond Centre
Cambridge Suites Hotel

York Street
Bay Street
Younge Street
Adelaide Street

Toronto Stock Exchange
105 Adelaide W. West
11 Adelaide W.
104 Yonge
100 Yonge
One Financial Place
20 Victoria
25 Adelaide

2 First Canadian Pl.
First Canadian Pl.
1 First Canadian P.
Scotia Plaza
The Bank of Nova Scotia
King St. West
King Street

Standard Life Centre
Royal Trust Tower
Toronto Dominion Bank Pavilion
West
North
King Station

Toronto Dominion Centre
Toronto Dominion Bank Tower
Ernst & Young Tower
Design Exchange
Commerce Court
East

Commercial Union Tower
South
Wellington Street

95 Wellington West
Aetna Tower
North Tower
BCE Place
Bay Wellington Tower
Labatt House

Royal Bank Plaza
South Tower
The Galleria
22 Front St. West
Heritage Sq.
Hockey Hall of Fame

Royal York House
Canada Trust Tower
Front Street

Union Station

Union Station
VIA Rail Canada
GO Transit
Harbourfront Streetcar Station

Lake Ontario

Parliament Street to the Don Valley between Gerrard Street and Bloor Street has been gentrified and is now home to such celebrities as dancer Karen Kain.

Yorkville Originally a village outside the city. In the 1960s it became Toronto's Haight-Ashbury but is now a fashionable enclave of designer boutiques, galleries, cafés, and restaurants. North and west of Bloor Street and Yonge Street.

The Annex An architecturally unique residential community, which led the fight against the Spadina Expressway. From Bedford Road to Bathurst Street and from Bloor Street to Bernard Street.

Rosedale Named after Sheriff Jarvis's residence. Curving tree-lined streets and elegant homes are the hallmarks of this leafy suburb. Northeast of Yonge Street and Bloor Street to Castle Frank and the Moore Park Ravine. Synonymous with the wealthy elite.

Forest Hill The second prime residential area and home to Upper Canada College and Bishop Strachan School for girls. Stretches west of Avenue Road between St. Clair Avenue and Eglinton Avenue.

The Beaches Communal, youthful, and cozy. The boardwalk and beach make it a relaxing casual neighborhood. Only 15 minutes from downtown at the end of the Queen Street East streetcar (trolley) line.

The East End—the Danforth Largely a Greek and Indian community. Here you'll find a number of restaurants, shops, and cafés catering to both communities. A continuation of Bloor Street across the Don Valley Viaduct.

North York Recent redevelopment of this community about 8 miles north of Toronto's Queen Street has made this one of the hottest real estate markets in the country.

2 Getting Around

By Public Transportation

Public transit is operated by the **Toronto Transit Commission (TTC)** (☎ **416/393-4636** daily from 7am to 10pm for information), which provides an overall interconnecting subway, bus, and streetcar system.

Fares (including transfers to buses or streetcars) are $2 (or 10 tickets for $13) for adults, $1 (10 tickets for $6.50) for students 19 and under and seniors, and 50¢ (eight tickets for $2.50) for children under 12. You can purchase from any subway collector a special $5 day pass good for unlimited travel Monday to Friday after 9:30am and all day Saturday. On Sundays or holidays, a similar $5 pass may be used by up to six people (maximum of two adults).

For surface transportation you need a ticket, a token, or exact change. Tickets and tokens may be obtained at subway entrances or authorized stores that display the sign TTC TICKETS MAY BE PURCHASED HERE. Always obtain a transfer, just in case you need it. They are

The TTC Subway System

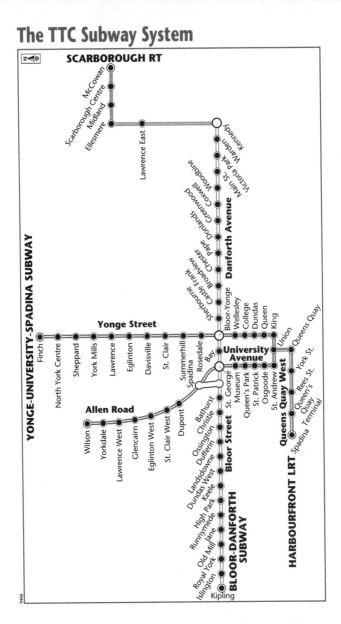

obtainable free of charge in the subways from a push-button machine just inside the entrance or directly from drivers on streetcars and buses.

THE SUBWAY It's a joy to ride—fast, quiet, and clean. It's a very simple system to use, too, consisting of two lines—Bloor-Danforth and Yonge-University-Spadina—designed basically in the form of a cross: The Bloor Street east-west line runs from Kipling Avenue in the west to Kennedy Road in the east, where it connects with Scarborough Rapid Transit traveling to Scarborough Centre and McCowan Road. The Yonge Street north-south line runs from Finch Avenue in the north to Union Station (Front Street) in the south. From here, it loops north along University Avenue and connects with the Bloor line at the St. George station. A Spadina extension runs north from St. George to Wilson Avenue.

A light rapid transit system connects downtown to Har-bourfront, running from Union Station along Queen's Quay to Spadina with stops at Queen's Quay ferry docks, York Street, Simcoe Street, and Rees Street. No transfer is needed from subway to LRT and vice versa.

The subway operates Monday through Friday from around 6am to around 1:30am and Sunday from 9am to 1:30am. From 1am to 5:30am a Blue Night Network operates on basic surface routes running about every 30 minutes. For route information, pick up a Ride Guide at subway entrances or call **416/393-4636.** Multilingual information is available. You can also use the automated information service at **416/393-8663.**

Smart commuters (and visitors) park their cars at subway terminal stations at Kipling, Islington, Finch, Wilson, Warden, Kennedy, York Mills, Victoria Park, and Keele. Certain conditions apply. Call **416/393-8663** for details. You'll have to get there very early, though.

BUSES & STREETCARS Where the subway leaves off, buses and streetcars take over to carry you east-west or north-south along the city's arteries. When you pay your fare (on bus, streetcar, or subway), always pick up a transfer, so that if you want to transfer to another mode of transportation, you won't have to pay another fare. For complete TTC information, call **416/393-4636.**

By Taxi

As usual, this is an expensive mode of transportation: $2.20 the minute you step in and then $1 for every additional kilometer. There's also a 10¢ charge for each bag. As you can see, cab fares can mount up, especially in rush hours. Nevertheless, if you need a cab you can hail one on the street (they also line up in front of the big hotels) or call one of the major companies: **Diamond** (☎ **416/366-6868**), **Yellow** (☎ **416/363-4141**), or **Metro** (☎ **416/363-5611**).

By Car

CAR RENTALS Prices on car rentals change so frequently and vary so widely that probably your best bet is to shop around using the *Yellow Pages.* Still, just to give you some idea, here are a couple of companies and their rates: **Budget,** 171 Bay St. (☎ **416/364-7104**), charges $42 (including 200 free kilometers) per day plus 12¢ per kilometer, or $210 per week (including 1,400 free kilometers), for a compact car. **Tilden,** 930 Yonge St. (☎ **416/925-4551**), charges $44 per day (including 200 free kilometers) plus 15¢ per kilometer, or $249 per week, for a small car; there are 10 Metro locations. Always ask about special weekend rates and other discounts.

Note: If you're under 25, check with the company—many will rent on a cash-only basis, some only if you have a credit card, and others will not rent to you at all.

DRIVING & PARKING   Driving and parking in the city can be very frustrating because the traffic moves slowly downtown and parking costs are extremely high.

Parking downtown runs about $4 per half hour, with a $15 to $17 maximum. After 6pm and on Sunday, rates go down to around $6. Generally the city-owned lots, marked with a big green "P," are slightly cheaper. Observe the parking restrictions—otherwise the city will tow your car away. Still, if you can't do without your car, note the following:

You can turn right on a red light after coming to a full stop and checking the intersection unless there is a sign forbidding such turns. Watch carefully also for one-way streets and no-left- and no-right-turn signs. The driver and front-seat passenger must wear their seatbelts (if you're caught not wearing yours, you'll pay a substantial fine). The speed limit within the city is 30 m.p.h. (50kmh). You must stop at pedestrian crosswalks. If you are following a streetcar and it stops, you must stop well back from the rear doors so that passengers can exit easily and safely. (Where there are concrete safety islands in the middle of the street for streetcar stops, this rule does not apply, but exercise care nonetheless.) Radar detectors are illegal.

The **Canadian Automobile Association (CAA),** 60 Commerce Valley Dr. E., Thornhill (☎ **905/771-3111**), provides aid to any driver who is a member of AAA.

By Ferry

Metro Parks operates the ferries that travel to the Toronto Islands. Call **392-8193** for schedules and information.

By Bicycle

You can secure a pamphlet outlining biking routes from the Toronto Convention and Visitor's Office. The Toronto Islands, the Beaches, Harbourfront/Lakefront/Sunnyside, and High Park are all great biking areas.

You can **rent bicycles** at Harbourfront right across from Queen's Quay; on Centre Island from Toronto Island Bicycle Rental (☎ **203-0009**); at High Park Cycle and Sports, 1168 Bloor St. W. (☎ **532-7300**); and at Bicycle Transit, 2348 Lakeshore Blvd. (☎ **252-1393**).

Fast Facts: Toronto

Airlines   Here are a few useful airline addresses: Air Canada, 130 Bloor St. W., at Avenue Road (☎ **416/925-2311**); American Airlines, in the Royal York Hotel, 100 Front St. W., the Manulife

Center, 55 Bloor St. W., and 44 Gerrard St. W. (☎ **416/ 283-2243**); Canadian Airlines International, on the concourse level of the Toronto Dominion Centre, 69 Yonge St. (☎ **416/ 675-2211**); Northwest Airlines, in the Royal York Hotel, 100 Front St. W. (☎ toll free **800/225-2525**); United Airlines, at the airport (☎ toll free **800/241-6522**); and USAir, the Royal York Hotel, 100 Front St. W. (☎ **416/361-1560**).

Airport See "Orientation," earlier in this chapter.

Area Code Toronto's area code is **416;** Mississanga is now **905.**

Auto Rentals See "Getting Around," earlier in this chapter.

Buses See "Getting Around," earlier in this chapter.

Business Hours Banks are generally open Monday through Thursday from 10am to 3pm and Friday from 10am to 6pm. To get the most advantageous rate of exchange, go to a bank. Most government and corporate offices are open Monday through Friday from 9am to 5pm. Stores are generally open Monday through Wednesday from 9:30 or 10am to 6pm and Saturday and Sunday from 10am to 5pm, with extended hours (until 8 to 9:30pm) on Thursday and usually Friday.

Car Rentals See "Getting Around," earlier in this chapter.

Climate See "Timing Your Trip" in Chapter 2.

Currency See "Information, Entry Requirements & Money" in Chapter 2.

Currency Exchange The best place to change your currency is at a bank. Currency can also be conveniently exchanged at the airport.

Dentist The Royal College of Dental Surgeons (☎ **916-6555**) offers emergency after-hours dental care. Otherwise, ask at the front desk or the concierge at your hotel. (See also "Medical Services," below.)

Doctor The College of Physicians and Surgeons, 80 College St. (☎ **961-1711**), operates a referral service from 9am to 5pm.

Documents Required See "Information, Entry Requirements & Money" in Chapter 2.

Driving Rules See "Getting Around," earlier in this chapter.

Drugstores Look under "Pharmacies" in the *Yellow Pages.* Shoppers Drug Mart, at 360 Bloor St. W., at Spadina Avenue, stays open Monday through Friday until midnight. For the late-night pharmacy closest to you, call **800/363-1040.** They operate many other branches downtown. The other big chain is Pharma Plus, with a store at 68 Wellesley St., at Church Street (☎ **924-7760**), which is open daily from 8am to midnight.

Electricity Same as in the United States—110 volts, 50 cycles, AC.

Embassies/Consulates   All embassies are in Ottawa, the national capital. However, many nations maintain consulates in Toronto, including the following: Australian Consulate-General, 175 Bloor St. E. (☎ **323-1155** or **323-3919**); British Consulate-General, 777 Bay St. at College (☎ **593-1267**); and the United States Consulate, 360 University Ave. (☎ **595-1700**).

Emergencies   Call **911** for fire, police, and ambulance.

Etiquette   At Confederation, Canadians opted for peace, order, and good government (as opposed to life, liberty, and the pursuit of happiness)—and it shows. You'll see respect for the individual expressed in terms of consideration for others and the community as a whole. Canadians will appreciate you more if you behave with decorum in public. Don't litter; don't push and shove; don't cause a ruckus. Although they will probably not initiate a conversation, being naturally reserved, they will welcome it if you do. I have always found Canadians very helpful. On a recent visit to Toronto with a wheelchair-bound friend, I never once had to ask for help. It was always offered before I could ask, and often people would retrace their steps to assist me in carrying the chair up a flight of steps.

Eyeglasses   Two offices of A-1 Public Optical, 69 Queen St. E., at Church Street (☎ **364-0740**), and at 750 Dundas St. W., at Bathurst Street (☎ **860-1550**), offer one-hour service, depending on the prescription.

Hairdressers/Barbers   For expensive coiffuring, try the Vidal Sassoon Salon, 37 Avenue Rd. (☎ **920-1333**), or Choppers Hair Design, 89 Bloor St. W. (☎ **928-9199**). There are, of course, plenty of more modest salons like the small one in Village by the Grange. Ask at your hotel for a recommendation.

Holidays   See "Timing Your Trip" in Chapter 2.

Hospitals   Try Toronto General Hospital, 200 Elizabeth St. (emergency ☎ **340-3948**).

Hotlines   Help is available from the following: rape crisis (☎ **597-8808**), assault victims (☎ **863-0511**), drug/alcohol crisis (☎ **595-6000**), and suicide prevention (☎ **285-0100** or **598-1121**).

Information   See "Information, Entry Requirements & Money" in Chapter 2 and also "Orientation," earlier in this chapter.

Laundry/Dry Cleaning   The following are conveniently located self-service laundromats: Bloor Laundromat, 598 Bloor St. W., at Bathurst Street (☎ **588-6600**); and Speedy Automatic Coin Wash, 568 Church St., at Wellesley Street (☎ **922-1147**).

For one-hour dry cleaning, try One-hour Dry Cleaner, 987 Bay St. (☎ **966-6868**); or Best Serve-One Hour Cleaners, 531 Yonge St., at Wellesley Street (☎ **921-9016**), which gives this service until 10am. It's open from 7am to 6pm Monday through

Saturday. One-hour dry cleaning is also available at Parliament One-Hour Cleaning, 436 Parliament St., at Spruce Street, near Carlton Street (☎ **923-5276**).

Libraries   Metro Library is at 789 Yonge St., north of Bloor Street (☎ **393-7000**).

Liquor/Liquor Laws   Liquor is sold at Liquor Control Board of Ontario (LCBO) stores, open Monday through Saturday. Most are open from 10am to 6pm (some stay open evenings). Call **365-5900** for locations. These stores sell liquor, wine, and some beers. Check the *White Pages* under "Liquor Control Board" for locations. Convenient locations include: College Park, First Canadian Place, Manulife Centre, Eaton Centre, Union Station, and Yonge and Wellesley.

True wine lovers, though, will want to check out Vintages stores (also operated by the LCBO), which carry a more extensive and more specialized selection of wines. The most convenient downtown locations are in the lower-level concourse of Hazelton Lanes (☎ **924-9463**) and at Queen's Quay (☎ **864-6777**). Look also for the Wine Rack at 560 Queen St. W. (☎ **363-3647**) and at Wellesley and Church (☎ **923-9393**).

Beer is sold at Brewers Retail Stores, most of which are open Monday through Friday from 10am to 10pm and Saturday from 10am to 8pm. Check the *Yellow Pages* under "Beer and Ale" for locations. Convenient downtown locations include: Church and Wellesley, College and Bathurst, and Bloor and Spadina.

Some quiddities of the local law: Drinking hours are 11am to 1am Monday through Saturday and noon to 11pm Sunday (cocktail lounges are not usually licensed to sell liquor on Sunday; dining rooms are). The minimum drinking age is 19.

Lost Property   The TTC Lost Articles Office is at the Bay Street subway station (☎ **393-4100**), open Monday through Friday from 8am to 5:30pm.

Luggage Storage/Lockers   Lockers are available at Union Station.

Mail   Postage for letters and postcards to the United States costs 50¢; to overseas, 88¢. Mailing letters and postcards within Canada costs 43¢. Call **416/506-0938** for most current rates.

Maps   Available at convenience and book stores. Or try Canada Map Company, 211 Yonge St., north of Queen Street (☎ **362-9297**), or Open Air Books and Maps, 25 Toronto St., near Yonge and Adelaide streets (☎ **363-0719**).

Medical Services   For medical or dental problems, the Toronto General Hospital, with an entrance at 150 Gerrard St. W., as well as the main entrance at 200 Elizabeth St., provides 24-hour emergency service (☎ **340-3948**).

Money   See "Information, Entry Requirements & Money" in Chapter 2.

Newspapers/Magazines The three daily newspapers are the *Globe and Mail,* the *Toronto Star,* and the *Toronto Sun. Eye* and *Now* are the arts-and-entertainment weeklies of the moment. In addition, there are many English-language ethnic Toronto newspapers serving the Portuguese, Hungarian, Italian, East Indian, Korean, Chinese, and Caribbean communities. *Toronto Life* is the major monthly city magazine. *Where Toronto* is usually provided free in your hotel room.

Some of the best newsmagazine selections can be found at the Book Cellar and Maison de Presse, both in Yorkville; Coles the World's Biggest Bookstore and Pages on Queen Street West; and Lichtman's News and Books, at Yonge and Bloor streets, Yonge and Richmond streets, the Atrium on Bay Street, Yonge Street and Eglinton Avenue, and 1430 Yonge St.

Photographic Needs For major repairs there's the Camera Repair Centre, 1162 Yonge St., north of the Rosedale subway station (☎ **923-8143**).

Convenient downtown photo stores include Black's Camera, in the Eaton Centre (☎ **598-1596**); the Manulife Centre, 2 Bloor St. W. (☎ **928-1520**); and at many other locations. There's also the Japan Camera Centre, in the Eaton Centre (☎ **598-1474**); College Park (☎ **598-1133**); BCE Place (☎ **777-9909**); and other locations. Vistek, 496 Queen St. E. (☎ **365-1777**), is good for everything—repairs, camera, film, and lab.

Police In a life-threatening emergency, call **911.** For all other matters you can reach the Metro police at **324-2222.**

Post Office The post office has been withdrawing from traditional direct customer service. Postal services can now be found at convenience and drug stores like Shopper's Drug Mart and others. Look for the sign in the window indicating such services. There are also post office windows open throughout the city in Atrium on Bay (☎ **506-0911**), Commerce Court (☎ **956-7452**), the TD Centre (☎ **360-7105**), and at 36 Adelaide St. W. (☎ **360-7287**).

Radio The programming of the Canadian Broadcasting Corporation is one of the joys, as far as I'm concerned, of traveling in Canada. It offers a great mix of intelligent discussion and commentary as well as drama and music. In Toronto the CBC broadcasts on 740 AM and 94.1 FM.

CHIN, at 1540 AM and 100.7 FM, will get you in touch with the ethnic/multicultural scene in the city.

Religious Services Toronto has houses of worship for all major faiths, including the following: St. James Cathedral (Anglican), 65 Church St., at King Street (☎ **364-7865**); Rosedale Baptist Church, 877 Yonge St. (☎ **926-0732**); Zen Buddhist Temple, 86 Vaughan Rd. (☎ **658-0137**); Church of the Mother of God Proussa (Greek Orthodox), 461 Richmond St. E. (☎ **364-8918**); Beth Sholom Synagogue, 1445 Eglinton Ave. W. (☎ **783-6103**);

St. George's Lutheran Church, 410 College St. (☎ **921-2687**); St. Andrew's Presbyterian Church, 75 Simcoe St., at King Street (☎ **593-5600**); and St. Michael's Cathedral (Roman Catholic), 200 Church St. (☎ **364-0234**).

Restrooms Public restrooms are found in major shopping complexes like Eatons, the Manulife Centre, the Holt Renfrew Centre, the Colonnade, and similar convenient locations. They are invariably clean and well kept. You can also use hotel and restaurant facilities.

Safety As large cities go, Toronto is generally safe. But there are precautions that you should take whenever you're traveling in an unfamiliar city or country. Stay alert and be aware of your immediate surroundings. Wear a money belt and keep a close eye on your possessions. Be particularly careful with cameras, purses, and wallets, all favorite targets of thieves and pickpockets. Be especially careful walking on dark streets and in parks after dark. Every society has its criminals. It's your responsibility to be aware and alert even in the most heavily touristed areas.

Shoe Repairs For while-you-wait service, go to Mr. Presto at Royal Bank Plaza (☎ **860-1712**); or to any of the many Moneysworth outlets: BCE Place (☎ **869-1475**); 33 Bloor St. E. (☎ **922-6534**); First Canadian Place (☎ **362-7310**); TD Centre (☎ **861-0163**); or Eaton Centre (☎ **593-8745**).

Taxes The provincial retail sales tax is 8%; there's also a 5% tax on hotel/motel rooms and a national 7% goods and services tax (GST).

In general, nonresidents may apply for a refund of these taxes for nondisposable merchandise that will be exported for use provided they were removed from Canada within 60 days of purchase. Note, though, that the following do not qualify for rebate: meals and restaurant charges, alcohol, tobacco, gas, car rentals, and such services as dry cleaning and shoe repair. The quickest and easiest way to secure the refund is to stop in at a duty-free shop at the border. You must have proper receipts with GST registration numbers. Or you can apply through the mail but it will take about four weeks to receive your refund. For an application form and information, write or call Revenue Canada, Customs and Excise, Visitor Rebate Program, Ottawa, Canada K1A 1J5 (☎ **613/ 991-3346**), *well in advance* of your trip. You can also contact Ontario Travel, 77 Bloor St. W., Queen's Park, Toronto, ON, M7A 2R9 (☎ **416/314-0944,** or toll free **800/668-2746**).

For information on the new GST, call **416/973-1000.**

Taxis See "Getting Around" earlier in this chapter.

Telephone A local call from a telephone booth costs 25¢. Watch out for hotel surcharges on local and long-distance calls; often a local call will cost at least $1 from a hotel room.

Time Toronto is on eastern standard time. Daylight saving time is in effect April through October.

Tipping   Basically it's the same as in the United States: 15% in restaurants, 15% to 20% for taxis, and $1 per bag for porters.

Transit Information   For information on the subway, bus, and streetcar system, call **393-4636.**

Useful Telephone Numbers   Call **283-1010** for the "Talking Yellow Pages" and then follow the instructions for securing the latest business news, stock market report, events calendar, "What's On for Kids," national sports report, and weather.

---

3   Networks & Resources

FOR STUDENTS   Toronto has several major colleges as well as the large and sprawling University of Toronto.

George Brown College of Applied Arts and Technology (☎ **867-2000**) has several campuses around town, including the St. James campus at 200 King St. E.; the Kensington Campus near the Kensington Market at 21 Nassau St.; the Nightingale Campus at 2 Murray St., near University Avenue and Dundas Street; and the campus at Casa Loma, 160 Kendal Ave., at Davenport Road and Spadina Avenue. Schools include theater and dance schools. The college bookstores are at 200 King St. E. (☎ **867-2365**) and at 160 Kendal Ave. (☎ **944-4440**).

Ryerson Polytechnical Institute (☎ **979-5000**) is located at 350 Victoria St., at Gould Street. Here are some useful telephone numbers:

Student information (☎ **979-5036**)
Bookstore (☎ **979-5116**)
CKLN radio, 380 Victoria St. (☎ **595-1477**)
The Ryersonian newspaper (☎ **979-5323**)
Theater box office (☎ **977-1055**)
Women's center (☎ **598-9838**)

The **University of Toronto,** Simcoe Hall, King's College Circle, Toronto, ON, M5S 1A1 (☎ **416/978-8638** or **978-4111** for tour information), is the largest university in Canada, with 52,500 students (41,000 full-time). It offers many activities and events year round that any visitor can attend—lectures, seminars, concerts, and more. U of T Day is usually celebrated in the middle of October, when the university holds open house to the community and also celebrates with a children's fair and the annual homecoming football game and parade.

Downtown, the main **St. George Campus** university buildings are located in an area stretching from College Street to Bloor Street and from University Avenue to Spadina Avenue. Composed of several separate colleges, most of which are on the downtown campus, the university also operates **Erindale College** on Mississauga Road North in Mississauga and **Scarborough College** on Military Trail in Scarborough.

Some useful university addresses and telephone numbers include the following:

Libraries: John P. Robarts Research Library (☎ **978-2294**); Hart House (☎ **978-4411**); University College (☎ **978-3170**).

Student Affairs: Dental Clinic (☎ **979-4335**); information and events (☎ **978-8638**): Hart House (☎ **978-4732**); International Student Centre, 33 St. George St. (☎ **978-2564**); Students Association, 119 St. George St. (☎ **598-3110**); U of T Gays and Lesbians, 315 Bloor St. W. (☎ **971-7880**); Koffler Student Services Centre, 214 College St.

Theaters and Sports: Athletic tickets (☎ **978-4112**); Hart House Theatre (☎ **978-8668**); Macmillan Theatre and Walter Hall, Faculty of Music (☎ **978-3774**); Varsity Arena Stadium (☎ **978-7388**).

Publications and Radio: Bookstore, 214 College St. (☎ **978-7900**); *Bulletin,* 45 Willcocks St. (☎ **978-7016**); *The Varsity,* 44 St. George St. (☎ **979-2831**); *U of T* magazine, 21 King's College Circle (☎ **978-2106**); U of T Radio, 91 St. George St. (☎ **595-0909**).

FOR GAY MEN & LESBIANS   Any gay man or lesbian will find the following resources useful. First, pick up a copy of *Xtra!,* available free at many bookstores, including the **Gay Liberation Bookstore/Glad Day Bookshop,** 598A Yonge St., 2nd floor (☎ **961-4161**), open Monday to Friday from 10am to 9pm, Saturday until 7pm, and Sunday from noon until 6pm.

For information, call the **Gay Phone Line** (☎ **964-6600**) or **Tel-Xtra** (☎ **925-9872**).

For political and community information, contact **Gay & Lesbian Youth Toronto** (☎ **591-6749**) or the **Coalition for Lesbian and Gay Rights,** 736 Bathurst St. (☎ **533-6824**).

FOR WOMEN   For books and information on the feminist scene, stop by the **Toronto Women's Bookstore,** 73 Harbord St., at Spadina (☎ **922-8744**). It's open Monday through Thursday and Saturday from 10:30am to 6pm, Friday until 9pm, and Sunday from noon to 5pm.

There's also a **Women's Crisis Line** (☎ **534-7507**), operated by the city. For general community/political information, secure a copy of the local women's publication, **VOICE,** 152 Arlington St. (☎ **656-4949**).

4

Toronto Accommodations

ALTHOUGH TORONTO HAS MANY FINE HOTELS, IT'S NOT EASY TO FIND good-value accommodations downtown. The city is expensive. Most of the top hotels are pricey and cater to a business clientele; at even the more moderate establishments you can expect to pay $80 to $100 per day; budget hotels, which are few, charge less than $80, while nonhotel accommodations, like university dorms, start at $45 to $50 per night. Bed-and-breakfasts are a good budget bet, but even they are creeping upward in price.

The situation is not helped by a 5% accommodations tax and the new national 7% GST.

There are some things that you can do to combat the situation. I cannot stress enough how important it is to ask for a discount. Hotel rates move up and down depending on the traffic—in fact, hotels are beginning to apply the same yield management techniques that airlines have been using successfully, so that rates go up and down depending on the occupancy. For example, a single room listed at $199 could rent for as little as $130. If a room goes unsold the revenue is lost forever. The management would much prefer to sell a room than not, so don't be ashamed to ask. State what you're prepared to pay and see what happens. If business is slow, it will work; if it's not, it won't.

Take advantage of special discounts. Always ask about discounts for special groups of people—corporate personnel, government employees, the military, seniors, students—whatever group to which you legitimately belong. Also ask about seasonal discounts, especially summer rates and weekend packages, which can help you secure some great bargains even at the most luxurious establishments.

Remember, too, that the prices quoted here are so-called rack rates—the prices quoted to walk-ins. These can be as much as 40% higher than other discounted rates—government, corporate, and so on. Again, ask for the discount.

In addition, always ask about parking charges and surcharges on local and long-distance phone calls. Both can make a big difference in your bill.

In the pages that follow I have categorized my favorites according to price and location. Downtown runs from the lakeshore to College/Carlton Street between Spadina Avenue and Jarvis Street; midtown refers to the area north of College/Carlton Street to where Dupont crosses Yonge Street, also between Spadina and Jarvis; uptown, west, and east designate areas outside the city core. I have included a selection of airport hotels because "the Strip," as it's called, has about 20 hotels and functions as a large entertainment center, not only for visitors but also for natives who think nothing of popping out there to a dance club or dining spot.

AN IMPORTANT NOTE ON PRICES   The price brackets for a double room are roughly as follows: very expensive, $175 and up per day; expensive, from $100 to $175; moderate, from $70 to $100; budget, less than $65. I emphasize that these are only very rough categories, and subtle distinctions of taste, clientele, and reputation must also be taken into account.

Unless stated otherwise, *the prices cited in this guide are given in Canadian dollars,* which is good news for you because the Canadian dollar is worth 35% less than the American dollar but buys just about as much. As we go to press, $1 Canadian is worth 74¢ U.S., which means that your $100-a-night hotel room will cost only $74 U.S. a night, your $50 dinner for two will cost only $37 U.S., and your $5 breakfast will cost only $3.70 U.S.

Note: The accommodations tax is 5%, and the goods and services tax is 7%, but both are refunded to nonresidents upon application (see "Taxes" in "Fast Facts: Toronto" in Chapter 3).

BED & BREAKFAST   For interesting, truly personal accommodations, contact **Toronto Bed & Breakfast,** 253 College St. (P.O. Box 269), Toronto, ON, M5T 1R5 (☎ **416/588-8800** Monday to Friday from 9am to noon and 2 to 7pm), for their list of homes offering bed-and-breakfast accommodations within the city for an average $60 to $70 per night double. The association will reserve for you, or you can choose an establishment and make all the arrangements yourself.

You can also contact **Metropolitan Bed and Breakfast Registry of Toronto,** 615 Mount Pleasant Rd., Suite 269, Toronto, ON, M4S 3C5 (☎ **416/964-2566;** fax 416/537-0233), which lists close to 40 lovely bed-and-breakfast accommodations, ranging from $55 and up double. Include $2 for postage and handling when you write requesting a booklet. They will make reservations for you.

Other organizations to try include the **Downtown Toronto Association of Bed and Breakfast Guesthouses,** P.O. Box 190, Station B, Toronto, ON, M5T 2W1 (☎ **416/368-1420;** fax 416/368-1653). This association represents about 30 B&Bs and is operated by Linda Lippa, an enthusiastic B&B host herself who has a spacious Victorian home where she welcomes guests. The best time to call is between 8:30am and 7pm. All homes are no-smoking. Room prices range from $45 to $65 single and $55 to $75 double.

Bed & Breakfast Accommodators, 223 Strathmore Blvd., Toronto, ON, M4J 1P4 (☎ **416/461-7095**), offers nine rooms with three shared baths. Facilities include a kitchen and daily maid service. Breakfast is included. It's located off Greenwood Avenue, convenient to the Greenwood subway stop. Rates are $45 single and $55 double. Fully furnished two- and three-bedroom apartments are also available.

Bed and Breakfast Homes of Toronto, P.O. Box 46093, College Park Post Office, ON, M5B 2L8 (☎ **416/363-6362**), represents about 20 homes with doubles starting at $45. The organization lets you speak directly to the hosts before booking.

1 Downtown

The downtown area runs from the lakefront to College/Carlton Street between Spadina Avenue and Jarvis Street.

Very Expensive

Cambridge Suites Hotel, 15 Richmond St. E., close to the corner of Yonge Street, Toronto, ON, M5C 1N2. ☎ **416/368-1990,** or toll free **800/463-1990.** Fax 416/601-3751. 230 suites. A/C MINIBAR TV TEL **Subway:** Queen.

Rates (including continental breakfast): $200 single; $220 double. **Parking:** $14.

Ideally situated downtown, this all-suite hotel features comfortable accommodations and the extra-special conveniences that make all the difference to the traveler. Each large 550-square-foot suite has a refrigerator, a microwave, and dishes, along with a supply of coffee, tea, and cookies. If you like, you can leave a list and your grocery shopping will be done for you. The furnishings are extremely comfortable and include a couch, armchairs, and a coffee table. (In some cases, french doors separate the living area from the bedroom.) There are two TVs and two telephones in each suite, with hookups for conference calls and a computer. There's also a dressing area with a full-length mirror and a marble bathroom, equipped with a hairdryer and a full complement of amenities. The penthouse luxury suites are duplexes that have Jacuzzis.

Dining/Entertainment: Facilities include a small, comfortable bar and a fine dining room that serves reasonably priced entrées at dinner, such as salmon teriyaki or breast of chicken with cilantro and lime beurre blanc.

Services: Daily maid service, valet, concierge.

Facilities: Business center; laundry; convenience store; fitness center, boasting a fine view of the city and equipped with whirlpool; exercise room and sauna.

Hilton International, 145 Richmond St. W., Toronto, ON, M5H 3M6. ☎ **416/869-3456,** or toll free **800/445-8667.** Fax 416/869-1478. 601 rms and suites. A/C MINIBAR TV TEL **Subway:** Osgoode.

Rates: $160 single; $180 double. Extra person $20. One child under 18 stays free in parents' room. Weekend packages available. **Parking:** $17 overnight.

If you approach the Hilton from the rear you'll see the steam rising from this plush hotel's show pool, just one of the luxury facilities available at this stylish, 32-story, $40-million establishment. Part of the Hilton hotels chain, it is conveniently located near the Convention Centre.

If you wish, you can take a glass-enclosed elevator to your room, which will be large and impeccably decorated with all the expected conveniences—phone, color TV, AM/FM radio, and individual temperature control—plus such unusual touches as scales and alarm clocks. Rooms are currently being refurbished in shades of jade and rose.

Dining/Entertainment: Trees 20 feet tall separate the lobby from the Garden Court restaurant, where you can enjoy breakfast, lunch, afternoon tea, or dinner while seated on a cushioned rattan chair. Barristers, as might be expected, has a clubby atmosphere, with wonderful leather armchairs and couches.

Services: 24-hour room service, concierge, laundry/valet, babysitting.

Facilities: Heated indoor pool, sauna, whirlpool, exercise room, massage specialist, executive business center.

King Edward Hotel, 37 King St. E., Toronto, ON, M5C 2E9.
☎ **416/863-9700.** Fax 416/367-5515. 312 rms and suites.
A/C MINIBAR TV TEL **Subway:** King.
Rates: $210–$230 single; $230–$255 double; from $370 suite. Weekend packages $140–$150 per night for room and valet parking. **Parking:** $24.

Affectionately known as The King Eddy, this is the city's oldest hotel. In its heyday it welcomed such guests as Edward, Prince of Wales, Rudolph Valentino, Charles de Gaulle, Richard Burton and Liz Taylor, the Beatles, and anybody who was anybody in Toronto.

It was built in 1903 by distiller George Gooderham, who was then the richest man in Toronto. In 1981 it underwent a $40 million renovation that restored all of the architectural features—marble Corinthian columns, sculpted stucco, and the glass-domed rotunda above the lobby.

The 312 rooms are extremely spacious and beautifully decorated. Each comes fully equipped with a remote-control color TV; telephones in the bedroom and bathroom; a clock-radio; and such niceties as complimentary newspaper delivery, bathrobes, super-fluffy towels sans monogram, shampoo, perfume, and marble bathtubs.

Dining/Entertainment: Traditional English afternoon tea—complete with clotted cream, strawberry preserves, and cucumber finger sandwiches—is served in the lobby. The famous old Victoria Room, a refuge for the well-to-do, has been turned into the Café Victoria, where baroque plasterwork and etched glass are combined and a light, airy feel is imparted by many tall shrubs. The Consort Bar, on the main floor, has ceiling-high windows offering lovely views of King Street. For formal dining, Chiaro's specializes in fine North American and continental cuisine with main dishes priced from $21 to $30.

Services: 24-hour room service, concierge, laundry/valet, complimentary shoeshine and newspaper, nightly turndown.

Facilities: Health club with masseuse.

Royal York, 100 Front St. W., Toronto, ON, M5J 1E3.
☎ **416/863-6333,** or toll free **800/828-7447, 800/441-1414** in the U.S. 1,365 rms, 191 suites. A/C MINIBAR TV TEL **Subway:** Union.
Rates: $210 single; $225 double. Entrée Gold service $30 extra. Many special packages available. **Parking:** $17.

To many citizens and regular visitors, the Royal York *is* Toronto, because in its 34 banquet and meeting rooms many of the city's

Downtown Toronto Accommodations

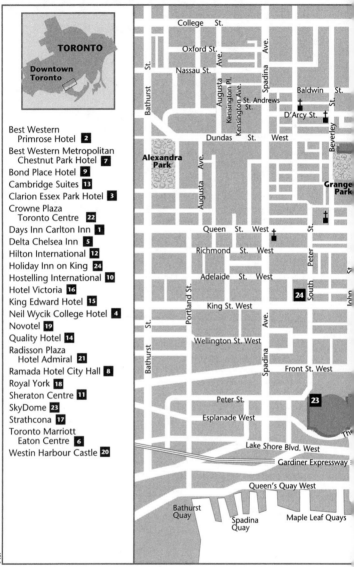

Best Western
   Primrose Hotel **2**
Best Western Metropolitan
   Chestnut Park Hotel **7**
Bond Place Hotel **9**
Cambridge Suites **13**
Clarion Essex Park Hotel **3**
Crowne Plaza
   Toronto Centre **22**
Days Inn Carlton Inn **1**
Delta Chelsea Inn **5**
Hilton International **12**
Holiday Inn on King **24**
Hostelling International **10**
Hotel Victoria **16**
King Edward Hotel **15**
Neil Wycik College Hotel **4**
Novotel **19**
Quality Hotel **14**
Radisson Plaza
   Hotel Admiral **21**
Ramada Hotel City Hall **8**
Royal York **18**
Sheraton Centre **11**
SkyDome **23**
Strathcona **17**
Toronto Marriott
   Eaton Centre **6**
Westin Harbour Castle **20**

historical and social events have taken place. It is by any measure a huge enterprise—it's a major convention hotel and, as such, is not to everyone's taste. Still, there is a magnificence to this hotel, which opened in 1929 and has hosted a raft of royalty, heads of state, and celebrities. The lobby itself is vast, impressive, and crowned by an incredible inlay coffered ceiling that is lit by large cast-bronze chandeliers. If you stay here, do go down and look at some of the

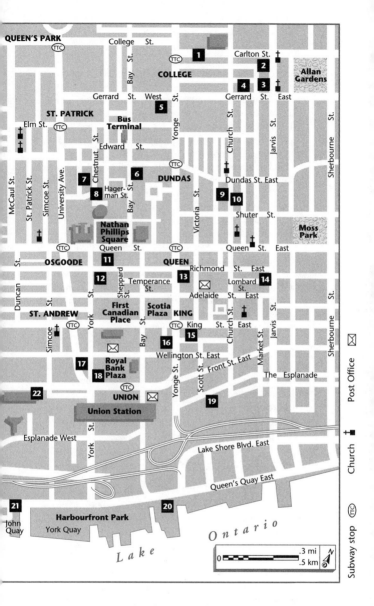

banquet rooms, several of which have splendid ceiling murals, and the series of provincial meeting rooms, each with a unique decor.

The statistics are mind-boggling—for example, the Royal York can sleep 2,800 guests; it contains ⅛ mile of carpeting; and it can accommodate 10,000 people at one meal sitting. The kitchen bakes 10,000 rolls daily; uses 18,000 eggs per week; and washes 25,000 pieces of china and 45,000 pieces of silverware daily.

The hotel has recently undergone major renovations. Rooms vary in size, but a standard room will have a king-size bed. The decor varies but tends to warm florals or else a combination of jade and rose with antique reproduction furnishings that always include an armchair and a well-lit desk. Nice features are solid-wood doors, windows that open, and wall moldings. Rooms for travelers with disabilities are exceptionally well equipped for wheelchair guests and for the deaf and blind. Entrée Gold provides a superior room on a private floor with separate check-in, private lounge, complimentary breakfast and newspaper, and nightly turndown.

Dining/Entertainment: The Royal York boasts an incredible 10 restaurants and lounges. The Acadian Room offers continental cuisine in an elegant atmosphere. For a show of Japanese finesse there's a Benihana steakhouse. The Gazebo affords a gardenlike setting for lunch; York's Kitchen is open for breakfast and lunch featuring buffets; York's Deli and Bakery offers an array of salads, soups, hot dishes, and super-sized sandwiches. Muffin on the Run has an extensive selection of muffins. Piper's Bar & Eatz has a full range of drinks, tavern menu, and entertaining singing waiters. The Lobby Bar features a sports screen; the Library Bar is a more intimate and cozy meeting spot. Downstairs you'll find the Black Knight karaoke bar; Dick Turpin's, an English-style pub with sing-along entertainment; and the small York Station bar.

Services: Room service (available from 6am to 12:45am), concierge.

Facilities: Skylit indoor lap pool with hand-painted trompe l'oeil murals and potted palms, exercise room, saunas, steam rooms and whirlpool, barbershop and beauty salon, shopping arcade with an American Express Travel Centre, business center.

The Sheraton Centre, 123 Queen St. W., Toronto, ON, M5H 2M9. ☎ **416/361-1000,** or toll free **800/325-3535.** Fax 416/947-4854. 1,382 rms, 79 suites. A/C MINIBAR TV TEL **Subway:** Osgoode. **Rates:** $185–$210 single; $195–$235 double. Extra person $20; roll-away bed $10. Two children under 18 stay free in parents' room. Various packages available. **Parking:** $20 a day.

A city in itself, the Sheraton Centre contains more than 40 shops in the Plaza, six restaurants and bars, and two movie theaters. It's conveniently located at the heart of the city's underground passageways, right across from City Hall. Behind the lobby, you'll even find two acres of landscaped gardens with a waterfall and summer terrace.

In this 43-story complex there are more than a thousand spacious rooms, all attractively furnished and well equipped. The Towers rooms, which are more expensive, offer additional amenities—bathrobes, additional telephone in the bathroom, a private elevator and reception area, and complimentary continental breakfast and evening hors d'oeuvres. All the rooms have recently been refurbished as part of a $47 million renovation. Nice features include coffeemakers and irons and ironing boards.

Dining/Entertainment: In the shopping concourse you'll find an authentic-looking English pub (shipped from England in sections) called Good Queen Bess, complete with toby jugs, cozy fireplaces, and mugs of Newcastle brown. At the Reunion bar in the lobby, where you'll be served great drinks and snacks, you'll find a dance floor, fooz ball, and 13 thirty-inch video monitors sharing the space with you. The Long Bar provides off-track betting and a great view of City Hall. Postcards presents cuisine from around the world, with regular special promotions featuring breakfasts, luncheon buffets, and dinners from the country of the moment, along with a regular all-day menu.

Services: 24-hour room service, laundry/valet, babysitting available.

Facilities: Indoor/outdoor pool, sauna, games room, hot tub, exercise room, shopping mall, two movie theaters.

Skydome, 1 Blue Jays Way, Toronto, ON, M5V 1J4.

☎ **416/360-7100.** Fax 416/341-5090. 346 rms. A/C MINIBAR TV TEL **Subway:** Union.

Rates: City view, $110–$210 single or double; field side, from $300 standard room, from $400 deluxe room.

For sports fans and baseball fans in particular, this is hotel heaven. Imagine having a room that overlooks the bullpen and the splendid green of the park, as do 70 rooms of this hotel located right inside the SkyDome stadium.

Standard rooms come with a view window, more expensive field-side rooms have raised living areas, and then there are the suites. The city-view rooms are the least expensive. Each unit has modern furnishings and is equipped with a telephone in the bathroom and full amenities, including a hairdryer, coffeemaker, and clock-radio.

Dining/Entertainment: Café on the Green overlooks the field, and, adjacent to the hotel, so do Sightlines and the Hard Rock Café.

Services: 24-hour room service, laundry/valet, concierge.

Facilities: Fitness center with pool, squash courts, sauna, and exercise room.

★ **Westin Harbour Castle,** 1 Harbour Square, Toronto, ON, M5J 1A6. ☎ **416/869-1600,** or toll free **800/228-3000.** Fax 416/869-0573. 922 rms, 56 suites. A/C MINIBAR TV TEL **Subway:** Union; then LRT to the hotel.

Rates: $190–$210 single; $210–$230 double. Extra person $20. Children stay free in parents' room. Weekend packages (double occupancy) and special long-term rates available. **Parking:** $18.

The Harbour Castle is located right on the lakefront, ideally situated for the Harbourfront and linked to downtown by the LRT. The rooms are located in two towers joined at the base by a five-story podium. Marble, oak, and crystal adorn the spacious lobby, which commands a great harbor view. The hotel has recently undergone a $50 million facelift.

Each room has a view of the lake and is furnished with a remote-control color TV featuring in-room movies, a bathroom telephone, a marble-top desk and night table, a table and floor lamps, and color-coordinated fabrics. There are 442 no-smoking rooms.

Dining/Entertainment: The moderately priced Regatta Restaurant and Terrace overlooking the harbor serves breakfast, lunch, and dinner. The Lighthouse, a revolving restaurant on the 37th floor, reached via a glass-walled elevator, provides fabulous views during lunch, brunch, or dinner. Tea is served in the lobby lounge, along with cocktails and a continental breakfast. Off the main lobby, the Chartroom offers a quiet haven for a drink.

Services: 24-hour room service, concierge, laundry/valet, guest-room voice mail, beauty shop.

Facilities: Fitness center with indoor pool, whirlpool, sauna, steamroom, squash courts, tennis court, massage clinic, shopping arcade.

Expensive

Best Western Metropolitan Chestnut Park Hotel,

108 Chestnut St., Toronto, ON, M5G 1R3. ☎ **416/977-5000,** or toll free **800/668-6600.** Fax 416/977-9513. 500 rms, 22 suites. A/C MINIBAR TV TEL **Subway:** St. Patrick.

Rates: $150 single; $190 double. Children under 16 stay free in parents' room. **Parking:** $15.

The Chestnut Park is conveniently located two blocks from the Eaton Centre on Chestnut Street, just off Dundas Street between Bay Street and University Avenue. The Canadian Museum of Textiles is connected to the hotel via a walkway. The ambience is modern, with many Oriental decorative furnishings in the lobby and throughout.

An Important Note on Prices

Unless stated otherwise, the prices cited in this guide are given in Canadian dollars, which is good news for U.S. travelers because the Canadian dollar is worth 26% less than the American dollar, but buys nearly as much. As we go to press, $1 Canadian is worth 74¢ U.S., which means that your $100-a-night hotel room will cost only U.S. $74, and your $6 breakfast costs only U.S. $4.44.

Here's a quick table of equivalents:

Canadian$	U.S.$
$1	$0.74
5	$3.70
10	$7.40
20	$14.80
50	$37.00
100	$74.00
200	$148.00

The rooms are spiffily furnished and equipped with telephones with computer- and fax-compatible jacks, safes, color TVs, and bathrobes.

Dining/Entertainment: Tapestries is open for breakfast, lunch, and dinner. The Alibi Restaurant/Bar overlooks the lobby.

Services: 24-hour room service, concierge, valet.

Facilities: Indoor swimming pool, health club with sauna and exercise room, business center.

Clarion Essex Park Hotel, 300 Jarvis St., just south of Carlton, Toronto, ON, M5B 2C5. ☎ **416/977-4823,** or toll free **800/567-2233.** Fax 416/977-4830. 58 rms, 44 suites. A/C MINIBAR TV TEL

Rates: $110–$135 single or double. **Parking:** $10.

Conveniently located within walking distance of the Eaton Centre, Pantages Theatre, and City Hall, the Clarion Essex Park has been transformed in a recent renovation. The lobby is sheathed in marble and accented with Oriental screens and fresh flowers, and the whole place has been turned into a very comfortable moderately priced facility. All rooms have queen- or king-size beds, and each is nicely furnished with a sofa, a desk, and a coffee table and fully equipped with a push-button phone, a cable color TV housed in a cabinet, and a fully tiled bathroom with a hairdryer and all the amenities. Closets are large.

Dining/Entertainment: The Clarion has a restaurant/bistro with a bar.

Services: Room service (available from 7am to 10pm).

Facilities: Indoor pool, sauna, whirlpool, fitness center, squash courts, and billiards room.

Crowne Plaza Toronto Centre, 225 Front St. W., Toronto, ON, M5V 2X3. ☎ **416/597-1400,** or toll free **800/HOLIDAY.** Fax 416/597-8128. 549 rms, 38 suites. A/C MINIBAR TV TEL **Subway:** Union.

Rates: $150 single or double. Extra person $20. Weekend packages available. **Parking:** $21.

The Crowne Plaza Toronto Centre, attached to the Convention Centre, is ideally located for the CN Tower, SkyDome, Roy Thomson Hall, and the theater district. Rose marble, cherry wood, and polished bronze are used throughout the lobby. The 25-story tower slopes back and upward from the main entrance, creating a garden court, which accommodates a lounge and café.

The rooms, decorated in dusky rose or muted green, are finely appointed, with marble bathroom counters, writing desks, and elegant table lamps, and feature such residential touches as draped tables and matching window valances. All feature color TVs, clock-radios, individual climate control, two telephone lines, and hairdryers. No-smoking rooms are available.

Entrée Gold accommodations offer additional amenities— complimentary breakfast, cocktail canapés, and shoeshine, as well as private check-in and honor bar and nightly turndown.

Dining/Entertainment: The Trellis Lounge, decorated with trees and plants, is well known for its Sunday brunch and after-theater menu. In the elegant Chanterelles, imaginative main courses range from $20 to $29. Luncheon prices range from $11 to $15. A special pretheater menu is offered. The Trellis Bistro offers casual dining.

Services: 24-hour room service, concierge, laundry/valet.

Facilities: Indoor pool, whirlpool, saunas, well-equipped exercise room, squash courts, sundeck.

Days Inn Carlton Inn, 30 Carlton St., Toronto, ON, M5B 2E9.
☎ **416/977-6655,** or toll free **800/325-2525.** Fax 416/977-0502.
535 rms and suites. A/C TV TEL **Subway:** College.
Rates: $125 single; $135 double. Extra person $15. Children under 18 stay free in parents' room. Summer discounts available. **Parking:** $12.

Nicely furnished rooms with modern conveniences at fair prices are the hallmark of the Carlton Inn, a modern, centrally air-conditioned high-rise. Besides offering reasonably priced (for Toronto) accommodations, the inn is well located, only a few steps from Yonge Street, right next door to Maple Leaf Gardens.

All rooms contain color TVs with in-house movies. Refrigerators are available on request.

Dining/Entertainment: There is a lounge, a sports bar, and a restaurant.

Services: Laundry/valet.

Facilities: Indoor pool, saunas, hair salon, car rental.

Delta Chelsea Inn, 33 Gerrard St. W., Toronto, ON, M5G 1Z4.
☎ **416/595-1975,** or toll free **800/268-1133.** Fax 416/585-4362.
1,538 rms, 50 suites. A/C TV TEL **Subway:** College.
Rates: $150 single; $190 double; from $225 suite. Extra person $15. Children under 18 share parents' room free. Weekend packages available. Seniors $95. **Parking:** $15—but only 300 spaces.

The Delta Chelsea, located between Yonge and Bay streets, is still one of Toronto's best buys—particularly for families and on weekends—although prices have risen considerably in recent years. The crowded scene in the lobby, though, testifies to its continued popularity.

All rooms have color TVs with in-room movies; push-button phones; and bright, modern furnishings. Some rooms have kitchenettes. The new south tower opened in late fall 1990, with 600 rooms featuring dual phones with data jacks, call waiting, and conference-call features. The new tower also contains a penthouse lounge, a business center, and more dining facilities.

The hotel more recently opened a special business floor where rooms contain ergonomic chairs, cordless phones, and speakers in the bathrooms. Guests staying here receive such amenities as free local calls, the *Globe and Mail,* and access to a business center located on the same floor—all for only $15 over regular room rates.

Dining/Entertainment: Wittles offers fine, elegant dining. The Express Café is a self-service cafeteria with very reasonable prices. The Garden offers an extensive range of items—deli, sandwiches, pizza, and roast chicken, as well as baked items. The restaurants offer a good-value children's menu, and children under 7 eat free. The Chelsea Bun, which serves lunch buffets and Sunday brunch, offers live entertainment daily and Dixieland jazz on Saturday afternoon.

Services: 24-hour room service; babysitting; laundry/valet pickup; Special Signature service including additional amenities like complimentary breakfast and newspaper, minibar, bathrobe.

Facilities: Swimming pool, whirlpool, sauna, exercise room, lounge, games room with pool tables, beauty salon, business center, and—a blessing for parents—a children's creative center where 3- to 8-year-olds can play under expert supervision (it's open until 10pm on Friday and Saturday, and there's a nominal charge).

Holiday Inn on King, 370 King St. W. (at Peter), Toronto, ON, M5V 1J9. ☎ **416/599-4000.** 405 rms, 20 suites. A/C TV TEL **Subway:** St. Andrew.

Rates: From $110 single or double. Extra person $15. **Parking:** $11.

Housed in an odd-looking Miami-style building, the Holiday Inn is well located for the theater district, the CN Tower, and SkyDome. The rooms are pleasantly furnished in pastels, with sage-green carpeting and floral bedspreads; each is fully equipped with a push-button phone, a clock-radio, a TV on a stand, a wet bar, and a decently lit desk. Many have balconies. The bathrooms have a number of amenities, including hairdryers.

Dining/Entertainment: The Holiday Inn offers two restaurants and a lounge.

Facilities: Outdoor pool, sauna, fitness center.

Novotel, 45 The Esplanade, Toronto, ON, M5E 1W2. ☎ **416/367-8900,** or toll free **800/668-6835.** Fax 416/360-8285. 262 rms, 8 suites. A/C MINIBAR TV TEL **Subway:** Union.

Rates: From $125 single or double. **Parking:** $10.50.

Located just off Yonge Street near the St. Lawrence Centre and O'Keefe Centre, the Novotel is an ultramodern hotel, built in French Renaissance style with a Palladian entrance leading to a marble lobby with oak and Oriental decorative accents.

The rooms are nicely appointed with all the expected conveniences, each including a remote-control TV, two telephones, a hairdryer, a minibar, a radio/TV speaker in the bathroom, and skirt hangers.

Dining/Entertainment: The Café Nicole serves breakfast, lunch, and dinner. Main courses include lamb filet with rosemary and steak frites with aioli, priced from $13 to $17. A quick buffet breakfast is available.

Services: Room service (available from 6am to midnight), concierge, laundry/valet, shuttle to airport.

Facilities: Indoor pool, sauna, whirlpool, exercise room.

★ **Radisson Plaza Hotel Admiral,** 249 Queen's Quay W., Toronto, ON, M5J 2N5. ☎ **416/364-5444,** or toll free **800/333-3333.** Fax 416/364-2975. 140 rms, 17 suites. A/C MINIBAR TV TEL **Subway:** Union.

Rates: $140–$180 single or double. Extra person $20. Weekend packages available. **Parking:** $11.

As the name and the harborfront location suggest, the Hotel Admiral has a strong nautical flavor. The lobby combines polished woods and downtown Toronto brass with nautical paintings. The horseshoe-shaped roofdeck comes complete with pool and cabana-style bar/terrace.

The rooms are elegantly furnished with campaign-style chests of drawers with brass trimmings, marble-top side tables, and desks, all set on jade carpets. Extra amenities include two phones, a hairdryer and clothes line in the bathroom, a clock-radio, a minibar, and a complimentary newspaper.

Dining/Entertainment: The Commodore's Dining Room, which looks out onto Lake Ontario and the waterfront, serves classic continental cuisine, with main courses ranging from $20 to $32. The Galley serves a more modest menu, priced from $8 to $16. The adjacent Bosun's Bar also offers light snacks.

Services: 24-hour room service, concierge, complimentary newspaper delivery.

Facilities: Outdoor swimming pool, whirlpool, squash court.

Ramada Hotel City Hall, 89 Chestnut St., Toronto, ON, M5G 1R1. ☎ **416/977-0707.** Fax 416/977-1136. 717 rms and suites. A/C TV TEL **Subway:** Dundas or University.

Rates: $135 single; $150 double. Extra person $15. Children under 19 stay free in parents' room. **Parking:** $13.

The Ramada Hotel City Hall, right behind City Hall, has all the earmarks of the chain, plus a little extra. The rooms have recently been upgraded, with such nice amenities as hairdryers. Each room is large and well furnished, with a console control panel by the bed for the color TV and radio, a vanity mirror or sink outside the bathroom, and individual climate control.

Dining/Entertainment: The Dewey Secombe and Howe Lounge offers pool and snacks in the evening. The Chestnut Tree restaurant on the main floor offers all-day dining.

Services: Room service (available from 6am to 11pm), concierge, babysitting.

Facilities: Indoor and outdoor pools, sauna, exercise room, sun terrace, business center.

Toronto Marriott Eaton Centre, 525 Bay St., at Dundas, Toronto, ON, M5G 2L2. ☎ **416/597-9200.** Fax 416/597-9211. 459 rms and suites. A/C MINIBAR TV TEL **Subway:** Dundas.

Rates: $140 single or double. If you book 21 days in advance a special reduced rate of $108 is available, but this rate requires prepayment and allows for no changes or cancellations.

A brand-new hotel with all the hallmarks of the Marriott chain is conveniently located alongside Eaton Centre. In addition to the amenities listed above, rooms contain clock-radios and attractive furnishings. No-smoking rooms and rooms for those with disabilities are available, too.

Dining/Entertainment: The Parkside atrium is for all-day dining, while J.W.'s offers more intimate service. Characters bar features billiards and table games as well as music and sporting events; the lobby bar is more relaxing.

Services: 24-hour room service, concierge, babysitting.

Facilities: Indoor rooftop swimming pool, whirlpool, sauna, health club.

Moderate

Best Western Primrose Hotel, 111 Carlton St. (between Church and Jarvis sts.), Toronto, ON, M5B 2G3. ☎ **416/977-8000,** or toll free **800/268-8082.** Fax 416/977-6323. 338 rms, 4 suites. A/C TV TEL **Subway:** College.

Rates: $129–$149 single or double. Extra person $10. Weekend packages available (except July–Sept). **Parking:** $10.

The Primrose offers spacious rooms, all with wall-to-wall carpeting and color-coordinated furnishings, color TVs, and individual climate control. About 25% contain king-size beds and sofas; the rest have two double beds.

Dining/Entertainment: The downstairs coffee shop charmingly evokes the atmosphere of a Viennese café with its painted-wood decor. For relaxing there's the One Eleven Lounge.

Services: Room service (available from 7am to 11pm), laundry/valet, complimentary newspaper.

Facilities: Outdoor heated pool and sauna.

Bond Place Hotel, 65 Dundas St. E., Toronto, ON, M5B 2G8. ☎ **416/362-6061.** Fax 416/360-6406. 286 rms and suites. A/C TV TEL **Subway:** Dundas.

Rates: $60–$90 single or double. Extra person $15. Weekend packages available. **Parking:** $11.

Ideally located just a block from the Eaton Centre and adjacent to the Pantages and Elgin theaters, the Bond Place Hotel is an independently owned, medium-size modern establishment offering all the appurtenances of a first-class hotel at reasonable prices.

The rooms, all pleasantly decorated in pastels with bamboo furniture and wall-to-wall carpeting, each contain a color TV with in-house movies available, individual climate control, and a direct-dial phone.

Dining/Entertainment: Off the lobby, the Garden Café serves from 7am to midnight daily. Downstairs, Freddy's offers a weekday buffet lunch, then turns into a piano bar at night (where you can enjoy complimentary hors d'oeuvres from 5:30 to 6:30pm).

Services: Room service (available from 7am to 10pm), laundry/valet.

Hotel Victoria, 56 Yonge St., Toronto, ON, M5E 1G5. ☎ **416/363-1666.** Fax 416/363-7327. 48 rms and suites. A/C TV TEL **Subway:** King.

Rates: $80–$105 single; $110 double. Extra person $15. Ask about special summer discounts.

In search of a small, personal hotel? Try the Hotel Victoria, with only 48 rooms spread over six floors. It's only two blocks from O'Keefe Centre. The lobby is small and elegant, and renovation has retained the marble columns, staircase, and decorative moldings of an earlier era.

The rooms are either standard or select (the latter are larger). Furnishings are modern and combined with a green-and-beige decor. Each room contains a color TV, a private bath, and a clock-radio. Some have coffeemakers and minirefrigerators. A complimentary *Globe and Mail* and free local phone calls are included in the price of a room.

Dining/Entertainment: There's an attractive restaurant and lounge, as well as a lobby bar.

Services: Room service (available from 7am to 2pm), laundry/valet, complimentary newspaper.

Quality Hotel, 111 Lombard St. (between Adelaide and Richmond sts.), Toronto, ON, M5C 2T9. ☎ **416/367-5555.** Fax 416/367-3470. 194 rms and suites. A/C TV TEL Subway: King or Queen.
Rates: $85 single; $95 double. **Parking:** $9.

Formerly a Journey's End, the Quality Hotel has modern rooms fully appointed with color TVs and jade-and-rose or gray-blue decor. Features include complimentary local phone calls, morning coffee, and newspaper.

Budget

Hostelling International, 223 Church St., Toronto, ON, M5B 1Y7. ☎ **416/368-0207.** Fax 416/368-6499. 175 beds. A/C **Subway:** Dundas.
Rates: $18 per person in a dormitory; $23 per person in a semiprivate room.

Located downtown between Queen and Dundas streets, the hostel contains 175 beds in dormitory style (6 to 10 beds per room) and semiprivate accommodations. There's a comfortable lounge with a couch and TV, a kitchen, and laundry facilities. The hostel is open 24 hours. Washrooms are on every floor. The Passport Cafe offers reasonably priced meals as well as pool, darts, and an outdoor patio.

Neil Wycik College Hotel, 96 Gerrard St. E. (1 block east of Yonge), Toronto, ON, M5B 1G7. ☎ **416/977-2320,** or toll free **800/268-4358** in Canada and the northeastern U.S. Fax 416/977-2809. 300 rms. **Subway:** College.
Rates: $30 single; $40–$42 double. **Parking:** $8 nearby.
Open: Mid-May to late Aug.

From mid–May to late August, the Neil Wycik College Hotel offers basic, clean accommodations to tourists and families at extremely reasonable rates. Since these are primarily student accommodations, rooms have no air-conditioning and no TVs and contain only the most essential furniture—a bed, chair, and desk. Each unit contains five bedrooms (singles, twins, and a family room), two washrooms, and a common room. Linen, towels, and daily housekeeping are provided. The facilities include a TV lounge, a rooftop sundeck, a sauna, a laundry room, and a cafeteria.

The Strathcona, 60 York St., Toronto, ON, M5J 1S8.
☎ **416/363-3321.** Fax 416/363-4679. 196 rms and suites.
A/C TV TEL **Subway:** Union.
Rates: $60–$65 single; $70–$75 double.

Currently one of Toronto's best buys—if not the only good deal— the Strathcona is located right across from the Royal York Hotel, within easy reach of all downtown attractions. Although the rooms are small, they have recently been refurbished and furnished with modern blond-wood furniture, gray carpeting, and brass floor lamps. Each has a phone, a color TV, and a private bath.

The coffee shop/restaurant is open daily; there's also a luncheon snack bar and a lounge with a large-screen TV for sports watching. Room service is offered from 6am to 7pm. Great location, great price.

2 Midtown

The midtown area runs north from College/Carlton Street between Spadina Avenue and Jarvis Street, to where Dupont crosses Yonge Street.

Very Expensive

⭐ **The Four Seasons Hotel,** 21 Avenue Rd., Toronto, ON, M5R 2G1. ☎ **416/964-0411,** or toll free **800/268-6282.** Fax 416/964-2301. 210 rms, 170 suites. A/C MINIBAR TV TEL **Subway:** Bay.

Family-Friendly Hotels

Delta Chelsea Inn (see p. 62) The Chelsea Chum Club for kids aged 3 to 12 sponsors special activities in the Children's Creative Centre and throughout the hotel. When they check in at the lifesize gingerbread house they get a registration card and passport. Children under 6 eat free; there are special menus for the older set. All this goes a long way toward creating a smooth family stay.

Inn on the Park (see p. 80) Swings, ice skating, bicycles, and a video room make this a miniparadise for kids of all ages. The hotel operates an Inn Kids supervised recreational program for those aged 5 to 12 and even sponsors special themed weekends for them.

The Four Seasons (see p. 67) Free bicycles, video games, and the pool should keep them occupied. The meals served in Animal World wicker baskets or on Sesame Street plates, and the complimentary room-service cookies and milk on arrival will make them feel special. Housekeeping provides all the amenities parents need.

Rates: $225–$290 single; $255–$315 double; from $335 suite. Weekend rates available. **Parking:** $15.

Located in the heart of the Bloor-Yorkville area, the Four Seasons has a well-deserved reputation for highly personal service, quiet but unimpeachable style, and total comfort. The lobby, with its marble and granite floors, Savonnerie carpets, and stunning fresh-flower arrangements, epitomizes this style.

The spacious rooms are furnished with king-size, queen-size, or twin beds and boast dressing rooms and marble bathrooms. The table lamps are porcelain, the furnishings elegant, and the fabrics plush. All rooms are air-conditioned and have remote-control color TVs, AM/FM radios, and terry-cloth bathrobes. Extra amenities include hairdryers, makeup and full-length mirrors, tie bars, closet safes, and windows that open. Corner rooms have balconies. Four Seasons Executive Suites each have an additional seating area separated from the bedroom by French doors, two TVs, and a deluxe telephone with two lines and conference-call capacity. No-smoking rooms and special rooms for those with disabilities are available.

Dining/Entertainment: Truffles, on the second floor, has been named one of the world's 10 great hotel restaurants. Two sculptures of Uffizi wild boars adorn the entrance to the lavish dining area which features murals, ceramics, and furniture designed by Canadian artists. Only the finest materials have been used in the design elements, like the curly maple walls and the magnificent marquetry floor crafted from 11,000 pieces of walnut, oak, jojoba, and purple-heart wood. The tables are amply spaced and the cuisine is extraordinary. Start with the lobster salad with winter leaves, cucumber and chive puree, orange port and ginger dressing; the ravioli filled with shrimp, sweet garlic, and vegetables in a Provence herb-and-tomato broth; or the crab soup, which is amazing—a clear broth with lemon balm, shaved fennel, coriander, and ginger. Follow with the grilled swordfish Provençal with two sauces: red wine shallot sauce and dill caper sauce with olives. You might also choose medallions of veal tenderloin with creamed mushrooms, sautéed spinach, and a morel sauce. At the conclusion, treat yourself to a sampling platter of desserts or the restaurant's signature chocolate confection—semisweet and milk-chocolate fudge pyramids, candied oranges, and grenadine sauce.

The Studio Cafe, which has become one of the city's places to see and be seen, serves meals all day. It features an open kitchen, is filled with light and beautifully decorated with modern Italian furnishings—including some gorgeous Gianni Versace fabrics on the tables. The decor includes display cases filled with original glass artworks, which are for sale with prices ranging from $100 (for smaller paperweights) to $4,000 (for large vases). Labels in the display cases identify the artists and where they can be contacted. The menu is inspired by the Mediterranean and offers a variety of gourmet pizzas (delicious!), pastas, salads, and light entrées—like grilled red snapper with a ragout of vegetables or chicken stir-fry with

Shanghaianese noodles. A luncheon buffet and evening hors d'oeuvres are served in La Serre, which also features entertainment in the evenings. The Lobby Bar serves a traditional afternoon tea. There are special kids' menus, too, with meals served either in Animal World wicker baskets or on Sesame Street plates.

Services: 24-hour concierge, 24-hour room service and valet pickup, one-hour pressing, complimentary shoeshine, twice-daily maid service, babysitting, doctor on call, children's activities, weekday courtesy limo to downtown, complimentary coffee and newspaper.

Facilities: Business center; health club with indoor/outdoor pool, whirlpool, Universal equipment, and massage; free bicycles and video-game units for children.

Inter-Continental, 220 Bloor St. W., Toronto, ON, M5S 1T8. ☎ **416/960-5200.** Fax 416/920-8269. 209 rms. A/C MINIBAR TV TEL **Subway:** St. George.

Rates: $195–$240 single; $210–$270 double. **Parking:** $22 valet.

The Inter-Continental, conveniently located on Bloor Street at St. George, is small enough to provide excellent, very personal service from the minute you enter the small but rich-looking marble lobby. The rooms are spacious and well furnished with comfortable French-style armchairs and love seats. The marble bathrooms, with separate showers, are large and equipped with every kind of amenity—each has a dual-line telephone with personal computer/fax hookup; a clothesline; large fluffy towels; a bathrobe; a scale; and a full range of soaps, lotions, and more. Extra special room features include closet lights, a large desk-table, a clock-radio, a full-length mirror, and windows that open.

Dining/Entertainment: Signatures offers fine dining with dinner entrées priced from $18 to $25. It also offers one of the best brunches in town. The attractive, comfortable Harmony Lounge, with its marble bar, fireplace, and cherry paneling, is a pleasant retreat for afternoon tea or cocktails accompanied by piano entertainment. From here, French doors lead out to an inviting patio.

Services: 24-hour room service, laundry/valet, twice-daily maid service, nightly turndown, concierge, complimentary shoeshine and newspaper.

Facilities: Lap pool with adjacent patio; fitness room with treadmill, bikes, Stairmaster, and Paramount equipment; sauna and massage room; business center.

The Park Plaza, 4 Avenue Rd., Toronto, ON, M5R 2E8. ☎ **416/924-5471,** or toll free **800/268-4927.** Fax 416/924-4933. 224 rms, 40 suites. A/C MINIBAR TV TEL **Subway:** Museum or Bay.

Rates: Prince Arthur Tower, $190 single or double; Plaza Tower, $255 single or double. Extra person $15. Weekend and other packages available. Children under 18 stay free in parents' room. **Parking:** $17.

The Park Plaza, located in fashionable Yorkville, is close to the ROM and the planetarium. All 64 rooms and 20 suites in the original Plaza

Tower, built in 1935, have been completely renovated and redecorated to exceptionally high standards. The rooms are very tastefully furnished in a candy-stripe style, with brass and glass accents. Each is fully equipped with the latest conveniences, including clock-radio, two push-button phones (one in the bathroom), louvered closets, and full-length mirror. The marble bathroom has a hairdryer, makeup mirror, bathrobe, and full amenities. Suites have additional features such as scales and two-line telephones that can be hooked up to faxes and personal computers. The Plaza Tower rooms are more expensive than the 180 rooms in the Prince Arthur Tower because they are more lavish. The latter rooms, though, are large and well furnished, with full facilities, including TVs, push-button phones, hairdryers, and minibars.

Dining/Entertainment: The Prince Arthur Garden Restaurant is a popular city breakfast/brunch and lunch spot. Chandeliers ring the room, and there's always a brilliant floral centerpiece. The main dining room, the Roof Restaurant, is on the 18th floor, adjacent to the lounge that has attracted so many Toronto literati. Their books are showcased and portrait sketches of them grace the wall of this comfortable room. The inviting couches, wood-burning fireplace, and marble-top tables make it a perfect venue for viewing the city's skyline. In summer, the outdoor terrace is great for twilight dining. Main dishes in the dining room range from $20 to $28.

Services: 24-hour room service, laundry/valet, complimentary newspaper and shoeshine, concierge.

Facilities: Business center; fitness room.

Sutton Place Grande Le Meridien, 955 Bay St., Toronto, ON, M5S 2A2. ☎ **416/924-9221,** or toll free **800/268-3790.** Fax 416/924-1778. 208 rms, 72 suites. A/C MINIBAR TV TEL **Subway:** Museum or Wellesley.

Rates: $265 single; $295 double; from $270 suite. Extra person $20. Children under 18 stay free in parents' room. Weekend rates available. **Parking:** $19.

A small luxury hotel, the Sutton Place attracts a celebrity/entertainer and business clientele. It has a European flair that is exhibited in the decor and the service. Throughout the public areas you will find antiques, old-master paintings, 18th-century Gobelins, Oriental carpets, and crystal chandeliers. The very spacious rooms are luxuriously furnished in a French style and each contains a couch and desk. All have remote-control color TVs and hairdryers. The suites have bathrobes and also, for business travelers, two telephones allowing-hookup to a fax or PC.

Dining/Entertainment: The Sansouci is one of the city's most beautiful dining rooms with its Gobelins, fresh-flower arrangements, silver, and crystal. Breakfast, lunch, and dinner are served here, and there's a spectacular brunch on Sunday ($28.95 per person). The à la carte dinner menu is modestly priced. Start with gingered shrimp, oysters, or the chicken liver pâté and follow with one of the half-dozen entrées like chicken breast with Pommery mustard crust, salmon with tomato sauce, or pork tenderloin with glazed apples. Prices range from $10 to $16. Alexandra's is a comfortable piano lounge where light lunches are served and you can dance in the evening. It's open from 11am to 1am daily. Stop 33 is one of the city's most romantic dining spots, too.

Services: 24-hour room service, valet pickup, complimentary newspaper and shoeshine, twice-daily maid service, concierge, beauty salon, limousine to the financial district.

Facilities: Indoor pool with sundeck, sauna, massage, fully equipped fitness center, business center.

Expensive

Hotel Plaza II, 90 Bloor St. E., Toronto, ON, M4W 1A7.
☎ **416/961-8000,** or toll free **800/267-6116.** Fax 416/961-4635. 238 rms, 18 suites. A/C MINIBAR TV TEL **Subway:** Bloor.
Rates: $145 single; from $160 double; from $250 suite. Extra person $15. Children under 18 stay free in parents' room. Weekend packages available. **Parking:** $17.

Occupying the 7th to 12th floors of a multiuse complex, the Hotel Plaza II is designed around an inner cobblestone courtyard with flowers, shrubbery, and trees. The lobby is on the street level.

All the rooms have double beds and are tastefully decorated. Appointments include the standard ones listed above as well as clock-radios, makeup mirrors, hairdryers, and in-house movies. Plaza Club rooms have a concierge and private lounge.

Dining/Entertainment: The restaurant, Matisse, pays homage to the artist with floor-to-ceiling replicas of his paintings. It serves all day, featuring California-style cuisine with European accents. There's also a bar.

Services: Room service (7am to 11pm), laundry/valet, complimentary shoeshine, nightly turndown.

Facilities: Squash, pool, sauna, and whirlpool facilities in the Bloor Park Club in the building.

Comfort Hotel, 15 Charles St. E., Toronto, ON, M4Y 1S1.
☎ **416/924-7381,** or toll free **800/263-7142** in the U.S. and Canada. Fax 416/927-1369. 113 rms. A/C TV TEL **Subway:** Bloor.
Rates: $94 single or double. Weekend rates available. **Parking:** $8.

The Comfort Hotel is a small, pleasant place. The rooms are large; they're furnished with light-oak pieces and have full amenities.

The restaurant, which is plush and comfortable day or night, serves a continental dinner menu. Prices begin at $11.50. Piano entertainment is provided on weekends. The hotel is ideally situated less than 100 yards off Yonge Street and only two blocks south of Bloor. A fully equipped health club is nearby and open to hotel guests.

Journey's End, 280 Bloor St. W. (at St. George), Toronto, ON, M5S 1T8. ☎ **416/968-0010**). 214 rms. A/C TV TEL
Rates: $86 single; $98 double. Weekend and other packages available. **Parking:** $11.50.

Midtown Toronto Accommodations

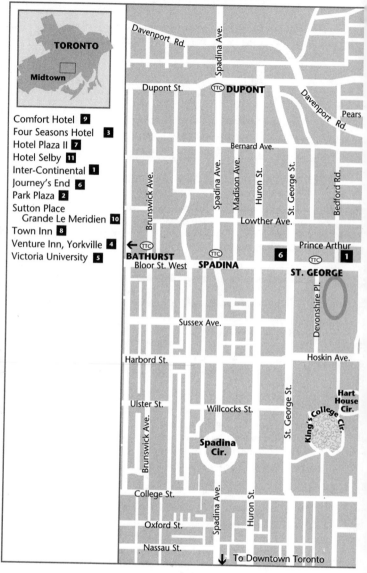

Comfort Hotel **9**
Four Seasons Hotel **3**
Hotel Plaza II **7**
Hotel Selby **11**
Inter-Continental **1**
Journey's End **6**
Park Plaza **2**
Sutton Place
   Grande Le Meridien **10**
Town Inn **8**
Venture Inn, Yorkville **4**
Victoria University **5**

Part of the budget chain, this hotel is only a few blocks west of the
Inter-Continental and represents a great value for the location. Rooms
are modern and well equipped, with remote-control cable TVs and
modern light furnishings, including useful well-lit worktables.
Restaurant and coffee shop, too.

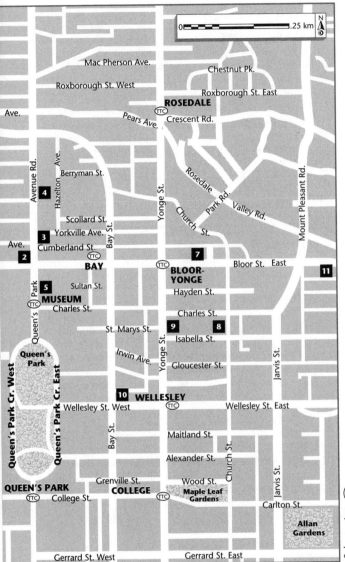

The Town Inn, 620 Church St. (at Charles St.), Toronto, ON, M4Y
2G2. ☎ **416/964-3311,** or toll free **800/387-2755.** 200 suites.
A/C TV TEL **Subway:** Bloor.

Rates: $125–$150 single or double; $195–$225 two-bedroom suite
accommodating up to four. Extra person $15. Children under 12 stay
free in parents' room. **Parking:** $13.

Since the Town Inn was originally built as an apartment house, all units are suites, each with a bedroom, living room, dining area, kitchenette, and balcony. They also feature color TVs with in-house movies and individual climate control. Other extras include laundry/valet service, an indoor swimming pool with a solarium roof, saunas, and an outdoor tennis court.

Venture Inn, Yorkville, 89 Avenue Rd., Toronto, ON, M5R 2G3. ☎ **416/964-1220,** or toll free **800/387-3933.** Fax 416/964-8692. 71 rms. A/C TV TEL **Subway:** Bloor, Bay or St. George.

Rates (including continental breakfast): $95 single; $110 double. Extra person $10. **Parking:** $6.

The Venture Inn, with its modern rooms featuring pine accents, has a high-priced location in Yorkville, but it charges only moderate prices. Laundry and dry cleaning services are available.

Budget

Hotel Selby, 592 Sherbourne St., Toronto, ON, M4X 1L4. ☎ **416/921-3142.** 67 rms (59 with bath). A/C

Rates (including continental breakfast): $60–$85 single or double; $100–$125 suite. **Parking:** Limited free parking on first-come first-serve basis; otherwise you pay.

This hotel, located in a large heritage Victorian, represents a great downtown bargain. Downstairs at the front desk there's a comfortable lobby sitting area with a chandelier and a fireplace. The rooms are individually decorated with an eclectic mix of furniture. Ceilings are high, making the rooms airy and dramatic; many have stucco decoration and moldings. In several rooms the old bathroom fixtures have been retained. Room 303, for example, the Gooderham Suite, is very large and boasts a fireplace. Furnishings include a couch, a TV, and a push-button phone. There's a large walk-in closet, and the bathroom has a clawfoot tub and pedestal sink. The Hemingway Suite has a brass-hooded fireplace, an oak dresser, a couple of wingbacks, and a small tub with a shower in the bathroom. Room 401 has an old-fashioned burled-wood bed, angled ceilings, track lighting, and a pair of leatherette wingbacks. Facilities include a restaurant and a piano bar that attracts both a gay and straight crowd. There's also a coin laundry on premises. Guests have access to a nearby health club for a small charge.

Victoria University, 140 Charles St. W., Toronto, ON, M5S 1K9. ☎ **416/585-4524.** 425 rms (none with bath). **Subway:** Museum.
Rates (including breakfast): $44 single; $62 double. Discounts available for seniors and students.
Open: Early May to late Aug.

Summer visitors (early May to late August) can stay at Victoria University, right across from the Royal Ontario Museum, in a 425-room university residence. Each accommodation is furnished as a study/bedroom and is supplied with fresh linen, towels, and soap.

Bathrooms are down the hall. Guests enjoy free local calls and use of laundry facilities as well as access to the dining and athletic facilities, which include tennis courts.

3 Uptown

Best Western Roehampton Hotel, 808 Mount Pleasant Rd., Toronto, ON, M4P 2L2. ☎ **416/487-5101,** or toll free **800/387-8899.** Fax 416/487-5390. 110 rms and suites. A/C TV TEL **Subway:** Eglinton.

Rates: From $75 single or double. Special discount packages available. **Parking:** $6.45.

Situated at the center of the Eglinton Avenue business district, the Roehampton has spacious, recently renovated rooms. The corner rooms are especially large and attractive, with pleasant views. All units are well equipped with color TVs and individual climate control; some have refrigerators.

Dining/Entertainment: Champs sports lounge/restaurant serves an all-day menu.

Services: Room service (available from 7am to 11pm), laundry/valet.

Facilities: Outdoor rooftop pool and sundeck.

The Bradgate Arms, 54 Foxbar Rd., Toronto, ON, M4V 2G6. ☎ **416/968-1331,** or toll free **800/268-7171.** Fax 416/968-3743. 110 rms and suites. A/C MINIBAR TV TEL **Subway:** St. Clair.

Rates: $170–$190 single or double. Weekend rates available. **Parking:** Free.

The Bradgate Arms, tucked away on a side street off Avenue Road at St. Clair Avenue, has a tranquil, secluded air. It was created by joining two apartment houses, which are now linked by a pink marble atrium lobby filled with trees and a fountain. The large rooms are well furnished with solid pieces and feature minibars and wet bars.

Dining/Entertainment: Avenues has a good reputation, and there's also a cozy piano lounge.

Services: Room service (available from 7am to 11:30pm), laundry/valet.

Facilities: Whirlpool at affiliated health club, exercise room, and library.

4 At the Airport

Very Expensive

Bristol Place Hotel, 950 Dixon Rd., Rexdale, ON, M9W 5N4. ☎ **416/675-9444.** Fax 416/675-4426. 286 rms and suites. A/C MINIBAR TV TEL **Subway:** Kipling.

Rates: $125 single or double; from $285 suite. Extra person $15. Children under 18 stay free in parents' room. Special packages available. **Parking:** Free.

For really personal service—the kind that caters to the idiosyncrasies of each guest—and ultrachic surroundings, try the Bristol Place, a select hotel where contemporary architecture and facilities blend with old-fashioned attention to detail and service. Outside, the red-brick building is striking enough, but step into the lobby and it's stunning. It soars three stories to a skylit ceiling through which the sun dances on the trees, sculptures, mosaics, and contemporary wall hangings. The sound of the waterfall alone made me want to stay.

And now the rooms. The regular rooms are beautifully designed, decorated, and appointed. Each has custom-made contemporary furniture, double or king-size beds, geometric design throws, two telephones, a color TV, a bedside console, an alarm clock, and large parlor lights in the bathroom.

Dining/Entertainment: Le Café, raised slightly to overlook the lobby, is a plush coffee shop with comfortable banquettes and handmade ceramic tiles. Zachary's dining room is delightfully contemporary and graced with a kaleidoscopic tapestry hung over white tile. The dinner specialties cost $21 to $30 for such dishes as salmon with truffle sauce and breast of pheasant on braised green vegetables. The buffet brunch is $21.50.

Services: 24-hour room service, laundry/valet, concierge, supervised kids' program.

Facilities: Indoor/outdoor pool with skylight dome and sundeck; flower gardens; reflecting pools; children's play area; health club with exercise room, sunroom, sauna.

Expensive

Regal Constellation Hotel, 900 Dixon Rd., Etobicoke, ON, M9W 1J7. ☎ **905/675-1500.** Fax 905/675-4611. 708 rms and suites. A/C TV TEL **Subway:** Kipling.

Rates: $110–$130 single; $130–$150 double. Extra person $15. Children under 16 stay free in parents' room. Weekend and honeymoon packages available. **Parking:** Free.

Providing top-notch facilities and personal service, the Constellation has a certain traditional elegance—former Prime Minister Lester Pearson liked to stay here when he came to Toronto, and so do many celebrities.

Although built almost 30 years ago, the Constellation has expanded so often that its rooms offer a myriad of different styles. Color schemes run from beige-brown to green. Every room is a minisuite featuring L-shaped sofas, large desks, king-size or twin/double-bed arrangements, and a color TV with in-house movies.

Dining/Entertainment: The hotel is a veritable entertainment complex. At the Woodbine Pub you can dance to DJ entertainment. The Regal also has a Chinese restaurant and the Atrium off the main lobby for all-day dining. At night you can sit under a spreading banyan tree overlooking a tropical garden and enjoy a cocktail or dance in the Banyan Tree bar.

Services: 24-hour room service, dry cleaning, concierge, babysitting.

Facilities: Indoor/outdoor pool (shaped like a river around a tropical island reached by small wooden footbridges), banking facilities, hair salon, amphitheater, full recreation complex with exercise room and saunas.

Sheraton Gateway at Terminal Three, Toronto AMF,
Box 3000, Toronto, ON, L5P 1C4. ☎ **905/672-7000,** or toll free **800/565-0010.** Fax 905/672-7100. 483 rms.
A/C MINIBAR TV TEL

Rates: $160 single or double. **Parking:** Free.

Connected by skywalk to Terminal 3, this is the most convenient place to stay at the airport. All rooms are soundproofed and luxuriously decorated; they contain all the amenities, including hairdryers. For travelers it's also convenient to be able to view flight departure and arrival times on your own personal TV.

Dining/Entertainment: Three buffets are served daily in the Café Suisse while the Mahogany Grill is reserved for fine dining. There's also a bar/lounge featuring nightly piano entertainment.

Services: Room service from 5am to 1am, hair salon.

Facilities: Indoor pool, whirlpool, and exercise center.

Toronto Airport Hilton International, 5875 Airport Rd.,
Mississauga, ON, L4V 1N1. ☎ **905/677-9900,** or toll free **800/268-9275.** Fax 416/677-7782. 413 rms, 154 minisuites.
A/C MINIBAR TV TEL **Directions:** Take the Gardiner Expressway west to Hwy. 427 north, to Airport Expressway (Dixon Rd. exit).
Rates: $110–$135 single; $140–$160 double; minisuites from $170 single, $190 double. Extra person $25. Children stay free in parents' room. Weekend packages available. **Parking:** Free.

The Airport Hilton has all the comfort and conveniences associated with the name. A 12-story tower added to the hotel contains all minisuites, each featuring separate bedroom, bathroom, and parlor areas. Each minisuite comes fully equipped with a king-size bed, a sofa bed, two color TVs, three telephones, a table for working or dining, a minibar, a hairdryer, a bathrobe, and individually controlled air-conditioning and heating. The 259 rooms contain all the expected appurtenances: queen-size beds, bedside remote-control consoles, color TVs with in-house movies, louvered closets, bathrooms with telephones, and minibars.

Dining/Entertainment: Misty's club is well known for its musically themed evenings—from country to reggae (Wed to Sun). The Harvest Restaurant/Café features international cuisine; E Ting's, a cozy intimate restaurant next door to Misty's, offers light meals and finger food.

Services: 24-hour room service, laundry/valet, babysitting.

Facilities: Outdoor heated pool with poolside deck, squash and racquetball courts, exercise room, business services.

Moderate

Best Western Carlton Place Hotel, 33 Carlson Court, Toronto, ON, M9W 6H5. ☎ **416/675-1234,** or toll free **800/528-1234.** Fax 416/675-3436. 524 rms. A/C TV TEL **Subway:** Kipling.
Rates: $90–$103 single; $100–$115 double. Extra person $10.

Best Western's Carlton Place Hotel offers modern rooms, each equipped with two telephones, a hairdryer, and the other usual amenities listed above; some rooms have minibars. The public areas have that light-pine, wicker, and tile look. Apples restaurant offers all-day dining. There's also 24-hour room service, an indoor swimming pool, a sauna, and whirlpool.

Days Inn, 6257 Airport Rd., Mississauga, ON, L4V 1N1.
☎ **905/678-1400,** or toll free **800/325-2525** in the northeastern U.S. and eastern Canada. Fax 905/678-9130. 200 rms. A/C TV TEL **Subway:** Kipling.
Rates: $97 single; $107 double. Extra person $10. Children under 18 stay free in parents' room. Weekend packages available. **Parking:** Free.

The Days Inn offers facilities similar to those of the larger hotels on the airport strip but at lower prices. It's a small, friendly place set in a streamlined seven-story block. The lobby has a comfy air with its natural-stone fireplace.

The rooms are bright and airy and feature natural-pine furniture, beige-and-brown color schemes, color TVs, phones, individual climate control, and a vanity outside each bathroom.

Dining/Entertainment: In the Steak and Burger, carefully tended plants and flowers are set in an actual greenhouse wall and are complemented by exposed brick and a host of Canadian artifacts— a steeple clock, Staffordshire figures, and other ceramics.

Services: Room service (available from 6am to 11pm).

Facilities: Indoor pool, fitness center, and squash courts (available at an affiliated health club).

Delta's Meadowvale Inn, 6750 Mississauga Rd. (at Hwy. 401), Mississauga, ON, L5N 2L3. ☎ **905/821-1981.** Fax 905/542-4036. 374 rms, 5 suites. A/C TV TEL **Subway:** Yorkdale; then GO bus to the hotel.
Rates: $190 single or double. Weekend packages available. **Parking:** Free.

At Delta's, they've created a cozy rustic ambience by using a lot of wood and brass and placing a fireplace in the lobby. Here you'll find 374 fully appointed rooms with balconies. Fifteen executive rooms have turndown service, complimentary newspapers, bathrobes, and other extra amenities.

Services: 24-hour room service, laundry/valet.

Facilities: Indoor pool; indoor tennis, racquetball, and squash courts; exercise room; creative center for children.

Ramada Airport West, 5444 Dixie Rd. (at Hwy. 401), Mississauga, ON, L4W 2L2. ☎ **905/624-1144,** or toll free **800/737-3211.** Fax 416/624-9477. 289 rms, 8 suites. A/C TV TEL **Subway:** Kipling.

Rates: $160–$170 single or double. Extra person $10. Weekend rates are lower. **Parking:** Free.

Located on a six-acre woodland site 10 minutes from the airport, the Ramada Airport West has natural-oak walls and trim in the lobby, plenty of plants scattered throughout, and clean, comfortable rooms.

Dining/Entertainment: Chardonnay Grill and Lounge.

Services: 24-hour room service, laundry/valet, babysitting.

Facilities: Indoor pool, sauna, exercise room, beauty salon.

Venture Inn at the Airport, 925 Dixon Rd., Etobicoke, ON, M9W 1J8. ☎ **416/674-2222,** or toll free **800/387-3933.** Fax 416/674-5757. 283 rms. A/C TV TEL **Directions:** Take the Gardiner Expressway west to Hwy. 427 north, to Airport Expressway (Dixon Rd. exit).

Rates (including breakfast): $90 single; $100 double. Extra person $10. **Parking:** Free.

This hotel is part of the moderately priced Venture Inn chain, which features modern rooms furnished country style. Complimentary breakfast is available, but there is no restaurant/lounge on the premises, although Pat and Mario's is connected to the hotel and there are and plenty of others nearby. Facilities include an indoor pool, sauna, and whirlpool.

Budget

Comfort Inn–Airport, 240 Belfield Rd., Rexdale, ON, M9W 1H3. ☎ **416/241-8513.** Fax 416/249-4203. 122 rms. A/C TV TEL **Directions:** Take Hwy. 27 north to Belfield Rd.

Rates: $65 single; $70 double. Extra person $8. **Parking:** Free.

Also off the airport strip but close enough to be convenient, the Comfort Inn–Airport has modern rooms with up-to-date, color-coordinated decor and pine furnishings, plus individual climate control, color TVs, and phones. A restaurant is planned for 1995.

5 Metro West

While this is not the most salubrious area in which to stay, it does have some low-cost motels. The establishment listed below is the best of the lot.

Budget

The Silver Moon, 2157 Lakeshore Blvd. W., Toronto, ON, M8V 1A1. ☎ **416/252-5051.** 24 rms. A/C TV TEL **Directions:** Take the Queen St. streetcar (no. 501) west to the end of the line.

Rates: $50 single; $60 double. **Parking:** Free.

Along Lakeshore Boulevard stretches a whole motel row's worth of accommodations that saw their heyday when Highway 2 was the main route into the city. Today only a few of these motels, such as the Silver Moon, deserve a mention, primarily for clean but basic accommodations. Free local calls are a plus.

6 Metro East

The accommodations listed here are conveniently located for the Metro Zoo; the science center; and Scarborough Town Centre, a vast shopping mall.

In addition to the three outstanding accommodations and the university accommodations listed below, there are a number of chain hotels located in this area, including the following: Embassy Suites, Holiday Inn, Radisson, Ramada, and Sheraton. Most of them charge more than $100 a night and have few exceptional features. A couple, though, have moderately priced rooms and therefore have also been included.

Very Expensive ─────────────────────────

★ **The Four Seasons' Inn on the Park,** 1100 Eglinton Ave. E., Don Mills, ON, M3C 1H8. ☎ **416/444-2561,** or toll free **800/332-3442** in the U.S., **800/268-6282** in Canada. Fax 416/446-3308. 540 rms, 28 suites. A/C MINIBAR TV TEL **Subway:** Eglinton.

Rates: $120–$180 single or double; from $200 suite. Extra person $20. Two children under 18 stay free in parents' room. Weekend packages available. **Parking:** Free.

The Four Seasons Inn is a luxury hotel/resort only 15 minutes from downtown via the Don Valley Parkway—conveniently located only minutes from the Ontario Science Centre. Set on 600 acres of parkland, the inn takes advantage of its natural setting: A lounge faces west to capture the magnificent sunsets, and a landscaped two-acre courtyard has Douglas firs, silver birches, a rock garden, and a duck pond, all crisscrossed by walkways and dotted with benches. Beautiful in summer, picturesque in fall.

The rooms, located in a 14-story low-rise and a 21-story tower, have beautiful views (those facing west have balconies). All are superbly decorated with contemporary pieces and have those extra little features like alarm clocks, hairdryers, and bathrobes, as well as the usual color TVs with in-house movies, phones, and individual climate control.

Dining/Entertainment: The Terrace Lounge, a comfy piano bar, features a salad-bar lunch and cocktail-hour snacks. During the summer months, the Cabana, the poolside restaurant, is open for pleasant outdoor dining. A stylish garden atmosphere is the backdrop for sophisticated continental cuisine in Seasons, the hotel's premier dining room, which serves such specialties as balsamic-scented breast of chicken with multigrain pilaf, or pan-seared filet of beef with roasted shallots, red wine, and crisp potato cake, priced from $20 to $29. For casual all-day dining, there's the Harvest Room. All the restaurants feature alternative cuisine for the health-conscious.

Services: 24-hour room service, 24-hour concierge, twice-daily maid service, complimentary shoeshine, laundry/valet, one-hour pressing.

Facilities: Indoor, outdoor, and diving pools; games room with video games and pinball; badminton; volleyball; shuffleboard; racquet club with tennis, squash, and racquetball courts; health club with saunas and gym; bicycling and cross-country skiing; Innkidz, a supervised free program for children 5 to 12 (in summer it's offered daily from 9:30am to 4:30pm; in winter, it's offered only on weekends and special holidays); business center; beauty salon, and other boutiques.

Prince Hotel, 900 York Mills Rd., Don Mills, ON, M3B 3H2.
☎ **416/444-2511,** or toll free **800/323-7500** in the U.S.,
800/268-7677 in Canada. Fax 416/444-9597. 406 rms and suites.
A/C MINIBAR TV TEL **Subway:** York Mills.
Rates: $165–$180 single; $185–$210 double. Extra person $15.
Children under 18 stay free in parents' room. Weekend packages available. **Parking:** Free.

The other luxury resort hotel in this area is much quieter, having an almost ethereal serenity, which may derive from its Japanese connections. The Prince Hotel, located 20 minutes from downtown, is set in 15 acres of private parkland where you can wander nature trails.

A warm and soft decor will greet you in your room, which may have a beautiful bay window or balcony. Each of the oversize rooms has a marble bathroom with hairdryer, a color TV with in-house movies, two telephones, and an in-room safe.

Dining/Entertainment: Le Continental features a walk-in cellar and fine cuisine with main courses priced from $18.50 to $27. Katsura, the specialty restaurant, has four separate dining areas, a tempura counter and sushi bar, tatami-style dining, teppanyaki-style cuisine, and a robata bar. Complete dinners range from $32.50 to $45. The Coffee Garden restaurant overlooks a grove of 30-foot-tall trees, as does the Brandy Tree, a sophisticated piano bar, restfully decorated in gray and plum.

Services: 24-hour room service, laundry/valet, nightly turndown, concierge, babysitting.

Facilities: Outdoor heated pool, sauna, tennis courts, fitness center, games room, putting green, nature trails.

Moderate

Travelodge Scarborough, 20 Milner Business Court, Scarborough, ON, M1B 3C6. ☎ **416/299-9500,** or toll free **800/667-3529.** Fax 416/299-6172. 160 rms. A/C TV TEL **Subway:** Scarborough Town Center.
Rates: $65 single; $70 double. **Parking:** Free.

The Travelodge has rooms containing color TVs with in-room movies, individual climate control, and attractive furnishings. There are a restaurant/lounge and an indoor pool and whirlpool.

Venture Inn, 50 Estate Dr. (Markham Rd. and Hwy. 401), Scarborough, ON, M1H 2Z1. ☎ **416/439-9666,** or toll free **800/387-3933.** 136 rms. A/C TV TEL **Subway:** McCowan.

Rates (including continental breakfast): $70 single; $80 double. Children under 19 stay free in parents' room. **Parking:** Free.

The Venture Inn has pleasantly decorated rooms with the chain's country-pine look. Restaurants are nearby.

Budget

University of Toronto in Scarborough, Student Village,

Scarborough Campus, University of Toronto, 1265 Military Trail, Scarborough, ON, M1C 1A4. ☎ **416/287-7369. Directions:** Take the subway to Kennedy, then the Scarborough Rapid Transit to Ellesmere, then bus no. 95 or 95B to the college entrance.

Rates: $140 for two-night minimum stay per town house. Family rates available. **Parking:** Free. **Open:** Mid–May to the end of Aug.

From mid–May to the end of August, the University of Toronto in Scarborough, Student Village, has accommodations available in town houses that sleep four to six people and contain equipped kitchens. None has air-conditioning, a TV, or a telephone. There is a cafeteria, a pub, and a recreation center (with squash and tennis courts, a gym, and an exercise room) as well as a laundry, a bank, and a bookstore on campus.

A Lovely Rural/City Retreat

The Guild Inn, 201 Guildwood Pkwy., Scarborough, ON, M1E 1P6. ☎ **416/261-3331,** or toll free **800/877-1133.** Fax 416/261-5675. 90 rms, 5 suites. A/C TV TEL **Subway:** Kennedy.

Rates: Main inn, $65 single or double, $10 per extra person; new wing, $85 single or double. Children under 12 stay free in parents' room. Special packages available. **Parking:** Free.

If you want to stay in a unique and beautiful setting, then try the Guild Inn, just 10 miles (about 20 minutes) outside the city. Enter through the broad iron gates and follow the circular drive, which is shaded by trees and bordered with flowers. The original entrance hall retains the character of an English manor, with its broad staircase, oak beams, and wrought-iron chandeliers.

The 90-acre grounds are dotted with historic architectural fragments, remnants from the Guild of All Arts, which once occupied the property. So many visitors were attracted by the Guild's collections and workshops that dining facilities and guest rooms were added, until the Guild became a flourishing country inn. During these halcyon years many notables visited, including Queen Juliana of the Netherlands, Dorothy and Lillian Gish, Moira Shearer, Rex Harrison, Sir John Gielgud, and Lilli Palmer.

The gardens at the rear sweep down to the Scarborough Bluffs, rising 200 feet above Lake Ontario, and for a room with this view you'll pay a little extra. The original central section of the inn was built in 1914, and the rooms here have been renovated. All 90 rooms have air-conditioning, AM/FM radios, color TVs, and private balconies.

Dining/Entertainment: The dining room is still a popular gathering place for Sunday brunch ($17), and it serves primarily grills, roasts, and seafood, priced from $13 to $20. In summer, tea is served outdoors in the garden, and there's a lovely veranda for cocktails.

Facilities: Outdoor swimming pool, tennis court, games room, exercise room, nature trails.

5

Toronto Dining

THE MULTICULTURAL MOSAIC OF THE CITY MAKES DINING IN TORONTO A delightful round-the-world experience that can be enjoyed for only a moderate price. Of course, you can eat at the fashionable hot spots, and by all means do so, but more fun, in my opinion, is to explore the city's neighborhoods and visit the ethnic dining spots in Little Italy, Little Portugal, Chinatown, and Greektown. Another charming and welcome aspect of the city dining scene is the incredible number of outdoor dining spots and the tolerance extended to those of us who just want to linger for a few hours over an iced coffee or a lemonade. It's refreshing and very European in flavor. Supposedly there are 5,000-plus restaurants in the city. Below is a quick-reference list of 130 or so of my favorites organized by cuisine (with the neighborhood and an abbreviation of the price category in parentheses), followed by writeups of each establishment categorized according to location and price.

SOME DINING NOTES   Although dining in Toronto can be expensive, it usually seems that way not so much because of the food but because of the extras—like the 8% provincial sales tax on meals and the 7% GST. In addition, wine prices are higher than those in the United States, largely because of the tax on all imported wines. So you will pay as much as $6 for a glass of house wine in the better restaurants and as much as $25 for a one-liter carafe. Most wine lists start in the $20 range. There's also a 10% tax on all alcohol—keep in mind that the prices quoted often do not reflect that tax. Just be aware of these facts.

Prices are rather broad categories: At luxury (or very expensive) establishments expect to pay $125 and up for dinner for two without wine; expensive, $80 to $100; moderate, $50 to $70; and at inexpensive or budget establishments, under $30. These, I stress, are only rough guidelines, and at many of the moderately priced and budget-priced establishments you can pay much less by choosing carefully.

The abbreviations which appear in the list of restaurants by cuisine can be translated as: VE=Very Expensive; E=Expensive; M=Moderate; I=Inexpensive.

Unless stated otherwise, *the prices cited here are given in Canadian dollars*—good news for Americans because the Canadian dollar is worth 35% less than the American dollar but buys just about as much. As we go to press, $1 Canadian is worth 74¢ U.S., which means that your $50 dinner for two will cost only $37 U.S., and your $5 breakfast will cost only $3.70 U.S.

Locations are as follows: **Downtown** refers roughly to streets from the waterfront to and including College/Carlton Street between Spadina Avenue and Jarvis Street; **midtown** refers to the area north of College/Carlton Street to Davenport and Yonge streets and also between Spadina and Jarvis; I have also further subdivided both of these sections into west and east. **Uptown** covers Yonge/Davenport Street and north.

1 Restaurants by Cuisine

Asian/European
Lotus (Downtown West, VE)

Burgers
Hughie's Burgers (Downtown West, IE)
Toby's Goodeats (Midtown West, IE)

Cajun
Bayou Bistro (Downtown West, M)
N'Awlins (Downtown West, M)
Southern Accent (Midtown West, M)

California
Acqua (Downtown East, E)
Left Bank (Downtown West, M)

Canadian/International
Fred's Not Here Smokehouse
  and Grill (Downtown West, M)
Red Tomato (Downtown West, M)

Caribbean
Kensington Patty Palace (Downtown West, IE)

Chinese
Kowloon Dim Sum (Downtown West, IE)
Lee Garden (Downtown West, IE)
Pink Pearl (Downtown West, M)
Saigon Palace (Downtown West, IE)
The Eating Counter (Downtown West, IE)
Wah Sing (Downtown West, IE)
Young Lok Gardens (Downtown West, IE)

Coffee
Café Miró (Midtown East/The East End, IE)
Chez Cappuccino (Midtown West, IE)

Continental
Arlequin (Midtown West, M)
Biffi's Bistro (Uptown, M)
Bofinger (Uptown, M)
Chiaro's (Uptown/Hotel Dining, VE)
Encore (Downtown East, E)
Herbs (Uptown, M)
Jacques Bistro du Park (Midtown West, M)
Lakes (Midtown West, M)
La Maquette (Downtown East, E)

Mildred Pierce (Downtown West, M)
Movenpick Bistretto (Midtown West, M)
Movenpick Marche (Downtown East, IE)
Palmerston (Midtown West, M)
Peter Pan (Downtown West, M)
Rivoli (Downtown West, IE)
The Roof Restaurant (Uptown/Hotel Dining, VE)
Scaramouche (Uptown, E)
Seasons (Uptown/Hotel Dining, E)
Trapper's (Uptown, M)
Truffles (Uptown/Hotel Dining, VE)

Crepes
Le Papillon (Downtown East, IE)

Deli
The Bagel (Downtown West, IE)
Shopsy's (Downtown East, IE)

Desserts
Just Desserts (Uptown, IE)

Eclectic
Mildred Pierce (Downtown West, M)
Jump Cafe and Bar (Downtown West, E)

French
Bistro 990 (Midtown West, E)
Brasserie Les Artistes (Downtown East, M)
Brownes Bistro (Uptown, M)
Chiaro's (Uptown/Hotel Dining, VE)
La Bodega (Downtown West, M)
Le Bistingo (Downtown West, M)
La Grenouille (Uptown, M)
Le Paradis (Uptown, M)
Le Rendez-Vous (Midtown West, M)
Le Select (Downtown West, M)
Mildred Pierce (Downtown West, M)
Opus (Midtown West, E)
St. Tropez (Downtown West, M)
Taro Grill (Downtown West, M)
Yves Bistro (Midtown West, M)

Fusion (Asian/Caribbean/Mediterranean)
New Avec (Downtown West, E)

Greek
Astoria (Midtown East/The East End, IE)
Myth (Midtown East/The East End, IE)

Omonia (Midtown East/The East End, IE)
Ouzeri (Midtown East/The East End, IE)
Ilan on the Danforth (Midtown East/The East End, IE)

Indian

The Bombay Palace (Downtown East, IE)
Indian Rice Factory (Midtown West, IE)
The Moghul (Downtown West, IE)
Raja Sahib (Downtown West, IE)

International

The Groaning Board (Downtown West, IE)
N 44 (Uptown, E)
Queen Mother Cafe (Downtown West, IE)
Red Tomato (Downtown West, M)

Italian

Acqua (Downtown East, E)
Bar Italia (Midtown West, IE)
Biagio (Downtown East, E)
Centro (Uptown, E)
Coppi (Uptown, M)
Grano (Uptown, M)
Grappa (Midtown West, M)
Il Fornello (Downtown West, IE)
Il Posto (Midtown West, M)
La Fenice (Downtown West, E)
Maccheroni (Downtown East, IE)
Myth (Midtown East/The East End, IE)
N'Awlins (Downtown West, M)
The Old Spaghetti Factory (Downtown East, IE)
The Organ Grinder (Downtown East, IE)
Orso (Downtown West, E)
Pronto (Uptown, E)
Spiaggia (Downtown East, M)
Splendido Bar and Grill (Midtown West, E)
Trattoria Giancarlo (Midtown West, M)

Japanese

Fune (Downtown West, M)
Masa (Downtown West, M)
Mori (Midtown West, IE)
Nami Japanese Seafood (Downtown East, E)
Takesushi (Downtown East, M)

Light Fare

Bloor Street Diner (Midtown East, IE)
Brownes Bistro (Uptown, M)
Café Miró (Midtown East/The East End, IE)
Chez Cappuccino (Midtown West, IE)

Laotian
Vanipha (Downtown West, IE)

Malaysian
Ole Malacca (Downtown West, M)

Mediterranean
Opus (Midtown West, E)
Taro Grill (Downtown West, M)

Middle Eastern
Aïda's Falafel (Midtown West, IE)
Jerusalem (Uptown, IE)
Kensington Kitchen (Midtown West, IE)

North American
The Senator (Downtown East, M)

Nouvelle
Zachary's (Uptown)

Peruvian
The Boulevard Café (Midtown West, IE)

Portuguese
Chiado (Midtown West, M)
The Boat (Downtown West, M)

Québecois
Montréal Bistro and Jazz Club (Downtown East, M)

Seafood
Filet of Sole (Downtown West, M)
Joso's (Midtown West, M)
The Lobster Trap (Uptown, E)
The Old Fish Market (Downtown East, IE)
Whistling Oyster Seafood Cafe (Downtown West, M)

Steak
Barberian's (Downtown West, E)

Thai
Bangkok Garden (Downtown West, E)
Thai Magic (Uptown, M)
Vanipha (Downtown West, IE)
Young Thailand (Downtown East, IE)

Vegetarian
Annapurna Restaurant (Midtown West, IE)
Earthtones Vegetarian Restaurant (Downtown West, IE)
Free Times Café (Downtown West, IE)

Vietnamese
Saigon Palace (Downtown West, IE)

2 Downtown West

There's plenty of pleasurable and reasonable dining to choose from in this area; one of the best streets on which to look for a selection of reasonably priced bistros frequented by artists and young professionals is Queen Street West. Dining in the theater district is, as in most other cities, fraught with pitfalls—high prices and poor quality—but I describe some exceptions below.

Very Expensive

★ **Lotus,** 96 Tecumseh St. ☎ **368-7620.**

Cuisine: ASIAN/EUROPEAN. **Reservations:** Imperative—at least two weeks in advance.
Prices: Main courses $28. AE, MC, V.
Open: Dinner Tues–Sat 6–10pm.

Located off King, west of Bathurst, Lotus focuses on its menu—not its ambience. The storefront's decor is plain, with a tiny bar, a blush of color on one wall, and some herbed vinegar for decorative accent. That's it. But the quality and inspiration that has gone into the food has won chef Su Sur Lee accolades—which means that this small restaurant is booked a long time in advance. Su Sur Lee hails from Hong Kong and he creatively combines European and Asian styles and flavors to produce such thrilling dishes as quick-sautéed large shrimps in a Thai green curry sauce with fresh mango, chop suey vegetables, and an orange-pepper rice-noodle cake; or organic crispy-skin duck breast with raspberry wildflower honey and lavender glaze, roasted squash, and young potato and hazelnut homefries.

The menu changes daily. Among the appetizers you might find such delicately flavored dishes as sautéed wild chanterelle and red-lobster mushrooms with green garlic butter and spinach spaetzle; or seared foie gras with beet-and-apple compote, topped with carrot vinaigrette and mustard oil. The desserts, which currently cost $8, range from a classic baked raspberry tart in a light custard with white chocolate ice cream to Peking-style fig fritters with caramel ice cream, mango purée, and hot chocolate sauce.

Expensive

Bangkok Garden, 18 Elm St. ☎ **977-6748.**

Cuisine: THAI. **Reservations:** Recommended.
Prices: Main courses $17–$20; all-you-can-eat lunch buffet $10. AE, MC, V.
Open: Restaurant, lunch Mon–Fri 11:30am–2:30pm; dinner Mon–Sat 5:30–10:30pm. Brass Flamingo bar, Mon–Sat 11:30am–11pm.

Bangkok Garden offers Thai cuisine in a lush dining room fashioned out of teak. You may dine either in the tropical Garden, complete with flowing river stocked with fish, or on the Veranda, where Somerset Maugham would feel right at home. A spirit house, bronze nagas, and porcelain jardinieres add to the exotic ambience throughout.

Those unfamiliar with Thai food might try one of the special dinners for $37 and up, so that you can sample a selection of appetizers, shrimp soup flavored with lemon grass, three pagodas curry, stir-fried glass noodles, green beans with shrimp, rice, fruit, and Thai sweets. A la carte dishes include smooth curries made with chili, lime, and coconut milk; chicken richly flavored with tamarind; and fish steamed with ginger. Try something from the noodle bar, seasoning your choices to your own particular taste with spring onions, fresh coriander leaves, salted turnip, chili vinegar, and many other exotic flavors. For dessert, try mango sticky rice.

⭐ **Barberian's,** 7 Elm St. ☎ **597-0225** or **597-0335.**
Cuisine: STEAK. **Reservations:** Required.
Prices: Main courses $19–$30. AE, DC, MC, V.
Open: Lunch Mon–Fri noon–2:30pm; dinner daily 5pm–midnight.

Steak houses, as far as I'm concerned, are usually rather dull establishments, but Barberian's is the best and brightest in town. The front half, both inside and out, remains essentially as built in 1860, and the three cozy interconnected rooms house a superb collection of Canadiana that includes several originals by the Group of Seven; a bust of Canada's first prime minister, Sir John A. Macdonald; one of the original grandfather clocks made in Canada; along with pre-Confederation money, coal-oil lamps, and firearms. Despite the traditional air, Barberian's exudes friendliness and lightness of touch.

Nonchalance does not extend to the food, however, which focuses on 10 or so steak and seafood dishes, all well worth the price. After 10pm a fondue and dessert menu awaits the after-theater or late diner.

⭐ **La Fenice,** 319 King St. W. ☎ **585-2377.**
Cuisine: ITALIAN. **Reservations:** Recommended.
Prices: Main courses $14–$24. AE, DC, MC, V.
Open: Lunch Mon–Fri noon–2:30pm; dinner Mon–Sat 5:30–11pm.

Really fresh ingredients and fine authentic olive oil are the hallmarks of the cuisine at La Fenice, where a plate of assorted appetizers will include pungent roast peppers, crisp-fried zucchini, squid, and a roast veal in tuna sauce (*vitello tonnato*). There are 18 or more pasta dishes—tagliatelle burro and basilico with fragrant basil sauce and also seafood risotto—along with a fine selection of Provimi veal, chicken, and fresh fish dishes. Dessert offerings include a refreshing raspberry sherbet, zabaglione, tiramisu, and fresh strawberries and other fruits in season.

Jump Cafe and Bar, 1 Wellington St. W. ☎ **363-3400.**
Cuisine: ECLECTIC. **Reservations:** Recommended for lunch and dinner.
Prices: Main courses $17–$20. AE, DC, ER, MC, V.
Open: Lunch Mon–Fri 11:30am–5pm; dinner Mon–Sat 5–11:30pm.

A little hard to find, tucked away in Commerce Court, this is one of the latest power-dining spots. It vibrates with energy. The streamlined atrium dining room has polished granite floors and warm maple tables; the grand space is broken up by palm and other strategically placed trees and shrubs. The small bar area to the left of the entrance is presided over by a bust of Bacchus and features a good selection of single malts and grappas. In summer it's pleasant to sit out in Commerce Court.

In addition to the fresh daily specials, the menu features about six dishes like oven-roasted chicken marinated in anchote spice on buttermilk whipped potatoes; passion-glazed Atlantic salmon on wilted spinach, with sweet corn and shiitake caps in an orange miso butter; or roast rack of lamb with clove mustard herb crust, sweet yam ratatouille, green mustard aioli, and tarragon pan juices. There are also pizzas and pastas available. To start try the mussels steamed with lime leaf, coconut milk, garam masala, tomato, and coriander, or perhaps the oak-smoked salmon on a warm salad of new potatoes with mustard dressing, green onion, capers, and dill sour cream. Among the desserts, I lust after the caramelized banana and chocolate bread pudding, but you may be seduced by the maple-glazed pecan pie with a Kentucky bourbon crème anglaise, the tiramisu, or the dark chocolate fudge cake with white chocolate ice cream and Bailey's Irish cream.

New Avec, 330 Adelaide St. W., (between Peter Street and Drummond Place). ☎ **591-2102.**
Cuisine: FUSION (ASIAN/CARIBBEAN/MEDITERRANEAN). **Reservations:** Recommended.
Prices: Main courses $17.50–$24. AE, DC, ER, MC, V.
Open: Mon–Thurs 6–11pm, Fri–Sat 6pm–midnight.

This is the latest exciting arena in which chef Greg Couillard has chosen to demonstrate his cooking brilliance. The traditional favorites are still on the menu: the spicy, thick, wonderfully flavored jump-up soup with hot and sweet peppers, okra, and black-eyed peas; and jerk chicken with coconut milk and cilantro. He continues to marry Asian and European cuisine, producing such dishes as glazed duck with raspberry soy sauce. You'll enjoy a golden, sunwashed atmosphere redolent of the Mediterranean. To cap it all off the upholstered chairs are covered in a celebratory sun and moon design.

★ **Orso,** 106 John St. ☎ **596-1989.**
Cuisine: ITALIAN. **Reservations:** Recommended for both lunch and dinner.
Prices: Main courses $17–$28.50. AE, DC, MC, V.
Open: Mon–Sat 11:30am–midnight, Sun 5–10:30pm.

Orso, a cozy Italian bistro with an elegant small bar up front, is located in a brick town house in the theater district. Pink marble floors, low ceilings, and framed paintings make for an intimate ambience. The menu is the same at lunch and dinner. At lunch you might opt for one of the 10 or so appetizers, such as grilled smoked salmon with ginger mayonnaise, or warm spinach, arugula, and radicchio salad with roasted prosciutto, potato, and balsamic vinegar. Or try one of the half dozen delicious crisp-crusted pizzas topped variously with gorgonzola, prosciutto, and sun-dried tomato, or with onion, black olives, mushrooms, parmesan, pancetta, and tomato, to select only two. At dinner you could do the same or choose a pasta dish or a main course such as salmon with sautéed red kale, lemon, and black olive butter; roasted quail with grappa and braised red cabbage; or grilled lamb chops with port rosemary and grilled endive.

Moderate

Bayou Bistro, 275 Queen St. ☎ 977-7222.

Cuisine: CAJUN. **Reservations:** Recommended, especially at lunch.
Prices: Main courses $7–$10 at lunch, $12–$16 at dinner. AE, DC, MC, V.
Open: Lunch Mon–Fri 11:30am–2:30pm; dinner Mon–Thurs 5–10:30pm, Fri–Sat 5–11pm.

Bayou Bistro is a popular spot where the desserts are everyone's downfall—deep-fried ice cream with apple bourbon sauce, peanut-butter pie, and great sorbets, all freshly made. Start with crab cakes or a thick gumbo and follow with blackened swordfish, shrimp Creole, or Cajun sirloin steak. There's always a pasta of the day, along with such dishes as veal Oscar and chicken with hot mango chutney and sautéed banana. The atmosphere is light, modern, and informal—with bricks, poster art, and a maple bar.

The Boat, 158 Augusta Ave. ☎ 593-9218.

Cuisine: PORTUGUESE. **Reservations:** Recommended at dinner.
Prices: Main courses $10–$20. AE, MC, V.
Open: Lunch Tues–Sat 11:30am–3pm; dinner Tues–Sat 5pm–1am, Sun 5–10pm.

In the heart of Kensington Market, the Boat serves up typical Portuguese fare and entertainment. The emphasis is on seafood—whole Dover sole meunière; steamed crab; cod in a casserole with green peppers, onions, and tomato sauce; and mixed seafood plate containing lobster tail, shrimp, clam, squid, and Alaskan king crab. These are supplemented by pork alentejo and barbecued chicken Portuguese style.

Filet of Sole, 11 Duncan St. ☎ 598-3256.

Cuisine: SEAFOOD. **Reservations:** Required two days in advance.
Prices: Main courses $10–$28. AE, DC, MC, V.
Open: Lunch Mon–Fri noon–2:30pm; dinner daily 5–11pm.

Conveniently located near the CN Tower and the theater district, this must be Toronto's favorite seafood restaurant. Here you'll find an oyster bar and an extensive seafood menu that also features daily specials. The restaurant serves everything from fish-and-chips to lobster with rice and vegetable. Most of the dishes are in the $13-to-$18 range for bluefish, monkfish, red snapper, salmon, swordfish, tuna, mahimahi, and many other varieties. For nonfish lovers there's sirloin steak and roasted chicken. The dessert specialty is the frozen meringue basket filled with Grand Marnier, chocolate-pecan ice cream, fresh strawberries, and strawberry sauce—not to mention the chocolate truffle mousse and hot almond crepes.

Fred's Not Here Smokehouse and Grill, 321 King St. W.
☎ 971-9155.

Cuisine: CANADIAN/INTERNATIONAL. **Reservations:** Recommended.
Prices: Main courses $8–$14 at lunch, $14–$24 at dinner. AE, DC,
MC, V.
Open: Lunch Mon–Fri noon–2pm; dinner Mon–Sat 6–10pm.

Upstairs above Red Tomato, this restaurant has a more sedate atmosphere and more formal and expensive food than its cousin below. The menu, though, is equally extensive, presenting an array of fish and meat choices—from grilled loin of lamb with a honey, rosemary, and ginger glaze to sautéed jumbo shrimp with smoked jalapeño-tequila sauce, served with black pasta. Other choices range from a pan-roasted stuffed Québec pheasant with a sauce of wild mushrooms, brandy, and cream to a plain steak or lobster. The equally eclectic appetizers might include crispy Thai noodles along with pâté, coconut shrimp, and more. Favorites among the desserts are the pâté of white and dark chocolate with pistachio sauce and the banana fritters with caramel ice cream and chocolate sauce.

Fune, 100 Simcoe St. ☎ 599-3868.

Cuisine: JAPANESE. **Reservations:** Recommended.
Prices: Main courses $9–$14. AE, DC, MC, V.
Open: Lunch Mon–Fri noon–2:30pm; dinner Sun–Thurs 5–11pm, Fri–Sat 5pm–midnight.

The fun and focal point of this dining room is the 40-seat sushi bar on which an endless procession of small barges laden with freshly made sushi and sashimi float around an oval water-filled canal. There is also a selection of udon dishes and familiar favorites like tonkatsu, tempura, and teriyaki, as well as luncheon and dinner buffets. The fun starts at 10pm, when the karaoke entertainment begins, and it goes on until 1am (1:30am on Friday and Saturday).

An Important Note On Prices

Unless stated otherwise, **the prices cited in this guide are given in Canadian dollars,** which is good news for U.S. travelers because the Canadian dollar is worth 26% less than the American dollar, but buys nearly as much. As we go to press, $1 Canadian is worth 74¢ U.S., which means that your $100-a-night hotel room will cost only U.S. $74, and your $6 breakfast costs only U.S. $4.44.

Here's a quick table of equivalents:

Canadian $	U.S. $
$1	$0.74
5	$3.70
10	$7.40
20	$14.80
50	$37.00
100	$74.00
200	$148.00

La Bodega, 30 Baldwin St. ☎ **977-1287.**

> **Cuisine:** FRENCH. **Reservations:** Recommended for dinner.
> **Prices:** Main courses $17–$26; prix fixe $17.50. AE, DC, ER, MC, V.
> **Open:** Lunch Mon–Fri noon–2:30pm; dinner Mon–Sat 5–11pm.

Ensconced in an elegant town house, La Bodega, two blocks south of College and two west of University Avenue, is still a favorite because it serves fine fresh food at moderate prices in a very comfortable atmosphere. Every day, the specials, usually inspired by the freshest produce at the market, are written on the blackboard menu. There's usually a dozen or so interesting choices, including several fresh fish dishes. For example, on my last visit the chef was offering monkfish with lobster sauce cardinale, and venison in a cognac sauce. The best bet of all, though, is the prix fixe for $17.50 for dinner, offering a choice of two set menus—one meat, the other fish—with soup or salad and tea or coffee. In summer the patio, with tables covered in red gingham and bearing multicolored umbrellas, is a popular dining spot.

At lunchtime, when the restaurant is especially popular, there's lighter fare with such things as coq au vin, tourtière, and salade niçoise, and a prix fixe for $11.85.

The dining rooms are quite fetching. The walls are graced with French tapestries and the windows with lace curtains. French music adds a certain Gallic air. There's a definite glow about the place.

Le Bistingo, 349 Queen St. W. ☎ **598-3490.**

> **Cuisine:** FRENCH. **Reservations:** Recommended.
> **Prices:** Main courses $10–$16 at lunch, $14–$28 at dinner. AE, MC, V.
> **Open:** Lunch Mon–Fri 11am–2:30pm; dinner Mon–Sat 5:30–10:30pm.

Le Bistingo is simple and sleek, containing tables set with pristine white tablecloths. The atmosphere is intimate yet not ornate, and the food is simple, fresh, and moderately priced.

At dinner you might enjoy the grilled red snapper with a ragout of clams and shrimp, chicken with five spices and Chinese noodles, or roast rack of lamb with basil aioli and Yukon gold potato mousseline. Appetizers are also appealing, like the salad of duck confit, asparagus, field mushrooms, and baby greens; or the hot escargots in a Chinese wrapper with nuoc man sauce. Finish with the warm apple tart that slips down easily with the accompanying Calvados ice cream or the profiteroles with espresso ice cream and caramel sauce.

⭐ **Le Select,** 328 Queen St. W. ☎ **596-6406.**

> **Cuisine:** FRENCH. **Reservations:** Recommended.
> **Prices:** Main courses average $9 at lunch, $13–$18 at dinner; fixed-price meal $16. AE, DC, MC, V.
> **Open:** Mon–Thurs 11:30am–11:30pm, Fri–Sat 11:30am–midnight, Sun noon–10:30pm.

People throng the entrance of Le Select, a real bistro decorated in Paris Left Bank style, complete with an authentic zinc bar, breakfronts, fringed fabric lampshades over the tables, tollware, French posters, and a jazz background to set the scene.

What draws the young artistic crowd here is the chance to dine on moderately priced but good French food—from mussels steamed in white wine and shallots to pork filet with green peppercorn sauce. Most dishes, such as the filet of salmon with dill and Pernod, average under $10. Among the selections the day I visited were beef tongue with capers and gherkins in a warm vinaigrette and also a turkey drumstick with braised cabbage. For dessert there was fruit tart and chocolate mousse.

Left Bank, 567 Queen St. W., just east of Portland St. on the south side of the street. ☎ **504-1626.**

Cuisine: CALIFORNIA. **Reservations:** Recommended for dinner.
Prices: Main courses $13–$22. 50. AE, MC, V.
Open: Lunch Mon–Fri noon–3:30pm; dinner daily 6–11pm.

The heavy tapestries and ornate carved French doors and bar give this room a rich French Renaissance feel that's more akin to the Loire Valley than to the Left Bank. Equally surprising is the American cuisine served here. The 10 or so main courses range from penne with white beans, yellow tomatoes, sage pesto, and mascarpone cheese to broiled Cuban rock lobster tail with roasted corn, whipped sweet potatoes, and ancho chili butter. To start try the warm ginger scallion crepe stuffed with stir-fried lobster, mango, cucumber, and wild mushrooms, served with sweet miso butter; or the crispy fried bluepoint oysters served in the half shell with apple-smoked bacon and sour cream dressing. There's a pool/billiard room downstairs.

Masa, 205 Richmond St. W. ☎ **977-9519.**

Cuisine: JAPANESE. **Reservations:** Recommended.
Prices: Sushi $2.50 per piece; appetizers $3.50–$5; fixed-price dinners $14–$39. AE, DC, MC, V.
Open: Lunch Mon–Fri noon–2:30pm; dinner Mon–Sat 5–11pm. Sun 5–10pm.

Masa is well known to Toronto aficionados of Japanese cuisine. Seat yourself at the sushi bar and choose from a huge assortment or dine Western or tatami style. Sake containers, Japanese prints, fans, and screens are scattered around the large room. There's a full range of appetizers—sliced fishcake, oysters in rice vinegar, and seaweed-pasted crab leg, to name only a few. Or you can preface your dinner with one of the many fascinating soups—Tororo seaweed soup, for instance. The best deals, though, are the fixed-price dinners, which will include clear soup; a small appetizer; rice; and such main courses as salmon teriyaki, raw tuna sashimi, or garlic beef yakiniku. Don't miss the mitsu mame dessert—seaweed jelly with black peas.

Mildred Pierce, 99 Sudbury St. ☎ **588-5695.**

Cuisine: FRENCH/CONTINENTAL/ECLECTIC. **Reservations:** Not accepted. **Directions:** Take Queen West to Dovercourt. Turn left, then right on Sudbury. The restaurant is located on the left at the back of a parking lot attached to Studio 99.
Prices: Main courses $13–$18. ER, MC, V.

Open: Lunch Mon–Fri noon–3pm, Sat–Sun 11am–3pm; dinner Sun–Thurs 6–10pm, Fri–Sat 6–11pm.

This atmospheric spot, which resembles a movie set, is worth seeking out. From the handful of tables outside you have a great view of the CN Tower and the downtown skyline. The outdoor terrace is awaft in billowing cloth screens and climbing shrubs. Inside, the room has a theatrical flair with gilt decorations, huge chandeliers created from God knows what, large semicircular banquettes, and glowing faux copper tables, all set against antiqued walls. At the back of the room stands a large arch with the following moniker above: Pearly Gates, Canadian Entrance.

Out of the open kitchen comes a variety of fine daily specials like the loin of pork with a cabernet-cassis sauce and chutney accompaniment. The menu features six or so main courses that range from linguine tossed in virgin olive oil and topped with grilled Bartlett pears, grilled leeks, and crumbled Stilton cheese to rack of lamb au jus served with tabbouleh in a phyllo pastry cup and a lemon-tahini aioli. My favorite dish, though, is a baked filet of salmon with a plum-miso sauce arranged on a nest of stir-fried noodles with arame seaweed, green onion, and carrot julienne garnished with wasabe and pickled ginger. Start with the steamed mussels in coconut milk, lemon grass, and Thai herbs and spices or the tiger shrimp dumplings, deep-fried and served with fresh mango, saffron-coconut milk sauce, and a hot chili-oil dip.

Depending on your passions, you'll want to save some room for dessert. I can recommend the pear tarte Tatin served with brandied caramel sauce and vanilla ice cream but you might prefer the chocolate-pistachio pâté served with white and dark chocolate sauce or the profiteroles filled with vanilla ice cream and drizzled with chocolate sauce.

N'Awlins, 299 King St. W. ☎ 595-1958.

Cuisine: CAJUN/ITALIAN. **Reservations:** Recommended at dinner.
Prices: Main courses $15–$20. AE, DC, MC, V.
Open: Mon–Fri noon–11pm, Sat–Sun 5–11pm.

Jazz is played here every night and the walls are studded top to bottom with photographs of historic and contemporary jazz greats. There's a long narrow bar in back and outdoor dining, too. The cuisine complements the ambience—witness the blackened chicken breast and grilled Cajun chicken. Other dishes are more eclectic like the tiger shrimp sautéed with garlic, leeks, and white wine on a bed of rice, or veal stuffed with spinach and mushrooms topped with a pesto cream sauce. There are pasta dishes, too—linguine with grilled chicken and red and yellow peppers in a white wine pesto sauce, or fusilli with bacon, chicken, and leeks in a white wine/pink cream sauce. The same dichotomy appears on the appetizer menu: Cajun calamari, Creole tiger shrimp, Cajun chicken livers, and medallions of alligator meat dusted in a Cajun seasoning served with dipping sauce are listed along with grilled sea scallops served with an orange brandy sauce or the tiger shrimp sautéed in a coconut cream sauce.

★ **Ole Malacca,** 49 Baldwin St. (at the corner of McCaul and Beverley sts.). ☎ **340-1112.**
Cuisine: MALAYSIAN. **Reservations:** Recommended.
Prices: Main courses $8–$16. AE, MC, V.
Open: Lunch Mon–Fri 11:30am–2:30pm; dinner Mon–Thurs 5–10pm, Fri–Sat 5–11pm.

Ole Malacca is a very appealing restaurant. Comfortable, welcoming, and furnished with bamboo/rattan and paper lanterns, it's full of Southeast Asian atmosphere. So is the spicy food, such as tiger prawns with garlic, ginger, and chili with brandy; filet of sole with curry coconut; or chicken with brandy-soy sauce. Try one of the sambals (based on shrimp paste) or the satays (cooked on a hibachi at the table). *Gado gado Bali* (slivers of cucumber, bean sprouts, hard-boiled egg, and slivers of chicken topped with spicy peanut sauce) is enough for three. A great way to sample the cuisine is to go for the luncheon buffet, which features more than 20 dishes.

Peter Pan, 373 Queen St. W. ☎ **593-0917.**
Cuisine: CONTINENTAL. **Reservations:** Recommended for parties of six or more.
Prices: Main courses $10–$14. AE, MC, V.
Open: Lunch Mon–Sat noon–2:30pm; dinner Sun–Wed 6pm–midnight, Thurs–Sat 6pm–1am; brunch Sun noon–4pm.

Peter Pan still remains a favorite of many who know this moderately priced gourmet find intimately. A bare-bones 1930s look with tin ceilings and high booths lit by art deco sconces provides the background. On the menu you'll find about a dozen appetizers, pizza, pasta, and fish of the day, and about a dozen main courses. The cuisine is imaginative, and often flavored with au courant Asian, Caribbean, and Mexican herbs and spices. For example, you might start with grilled calamari with jalapeño peppers, olive oil, and mixed greens or with mussels steamed with white wine, tomato, and gingered black beans. Follow with shrimp with vegetables, ginger, coriander, and lime; fusilli tossed in a tomato-basil broth with bacon, sweet peppers, mushrooms, black olives, and asiago cheese; or grilled chicken breast marinated in orange juice capers, olives, and raisins served with red onion marmalade, grilled yams, and vegetables. Desserts are always enticing, like the pear tart with almond cream or the Brazilian fig tart with kirsch sabayon.

Pink Pearl, 207 Queen's Quay W. ☎ **203-1233.**
Cuisine: CHINESE. **Reservations:** Recommended.
Prices: Main courses $10–$17. AE, DC, MC, V.
Open: Lunch daily 11am–3pm; dinner daily 5–11pm.

An attractive Chinese restaurant with views of Lake Ontario, Pink Pearl has been a local favorite for many years because of the quality of its food. To start there are several hors d'oeuvres and eight soups to select from, including shark's-fin soup with chicken. The specialties of the house range from braised lobster with ginger and green onion, and sliced chicken sautéed with pineapple and green peppers, to shrimps Szechuan style. There's an intriguing dish called rainbow chopped in crystal fold, consisting of finely chopped pork, Chinese sausage, mushroom, bamboo shoots, water chestnuts, celery, and carrot sautéed and served in crisp lettuce.

Another Pink Pearl can be found at 110 Bloor St. W. (☎ 975-1155).

Red Tomato, 321 King St. W. ☎ 971-6626.

Cuisine: CANADIAN/INTERNATIONAL. **Reservations:** Not needed.
Prices: Main courses $6–$14 at lunch, $6–$15 at dinner. AE, DC, MC, V.
Open: Mon–Fri 11:30am–12:30am, Sat noon–1am, Sun 4:30–10pm.

This popular bar/restaurant is famous for its hot-rocks cuisine—Korean beef, Jamaican jerk chicken, chicken with mango-chili salsa—all cooked the way it sounds. At night the downstairs space with its large central bar, video screens, wild murals, and exposed plumbing is filled with the young and not-so-young feasting on an array of small dishes—like the great spicy Yucatán shrimp; nachos; satay; and barbecued pork quesadillas with Brie, leeks, and pineapple. Afterward they can move onto something more substantial like steak or chicken fajitas, shrimp-and-scallop brochette, or a pasta or pizza dish.

St. Tropez, 315 King St. W. ☎ 591-3600.

Cuisine: FRENCH. **Reservations:** Recommended at dinner.
Prices: Main courses $10.75–$16.75. AE, DC, ER, MC, V.
Open: Mon–Wed 11:30am–11pm, Thurs–Sat 11:30am–midnight.

Stucco, mock shutters, and pale washes of color effect a country French atmosphere, which is further enriched by the table runners with their colorful fruit design. In summer the back courtyard, with its awning and vine-encrusted walls and statuary, is appealing. The bistro fare consists of such dishes as lamb with garlic and rosemary, salmon with lentils, chicken Dijon, and of course steak frites and a fish of the day. For dessert try the classic tarte Tatin or the clafoutis.

Taro Grill, 492 Queen St. W. (just west of Denison Ave. on the north side). ☎ 504-1320.

Cuisine: FRENCH/MEDITERRANEAN. **Reservations:** Not accepted.
Prices: Main courses $11–$16. MC, V.
Open: Lunch daily noon–4pm; dinner Sun–Thurs 6–11pm, Fri–Sat 6pm–midnight.

A small, distinctly hip spot (the multicolored mosaic floor, the red walls, and the jazz in the background are a dead giveaway). Head past the small bar and kitchen up front to the small dining area behind. The menu is short, featuring a pasta and fish of the day along with several pizzas and such dishes as breaded chicken breast stuffed with mushrooms and herbs served in a Dijon cream sauce, or lamb chops served in a rosemary wine glaze. Appetizers are similarly straightforward—warm goat cheese and walnut salad, steamed mussels, and other salads.

Whistling Oyster Seafood Cafe, 11 Duncan St. ☎ 598-7707.

Cuisine: SEAFOOD. **Reservations:** Recommended for lunch only.

Prices: Main courses $10–$23. AE, DC, ER, MC, V.
Open: Mon–Sat 11am–1am, Sun 4–11pm.

Downstairs at the Filet of Sole, the Whistling Oyster has a happy oyster hour and a happy dim sum hour on Sunday from 4:30 to 10pm. Enjoy 20 or so appetizers including a variety of fresh clams and oysters and such dishes as steamed clams in wine, tomato, and garlic; blackened tiger shrimp with mangoes and Thai coleslaw; conch fritters, and many more. Most items are under $3; everything is under $5. At other times there's an extensive shellfish and fish menu that runs from $10 for a coquille maison to $20 for Alaskan king crab legs.

Inexpensive

Earthtones Vegetarian Restaurant, 357 Queen St. W.
☎ 599-9054.
Cuisine: VEGETARIAN. **Reservations:** Not accepted.
Prices: Main courses $4–$7.50. MC, V.
Open: Mon–Sat 9am–10pm.

Earthtones consists of a small room with an outdoor patio and polished wood tables—plain and simple, like the food. You'll find piping-hot soups made daily, ratatouille, vegetarian chili, quiche, omelets, all kinds of salads, sandwiches, and hummus—all under $5. Hot dishes are sold in small, medium, and large portions.

The Eating Counter, 21–23 Baldwin St. ☎ 977-7028.
Cuisine: CHINESE. **Reservations:** Accepted for parties of 4–10 only.
Prices: Main courses $7–$13. AE, DC, MC, V.
Open: Daily 11am–11pm.

Lines extend onto the street from the Eating Counter, near McCaul and Dundas streets. Many of the eager patrons here are Chinese who relish the perfectly cooked Cantonese fare—crisp fresh vegetables; noodles; barbecue specialties; and, a particular favorite, fresh lobster with ginger and green onions. Ask the waiter to recommend the freshest items of the day. The decor is nonexistent, but the food is good.

Free Times Café, 320 College St. ☎ 967-1078.
Cuisine: VEGETARIAN/INTERNATIONAL. **Reservations:** Not needed.
Prices: Daily specials $7–$8. AE, MC, V.
Open: Mon–Sat 11:30am–12:45am, Sun 11:30am–10:45pm.

The Free Times Café has a casual avant-garde ambience, displays original art, and also features folk and original acoustic music nightly. The food is reasonably priced and includes such daily specials as sole with veggie stir-fry and veggie curry with couscous. Fully licensed.

The Groaning Board, 287 King St. W. (at John). ☎ 595-7232.
Cuisine: INTERNATIONAL/NATURAL. **Reservations:** Recommended on weekends.
Prices: Main courses $6–$7. AE, MC, V.
Open: Daily 9am–1am.

One of the best entertainment buys in Toronto awaits you at the Groaning Board. Every night at 7 and 9pm, a selection of international award-winning commercials is shown from the Cannes and Venice festivals. The food is 40% vegetarian, 60% meat dishes, featuring everything from fish and chips, quiche, and steak to eggplant parmesan, lasagne, and Middle Eastern specialties.

Il Fornello, 214 King St. W. ☎ 977-2855.

Cuisine: ITALIAN. **Reservations:** Recommended.
Prices: Main courses $9–$13. MC, V.
Open: Mon–Fri noon–10pm, Sat–Sun 4–11pm.

Il Fornello is famous for its 50 varieties of pizza cooked in a wood-fired clay oven and for a variety of popular Italian dishes—pasta, veal, and chicken. Also featured is an alternative menu with nondairy, nonyeast, and low-cholesterol items. Five other locations, too.

Kensington Patty Palace, 172 Baldwin St. ☎ 596-6667.

Cuisine: CARIBBEAN.
Prices: Most items $2.50–$5. No credit cards.
Open: Mon–Wed and Sat 10am–6pm, Thurs–Fri 10am–7pm.

Folks line up here in the heart of the Kensington Market—and with good reason. For a few dollars you can secure some satisfying, tasty food that you can enjoy on the bench out front if you can find space. The beef, chicken, and goat rotis ($4.20) are famous; so, too, are the potato and chick-pea rotis, which are even cheaper. Beef, chicken, and vegetable patties are also available for $1 or less. For a real Jamaican experience try the salted codfish and *callallo* (a strong-flavored spinach). To round out your feast, take away some *totoes* (coconut cookies) or *gizzadas* (coconut tarts). This one's a real Toronto tradition.

Kowloon Dim Sum, 5 Baldwin St. ☎ 977-3773.

Cuisine: CHINESE.
Prices: Combination plates less than $6. AE, MC, V.
Open: Daily 10am–11pm.

Kowloon Dim Sum is a budget diner's delight for dim sum and barbecue specialties.

Lee Garden, 331 Spadina Ave. (between St. Andrews and Nassau sts.). ☎ 593-9524.

Cuisine: CHINESE. **Reservations:** Not accepted.
Prices: Main courses $8–$13. MC, V.
Open: Daily 4pm–midnight.

Lee Garden is known for its seafood specialties—like tiger shrimp with fresh pineapple; fresh oyster, clam, abalone, and crab cooked with green onion and ginger; or shrimp with pepper and eggplant. The menu also features such pork, beef, and chicken dishes as honey-orange back ribs, chicken in black-bean sauce, and beef with chili peppers. The duck with onion-lemon sauce is also popular.

The Moghul, 33 Elm St. (between Yonge and Bay sts.). ☎ 597-0522.

Cuisine: INDIAN. **Reservations:** Recommended, especially at dinner.
Prices: Main courses $8–$11. AE, DC, MC, V.
Open: Lunch Mon–Fri 11:30am–2:30pm; dinner Mon–Thurs 5–10:30pm, Fri–Sat 5–11pm, Sun 5–10pm.

Downtown Toronto Dining

Acqua **45**
Bangkok Garden **12**
Barberian's **13**
Bayou Bistro **25**
Biagio **42**
The Boat **5**
The Bombay Palace **47**
Earthtones Vegetarian **21**
The Eating Counter **8**
Encore **54**
Filet of Sole/Whistling Oyster **29**
Fred's Not Here/Red Tomato **33**
Free Times Café **1**
Fune **30**
The Groaning Board **38**
Il Fornello **36**
Jump Cafe and Bar **44**
Kensington Patty Palace **4**
Kowloon Dim Sum **9**
La Bodega **6**
La Fenice **32**
La Maquette **43**
Le Bistingo **22**
Lee Garden **3**
Left Bank **18**
Le Papillon **46**
Le Select **23**
Maccheroni **50**
Masa **26**
The Moghul **11**
Montréal Bistro and Jazz Club **41**
Movenpick **37**
Movenpick Marché **49**
Nami Japanese Seafood **40**
N'Awlins **15**
New Avec **27**
The Old Fish Market **48**
The Old Spaghetti Factory **52**
Ole Malacca **7**
The Organ Grinder **53**
Orso **31**
Peter Pan **19**
Pink Pearl **55**
Queen Mother Café **24**
Raja Sahib **28**
Red Tomato/Fred's Not Here **33**
Rivoli **20**

Saigon Palace **20**
St. Tropez **34**
Senator **14**
Takesushi **51**
Taro Grill **17**

Vanipha **16**
Wah Sing **10**
Whistling Oyster/Filet of Sole **29**
Young Lok Gardens **35**
Young Thailand **39**

The Moghul is a very comfortable Indian restaurant serving good curries. Try the hot vindaloo or a rogan josh or any of the other chicken, shrimp, and beef specialties. For those who prefer subtlety, the biryanis are also excellent.

Queen Mother Cafe, 208 Queen St. W. ☎ **598-4719.**

> **Cuisine:** INTERNATIONAL. **Reservations:** Not accepted.
> **Prices:** Most items $7–$10. AE, MC, V.

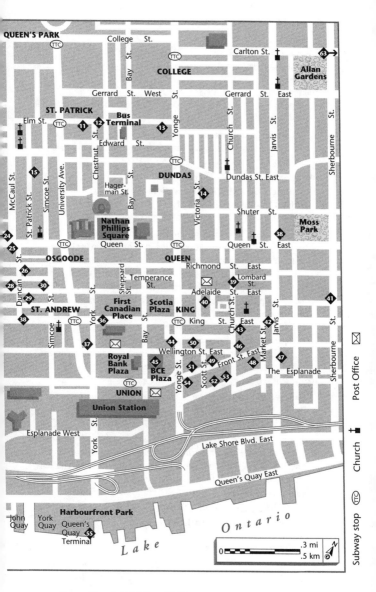

Open: Mon–Sat 11:30am–12:30am.

A simple restaurant with polished wood tables and bentwood chairs, this is another longtime favorite on Queen Street. Desserts are displayed in a counter in the back. The menu offers such Laotian-Thai items as crispy chicken with garlic, coriander, and black peppercorn served with lime coriander sauce, jumbo black tiger shrimp with chili-garlic dipping sauce; pad Thai (noodles with seafood and meat);

as well as burgers, sandwiches, and daily specials. Outdoor dining in summer.

Raja Sahib, 254 Adelaide St. W. ☎ 593-4756.

Cuisine: INDIAN. **Reservations:** Recommended for parties of four or more.

Prices: Main courses $8–$11. AE, DC, MC, V.

Open: Lunch Mon–Fri 11am–3pm; dinner Mon–Fri 5–11pm, Sat 4–11pm, Sun 5–10pm.

Raja Sahib, near Duncan, serves a variety of dishes priced under $11. Chicken tandoori, dansak, bhuna gosht, and chicken tikka are just some of the many dishes.

Rivoli, 332 Queen St. W. ☎ 597-0794.

Cuisine: CONTINENTAL. **Reservations:** Not accepted.

Prices: Main courses $9–$12. AE, MC, V.

Open: Lunch Mon–Sat noon–4pm; dinner Mon–Sat 6pm–1am.

Rivoli attracts an avant-garde crowd. Its dinner menu features nine or so eclectic specialties like pad Thai, passion shrimp (grilled marinated black tiger shrimp served with herbed mashed potatoes, mixed vegetable anise empanada, and southwestern roasted yellow pepper sauce), and something called "Hi Honey I'm home what's for dinner?"—a quarter chicken roasted with citrus chili glaze. Three or so daily specials supplement the menu—usually one pasta, one meat, and one fish dish. The lunch menu features sandwiches such as grilled cheese made with challah or pita stuffed with falafel. In summer the sidewalk patio is jammed. There's nightly avant-garde entertainment, and the decor is appropriately basic black.

Saigon Palace, 454 Spadina Ave. ☎ 968-1623.

Cuisine: CHINESE/VIETNAMESE. **Reservations:** Not needed.

Prices: Main courses less than $5. No credit cards.

Open: Sun–Thurs 9am–10pm, Fri–Sat 9am–11pm.

A super-budget eatery—a Vietnamese-style café with minimal decor—Saigon Palace has hardly anything on the menu over $5. There's a fine beef with noodle soup, pork chop, and curry chicken and steamed egg, each for $4. The place is filled with Chinese and Vietnamese residents.

Vanipha, 193 Augusta Ave. ☎ 340-0491.

Cuisine: THAI/LAO. **Reservations:** Accepted.

Prices: Most items $8–$10. V.

Open: Mon–Sat noon–11pm.

A Thai-Lao restaurant in a plain but comfortable step-down storefront, Vanipha serves some good cuisine. Try the pad Thai; grilled fish with tamarind sauce; chicken red curry; and, of course, the special treat—sticky rice.

Wah Sing, 41 Baldwin St. ☎ 596-1628.

Cuisine: CHINESE. **Reservations:** Accepted for large parties only.

Prices: Most items $7–$10. AE, MC, V.

Open: Sun–Thurs 11:30am–10pm, Fri–Sat 11:30am–11:30pm.

People come here to enjoy terrific seafood at reasonable prices—especially the lobster special, which is two lobsters for $15.95! There's plenty of other shellfish on the menu, like the mussels with black-bean sauce or the oysters with ginger sauce, along with duck, pork, noodles, and other traditional Chinese fare, too. The decor is minimal, but the food makes for crowds. Expect to wait.

Young Lok Gardens, 122 St. Patrick St. in Village by the Grange. ☎ 593-9819.

Cuisine: CHINESE. **Reservations:** Accepted for parties of six or more only.

Prices: Main courses $6–$12; lunch special $7. AE, MC, V.

Open: Mon–Fri 11:30am–10pm, Sat–Sun 11am–10pm.

One of Toronto's most highly rated and popular restaurants, Young Lok serves good Peking and Szechuan cuisine and tasty barbecue from the Mongolian grill. The atmosphere is casual and decorous at the same time, with bamboo lanterns and kites, fans, and umbrellas adding color to the scene. The latest addition is a fresh fish market where you can select a fish and either have it steamed Chinese style in black-bean sauce or ginger and scallion or have it grilled on the barbecue. Start with one of the clear soups, like seafood chowder or Chinese peasant soup, which is filled with tofu and chicken. Follow with Szechuan shrimp sautéed with cashew nuts; vegetables in a hot chili sauce; orange-spiced duck; or the Mongolian barbecue beef marinated in mustard, chili, wine, ginger, and plenty of garlic.

3 Downtown East

Expensive

Acqua, 10 Front St. W. ☎ 368-7171.

Cuisine: CALIFORNIA/ITALIAN. **Reservations:** Recommended.

Prices: Main courses $16–$19. AE, DC, ER, MC, V.

Open: Mon–Fri 11:30am–2:30pm and 5–11:30pm, Sat 5–11:30pm.

One of the trendiest and most dramatic Toronto restaurants, Acqua evokes the drama and color of Venice at carnival. A brilliant blue door leads into the bar; curvaceous tables stand under sail-like flags in the bar area (where you can dine), and there's also a courtyard dining area in the BCE building that is defined by striped poles reminiscent of those that line Venetian canals.

The cuisine is less easily defined. Charred rack of lamb with a rose and port wine sauce, and grilled swordfish with sweet corn and tomato relish served with basil mashed potatoes and roast peppers are just two of the main attractions. In addition, there are pizzas—like the one with prosciutto pesto, gold potatoes, arugula, and ricotta—or such pastas as fusilli with smoked salmon, chipotle peppers, and tomato vodka cream sauce. Start with Ontario goat cheese baked in pine-nut crust, served on roasted eggplant with tomatillo salsa, or blackened scallops with ginger mango relish. For dessert chocoholics won't be able to pass up the bittersweet chocolate pâté.

Biagio, 157 King St. E. ☎ **366-4040.**
Cuisine: ITALIAN. **Reservations:** Recommended.
Prices: Pasta and risotto $12–$16; main courses $15–$20. AE, DC, MC, V.
Open: Lunch Mon–Fri noon–2:30pm; dinner Mon–Sat 6–10:30pm.

This restaurant has one of the most beautiful, inviting courtyards in the whole city, as well as attractive high-ceilinged dining rooms and a separate bar inside. The menu features an array of extra-special pasta and risotto dishes. The lasagne arrives in a light-pink sauce studded with salmon, scallops, and shrimp, and the tagliolini comes with choice morsels of lobster. Risotto can be prepared with porcini; with saffron; with gorgonzola and parsley; with shrimp and arugula; or several other ways. For the more robust appetite there's a *bistecca al barolo e funghi* or a veal chop with wine, butter, and sage, and several other choices. To start, try the carpaccio or salmon marinated in dill and orange sauce.

Encore, 33 Yonge St. ☎ **947-0655.**
Cuisine: CONTINENTAL. **Reservations:** Recommended.
Prices: Pasta dishes $13–$16; main courses $9–$14 at lunch, $19–$23 at dinner. AE, MC, V.
Open: Lunch Mon–Fri 11:30am–2:30pm; dinner Mon–Sat 5:30pm–1am.

A sleek mirrored restaurant, Encore offers classic continental fare. At dinner there's a selection of pasta, fish, charcoal-grilled meats, and such specialties as pheasant with cassis-raspberry sauce or veal flamed with Calvados and served with sliced apples and cream. Lunch offers a similar selection at reduced prices. There's a pleasant bar where you can enjoy croissants stuffed with shrimp, lamb, pheasant, or any other filling of your choice.

La Maquette, 111 King St. E. ☎ **366-8191.**
Cuisine: CONTINENTAL. **Reservations:** Recommended.
Prices: Main courses $15–$25. AE, MC, V.
Open: Lunch Mon–Fri noon–2:30pm; dinner Mon–Sat 5:30–10:30pm.

You'll make a grand entrance through the lobby and up the staircase to reach La Maquette. The best option is the $20 prix fixe, which brings appetizer, entrée, dessert, and tea or coffee. You might opt for the salmon Wellington; beef tenderloin with horseradish crust with wild mushroom sauce; rack of lamb with honey mustard crust; or a seafood risotto. To start, try the scallops wrapped in nori and rice paper and served with wasabi and tomato coulis, or the asparagus in orange-tarragon butter. The menu, though, changes frequently. In summer, the outdoor dining area that overlooks the pocket park with a waterfall is particularly pleasant.

Nami Japanese Seafood, 55 Adelaide St. E. ☎ **362-7373.**
Cuisine: JAPANESE. **Reservations:** Recommended Thurs–Sat.
Prices: Sushi $4–$6; main courses $14–$29. AE, DC, MC, V.
Open: Lunch Mon–Fri noon–2:30pm; dinner Mon–Sat 6–10:30pm.

This atmospheric restaurant features sushi and such entrées as salmon teriyaki and bento. Up front there's a robata bar/sushi bar, and behind it is attractive booth seating or traditional tatami-style dining. The place attracts many Japanese, both businesspeople and families.

Start with kaki, ebi fry (oysters or shrimp), or beef sashimi—thinly sliced beef lightly coated and served with ponzu sauce. For a real treat order the tenshin bento, which provides an assortment of sushi and sashimi, or the Love Boat, which includes salad, miso, tempura, sushi, sashimi, salmon teriyaki, beef katsu, deep-fried chicken, and fruits.

Moderate

Brasserie Les Artistes, 243 Carlton St. at Parliament. ☎ 963-9433.

Cuisine: FRENCH. **Reservations:** Recommended.
Prices: Main courses $9–$14. AE, MC, V.
Open: Lunch Tues–Fri noon–2:30pm; dinner Mon–Thurs 5–10:30pm, Fri–Sat 5:30–11pm.

For a modest bistro-style meal, try this find in Cabbagetown. The atmosphere is casual and friendly, the wall art evokes Paris in the 1890s, and the tables are marble— -a suitable setting for the traditional moules marinière, steak and frites, escalope of veal aux fines herbes, and rack of lamb with fresh mint.

Montréal Bistro and Jazz Club, 65 Sherbourne St. (at Adelaide). ☎ 363-0179.

Cuisine: QUEBECOIS. **Reservations:** Recommended, especially on weekends.
Prices: Lunch specials $8; main courses $11–$16. AE, MC, V.
Open: Lunch Mon–Fri noon–2:30pm; dinner Mon–Thurs 6–10pm, Fri–Sat 6–11pm.

Montréal, at Adelaide and Sherbourne, is the place to try Québécois specialties, such as the famous pea soup and *tourtière*, a tasty meat pie. The food here is excellent and reasonably priced. Lunch specials include soup or salad and such main courses as veal roast with vegetables or linguine primavera. At night the specialties include rack of lamb, fettuccine with seafood, and braised rabbit in a Cajun sauce, with most items around $14. For dessert, try the special deep-fried ice cream with hot raspberry sauce. To the left of the entrance you'll find one of Toronto's best jazz clubs.

The Senator, 249 and 253 Victoria St. ☎ 364-7517.

Cuisine: NORTH AMERICAN. **Reservations:** Recommended for dinner in the dining room.
Prices: Main courses $6–$10 at lunch, $15–$22 at dinner. MC, V.
Open: Breakfast Mon–Fri 7:30–11:30am; lunch Mon–Fri 11:30am–3:30pm; dinner Tues–Sat 5–11:30pm (5–10pm in the diner), Sun 5–10pm; brunch Sat–Sun 8am–3pm.

In the diner, green leatherette booths, tiled floors, and down-home cuisine take you back to the 1940s at this local favorite, which is very conveniently located for the Pantages Theatre. Here you can still order a full breakfast of bacon and eggs, beans, home fries, and toast for $5. The luncheon menu features such comforting dishes as meat loaf, macaroni and cheese, fish and chips, liver and onions, burgers with fried onions and corn relish, and creamy rice pudding. And best of all you can perch on one of the stools and order up a rich and real old-fashioned milkshake.

The next-door dining room is decked out in mahogany, mirrors, and stained glass and affords customers access to enclosed velvet booths. Some of the same dishes make an appearance supplemented by such items as chicken breast with rosemary lemon sauce, prime rib, and seared yellowfin tuna with an olive, tomato, and red onion sherry vinaigrette. Find room for the desserts, which are good. The wine list is excellent too.

Spiaggia, 2318 Queen St. E. ☎ **699-4656.**

    Cuisine: ITALIAN. **Reservations:** Recommended.
    Prices: Pasta $10–$12; main courses $12–$14. AE, DC, MC, V.
    Open: Dinner only, Sun–Thurs 5–10pm, Fri–Sat 5–11pm.

A small, casual Beaches bistro, Spiaggia is filled with tables covered in blue gingham and glass. The short menu changes daily but will feature pastas, like fusilli with sausage and spicy tomato sauce or linguine with clam-and-mussel marinara, as well as more substantial dishes like veal with wild mushrooms and marsala. Desserts include tiramisu, chocolate-sambucca mousse, and a variety of gelati.

Takesushi, 22 Front St. ☎ **862-1891.**

    Cuisine: JAPANESE. **Reservations:** Recommended.
    Prices: Sushi combinations $16–$30; tempura and teriyaki dinners $13–$25. AE, DC, MC, V.
    Open: Lunch Mon–Fri noon–2:30pm; dinner Mon–Fri 5:30–10pm, Sat–Sun 5–10pm.

This fashionable Japanese restaurant specializes in sushi—for novices there's even a beginner's sushi: salmon marinated in vinegar and salt, and ebi or cooked shrimp sushi. Otherwise, you can order combinations such as a deluxe sushi, including eight nigiri and one makimono. Other sushi thrills include uni (sea urchin gonads) and kazunoko (herring roe soaked in sake, soy, and broth). Traditional tempura and teriyaki dinners are also available.

Inexpensive

The Bombay Palace, 71 Jarvis St. (between King and Adelaide sts.). ☎ **368-8048.**

    Cuisine: INDIAN. **Reservations:** Recommended.
    Prices: Main courses $9–$16. AE, DC, MC, V.
    Open: Lunch daily noon–3pm; dinner daily 6–10:30pm.

The Bombay Palace is plush, with its comfortable banquettes and exotic Indian statues and idols. For the real Indian cuisine-lover, there's an 18-dish daily buffet that includes bhuna gosht, tandoori chicken, salads, and vegetable curry. At night you can select from the à la carte menu or opt for a dinner like the Palace, which includes chicken tandoor, chicken tikka, tandoori prawns, seekh kebab, beef pasanda, pulao, vegetable, naan, chutney, and pickles—all for $17.

Le Papillon, 16 Church St. (between Front St. and Esplanade).
☎ **363-0838.**
Cuisine: CREPES. **Reservations:** Recommended on weekends.
Prices: Crepes $7–$10. AE, DC, MC, V.
Open: Lunch Tues–Fri noon–2:30pm; dinner Mon–Wed 5–10pm, Thurs
5–11pm, Fri 5pm–midnight; Sat 11:30am–midnight; Sun 11:30am–
10pm.

There'll probably be a line of eager young folks outside Le Papillon,
located just east of Jarvis Street, a pretty place to repair for a candlelit
dinner and crepes of all kinds. Exposed brick, mirrors, greenery, blue
gingham tablecloths, and modern lithographs set the tone. Before
you taste the imaginative crepes, start with a vegetable cocktail or a
bowl of onion soup and a salad. There are 16 savory crepes, ranging
from crepe Marie Claude (with sausages, apples, and Cheddar cheese)
to crepe Continental (chicken, mushrooms, and peppers in
béchamel). Then there are luscious dessert crepes, with sliced peaches,
apples, and cinnamon.

Maccheroni, 32 Wellington St. E. ☎ **867-9067.**
Cuisine: ITALIAN. **Reservations:** Accepted for large parties only.
Prices: Main courses $5–$8. AE, DC, ER, MC, V.
Open: Mon–Fri 11:30am–10pm, Sat 5–10pm.

Swathes of brilliant color—mustard yellow, periwinkle, orange, and
red—will transport you to the Mediterranean, as will the faux urns,
flowers, and fruit at this low-priced stage set, which serves adequate
if not exciting food. Start with the bruschetta or the crostini della
casa made with gorgonzola. You can follow with a variety of pasta
dishes—penne arrabiata, fettuccine Alfredo, lasagne, and fusilli
primavera—or pizza.

Movenpick Marche, in the galleria of BCE Place, Front St. E.
☎ **366-8986.**
Cuisine: CONTINENTAL. **Reservations:** Not accepted.
Prices: Main courses $5–$8. AE, DC, MC, V.
Open: Daily 9am–2am.

This large restaurant with a variety of seating areas is a relatively recent innovation in food merchandising. Pick up a tab at the entrance
and stroll through the bustling market, where various stands, carts,
and trolleys are set up displaying fresh foods and ingredients. Stop
at the rosticceria and select a meat for the chef to cook. Pause at the
seafood and raw bar and pick out a fish for the grill or peruse the
pasta bar. Then wander over to the bistro de vin and check out the
cases of wine or enjoy a boccalino of one of the open wines. The chefs
and staff are easily identifiable by their boaters as they stand behind
counters heaped with fresh salads, fish, meats, and pizzas. Ask and it
will be made before your very eyes—Cornish hens, Rösti with salmon,
steak, sausages, and more. A dependable place for breakfast, lunch,
or dinner.

⭐ **The Old Fish Market,** 12 Market St. ☎ **363-0334.**

Cuisine: SEAFOOD. **Reservations:** Recommended.
Prices: Main courses $9–$28. AE, MC, V.
Open: Coasters, Mon–Sat noon–1am, Sun 1:30–10pm. Restaurant, lunch Mon–Fri noon–2pm, Sat noon–2:30pm; dinner Mon–Fri 5–10pm, Sat 4:30–11pm, Sun 1:30–10pm.

The Old Fish Market, by the St. Lawrence Market, packs 'em in. On the ground floor there's an oyster bar and a large restaurant with comfortable booths and wooden tables, decorated with photographs of old salts and fishing scenes, plus such nautical regalia as lobster traps and foghorns. Upstairs you'll find Coasters, a black arborite shellfish bar where you can relax and eat while seated on low sofas. The decor consists of exposed brick and painted plumbing warmed by a huge fire blazing in the back during the winter. Coasters features daily specials, an oyster bar, cold and hot seafood appetizers, and imported beers.

Downstairs you'll get a selection of the freshest fish, pan-fried, broiled, or barbecued. Start with one of the chowders, then choose from the night's fresh offerings: rainbow trout, snapper, roughy, bluefish, mahimahi, or halibut, for example—all served with sourdough roll, mackerel pâté, house salad, and potatoes. Most dishes are $14 to $16, except for such items as a crab platter, lobster tails, and surf and turf.

The Old Spaghetti Factory, 54 The Esplanade. ☎ **864-9761.**

Cuisine: ITALIAN. **Reservations:** Required for parties of 10 or more.
Prices: Main courses $8–$12. AE, DC, MC, V.
Open: Mon–Thurs 11:30am–midnight, Fri–Sat 11:30am–1am, Sun 11:30am–11pm (winter closings an hour earlier).

The Old Spaghetti Factory turns out countless pasta favorites, such as spaghetti with tomato sauce or with meatballs, both including soup or salad, spumoni, and coffee or tea. Other dishes like veal parmigiana, chicken cacciatore, and lasagne supplement the menu. The huge space, seating 600, is cluttered with Canadiana—a good place for families with younger children.

The Organ Grinder, 58 The Esplanade. ☎ **364-6517.**

Cuisine: ITALIAN. **Reservations:** Accepted only for parties of 10 or more.
Prices: Most items $7–$12. AE, DC, MC, V.
Open: Mon–Fri noon–2pm and 5–10pm, Sat 11:30am–midnight, Sun 11:30am–10pm.

Kids love the Organ Grinder, a vast musical pizza parlor where an organist bashes out popular tunes on the theater pipe organ, which has a fascinating array of gadgets—submarine sirens, sleighbells, bird whistles, horse hooves, all kinds of drums, chimes, cymbals, and a glockenspiel—and over 1,000 pipes made of wood, zinc, lead, and tin. To the tunes of this rare monstrosity you can feast on standard Italian fare: pizza, lasagne, manicotti, veal parmigiana, and the other usual suspects.

Young Thailand, 81 Church St. (south of Lombard St.).
☎ **368-1368.**
    Cuisine: THAI. **Reservations:** Recommended.
    Prices: Main courses $7–$16. AE, DC, MC, V.
    Open: Lunch Mon–Fri 11:30am–3pm; dinner daily 5–11pm.

This large restaurant with minimal decor serves good Thai cuisine.
Beef, pork, chicken, and seafood dishes fill the menu—sliced beef in
hot spicy thick sauce; slices of chicken with shredded ginger, mushrooms, and onions; and pork with garlic, onions, chili pepper, and
sweet basil leaves. Sweet and sour fish and spicy shrimp are among
the close to 20 seafood dishes. Start with a stimulating tom kha kai
soup made with coconut milk, lemongrass, chili, and chicken or one
of the traditional salad or noodle dishes.

    There's another branch at 111 Gerrard St. E. between Jarvis and
Church (☎ **599-9099**).

4   Midtown West

There's plenty of fine dining here, but note that the area includes
Yorkville—and as with so many chic expensive shopping areas, dining in Yorkville is not always a pleasant experience. Here, rents are
high and consequently prices are high, but the quality sometimes just
doesn't match. That said, I have included in this section one or two
selections that can be relied upon to deliver quality at a decent price.

Expensive

Bistro 990, 990 Bay St. (at St. Joseph). ☎ **921-9990.**
    Cuisine: FRENCH. **Reservations:** Required.
    Prices: Appetizers $6–$12; main courses $16–$26. AE, ER, MC, V.
    Open: Lunch Mon–Fri noon–3pm; dinner Mon–Sat 6–11pm.

A celebrity hot spot, Bistro 990 could have been airlifted from the
French provinces with its French doors, lace curtains, and outdoor
café tables. The cuisine ranges from such traditional dishes as rack
of lamb Provençale, steak bordelaise, and half a roast chicken with
garlic mash to shrimp mango curry. Among the appetizers the tartare
of salmon is fresh-tasting, and the confit of duck a rich dish. Desserts change daily ranging from lemon tart, tarte Tatin, raspberry
cheesecake, and a selection of sorbets.

Opus, 37 Prince Arthur Ave. ☎ **921-3105.**
    Cuisine: FRENCH/MEDITERRANEAN. **Reservations:** Recommended.
    Prices: Main courses $18–$22.50. AE, MC, V.
    Open: Dinner daily 5:30–11pm.

A splashy place. Beyond the small Erté-decorated bar you'll enter a
series of small intimate rooms in a town house. The menu is short,
featuring about eight main courses like free-range chicken marinated
in lime juice and shoyu or monkfish in a red wine sauce. Other
dishes continue the eclectic theme: swordfish with pineapple and
sweet-and-sour sauce, bouillabaise, and rack of lamb with garlic

cream, or three fish layered with tomatoes, olives, and fresh basil. Whet the appetite with a fricassée of wild mushrooms with balsamic vinegar sauce or the terrine de foie gras with duck glaze.

⭐ **Splendido Bar and Grill,** 88 Harbord St. ☎ **929-7788.**
Cuisine: ITALIAN. **Reservations:** Recommended well in advance.
Prices: Pasta and pizza $8–$13; main courses $19–$25. AE, DC, ER, MC, V.
Open: Dinner daily 5–11pm.

Splendido is the city's current scene-stealer—and steal the scene it does, for it's an absolutely stunning dining room. Up front there's a black-gray granite bar. Behind stretches the dining room—a riot of brilliant yellow lit by a host of tiny, fairylike track lights while the walls are hung with huge flower canvases by Helen Lucas.

The food is Italian with international inspirations, and the menu changes monthly. Start with the unique antipasto of bacon-wrapped shrimp, coppa, peperonata, and bocconcini, with tomatoes and tapenade crostini; or the pistachio-crust sea scallops baked in a brick oven and served with mango chutney and fermented black-bean sauce. Follow with either pasta, pizza, or a main course. For example, you might choose the pizza with goat cheese, roasted ricotta, sun-dried tomatoes, olives, eggplant and oregano or the pasta ribbons with pancetta, mushroom, and peppered-vodka cream. Among the main courses, the corn-fried salmon with mashed potatoes, sweet corn relish, and arugula with citrus dressing is a special treat; so, too, is the beef tenderloin with mushroom duxelles, artichokes, fried ravioli, and barbecue butter sauce. It's a loud, lively place, so give it a pass if it's a romantic dinner you're seeking.

Moderate

Arlequin, 134 Avenue Rd. (between Davenport and Bernard sts.).
☎ **928-9521.**
Cuisine: CONTINENTAL. **Reservations:** Recommended.
Prices: Main courses $15–$18 at dinner. MC, V.
Open: Mon–Fri 11:30am–3pm; Mon–Sat 5:30–11pm.

Arlequin is a handsome small restaurant with a counter display of fabulous pâtés, cheeses, salads, and baked goods up front. The menu is keyed to market-fresh ingredients and might list quails with to-mato and rosemary, lamb with garlic and thyme glaze, or veal pavette with mushrooms and balsamic vinegar. The three-course prix fixe for $21.95 is an excellent value. At brunch the menu stretches to such dishes as lumache with scallops, shrimp, peppers, tomato, and basil pesto.

Chiado, 864 College St. (at Concord Ave.). ☎ **538-1910.**
Cuisine: PORTUGUESE. **Reservations:** Recommended.
Prices: Main courses $14–$20. AE, DC, MC, V.
Open: Lunch daily noon–3pm; dinner daily 5pm–midnight.

Chiado refers to the district in Lisbon that's filled with small bistrettos like this one. Beyond the appetizing display at the front of the room you'll discover a long, narrow, elegant dining room decorated with

French-style pink chairs and colorful art on the walls. In summer the storefront opens entirely onto the street, adding to the atmosphere. Among the appetizers the pinheta of salted cod and the marinated sardines with lemon and parsley will appeal to the true Portuguese; others might prefer the tiger shrimp served with sweet-pepper coulis. On the main menu a Portuguese might plump for the poached filet of cod or the bistretto-style steak with fried egg and fries, while a friend might go for the roast rack of lamb with red Douro wine sauce or the braised rabbit in Madeira sauce. To top it all off, choose the peach-coconut flan, chocolate mousse, pecan pie, or any of the other tempting desserts.

Grappa, 797 College St. (1¹/₂ blocks west of Beatrice). ☎ **535-3337.**
  Cuisine: ITALIAN. **Reservations:** Recommended at dinner.
  Prices: Main courses $11–$16. AE, ER, MC, V.
  Open: Dinner Tues–Sun 5–11pm.

Pass the small bar up front and enter the low-lit dining room, where the only decor is the oak curio cabinets filled with Barolos and other fine wines and a mural on the back wall depicting the vendange. The meal will start with a dish of black olives, crusty fresh bread, and olive oil. The food is fresh and good with such daily specials offered as a zuppa di pesce with shrimp, scallops, and mussels in a tomato-lemon broth. Other dishes you might find are salmon with cucumber vodka and dill cream or a strip loin with rosemary green peppercorn jus served with gnocchi. The pizza with gorgonzola, braised onions, wild mushrooms, and spinach is as piquant and appetizing as you can imagine. In addition, there are several pasta dishes like the robust cappellini puttanesca with shrimps, black olives, capers, and sun-dried tomatoes in white wine tomato sauce. Raspberry clafoutis, dark chocolate mousse cake, or tiramisu are just a few of the dessert musts.

Il Posto, 148 Yorkville Ave. ☎ **968-0469.**
  Cuisine: ITALIAN. **Reservations:** Recommended.
  Prices: Appetizers $5–$9; pasta $8–$11; main courses $16–$24. AE, MC, V.
  Open: Lunch Mon–Sat noon–2:30pm; dinner Mon–Sat 6–10:30pm.

Right in the heart of high-rent Yorkville, where restaurants are constantly opening and closing, Il Posto, tucked away in York Square, has thrived for many years and still offers a very attractive setting, both inside and outside on the brick terrace under a spreading maple tree. The dessert spread at the entrance is tempting enough— fresh raspberry tarts with kiwi, fresh strawberry and blueberry tarts, fresh oranges, and other delights. The menu features such Italian specialties as *pollo alla marsala* (chicken in a marsala wine sauce), *scaloppine pizzaiola* (veal cooked in a spicy tomato garlic sauce), beef with green peppercorns served with a brandy-flavored sauce, linguine with seafood or (even more delicious) with gorgonzola. There are also fish dishes and salads like arugula and endive and a special vitello tonnato. For dessert, besides the very special pastries, you might discover poached pears in chocolate, or of course the smooth, creamy zabaglione. The restaurant's beige walls, Italian prints, and classical music create a serene dining atmosphere that's enhanced even further by the handsome bouquets of fresh flowers.

Jacques Bistro du Parc, 126A Cumberland St. ☎ 961-1893.

Cuisine: CONTINENTAL. **Reservations:** Not needed.
Prices: Omelets $10–$12; other main courses $15–$18; prix fixe $15. AE, MC, V.
Open: Lunch Mon–Sat 11:30am–3pm; dinner daily 5–10:30pm.

Upstairs above a boutique in the heart of Yorkville, this spot specializes in omelets and bistro fare. Everything about the small room is tasteful—the fresh flowers on the bar and the French prints and pictures of Paris. But the patrons come for the omelets—10 selections—from simple fines herbes and bonne femme with bacon, mushrooms, and onion to gourmande with smoked salmon, sour cream, and chives. In addition there are a half dozen meat and fish dishes—coquilles St. Jacques in a California style with roasted green and red pepper, jalapeño, and tomato salsa or rack of lamb with Dijon mustard. And, of course, there are salads, soups, and quiches, too.

Joso's, 202 Davenport (just east of Avenue Road). ☎ 925-1903.

Cuisine: SEAFOOD. **Reservations:** Recommended.
Prices: Appetizers $4–$9; pasta $9–$14; main courses $14–$27. AE, MC, V.
Open: Lunch Mon–Sat 11:30am–3pm; dinner Mon–Sat 5:30–11pm.

Yugoslav Joseph Spralja—of Malka and Joso—has appeared on "The Tonight Show" and performed at Carnegie Hall, but since he gave up folk singing and playing the guitar because of an ulcer, he has taken to combing the fish markets for his restaurant, Joso's. Besides having a fascinating owner, this place has some interesting seafood and also a rather idiosyncratic decor (which might offend some, so I have to mention the erotic ceramic sculptures of golf-ball–bosomed females).

If you don't care a fig about such indelicate matters, but you do care about fresh seafood prepared to retain its flavor, then stop by Joso's. At dinner a selection of fresh fish will be presented to you, from which you can choose the specimen that appeals to you. It will then be grilled and served with a salad (such dishes are priced by the pound). Or you can have octopus steamed in garlic and parsley sauce, deep-fried squid with salad, or spaghetti with an octopus, clam, and squid tomato sauce. A selection of exotic coffees is available, along with a special baklava, and Italian ice creams and sorbets. Bentwood cane chairs and pale-lemon tablecloths complete the decor of the tiny downstairs room. A larger room upstairs is similarly appointed. Remember, this cosmopolitan bistro makes a very personal statement: You can either take it or leave it, but you should know about it.

Lakes, 1112 Yonge St. ☎ 966-0185.

Cuisine: CONTINENTAL. **Reservations:** Recommended at dinner.
Prices: Main courses $10–$16. AE, DC, MC, V.
Open: Mon–Wed noon–11:30pm, Thurs–Fri noon–1am, Sat 6pm–1am.

This bar and grill occupying a long, narrow room is the essence of comfort and good taste with its plush banquettes and art-covered walls.

The food reflects the same care and attention. There are only about seven main courses, supplemented by pasta dishes like shrimp and chicken tossed with rice noodles and peanuts in a spicy siracha sauce or more traditional angel hair pasta in tomato sauce with sun-dried tomatoes, black olives, and garlic. The heartier dishes include a slow-roasted chicken with basil and buttermilk mashed potatoes, Atlantic salmon in a black sesame crust with chive crème frâiche, and pork tenderloin with plum sauce and sweet corn risotto.

Le Rendez-Vous, 14 Prince Arthur Ave. ☎ 961-6111.

Cuisine: FRENCH. **Reservations:** Recommended.
Prices: Appetizers $5–$9; main courses $16–$22. AE, CB, MC, V.
Open: Lunch Mon–Fri noon–2:30pm; dinner daily 5:30–10pm.

At Le Rendez-Vous you'll find a variety of dining and decor in the classic French style. In summer the outdoor dining area is filled, along with the comfortable plant-filled atrium dining area. Rattan chairs, burgundy upholstery, and classical music provide atmosphere in the interior.

Dining choices range from fettuccine with smoked pheasant, golden tomatoes, pepper, and onions with balsamic vinegar and oil to rack of lamb with garlic and thyme au jus. Other appealing dishes include Dover sole prepared in a variety of ways, duck with five spices, and tiger shrimp with shallots and lemon. At lunch choices might include mushrooms stuffed with crab and topped with hollandaise along with egg and pasta dishes. For pre- or postdinner drinks, go downstairs to the wine cellar.

Movenpick Bistretto, 133 Yorkville Ave. ☎ 926-9545.

Cuisine: CONTINENTAL/SWISS. **Reservations:** Recommended at dinner, especially for small groups.
Prices: Main courses $8–$17.50. AE, DC, ER, MC, V.
Open: Mon–Sat 7:30am–2am, Sun 7:30am–1am.

At this popular place, where people line up for dinner, you won't find fine dining, but you will find excellent value and gigantic desserts. Just ask for the Design Dessert menu and you'll see what I mean. Although the menu features typical bistro fare like steak and frites, veal with mushroom cream sauce, and a croque-monsieur, my favorites are the Rösti dishes like the one topped with fresh slices of parmesan and prosciutto, mushrooms, peppers, and basil tomato sauce—all for $9.80, an amazing value. The fresh shellfish available is on display at the entrance—another very popular draw. This is one place in Yorkville where you'll receive value for your money in a bright lively atmosphere.

Palmerston, 488 College St. (just west of Markham St.).
☎ 922-9277.

Cuisine: CONTINENTAL. **Reservations:** Recommended at dinner.
Prices: Main courses $19–$28; prix fixe $18. AE, MC, V.
Open: Dinner daily 5:30–11pm. **Closed:** Mon in winter.

This small, intimate restaurant is a real gem. The cuisine is carefully prepared—simple classic dishes like coq au vin take on a really exotic, rich flavor here. Besides the à la carte menu there are daily specials offered; for example, on Monday shepherd's pie and on Thursday the justly lauded coq au vin.

Southern Accent, 595 Markham St. ☎ 416/536-3211.

Cuisine: CAJUN/CREOLE. **Reservations:** Recommended.
Prices: Appetizers $3–$8; main courses $14–$20. AE, ER, MC, V.
Open: Dinner daily 5–10:30pm; brunch Sun 11am–3pm. In summer lunch is served noon–3pm on the patio. **Closed:** Mon in winter.

Southern Accent has a real down-home feel. The background music is cool, the art interesting, and the floral tablecloths somehow funky. There are three areas to dine in—upstairs in the dining room, downstairs on the bar level, or out on the tent-covered brick patio. The menu features gumbo, jambalaya, shrimp étouffée, and blackened fish with lemon. At brunch the theme continues with beignets, Cajun pain perdu (the New Orleans version of French toast), and po'boy sandwiches. Oh, and don't miss the bread pudding.

★ Trattoria Giancarlo, 41–43 Clinton St. (at College). ☎ 533-9619.

Cuisine: ITALIAN. **Reservations:** Strongly recommended.
Prices: Pasta and rice $10–$12; main courses $16–$20. AE, MC, V.
Open: Dinner only, Mon–Sat 5:30–11pm.

This restaurant is one of my all-time favorite spots in Little Italy, if not in all the city, and I find myself returning here time after time. It's small and cozy and thoroughly Italian, with an outside dining area in summer. The tablecloths are covered with butcher paper, the floor is black-and-white tile, and the background music is opera or jazz.

For a real treat start with the fresh wild mushrooms brushed with herbs, garlic, and oil or the carpaccio of salmon. Follow with any one of six pasta dishes—perhaps spaghettini with shrimp and fra diavolo sauce or the risotto of the day. Good grilled fresh fish and meats are also part of the attraction, like the tender lamb brushed with lemon, rosemary, and fresh mint or the red snapper marinated in fresh thyme and bay, olive oil, and lemon. For dessert try the tiramisu, the crème caramel, or the delicious chocolate-raspberry tartufo. The evening somehow is always memorable and the welcome real.

Yves Bistro, 36A Prince Arthur Ave. ☎ 972-1010.

Cuisine: FRENCH. **Reservations:** Recommended.
Prices: Prix fixe $17.50 for main course and appetizer. MC, V.
Open: Lunch Mon–Fri noon–2pm; dinner Mon–Sat 5–10pm.

Comfortable, gracious, and made cozy by its mullioned windows, small serving bar, and brilliant sunflower mirrors, this bistro delivers good, well-priced food. Start with the mussels with basil and to-mato wine sauce, garlic and chili peppers, the chicken liver pâté with cognac, green peppercorns, chutney, cornichons, and melba toast, or the soup of the day. Among the 10 or so entrées you will find pasta, fish and meat—from a seafood Alfredo (fresh fettuccine with tiger shrimp, snow crabs, parmesan, and romano in a light cream sauce); to grilled lamb with thyme, garlic, mint, and red wine au jus; to medallions of pork tenderloin, poached pears, and Camembert cheese served with yam chips.

Inexpensive

For additional budget dining, see "Light, Casual & Fast Food" and "Dining Complexes" below in "Specialty Dining."

Aïda's Falafel, 553 Bloor St. W. ☎ 537-3700.

Cuisine: MIDDLE EASTERN. **Reservations:** Not needed.
Prices: Main courses $2–$6. No credit cards.
Open: Sun–Thurs 11am–1:30am, Fri–Sat 11am–3am.

Aïda's Falafel, on Bloor Street at Bathurst, is a small, unassuming restaurant with a couple of tables out front. Tabbouleh, falafel, and shish kebab cost $2 to $6. There's also a branch in the Beaches on Queen Street East at Woodbine.

Annapurna Restaurant, 1085 Bathurst St. (just south of Dupont). ☎ 537-8513.

Cuisine: VEGETARIAN/SOUTH INDIAN. **Reservations:** Not needed.
Prices: Most items less than $6. No credit cards.
Open: Mon–Tues and Thurs–Sat noon–9pm, Wed noon–6:30pm.

About two decades ago, Shivaram Trichur opened the Annapurna Restaurant, just south of Dupont. Beyond the counter, where you can purchase various goodies, including a loaf of banana bread, along with books on yoga and copies of *Meditation at the U.N.,* you'll find a room with no decor to speak of—but with some fine low-priced food. Enjoy the peaceful smoke-free atmosphere and the medieval background music along with the young, intellectual, and interesting crowd that gathers here.

Nothing on the menu is over $6.25, and for that amount you'll receive a veritable vegetarian feast—raita, *bonda* (gingery potato-and-vegetable balls dipped in chickpea batter and deep-fried), bhajia, samosas, pappadum, *sagu* (spinach-and-mixed-vegetable curry), potato masala, and rice or puris. My favorite choice is a *masala dosai,* a crepe filled with a spicy potato mixture and served with coconut chutney. Salads and vegetarian sandwiches supplement the South Indian dishes.

Bar Italia, 584 College St. ☎ 535-3621.

Cuisine: ITALIAN. **Reservations:** Not accepted.
Prices: Main courses $2–$7. V.
Open: Mon–Sat 8am–2am, Sun 9am–midnight.

The differences among various Canadian ethnic cultures can really be seen in the authentic ethnic establishments in Toronto. Bar Italia is one such place. Here you can savor an espresso and listen to the hiss of the cappuccino machine up front and the click of a cue against a billiard ball as folks play in the back area. The tables are marble-topped, the serving counter sports displays of fresh sunflowers, bread, and tomatoes. The chalkboard menu offers garlic-roasted bread with tomato basil chili paste, crostini gorgonzola, and pane and olives or a salad of arugula and mushrooms. There's a real Italian buzz here.

The Boulevard Café, 161 Harbord St. (between Spadina and Bathurst). ☎ 961-7676.

Cuisine: PERUVIAN. **Reservations:** Recommended for upstairs dining.
Prices: Main courses $10–$16. AE, MC, V.
Open: Tues–Sun 11:30am–3:30pm and 5:30–10:30pm; open daily in summer.

A favorite gathering spot for young creative types, the Boulevard Café is somehow reminiscent of Kathmandu in the 1960s, although the inspiration is Peru. Upstairs there's a dining room furnished with wooden banquettes softened by the addition of Peruvian cushions and South American wall hangings. The outside summer café is strung with colored lights and attracts an evening and late-night crowd. The menu features empanadas (spicy chicken or beef pastry); tangy shrimp in a spiced garlic, pimiento, and wine sauce; and *tamal verde* (spicy corn, coriander, and chicken pâté) to start. For the main course the major choice is *anticuchos*, marinated and char-broiled brochettes of your own choosing: sea bass, shrimp, pork tenderloin, beef, or chicken. Burgers, lamb chops, and steamed mussels are some of the other selections.

Chez Cappuccino, 3 Charles St. E. ☎ 925-6142.

Cuisine: COFFEE/LIGHT FARE.
Prices: Most items $2–$6. No credit cards.
Open: Daily 24 hrs.

Chez Cappuccino, just off Yonge Street, is a good way to start the day with a melt-in-the-mouth croissant, banana bread, or a bagel sandwich washed down with a smooth, frothy cappuccino. Specialty sandwiches include the half-foot-long version. Most items are around $2.

Indian Rice Factory, 414 Dupont St. ☎ 961-3472.

Cuisine: INDIAN. **Reservations:** Recommended.
Prices: Main courses $9–$15. AE, DC, MC, V.
Open: Mon–Sat noon–11pm, Sun 5–10pm.

A friend of mine raised in India swears by the Indian Rice Factory, operated by Mrs. Patel, who was born in the Punjab. It is an elegant place, with comfortable plush booths, a light-oak bar, and Indian artifacts. The food is decent and the prices are right. All the curries—chicken, beef, shrimp—are under $11. The restaurant also serves a wide selection of Indian vegetarian dishes, including *aloo gobi* (a curried mixture of potato and cauliflower), *matar paneer* (peas and cheese cooked with spices), *aloo palak* (spinach with potatoes), and a complete thali for $11.25 that includes a meat or vegetable main course, a vegetable of the day, dal, rice, chapati, raita, pappadum, and kachumber.

Kensington Kitchen, 124 Harbord St. ☎ 961-3404.

Cuisine: MIDDLE EASTERN. **Reservations:** Recommended.
Prices: Main courses $8–$12. AE, CB, DC, ER, MC, V.
Open: Mon–Sat 11:30am–11pm, Sun 11:30am–10pm.

A comfortable, casual place filled with an academic crowd, the Kensington Kitchen features minimal decor. A beaded-purse collection and a toy-airplane collection decorate the walls. There's a counter in the back for takeout. The menu is written bistro-style on a mirror and includes falafel, shish kebab, vegetarian chili, fish of the day, vegetable kebab on hummus, and daily pasta and other specials like the herb-crusted salmon with grilled red peppers, asparagus, and bok choy. There are two dining rooms—one upstairs, the other downstairs—but my favorite spot is on the deck out back under the spreading trees. There is a very well selected wine list.

★ **Mori,** 1280 Bay St. ☎ **961-1094.**

Cuisine: JAPANESE. **Reservations:** Recommended at dinner.
Prices: Main courses $7.50–$12. AE, MC, V.
Open: Lunch Mon–Sat noon–4pm; dinner Mon–Fri 4–10pm, Sat 4–11pm.

Mori, a tiny Japanese café with wrought-iron tables and deep-blue tablecloths, is great for budget dining. The attractions here are the sushi and other Japanese dishes like salmon teriyaki or chicken teriyaki, served with soup, oshitashi, and green tea. The variety of vegetarian sushi (spinach, carrot, and the like) is notable. So, too, is the vegetarian sukiyaki.

5   Midtown East/The East End

In the East End along Danforth Avenue you'll find yourself in a veritable Little Greece. Streets are lined with tavernas; bouzouki music spills out onto the sidewalk, and restaurant after restaurant bears a Greek name.

Astoria, 390 Danforth Ave. ☎ **463-2838.**

Cuisine: GREEK. **Reservations:** Not needed.
Prices: Main courses $8–$12. AE, MC, V.
Open: Mon–Wed and Fri–Sat 11am–1am, Sun and Thurs 11am–midnight.

Astoria is a little fancier than most of the Greek restaurants in the neighborhood, with its outdoor patio complete with fountain. The offerings include shish kebab, quails over charcoal, a 12-ounce New York steak, and broiled seafood.

Café Miró, 494 Danforth Ave. ☎ **466-4889.**

Cuisine: COFFEE/LIGHT FARE **Reservations:** Not accepted.
Prices: Main courses $5.95–$7.95. AE, MC.
Open: Lunch Wed–Mon noon–5pm; dinner Wed–Mon 6pm–midnight.

Brilliant bands of Miró colors stream around the bar—golden yellow, carmine, and an intense blue—while his art graces the walls of this atmospheric French-style café. Sit and savor one of the many different types of coffees or teas—caffe latte or a latte macchiato. If you like, you can order one of the 10 or so sandwiches or salad platters, or better yet, desserts like cappuccino dacquoise, key lime pie, or mango or pistachio gelati.

Midtown Toronto Dining

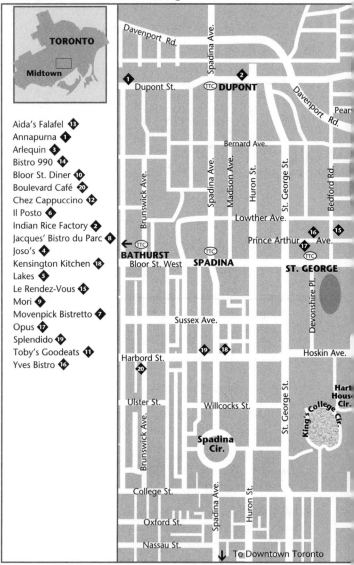

TORONTO

Midtown

Aida's Falafel 13
Annapurna 1
Arlequin 3
Bistro 990 14
Bloor St. Diner 10
Boulevard Café 20
Chez Cappuccino 12
Il Posto 6
Indian Rice Factory 2
Jacques' Bistro du Parc 8
Joso's 4
Kensington Kitchen 18
Lakes 5
Le Rendez-Vous 15
Mori 9
Movenpick Bistretto 7
Opus 17
Splendido 19
Toby's Goodeats 11
Yves Bistro 16

Myth, 417 Danforth Ave. (between Logan and Chester). ☎ **461-8383.**
   Cuisine: GREEK/ITALIAN. **Reservations:** Not accepted.
   Prices: Appetizers $4–$8; main courses $8–$11. AE, DC, MC, V.
   Open: Daily noon–4am.

   This large restaurant evokes the atmosphere of classical Greece, when
   huge sailing vessels plied the Mediterranean. Choose from among
   the long list of hot and cold appetizers or the handful of pasta dishes

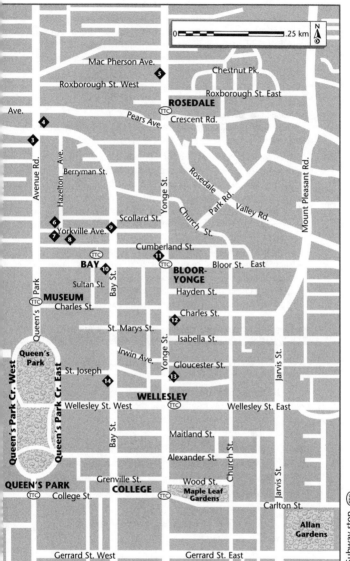

Subway stop (TTC)

and pizzas. The dramatic decor, video screens, and five pool tables attract a huge, young crowd at night.

Omonia, 426 Danforth Ave. (at Chester). ☎ **465-2129.**

    Cuisine: GREEK. **Reservations:** Not needed.
    Prices: Main courses $9–$12. AE, DC, ER, MC.
    Open: Daily 11am–1am.

Once one of the most popular local Greek restaurants, Omonia has a large outdoor dining area and up front, in the window, you can watch the lamb turning on a spit. Barbecued specialties, souvlaki, chicken, and pork selections are the main features. The Greek pictures, the patio, and the blue tablecloths provide an authentic ambience.

⭐ **Ouzeri**, 500A Danforth Ave. ☎ **778-0500.**
Cuisine: GREEK. **Reservations:** Not accepted.
Prices: Main courses $6–$10. AE, DISC, ER, MC, V.
Open: Daily noon–3am; lunch served until 3pm, dips and appetizers only served 4–5pm.

Ouzeri is the hot place out here—it's spirited, casual, and fun. People either jam the few small circular tables outside or occupy the tables inside, drinking one of the numerous international beers or wines by the glass. It's all très Athens, with tile floors, sun-drenched pastel hues, and eclectic art objects and art. The food is good and cheap. It runs the gamut from all kinds of seafood (prawns with feta and wine, sardines with mustard, calamari, broiled octopus) and all kinds of meat (pork, lamb, and beef kebabs) to rice, pasta, and phyllo pie dishes. Various snacks, too, complete the menu, like hummus, taramosalata, mushrooms à la grecque, and dolmades.

At lunch Ouzeri dishes out its version of dim sum, "meze sum"— hot and cold appetizers that are proffered on trays or wheeled by on

---

Family-Friendly Restaurants

Toby's Goodeats (see p. 133) Enough kid-appealing items to satisfy even the fussiest child. Lots of locations.

The Old Spaghetti Factory (see p. 110) The big warehouse, the carousel, the decor, the meatballs, and the spumoni should keep them happy. If not, they can wander next door and check out the sounds at The Organ Grinder.

The Organ Grinder (see p. 110) The organ, the pizza, and the rest of the young, energetic crowd will keep them marvelously entertained.

Movenpick Bistretto (see p. 115) caters to kids with a special menu, colored pencils, and drawing paper.

Fune (see p. 94) The sushi boats floating by at the sushi bar should pique your child's curiosity.

Jerusalem (see p. 128) Features lots of finger-licking Middle Eastern foods that kids find very palatable and fun to boot.

Kensington Kitchen (see p. 118) There are pita sandwiches, brownies, and other kid-friendly fare. The airplanes and other toys that decorate the walls only add to its attraction.

carts. Sunday brunch is a filling repast that begins with a buffet spread of appetizers and proceeds through cooked-to-order main courses. A frenetic, fun scene, especially at night.

Pan on the Danforth, 516 Danforth Ave. ☎ **466-8158.**

> **Cuisine:** GREEK. **Reservations:** Accepted for parties of six or more only.
> **Prices:** Main courses $11–$15. AE, MC, V.
> **Open:** Sun–Thurs 5pm–midnight, Fri–Sat 5pm–1am.

You can make a meal from the assortment of hot and cold appetizers that are offered at this exciting, energetically charged hot spot. There are about 20 to choose from—baby eggplant stuffed with onion, garlic, and roasted pine nuts; warm artichoke and potato in dill, lemon, and cream; or grilled marinated octopus served with lemon and thyme pesto. Among the more substantial dishes, enjoy the grilled loin of lamb with a fig and orange glaze, served with black olive mash and marinated artichokes. There's the traditional Greek favorite, moussaka, or a seafood dish like the swordfish, marinated and grilled in grape leaf and served with spinach orzo.

6   Uptown

Expensive

⭐ **Centro,** 2472 Yonge St. ☎ **483-2211.**

> **Cuisine:** ITALIAN. **Reservations:** Recommended.
> **Prices:** Main courses $19–$26. AE, DC, MC, V.
> **Open:** Dinner only, Mon–Sat 5–11:30pm.

Three blocks north of Eglinton Avenue, Centro exhibits grand Italian style—it's a huge space with dramatic columns, a balcony, a wine bar, brilliant murals, and ultramodern Milan-style furnishings.

The cuisine is Italian with a California accent. Among the dishes might be tapenade-crusted salmon served with couscous; grilled Provimi veal chop in pearl onion, garlic, mushroom, and chive sauce; or oriental fricassée of lobster on baby bok choy. There are also several pasta dishes as well as pizza fresh from the wood-burning oven. To start, try the peppered beef carpaccio or the warm herbed and pine-nut–crusted goat cheese. The international wine list is extraordinary.

The Lobster Trap, 1962 Avenue Rd. ☎ **787-3211.**

> **Cuisine:** SEAFOOD. **Reservations:** Recommended.
> **Prices:** Complete dinners $23.45–$31.50. AE, DC, MC, V.
> **Open:** Dinner only, daily 5–11pm.

People wend their way north to the Lobster Trap, just north of Lawrence Avenue, for one reason only—and that really should be stressed—it's the only place in the city where you can still pick out a 1-4-pound live lobster for an honest and fair price. You may even be sitting next to a celebrity in this dining room, where the tables have brown gingham tablecloths and most are sheltered under a shingled construction to evoke a maritime atmosphere.

For a dinner with clam chowder or lobster bisque, a salad, rolls and butter, french fries or rice, and a beverage, and a one-pound lobster, steamed or broiled and served with drawn butter, you will pay $23.45. Prices rise gradually to $27 for a 1½-pound crustacean. Other fish dinners are available, but stick to the lobster.

⭐ **N 44,** 2537 Yonge St. ☎ **487-4897.**
Cuisine: INTERNATIONAL. **Reservations:** Recommended.
Prices: Main courses $20–$27. AE, DC, MC, V.
Open: Dinner only, Mon–Sat 5–11pm.

Just south of Sherwood Avenue, this restaurant is housed in a dramatic space with soaring ceilings. In the back, chefs work in the glassed-in kitchen, which is etched with the compass logo (North 44° is Toronto's latitude). The atmosphere is enhanced by mirrors that sparkle and reflect the flowers displayed in the attached floral holders. The food is equally à la mode. On the dinner menu you might find roasted lamb with a pecan-mustard crust; grilled shellfish stew with lobster, scallops, shrimp, mussels, clams, tomato broth, ginger, black bean, and coriander; or strip steak with roasted garlic. Pizzas and pastas are also featured. Besides an extensive wine list, there's a number of wines by the glass. There's a pleasant mezzanine wine bar with piano entertainment Wednesday to Saturday.

⭐ **Pronto,** 692 Mount Pleasant Rd. ☎ **486-1111.**
Cuisine: ITALIAN. **Reservations:** Required.
Prices: Main courses $18–$25. AE, DC, MC, V.
Open: Dinner only, daily 5–11:30pm.

Behind its stucco facade, Pronto, just south of Eglinton Avenue, presents a striking and lovely low-ceilinged dining room that is alive and vibrant. In the back, behind a tiled counter, you can see the chefs in their crisp white toques preparing the food. At the center of the room there's always a lavish fresh-flower arrangement. A pianist adds to the atmosphere.

The cuisine matches the decor. The menu changes monthly, but among the appetizers (any of which can be ordered as a main course), you might find lamb sausage with polenta and mushrooms, mussels in white wine and garlic, or a ceviche of sea scallops. For a main course try (if it's available) the bouillabaisse, chock-full of the fresh fish of the day; the tenderloin of pork with sweet potatoes and sun-dried sour cherries; or the grilled lamb with apples and Calvados.

⭐ **Scaramouche,** 1 Benvenuto Place. ☎ **961-8011.**
Cuisine: CONTINENTAL. **Reservations:** Required.
Prices: Main courses $20–$28; pasta dishes $12–$15. AE, DC, MC, V.
Open: Main room, dinner only, Mon–Sat 6–10pm. Pasta bar, dinner only. Mon–Fri 6–11pm, Sat 6pm–midnight.

Scaramouche sustains its reputation as one of Toronto's top-class restaurants. A little difficult to find (it's located in the basement of an apartment building, four blocks south of St. Clair Avenue and Avenue Road), it's certainly worth seeking out. Try to secure a window seat, which grants a view of the downtown city skyline. The decor, the flower arrangements, and the careful presentation of the food make the experience special.

Although the menu changes frequently, it will feature a selection of hot and cold appetizers such as fresh calamari with shiitake mushrooms, sweet peppers, basil and olive oil broth, or warm sweetbread and mushroom terrine. Among the eight or so entrées you might enjoy pan-roasted Riesling-marinated quails; or hickory-smoked and -grilled salmon with wild rice fricassée, sweet peppers, pearl onions, smoked bacon, and escarole in horseradish white wine sauce. You can always select from the pasta bar menu, which offers similar appetizers and excitingly prepared fettuccine, linguine, lasagne, and cannelloni. Desserts, like the hazelnut bombe with warm sabayon or the coconut cream pie, are legendary.

Moderate

Biffi's Bistro, 699 Mount Pleasant Rd. ☎ **484-1142.**

> **Cuisine:** CONTINENTAL. **Reservations:** Recommended.
> **Prices:** Pasta $10–$11; main courses less than $10 at lunch, $13–$19 at dinner. AE, MC, V.
> **Open:** Downstairs, Mon–Fri noon–10pm, Sat 5pm–1am. Upstairs, Mon–Sat noon–1am.

A meal at Biffi's Bistro might start with the escargots en croûte or the fettuccine and follow with grilled salmon with crushed black peppercorns in a sauce of cream and fresh mint; filet mignon with wild mushrooms; veal with scallops and mustard-cream sauce; or cioppino. Among the pastas are rigatoni with porcini mushrooms or tagliatelle with clams, tomatoes, black olives, garlic, and white wine. Check out the mouth-watering desserts, especially the chocolate-raspberry tartufo filled with raspberry ice and topped with strega, the French silk pie, or the chocolate-and-amaretto pie with toasted almonds. At lunch, look for calves' liver with caramelized onions and parsley butter and also cannelloni.

Bofinger, 1507 Yonge St. ☎ **923-2300.**

> **Cuisine:** CONTINENTAL. **Reservations:** Required at lunch; recommended at dinner.
> **Prices:** Main courses $9–$19. AE, DC, MC, V.
> **Open:** Lunch daily 11:30am–2pm; dinner Sun–Wed 5:30–10pm, Thurs–Sat 5:30–11pm. All-day menu available in the lounge.

Bofinger, at St. Clair Avenue, has been designed as a spacious, mirrored, tiled, and muraled Parisian brasserie. At the front there's a bar set with marble tables. The dining areas have tables widely spaced on tile floors and set under a stained-glass paneled ceiling. The food is eclectic, with some dishes reflecting Caribbean/Asian accents and others the current simple bistro style. For example, there's a dish called jerk giant shrimp with green bananas, coconut, and papaya that shares the menu with steak and frites and Cajun strip loin. Pizzas and pastas are also available. Desserts are hard to resist, like the fresh raspberries served in a tulip pastry with raspberry sabayon.

Brownes Bistro, 1251 Yonge St. ☎ 924-8132.

Cuisine: FRENCH/LIGHT FARE. **Reservations:** Recommended.
Prices: Main courses $13–$18; pizza and pasta $9–$10. AE, MC, V.
Open: Lunch Mon–Fri noon–2pm; dinner Mon–Sat 6–11pm.

Just south of St. Clair Avenue is Brownes Bistro. The decor is rather nondescript, but the clientele is well-heeled and the food is well-flavored bistro fare. The menu might list fresh fish with lime coriander or lamb sausage with mashed potato and brown sauce. Pizza and pasta are also available.

Coppi, 3363 Yonge St. ☎ 484-4464.

Cuisine: ITALIAN. **Reservations:** Recommended at dinner.
Prices: Main courses $15–$20. AE, ER, MC, V.
Open: Mon–Fri noon–2pm, Sat 5:30–10:30pm.

Named after Fausto Coppi, the legendary Italian cyclist who died of malaria, this restaurant features poster-size photographs of Coppi at various stages of his career. The kitchen turns out grilled dishes along with pasta and risottos.

Grano, 2035 Yonge St. ☎ 440-1986.

Cuisine: ITALIAN. **Reservations:** Accepted for parties of six or more.
Prices: Main courses $9–$18. AE, DC, MC, V.
Open: Mon–Fri 10am–10:30pm, Sat 10am–11pm.

Grano is a wild Italian celebration—a celebration of down-to-earth food served in an atmosphere of washed Mediterranean pastels. It's casual and fun. The wine is served in tumblers; there's a courtyard out back; and the tables are painted in brilliant colors of mustard and cherry. The latest Italian art/posters decorate the walls, and large colorful majolica vessels abound. At the entrance the display counters are filled with a variety of antipasti, and any three (piccolo) or seven (grande) of these can be ordered, ranging in price from $10 for a small all-vegetable plate to $23 for a large plate of salmon carpaccio. In addition there are several pasta dishes, like the rigatoni siracusa with eggplant, peppers, olives, anchovies, and capers in a spicy tomato sauce and the gnocchi with a pink sauce. The meat or fish entrées change daily. To finish there's tiramisu, biscotti, and a variety of Italian custard-cream desserts.

Herbs, 3187 Yonge St. (north of Lawrence). ☎ 322-0487.

Cuisine: CONTINENTAL. **Reservations:** Recommended.
Prices: Main courses $11–$19. AE, DC, ER, MC, V.
Open: Lunch Mon–Fri 11:30am–2pm; dinner Mon–Thurs 5:30–10pm, Fri–Sat 5:30–11pm.

Brilliant colors and designs inspired by nature are the hallmarks of this appealing restaurant. Walls of brilliant yellow, burnt orange, and crimson serve as backdrops for paintings, which are actually for sale. Tables sport floral-design tablecloths of brilliant pink, mauve, and turquoise topped with butcher paper.

The food is eclectic. Among the eight or so main courses you might find pan-roasted Atlantic salmon wrapped in phyllo with a hoisin sauce; a confit of duck with red cabbage and grilled portobello mushroom on a potato galette; or fresh halibut with a grilled fresh pineapple and Mexican chili salsa. The desserts are sublime. You'll succumb to the lemon tart, served on a huge Villeroy & Boch china plate and artistically presented with figs, strawberries, and an intense raspberry and creme sorbet.

La Grenouille, 2387 Yonge St. ☎ 481-3093.

Cuisine: FRENCH. **Reservations:** Recommended.
Prices: Main courses $14–$20. AE, DC, MC, V.
Open: Lunch Mon–Fri noon–2:30pm; dinner Mon–Fri 5:30–10:30pm, Sat 5:30–11pm.

La Grenouille is a simple uptown French bistro serving reasonably priced, well-prepared food. The atmosphere is provided by candlelight, French music, and a sage-green neon sign reflecting against the storefront window. Select from the nine or so entrées—orange roughy in a shallot and butter sauce; rabbit in white wine with shallots, garlic, and mushrooms; and frog's legs, of course, sautéed in garlic butter and sprinkled with fresh parsley and lemon juice. There is a selection of soups, including a Mediterranean fish soup served with Emmenthal, croutons, and rouille; or you can begin with various salads and appetizers, including deep-fried breaded cheese croquettes on a coulis of fresh raspberries.

Le Paradis, 166 Bedford Rd. (north of Davenport). ☎ 921-0995.

Cuisine: FRENCH. **Reservations:** Recommended.
Prices: Main courses $8–$16.50; prix fixe $15.95. AE, MC, V.
Open: Lunch Mon–Fri noon–3pm; dinner Mon–Sat 6–11pm, Sun 5:30–10pm.

At night when the French doors are flung open to the street and Le Paradis is filled with chattering diners, you could swear that you're in a residential area of Paris. The room is long and narrow; and the banquettes and tables stretch alongside one wall, facing a bar on the other. European posters and photographs only add to the atmosphere. The offerings are typical bistro fare—chicken roasted with tarragon and flank steak with fries—with some regional specialties like pork chops roasted with green peppercorns and spices or lamb and beef sausage served on couscous. Many of the dishes, especially the seafood offerings, change daily and are listed on a blackboard. Typical appetizers include mussels and pâté. Best value is the three-course prix fixe.

Thai Magic, 1118 Yonge St. ☎ 968-7366.

Cuisine: THAI. **Reservations:** Recommended.
Prices: Main courses $8–$14 AE, MC, V.
Open: Lunch Mon–Fri 11:30am–2:30pm; dinner Mon–Sat 5:30–11pm.

Magical indeed is this long, narrow restaurant filled with orchids, Thai statuary, and artifacts. Warm mauves and greens make it even more inviting and a perfect backdrop for the sophisticated cuisine. Start with a combination plate of appetizers, *tom yum kai* (a really spicy soup flavored with lemon grass and containing succulent shrimp), or the familiar noodle dish pad Thai. For main courses there are stir-fries and curries (like the flavorsome chicken green curry or shrimp red curry with okra) as well as such dishes as chicken with basil, tamarind fish, coriander lobster, or shrimp lemon grass— the last a specialty that uses a unique family recipe.

Trapper's, 3479 Yonge St. ☎ 482-6211.

Cuisine: CONTINENTAL. **Reservations:** Recommended.
Prices: Main courses $13–$22 at dinner. AE, MC, V.
Open: Lunch Mon–Fri 11:30am–2:30pm; dinner Mon–Sat 5–10:30pm, Sun 5–9:30pm.

Trapper's, between Lawrence Avenue and York Mills Road, has a seasonally changing menu that features the best Canadian ingredients. Start with smoked Canadian salmon with Dijon sour cream, capers, and scallions, or Prince Edward Island mussels steamed in Innis Killin Riesling, chives, thyme, parsley, and garlic. Follow with charcoal-broiled marinated leg of venison with Pinot Noir ginger glaze, or filet of Muskoka trout seared in Acadian spices with a pineapple/red pepper/onion salsa. Pasta dishes are also offered; the barbecued steaks are a favorite.

Inexpensive

Jerusalem, 955 Eglinton Ave. W. ☎ 783-6494.

Cuisine: MIDDLE EASTERN. **Reservations:** Not accepted.
Prices: Appetizers less than $4; main courses $9–$13. AE, MC, V.
Open: Mon–Thurs noon–11pm, Fri–Sat noon–midnight, Sun noon–10pm.

At Jerusalem, just west of Bathurst Street, it's the food and prices that count. The decor is simple—just some hammered-brass tabletops on the walls—but the atmosphere is extremely warm, the service friendly and unhurried. All the appetizers are less than $4—falafel, kibbeh (a cracked-wheat roll stuffed with ground meat, onions, and pine nuts), various styles of hummus, tahini, and tabbouleh (a delicious blend of cracked wheat with chopped tomatoes, onions, parsley, mint, lemon, and olive oil). You can follow them with liver fried in garlic and hot-pepper sauce, siniyeh (mixed ground lamb and beef with onions, parsley, and pine nuts, oven baked with tahini sauce), and lamb or beef shish kebab.

7 Specialty Dining

Hotel Dining

Chiaro's, in the King Edward, 37 King St. E. ☎ 863-9700.

Cuisine: FRENCH/CONTINENTAL. **Reservations:** Recommended.
Prices: Appetizers $6–$15; main courses $19–$36. AE, CB, DC, MC, V.
Open: Lunch Mon–Fri noon–2pm; dinner Mon–Sat 6–10:30pm.

For formal dining, Chiaro's, decorated in stunning gray lacquer with etched-glass panels and French-style chairs, specializes in fine French and continental cuisine. Start with smoked salmon carved from the trolley or a terrine of forest mushrooms with venison carpaccio. You might follow with a poached Dover sole, rack of lamb with toasted hazelnuts, or lemon- and soya-marinated swordfish.

The Roof Restaurant, in the Park Plaza, 4 Avenue Rd. ☎ 924-4571.

Cuisine: CONTINENTAL. **Reservations:** Recommended.
Prices: Main courses $19–$23; three-course prix fixe $40. AE, MC, V.
Open: Dinner only, daily 5:30–10:30pm.

From this elegant room lit with brilliant chandeliers, you have a splendid view of the city out over the terrace. For a luxurious start, try the lobster-and-truffle ravioli with vanilla-and-champagne beurre blanc or the warm asparagus and wild mushroom tart layered with oyster and shiitake mushrooms. Follow with the grilled filet of salmon with orange and ginger glaze, or the rosemary roasted breast of chicken with shiitake and morel mushrooms in balsamic vinaigrette. Desserts are a delight to the eye and a disaster to the diet—decadent chocolate cheesecake and maple crème brûlée are two examples.

Seasons, in the Inn on the Park, 1100 Eglinton Ave. E. ☎ 444-2561.

Cuisine: CONTINENTAL. **Reservations:** Recommended.
Prices: Appetizers $5–$11; main courses $18–$25. AE, DC, MC, V.
Open: Lunch Mon–Fri noon–2:30pm; dinner daily 6–10pm; brunch Sun 10:30am–3pm.

A stylish garden atmosphere is the backdrop for sophisticated continental cuisine in Seasons. Start with grilled vegetable terrine with yellow corn polenta or salad of smoked duck and green asparagus with peppered red currant balsamic dressing. Then follow with crisp duckling with fried vegetable roll and hoisin sauce or broiled filet of red snapper in a coriander saffron broth. Alternative cuisine is featured for the health-conscious. At brunch there's a buffet with omelets cooked to order and hot dishes served.

Truffles, in the Four Seasons, 21 Avenue Rd. ☎ 964-0411.

Cuisine: CONTINENTAL. **Reservations:** Recommended.
Prices: Appetizers $7–$19; main courses $23–$35. AE, DC, MC, V.
Open: Dinner only, Mon–Sat 6–11pm.

Named one of the 10 best hotel restaurants in the world by *Hotel* magazine and carrying a 5-diamond AAA rating, Truffles is certainly the premier hotel dining room in the city. The room provides a lavish setting for some exquisite cuisine. Fine materials have been used in the design of all the elements—from the marquetry floor that's fashioned from 11,000 pieces of oak, jojoba, and purpleheart wood to the curly maple walls and the custom-designed cabinets, mirrors, ceramics, and other art pieces. The cuisine is imaginative, fresh, and flavor-filled. For those who have to watch their diets, the alternative cuisine is a welcome feature on the menu. Otherwise, you can start, say, with the lobster salad with winter leaves, cucumber, and chive puree, topped with orange port and ginger dressing; the ravioli filled with shrimp, sweet garlic, and vegetables in a Provence herb and tomato broth; or the crab soup, which is amazing—a clear broth with lemon balm, shaved fennel, coriander, and ginger. Follow with the grilled swordfish Provence style with two sauces: red wine shallot sauce or a dill caper sauce with olives. Or there are medallions of veal tenderloin with creamed mushrooms, sautéed spinach, and a morel sauce. At the conclusion, treat yourself to a sampling platter of desserts or the restaurant's signature "chocolate, chocolate"— semisweet and milk chocolate fudge pyramids, candied orange, and grenadine sauce.

Zachary's, in the Bristol Place, 950 Dixon Rd. ☎ **675-9444.**
Cuisine: NOUVELLE. **Reservations:** Recommended.
Prices: Appetizers $5–$10; main courses $18–$30. AE, DC, MC, V.
Open: Lunch Mon–Fri noon–2:30pm; dinner Mon–Sat 6–10pm; brunch Sun 11am–3pm.

For years Zachary's has been known as the one airport-area restaurant serving consistently good food. House specialties include fresh Dover sole, rack of lamb crusted with garlic and rosemary, and seared alligator filets. The hot-and-cold Sunday buffet brunch is also popular and famous for its distinguished dessert table and the chance to savor (among other things) a salmon-and-caviar omelet.

Dining Complexes

DRAGON CITY In the basement of Dragon City, the Asian shopping complex on Spadina Avenue at Dundas Street, you'll find tables surrounded by a series of counters frequented by the local Chinatown residents. You could be anywhere in Asia. The food offered is Indonesian, Japanese, Chinese, Taiwanese, noodles, and seafood. A real Toronto experience.

EATON CENTRE EATERIES For shoppers and cinema-goers, the Eaton Centre has a variety of dining experiences available, most of them moderately priced and most offering unsophisticated cuisine or food on the run. There are several food courts featuring a variety of ethnic and North American foods; local favorites like Toby's Goodeats for burgers, salads, and sandwiches; pubs like the Elephant & Castle, specializing in brews and such staples as shepherd's pie and fish-and-chips; and also a couple of fully licensed more leisurely dining establishments.

HARBOURFRONT DINING A great variety and some decent budget dining can be found in **Queen's Quay,** particularly upstairs with most items priced between $4 and $8. Croûtes and pita sandwiches can be found at **La Bouchée.** At **Pedro's** (☎ **203-0464**) you can choose among pizza (vegetarian even), spaghetti with all kinds of sauces, veal cutlet, lasagne, sausages, and a salad bar. All the items are under $8. The **Coyote Grill** (☎ **203-0504**) has burritos and nachos priced from $7 to $12.

Downstairs there are several restaurants, each one also operating an outdoor terrace/café from which you can watch the sailboats and other craft plying the harbor. **Fruiteria** (☎ **203-0274**) offers soups, salads, and fresh fruits of all sorts, with most items under $5.

Spinnakers (☎ **203-0559**) has an inside dining room as well, and a cocktail bar, too. Here you can enjoy fish-and-chips, baked halibut, salads, and more, priced from $8 to $17. **Baguette** (☎ **203-0287**) has chocolate-almond croissants, and makes tuna melts and other fare, all under $5.

Also on the Harbourfront on Pier 4 are **Wallymagoo's** (☎ **203-6248**), a nautical-theme restaurant known for its seafood, pizza, finger foods, and live entertainment; **Pier 4 Storehouse** (☎ **203-1440**), which features a raw bar and serves steak, seafood, and pasta priced from $15 to $27; **Whaler's Wharf** (☎ **203-5865**), featuring steak and seafood from a $10 catch of the day to $28 lobster. Open daily 4:30 to 11pm.

The **Water's Edge Patio and Bar** (☎ **203-0717**) overlooks Lake Ontario, has a huge outdoor bar, and serves fresh salads and grilled and barbecued items. It's jam-packed on weekends. Open 9am to 10pm. On weekends live entertainment goes on all day.

MOVENPICK   A veritable Swiss complex has been created at Movenpick, 165 York St., between Richmond and Adelaide (☎ **366-5234**).

The **Veranda Delicatessen** is a fine place to stop during the day for a tempting array of pastries, ice cream, truffles, cheeses, soup of the day, and sandwiches. Homemade breads, pastries, and Swiss chocolate truffles are available for takeout. Open Monday through Friday from 7:30am to 6pm, on Saturday from 10am to 6pm, and on Sunday from 10am to 4pm.

The tiled **Belle Terrasse,** filled with colorful potted plants, looks like an outdoor café and serves a variety of Swiss specialties, priced from $12 to $17, including Rahmschnitzel (pork schnitzel covered with a creamy mushroom sauce), Swiss bratwurst with Rosti, or tender veal liver sautéed in butter. Seafood, steaks, salads, curries, and various toasts complete the menu. Breakfast is served here from 7:30 to 11am. In the evenings specials are featured. Monday and Tuesday are pasta nights, all you can eat for $17; on Wednesday and Thursday a gourmet buffet ($26) is served; while on Friday and Saturday there's a fisherman's feast (from $30). On Sunday a brunch buffet is served ($25).

The wood-paneled **Rossli Restaurant,** decorated with horse saddlery (the name, in fact, means little horse), is for more formal dining. Start your meal with a Swiss barley soup with vegetables or air-dried beef and follow with one of the specialties from $15 to $20—veal in a white wine sauce with mushrooms, rack of lamb with flageolet beans, or sautéed beef tenderloin in mustard sauce. Seafood and steaks complete the menu. Save room for the tempting Swiss chocolate truffle cake. Open Monday through Saturday from 11:30am to 2pm and from 6pm.

And finally, there's the **Grape 'n' Cheese Wine Bar,** serving the complete menu and Swiss cheese fondue and raclette. Open Monday through Friday from 11am to 11pm and on Saturday from noon to 11pm.

VILLAGE BY THE GRANGE   Conveniently located south of the Art Gallery, Village by the Grange, at 71 McCaul St., contains the **International Food Market,** where you'll find everything from Chinese, Middle Eastern, Japanese, and Mexican fast food to Coney Island hot dogs and a booth specializing in schnitzels. Salads, burgers, Japanese specialties, meat pies, and more are also readily available. All the fare is around $5.

Light, Casual & Fast Food ─────────────────

The Bagel, 285 College St. ☎ 966-7555.

Cuisine: DELI.
Prices: Everything less than $9. V.
Open: Mon–Fri 7am–9pm, Sat 8am–9pm, Sun 8am–5pm.

You have to be a member of the "clean plate club" if you want to eat at the Bagel—otherwise the waitresses will scold you with "C'mon, eat already." Blintzes, bagels, lox, and cream cheese are the tops at this characterful spot, although special Asian-style dishes are also available, along with sandwiches and dinner plates.

Bloor Street Diner, 55 Bloor St. W. ☎ 928-3105.

Cuisine: LIGHT FARE.
Prices: Most items $4–$10.
Open: Daily 11am–3am.

The Bloor Street Diner is a convenient place to stop for a wide selection of reasonably priced food. The handmade floor, wall tiles, and pottery evoke a Provençal atmosphere. The restaurant offers several dining experiences. The espresso bar serves a variety of coffees, plus salads, panini sandwiches, and crepes. La Rotisserie features roasted meats, poultry, and fish prepared in Provence style. Le Café/Patio serves light bistro-style meals and stays open until 3am daily.

Hughie's Burgers, 22 Front St. W. ☎ 364-2242.

Cuisine: BURGERS.
Prices: Everything less than $8.50. AE, DC, MC, V.
Open: Mon–Thurs 11:30am–11:30pm, Fri–Sat 11:30am–midnight.

Hughie's offers a variety of burgers, sandwiches, and salads. There's even a 10-ouncer for $8.50. A popular, pleasant hangout, especially in early evening.

Shopsy's, 33 Yonge St. ☎ 365-3333.

Cuisine: DELI.
Prices: Sandwiches $5–$8. AE, DC, MC, V.
Open: Mon–Wed 7am–midnight, Thurs–Fri 7am–1am, Sat 8am–1am, Sun 8am–midnight.

Toronto's most famous deli was started in the garment district 72 years ago. Today, it's right across from the O'Keefe Centre. Shopsy's occupies spiffy quarters and sports an outdoor patio arrayed with brilliant yellow umbrellas. They serve huge stuffed deli sandwiches, the most traditional being the corned beef and pastrami. Good breakfast spot, too.

Toby's Goodeats, 93 Bloor St. W. ☎ 925-2171.

Cuisine: BURGERS.

Prices: Burgers $4–$7.50. AE, MC, V.

Open: Tues–Sat 11:30am–1am, Sun–Mon 11:30am–midnight.

Capture those childhood dreams of milkshakes, Coke floats, and a good burger along with the rest of the crowd at Toby's Goodeats, a 1950s-style hamburger joint. The decor suits: a schizophrenic combination of Formica tables, cookie jars, and funky posters, and the traditional brick-and-plants look. It's very crowded at lunchtime. A dozen burgers are priced from $4 to $6.50 for a 10-ouncer. In addition, there are salads, sandwiches, pizza, and pasta.

Toby's Goodeats can also be found at 1502 Yonge St. (☎ 921-1062), 2293 Yonge St. (☎ 481-9183), 725 Yonge St. (☎ 925-9908), in the Eaton Centre (☎ 591-6994), 542 Church St. (☎ 929-0411), and First Canadian Place (☎ 366-3953).

Breakfast/Brunch

Most people grab breakfast on the run and certainly in Toronto there are a zillion places to do that, many of them found on the lower floors of the major buildings and along the underground passageways that connect buildings. But there are some extra-special places to enjoy breakfast, if you have the time.

For years, **the Senator,** an institution, has been a breakfast hangout; for a more contemporary experience stop into **Chez Cappuccino,** 3 Charles St. E. (☎ 925-6142), where you can start the day with melt-in-the mouth croissants, banana bread, or a bagel sandwich washed down with a smooth, frothy cappuccino.

Nearly every restaurant in the city offers Saturday and Sunday brunch. Here are just a few of my favorites: the Prince Arthur Garden restaurant in the Park Plaza offers an innovative brunch menu featuring Italian, Mexican, Cajun, and Asian specialties; Sansouci at the Sutton Place hotel, 955 Bay St. (☎ 924-9221), makes for a spectacular setting for brunch; and the Boulevard Café, 161 Harbord St. (☎ 961-7676), spices up the traditional brunch with Peruvian specialties.

Desserts   Diet books, Optifast, and Weight Watchers may be ubiquitous, but bold enough to buck the trend, **Just Desserts,** 306 Davenport Rd. (☎ 922-6824), is open practically around the clock on weekends for those in need of that sugar fix. Around 50 desserts are available—as many as 14 different cheesecakes, 10 or so assorted pies, plus a whole array of gâteaux, tortes, meringues (all $4 to $5). I don't need to describe them—just go, order with a cappuccino or coffee, savor every bite, and feel bad afterward.

Enjoy them in a nostalgic atmosphere created by oak swivel chairs, black-tiled tables, and old-movie/Broadway melodies. While you're here you might like to purchase one of the many whimsical cookie jars.

Open from 8:30am to 3am on weekdays, to 5am on weekends.

Late-Night Dining **C'Est What,** 67 Front St. E. (☎ **867-9499**), stays open until 4am on weekends, serving snacks and bar food.

Greektown, out along the Danforth, hums until the early hours too, at such dining/drinking hot spots as Ouzeri, Myth, and others.

6

What to See & Do in Toronto

IT TAKES FIVE OR SIX DAYS TO REALLY SEE TORONTO'S HIGHLIGHTS. ALTHOUGH some of the major sights are centrally located, there are also several favorites outside the downtown core, and these take extra time and effort to reach. Ideally, you should spend one day each at Ontario Place, the Ontario Science Centre, Canada's Wonderland, and Harbourfront. In fact, that's what the kids will definitely want to do. Then there's also the zoo, which could take a whole day complete with a picnic.

The Art Gallery of Ontario, Chinatown, and the Royal Ontario Museum (ROM) could be combined in a pinch, but the day might be too museum-oriented for some. Ontario Place could conceivably be combined with Fort York and Exhibition Place. En route to Canada's Wonderland, you could stop in at Black Creek Pioneer Village, but I don't recommend that since it will cut into your time at Canada's Wonderland, which really requires a day.

As you can see, there are numerous major attractions in Toronto worthy of a whole day's visit. There are also many other downtown sights—the CN Tower, the Eaton Centre, Yorkville, Queen Street, City Hall, and Casa Loma—that any visitor will want to explore. Depending on your interests and whether you have children, there's enough to keep you going for several weeks in Toronto. But that said, below are a few suggestions.

Suggested Itineraries

If You Have Two Days

Day 1   Get to the Ontario Science Centre the minute it opens and then come back into town to spend the late afternoon/early evening at Harbourfront or Ontario Place.

Day 2   Start early at the Kensington Market and from there walk up to College Street and through the university area to the Royal Ontario Museum. Leave enough time to wander through Yorkville and browse in some of the stores and galleries before they close.

If You Have Three Days

Days 1–2   Spend the first two days as outlined above.

Day 3   Explore Chinatown and stop at the Art Gallery. Then pop over to the Eaton Centre and head down to Queen Street to explore Queen Street Village in the early evening.

There are a few recent additions to Toronto's cultural scene that visitors may want to take in: a new wing at the ROM that showcases eight centuries of European/Canadian decorative arts—highlights that dramatize the French and English aspects of early Canadian culture includes the French townhouse interior and the English gentleman's parlor; the New galleries at the Art Gallery of Ontario; and the striking murals and interior of the new Royal Princess of Wales theater. These-park afficionados and families may want to check out Wonderland's new rides and see the Star Wars characters that now enliven the park's byways. Looking forward to 1995, the Bata Shoe Museum plans to reopen with a splash in brand-new quarters designed by Raymond Moriyama.

If You Have Five Days

Days 1–3   Spend Days 1–3 as discussed above.

Day 4   Visit either Canada's Wonderland (if the family's in tow) or the McMichael Collection in Kleinburg. Black Creek Pioneer Village could be squeezed in, too.

Day 5   Take a trip to the Toronto Islands and while away the day among the lagoons, picnicking, relaxing, or bicycling.

1   The Top Attractions

Ontario Place, 955 Lakeshore Blvd. W. ☎ **314-9900** or **314-9811.**

When this 96-acre recreation complex on Lake Ontario opened in 1971, it seemed futuristic—and more than 20 years later it still does (admittedly, it was renovated in 1989). From a distance you'll see five steel-and-glass pods suspended on columns 105 feet above the lake; three artificial islands; and, alongside, a huge geodesic dome. The five pods contain a multimedia theater, a live children's theater, a high-technology exhibit, and displays that tell the story of Ontario in vivid kaleidoscopic detail. The dome houses Cinesphere, where a 60- by 80-foot screen shows specially made IMAX movies—currently "To Fly," "Africa, the Serengeti," and "Tropical Rainforest."

Under an enormous orange canopy, the Children's Village provides a well-supervised area where children under 12 can scramble over rope bridges; bounce on an enormous trampoline; slide down a twisting chute; and, most popular of all, squirt water pistols and garden hoses, swim, and generally drench one another in the water-play section. Afterward, parents can use the convenient changing room and washroom facilities before moving on to three specialty children's theaters.

A stroll around the complex reveals two marinas full of yachts and other craft; the HMCS *Haida,* a World War II and Korean War destroyer that can be toured; a 18-hole miniature golf course; and plenty of grassland for picnicking and general cavorting. There's a wide variety of restaurants and snack bars serving everything from Chinese, Irish, German, and Canadian food to hot dogs and hamburgers. And don't miss the wildest rides in town—the Wilderness Canoe Ride, the Water Slide, and bumper boats. Or for something more peaceful, there are pedal or remote-control boats.

At night the **Forum,** an outdoor amphitheater that accommodates 10,000 under the copper canopy and outside on the grassy slopes, comes alive. During the summer all manner of entertainments are held here, from the Toronto Symphony and National Ballet of Canada, to Tony Bennett, Dionne Warwick, and Bruce Cockburn. For tickets call **416/870-8000.**

Admission: Free, with some exceptions (like the Canadian National Exhibition). IMAX movies $5 adults, $2.50 seniors and children 12 and under.

Open: Mid–May to mid–Sept Mon–Sat 10:30am–midnight, Sun 10:30am–11pm. **Subway and Bus:** Located west of downtown, Ontario Place can be reached by taking the subway to Bathurst or Dufferin and buses south from there to Exhibition. Call TTC Information (☎ **393-4636**) for special bus service details. **Parking:** $9.

⭐ **Harbourfront Centre,** Queen's Quay W. ☎ **973-3000** for information on special events or **973-4000** for the box office.

The federal government took over a 96-acre strip of prime waterfront land in 1972 to preserve the waterfront vista—and since then Torontonians have rediscovered their lakeshore. Abandoned warehouses, shabby depots, and crumbling factories have been refurbished, and a tremendous urban park now stretches on and around the old piers.

The resulting Harbourfront has to be one of Toronto's most exciting happenings. Sailboats, motorboats, houseboats, ferries, and other craft ply the water or sit at anchor dockside, their happy denizens dining or drinking in one of the many waterside cafés, shopping, or attending one of the entertainment events that are very much part of the waterfront scene. It's a great place to spend the whole day.

Queen's Quay, at the foot of York Street, is the closest quay to town, and it's the first point you'll encounter as you approach from the Westin Harbour Castle. From here, boats depart for tours of the harbor and islands. An old renovated warehouse now houses a dance theater, plus two floors of shops, restaurants, and waterfront cafés.

After exploring Queen's Quay, walk west along the glorious waterfront promenade to **York Quay.** To get there you'll pass the **Power Plant,** a contemporary gallery, and behind it, the **Du Maurier Theatre Centre.** At **York Quay Centre** you can secure a lot of information on programming as well as entertain yourself in several galleries, including the **Craft Studio,** where you can watch artisans blow glass, throw pots, and make silk-screen prints. On the other side of the center you can attend one of the Molson Dry Front Music outdoor concerts, free all summer long at **Molson Place.** Also on the quay in the center is the **Water's Edge Cafe** overlooking a small pond for electric model boats and a children's play area.

From here, take the footbridge to John Quay, crossing over the sailboats moored below, to the stores and restaurants on Pier 4— **Wallymagoo's Marine Bar** and the **Pier 4 Storehouse.** Beyond on **Maple Leaf Quay** lies the **Nautical Centre.**

At the **Harbourside Boating Centre,** 283 Queen's Quay W., (☎ **203-3000**), you can rent sail and power boats as well as signing on for sailing lessons. For three hours, depending on size, sailboats cost from $45 to $125 and power boats from $60 to $180. Week-long and weekend sailing courses are offered.

The **Harbourfront Antiques Market,** at 390 Queen's Quay W., at the foot of Spadina Avenue (☎ **260-2626**), will keep antiques-lovers busy browsing for hours. More than 100 antiques dealers spread out their wares—jewelry, china, furniture, toys, and books. Indoor parking is adjacent to the market, and there's also a cafeteria that serves fresh salads, sandwiches, and desserts for that oft-needed rest stop. Open May through October, Tuesday through Friday from 11am to 6pm, Saturday from 10am to 6pm, and Sunday from 8 to 6pm; November through April, Tuesday through Friday from 11am to 5pm, Saturday 10am to 5pm, and Sunday from 8am to 6pm.

At the west end of the park stands **Bathurst Pier,** with a large sports field for romping around, plus two adventure playgrounds, one for older kids and the other (supervised) for 3- to 7-year-olds.

More than 4,000 events take place annually at Harbourfront, including a **Harbourfront Reading Festival,** held every Tuesday on York Quay, which attracts some very eminent writers. Other happenings include films, dance, theater, music, children's events, multicultural festivals, marine events, and other exciting programs. Two of the most important events are the annual **Children's Festival** and the **International Festival of Authors.** Most of the activities are free.

Train: Take the LRT from Union Station. **Bus:** Take the no. 77B bus from Union Station or the Spadina subway station; or the no. 6 or 6A bus to the foot of Bay Street and walk west.

★ The Toronto Islands

A stolid little ferry will take you across to 612 acres of island park crisscrossed by shady paths and quiet waterways—a glorious spot to walk, play tennis, cycle, feed the ducks, putter around in boats, picnic, or just sit.

Children will find **Centreville** (☎ **203-0405**), a 19-acre old-time amusement park, built and designed especially for them. But you won't find the usual neon signs, shrill hawkers, and the aroma of greasy hot-dog stands. Instead you'll find a turn-of-the-century village complete with Main Street, tiny shops, a firehouse, and even a small working farm where the kids can pet lambs and chicks and enjoy pony rides. They'll also love trying out the miniature antique cars, the fire engines, the old-fashioned train, the authentic 1890s carousel, the flume ride, and the aerial cars. Admission is free, but there is a charge for the rides. Open daily from mid–May to Labor Day, 10:30am to 6pm.

Ferries: Ferries, which operate all day, leave from the docks at the bottom of Bay Street. To get there, take a subway to Union Station and the Bay Street bus south. Round-trip fare $3 adults, $1.50 seniors and ages 15–19, $1 for children 15 and under. For ferry schedules, call **392-8193.**

Downtown

CN Tower, 301 Front St. W. ☎ **360-8500.**

As you approach the city, the first thing you'll notice is this slender needlelike structure and the tiny colored elevators that glide to the top of the 1,815-foot-high tower—the tallest free-standing structure in the world.

As you enter the base of the tower, just look up through the atrium to the top . . . yes, that's where you're going. Glass-walled elevators on the outside walls of the tower whisk you to the 1,136-foot-high seven-level sky pod in just under a minute. You can sometimes see all the way to Niagara Falls or even to Buffalo. One of the two observation levels is partially open to allow you to experience that dizzying sensation of height (vertigo sufferers beware).

The pod also contains broadcasting facilities and a revolving restaurant (for lunch, dinner, or Sunday brunch reservations at the revolving restaurant, call **362-5411**). Atop the tower sits a 335-foot antenna mast that took 31 weeks to erect with the aid of a giant Sikorsky helicopter; it took 55 lifts to complete the operation. Above the sky pod is the world's highest public observation gallery, the Space Deck, 1,465 feet above the ground.

While you're up there, don't worry that the elements might sweep it into the lake: It's built of contoured reinforced concrete covered with thick glass-reinforced plastic and is designed to keep ice accumulation to a minimum. The structure can withstand high winds, snow, ice, lightning, and earth tremors, which is probably more than you can say about your own house.

Another star attraction at the tower is the futuristic "The Tour of the Universe," a simulated spaceport that will project you into the year 2019. Kids love it as they buckle up on board the Hermes Shuttle and blast off to Jupiter.

The newest attractions at the tower are the **Mindwarp Theatre,** a simulator adventure and the **Q-Zar** tag game. The first begins with a wacky and interactive stroll through the theater and concludes with a thrilling trip through an abandoned mine shaft. The second is a live-action laser tag game. Each player aims to find and deactivate the opposing team members using an advanced laser handset.

Admission: Observation $12 adults, $8 seniors, $6.50 children 5–12. Mindwarp or Q-Zar $8, $7, and $6 respectively. Any two combinations $17, $13, $10; any four combinations $19.95, $14.95, and $11.95.

Open: Observation deck summer Mon–Sat 9am–midnight, Sun 10am–10pm; winter Sun–Thurs 10am–10pm, Fri–Sat 10am–11pm. The Mindwarp Theatre and Q-Zar summer daily 10am–10pm; winter Mon–Thurs 11am–7pm, Fri–Sat 10am–10pm, Sun 11am–7pm. **Subway:** Union, than walk west along Front Street.

IMPRESSIONS

A global psychiatrist, if asked to take a look at Toronto's rather unhealthy obsession with the CN Tower, would advise the city to take a cold shower and lie down on the couch for a spell.
—Allan Fotheringham, *Maclean's* (1975)

SkyDome, 1 Blue Jays Way, Suite 3000. ☎ **341-3663** or **341-2770** for tour information.

A gala event in 1989 was the opening of the downtown 53,000-seat SkyDome, home to the Toronto Blue Jays baseball team and the Toronto Argonauts football team. In 1992, Skydome became the first Canadian venue to host the World Series—in fact, the Blue Jays won the series both 1992 and 1993. The stadium itself represents an engineering feat, featuring the world's first fully retractable roof spanning more than eight acres and a gigantic video scoreboard. So large is it that you could fit a 31-story building inside the complex when the roof is closed. Indeed, there's already a spectacular 11-story hotel with 70 rooms facing directly onto the field in the complex. A film is shown, and walking tours are given of the complex.

Admission: Tours, $9 adults, $6 students 16 and under and seniors, free for children under 3.

Open: Tour schedule depends on events/sports schedule. **Subway:** Union.

⭐ **Art Gallery of Ontario,** 317 Dundas St. W., between McCaul and Beverley sts. ☎ **977-0414.**

The exterior gives no hint of the light and openness inside this beautifully designed gallery. The newly refurbished and expanded gallery is dramatic and the paintings are imaginatively displayed. The walls of the new galleries are stunning colors and throughout there are audiovisual presentations and computer terminals that provide information on particular paintings or schools of painters. There are several highlights not to be missed.

Although the European collections are fine, I would concentrate on the Canadian galleries. The galleries displaying the Group of Seven—Tom Thomson, F. H. Varley, Lawren Harris, and Emily Carr, and others—are extraordinary. In addition, there are other galleries showing the genesis of Canadian art from earlier artists like Cornelius Krieghoff, Paul Kane, and Paul Peel, to such moderns as Harold Town, Kenneth Lochhead, Jock MacDonals, Jack Bush, Michael Snow, and the Montréal Automatistes Riopelle and Borduas.

Also don't miss the galleries featuring Inuit art.

The **Henry Moore Sculpture Centre,** possessing more than 800 pieces (original plasters, bronzes, maquettes, woodcuts, lithographs, etchings, and drawings), is the largest public collection of his works. They were given to Toronto by the artist, supposedly because he was so moved by the citizens' enthusiasm for his work (remember, public donations bought the sculpture that decorates Nathan Phillips Square at City Hall). In one room, under a glass ceiling, 20 or so of his large works stand like silent prehistoric rock formations. Along the walls flanking a ramp are color photographs showing Moore's major sculptures in their natural locations, which fully reveal their magnificent dimensions.

The collection of European old masters ranges from the 14th century to the French impressionists and beyond. An octagonal room is filled with works by Pissarro, Monet, Boudin, Sisley, and

Downtown Toronto Attractions

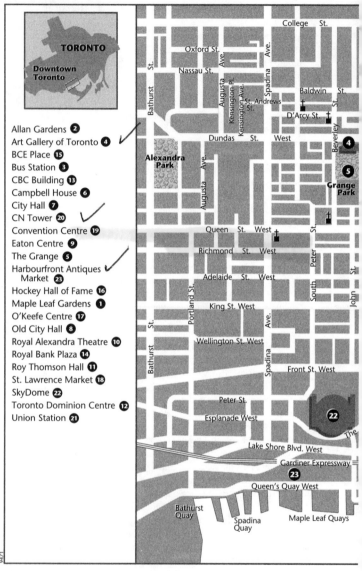

Renoir. De Kooning's *Two Women on a Wharf* and Karel Appel's *Black Landscape* are just two of the more modern examples. Among the sculpture you'll find Picasso's *Poupée* and Brancusi's *First Cry,* two beauties.

Behind the gallery and connected by an arcade stands the **Grange** (1817), Toronto's oldest surviving brick house. It was in fact the gallery's first permanent home. Originally the home of the Boulton

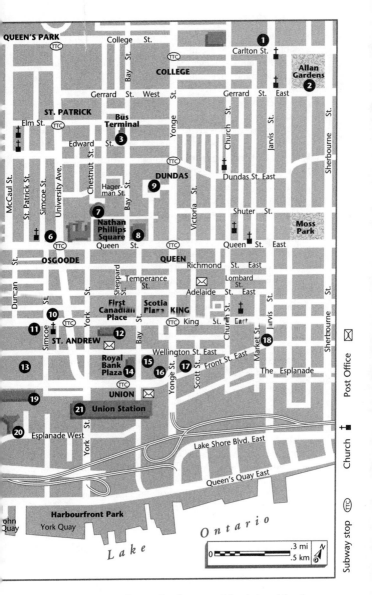

Subwaystop (TTC)   Church +■   Post Office ☒

family, it was a gathering place for many of the city's social and political leaders as well as for such eminent guests as Matthew Arnold, Prince Kropotkin, and Winston Churchill. Today it's a living museum of mid-19th-century Toronto life, having been meticulously restored and furnished to reflect the 1830s. Entrance is free with admission to the art gallery.

The gallery has an attractive restaurant/atrium bar open for lunch and dinner as well as a cafeteria, a gallery shop, plus a full program of films, concerts, and lectures.

Admission: $7.50 adults, $15 families (two adults plus children), $4 students and seniors, free for children under 12. Free on Wed 5–10pm.

Open: Wed 10am–10pm, Thurs–Mon 10am–5:30pm. The Grange is usually open the same hours. **Closed:** Christmas Day and New Year's Day. **Subway:** St. Patrick on the University line; or take the subway to Dundas and the streetcar west.

★ **Royal Ontario Museum,** 100 Queen's Park Crescent.
☎ **586-5549** or **586-5551** for 24-hour information.

The ROM, as it's affectionately called, recently completed a $55 million renovation and opened two new galleries in 1994. The Sigmund Samuel Canadiana Gallery displays more than 1,200 objects from the collection of early Canadian decorative arts and paintings revealing in a very concrete way the French and English contributions to Canadian culture. In the thematic historical displays you'll see the finest examples of glass, silver, woodenware, ceramics, toys, weather vanes, and more. In addition, the collection contains the famous McCrea models of buildings, farm implements, and tools, which provide a miniature representation of early rural Ontario life. The Gallery of Indigenous Peoples features changing exhibitions that explore the past and present cultures of indigenous peoples of Canada.

Among the museum's other highlights are the Roman Gallery (the most extensive collection in Canada), the world-class textile collection, nine life science galleries (devoted to evolution, mammals, reptiles, and botany), and the Discovery Gallery, which is in fact a minimuseum where kids and adults can touch authentic artifacts from Egyptian scarabs to English military helmets. The Bat Cave Gallery is a miniature replica of the St. Clair bat cave in Jamaica, complete with more than 4,000 very authentic-looking bat models. The Chinese collection is numbered among the top 10 in the world, and includes the Bishop White Gallery, which displays three impressive wall paintings of Buddhist and Daoist deities (ca. 1300) and 14 monumental wooden Buddhist sculptures dating from the 12th to 16th centuries. The Ming Tomb Gallery features elements from a Ming tomb—a series of gateways and guardian figures arranged in typical funerary order. Galleries are also devoted to Ontario and Canadiana, and to many other subjects. A favorite with the kids is the Dinosaur Gallery.

Admission (including admission to the George R. Gardiner Museum of Ceramic Art and the Astrocentre of the McLaughlin Planetarium): $7 adults, $4 seniors and students, $3.50 children 5–14, $15 families, free for children under 5; free for seniors all day on Tues, free for all Tues 4:30–8pm.

Open: Mon and Wed–Sat 10am–6pm, Tues 10am–8pm, Sun 11am–6pm. **Closed:** Easter, Christmas, and New Year's. **Subway:** Museum or St. George.

George R. Gardiner Museum of Ceramic Art, 111 Queen's Park. ☎ **586-8080.**

Across the street from the ROM, the George R. Gardiner Museum houses a diverse display of porcelain and pottery. There are four galleries. The pre-Columbian gallery contains fantastic Olmec and Mayan figures, plus objects from Ecuador, Colombia, and Peru. The majolica gallery displays modern and spectacular 16th- and 17th-century pieces from Florence, Faenza, and Venice. There's also a Delftware section displaying 17th-century chargers and other examples.

Upstairs the galleries feature 18th-century continental and English porcelain—Meissen, Sèvres, Worcester, Chelsea, Derby, and other great names. The collection includes more than 125 porcelain figurines from the commedia dell'arte as well as more than 100 porcelain scent bottles. Among other highlights are the pieces from the Swan Service—a 2,200-piece set that took four years (1737–41) to make. There's one oddity—a very prettily molded and painted bourdaloue (portable urinal).

Admission: (including admission to the Royal Ontario Museum) $7 adults, $4 seniors and students, $3.50 children, $15 families.

Open: Tues–Sat 10am–5pm, Sun 11am–5pm. From Victoria Day to Labor Day, it's open until 7:30pm on Tues. **Closed:** Christmas and New Year's Day.

★ **Ontario Science Centre,** 770 Don Mills Rd., Don Mills. ☎ **696-3127.**

Described as everything from the world's most technical fun fair to a hands-on museum of the 21st century, the Science Centre, at Eglinton Avenue East, holds a series of wonders for adult and child—no fewer than 700 hands-on experiments.

The building itself is another of architect Raymond Moriyama's miracles. Instead of flattening the ravine and bulldozing the trees on the site, Moriyama designed to the contours of the ravine so that a series of glass-enclosed escalators providing views of the natural surroundings take you down an escarpment to the main exhibition halls. Supposedly Moriyama built penalty clauses into the subcontractors' contracts for each and every tree destroyed!

Wherever you look there are things to touch, push, pull, or crank: Test your reflexes, balance, heart rate, and grip strength; play with computers and binary-system games and puzzles; shunt slides of butterfly wings, bedbugs, fish scales, or feathers under the microscope; tease your brain with a variety of optical illusions; land a spaceship on the moon; watch bees making honey; try to lift sponge building blocks with a mechanical grip; see how many lights you can light or how high you can elevate a balloon with your own pedal power. The fun goes on and on as you explore more than 700 participational exhibits in 10 themed exhibit halls. It's a wonder I ever made it home.

Throughout, there are small theaters showing film and slide shows, plus regular 20-minute presentations on lasers, metal casting, and high-voltage electricity (watch your friend's hair stand on end).

Facilities include a licensed restaurant and lounge, cafeteria, and science shop. By the way, with 1 million people visiting every year, the best time to get to the museum is promptly at 10am, so you can play without too much interference.

Admission: $7.50 adults, $5.50 young adults, $3 seniors and children 5–10, $17 families; children under 5 free. Parking is $4.

Open: Thurs–Tues 10am–6pm, Wed until 8pm. **Closed:** Christmas Day. **Subway:** Eglinton; then take the Eglinton bus east to Don Mills Road.

★ **The Metropolitan Zoo,** Meadowvale Rd., north of Hwy. 401, Scarborough. ☎ **392-5900.**

Covering 710 acres of woodland and meadow in Scarborough, the zoo contains some 5,000 animals and thousands of plants. Many of the plants and animals are housed in six pavilions (including Africa, Indo-Malaya, Australasia, and the Americas) or outdoors on four well-marked trails. It's a photographer's dream.

Six miles of walkways offer access to all areas of the zoo, or two modes of transportation can be used. During the warmer months the Zoomobile takes the zoo-goer around the major walkways, viewing the animals contained in outdoor facilities. The Monorail Ride, which runs year round, travels through the beautiful Rouge River Valley where animals native to Canada are displayed.

Facilities include restaurants, a gift shop, first aid, and a family center; strollers, wagons, and wheelchairs are also available. The zoo is equipped with ramps and washrooms for the disabled. The African pavilion is also equipped with an elevator for strollers and wheelchairs. There's ample parking and plenty of picnic areas with tables.

For zoo information, contact Metro Toronto Zoo, P.O. Box 280, West Hill, ON, M1E 4R5 (☎ **392-5900**). For transportation schedules, check with the TTC (☎ **393-4636**).

Did You Know . . . ?

- The first singing commercial was supposedly created by Torontonian Ernie Bushnell in 1926 for the local Jehovah's Witness radio station.

- Author Arthur Hailey (*Hotel, Airport*) worked as an assistant editor at *Bus and Truck Transport,* a Maclean-Hunter magazine.

- The Ontario Legislature sits on land that was originally occupied (appropriately, some say) by a lunatic asylum.

- Torontonian Norman Breakey invented the paint roller in 1940.

- The population of York (Toronto) was 703 in 1812.

- Canada's first postage stamp was created in Toronto by Sir Sanford Fleming in 1851.

Admission: $9.75 adults, $7 seniors and children 12–17, $5 children 4–11; children under 3 free.

Open: Summer daily 9:30am–7pm; winter daily 9:30am–4:30pm. Last admission is one hour before closing. **Closed:** Christmas Day. **Subway:** Kennedy; then take bus no. 86A north. **Directions:** By car from downtown, take the Don Valley Parkway to Highway 401 east and exit on Meadowvale Road.

⭐ **The McMichael Collection,** Islington Ave., Kleinburg. ☎ **905/893-1121.**

Located in Kleinburg, 25 miles north of the city, this collection of Canadian art is worth a visit for the setting alone.

You'll approach the gallery through quiet stands of pine trees until you reach a log-and-stone building specially designed to house the Canadian landscapes within. The lobby itself is a work of art: A pitched roof soars to a height of 27 feet on massive rafters of Douglas fir, and throughout the gallery panoramic windows look south over white pine, cedar, ash, and birch.

The gallery houses works by Canada's famous group of landscape painters, the "Group of Seven"—Arthur Lismer, Frederick Varley, and Lawren Harris, among others—as well as by Tom Thomson, David Milne, Emily Carr, and their contemporaries. These artists, inspired by the turn-of-the-century Canadian wilderness, particularly in Algonquin Park and northern Ontario, recorded its rugged landscape in highly individualistic styles.

An impressive collection of Inuit and contemporary Native Canadian art and sculpture is also on display.

Founded by Robert and Signe McMichael, the gallery began in 1965 when they donated their property, home, and collection to the Province of Ontario. Since then the collection has expanded to include over 5,000 works. Still, its unique atmosphere has been preserved—log-and-barnwood walls, fieldstone fireplaces, and homey decorative touches like hooked rugs and earthenware urns filled with flowers and dried leaves.

Admission: $6 adults, $3 seniors and students; children under 5 free.

Open: Apr–Oct daily 10am–5pm; Nov–Mar Tues–Sun 10am–4pm.

Canada's Wonderland, 9580 Jane St., Vaughan.

☎ **416/832-7000,** or **416/832-2205** for a recording, **416/832-8131** for concert information at the Kingswood Music Theatre. For information write P.O. Box 624, Vaughan, ON, L6A 1S6.

Nineteen miles (or 30 minutes) north of Toronto lies Canada's answer to Disney World.

The 300-acre park features more than 140 attractions, including 50 rides, a 10-acre waterpark, a participatory play area, and live shows. Among the most popular rides are Days of Thunder, which puts you in the driver's seat during a 200-mile-an-hour high-stakes stock car race; Jet Scream, a 360-degree looping starship; Vortex, Canada's only

Midtown Toronto Attractions

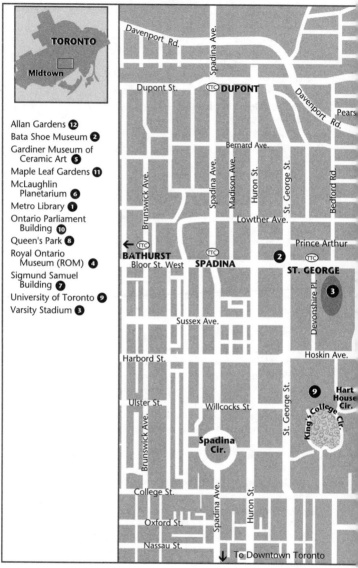

suspended roller coaster; The Bat, a backwards/forwards looping coaster; Skyrider, a stand-up looping coaster; and the Mighty Canadian Minebuster, the largest wooden roller coaster in the park. Splash Works has 16 water rides, from speed slides to tube rides and special scaled-down slides and pool for kids. At Timberwolf Falls riders plunge down a five-story waterfall. Shows range from the spectacular Paramount on Ice to a sea lion show. Top-name entertainers

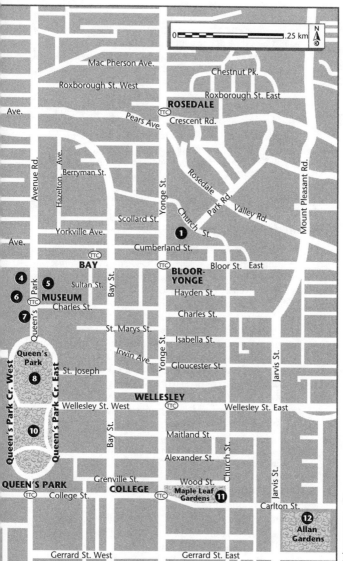

Subway stop ⓉⓉⒸ

appear at the Kingswood Theatre. To add to the thrills for kids and adults, Klingons, Vulcans, Romulans, and Bajorans (along with Hanna-Barbera characters) stroll around the park. Additional attractions include mini-golf, batting cages, restaurants, and shops.

You'll probably need eight hours to see everything. If you picnic on the grounds and forgo buying souvenirs, a family of four can do the park for about $90. Watch out, though, for the extra attractions not included in the admission pass, particularly the many "games of skill," which the kids love but the purse hates.

Admission: Pay One Price Passport, including a day's unlimited rides and shows (excluding food, games, merchandise, and the music theater), $29 adults, $14.45 children 3–6; children under 3 free. Grounds admission only is $18. Parking is $6.50.

Open: June–Labor Day daily 10am–10pm; May and Sept–Oct Sat–Sun 10am–8pm. **Closed:** Early Oct to early May. **Subway:** Yorkdale or York Mills; then GO Express Bus. **Directions:** By car, take Yonge Street north to Highway 401 and travel west to Highway 400. Go north on Highway 400 to the Rutherford Road exit and follow the signs. Exit at Major MacKenzie if you're coming south.

2 More Attractions

Architectural Highlights

City Hall, Queen St. W. ☎ 392-7341.

An architectural spectacle, City Hall houses the Mayor's office and the city's administrative offices. Daringly designed in the early 1960s by Finnish architect Viljo Revell, it consists of a low podium topped by the flying-saucer-shaped Council Chamber enfolded between two curved towers. Its interior is as dramatic as its exterior. A cafeteria and dining room are located in the basement.

In front stretches **Nathan Phillips Square** (named after the mayor who initiated the project), where in summer you can sit and contemplate the flower gardens, fountains, and reflecting pool (which doubles as a skating rink in winter), as well as listen to concerts. Here also stands Henry Moore's *Three-Way Piece No. 2,* locally referred to as *The Archer,* purchased through a public subscription fund, and the Peace Garden, commemorating Toronto's sesquicentennial in 1984. In contrast, to the east stands the **Old City Hall,** a green-copper-roofed Victorian Romanesque-style building.

Admission: Free.

Open: Self-guided tours Mon–Fri 8:30am–4:30pm. **Subway:** Queen; then walk west to Bay or take the Queen Street streetcar west one stop.

Eaton Centre, Dundas and Yonge sts. ☎ 598-8700.

Buttressed at both ends by 30-story skyscrapers, this high-tech center, which cost over $250 million, stretches from Dundas Street and Yonge Street south to Queen Street and encompasses six million square feet. **Eaton's Department Store** takes up one million square feet, and the rest is filled with over 320 stores and restaurants and 2 garages. Some 20 million people shop here annually.

Inside, the structure opens into the impressive **Galleria,** an 866-foot-long glass-domed arcade dotted with benches, orchids, palm trees, and fountains; it's further adorned by Michael Snow's soaring

Canada geese, entitled *Step Flight.* Three tiers rise above, reached by escalator and glass elevators, giving glorious views over this Crystal Palace and Milan-style masterpiece designed by Eb Zeidler (who also designed Ontario Place). Here, rain or shine, you can enjoy the sights, sounds, and aromas in comfort—don't be surprised by the twittering of the sparrows, some of whom have decided that this environment is as pleasant as the outdoors.

One more amazing fact about this construction: It was built around two of Toronto's oldest landmarks—**Trinity Church** (1847) and **Scadding House** (☎ **598-4521**), home of Trinity's rector, Dr. Scadding—because the public demanded that the developers allow the sun to continue to shine on the church's twin towers. It does!

Admission: Free.

Open: Mon–Fri 10am–9pm, Sat 9:30am–6pm, Sun noon–5pm. **Subway:** Dundas or Queen.

Metropolitan Toronto Reference Library, 789 Yonge St. ☎ **393-7000.**

If more libraries were built like this one, perhaps study would become more of a pastime and learning would come out of the dim and musty closets and into the world. Step inside—a pool and a waterfall gently screen out the street noise, and pine fencelike partitions, like those you find along sand dunes, undulate through the area. Step farther inside and the space opens dramatically to the sky. Every corner is flooded with light and air. I envy the citizens of Toronto their designer/architect Raymond Moriyama.

Admission: Free.

Open: Summer Mon–Thurs 9am–8pm, Fri 9am–6pm, Sat 9am–5pm; winter Mon–Thurs 9am–9pm, Fri 9am–6pm, Sat 9am–5pm, Sun 1:30–5pm. **Subway:** Bloor.

Frommer's Favorite Toronto Experiences

A Picnic on the Toronto Islands   A short ferry ride will transport you to another world of lagoons and rush-lined backwaters, miles away from the urban tarmac—a world of houseboats and bicycles, a place to stroll beside the weeping willows.

A Day at Harbourfront   Bring a model boat; watch artisans blowing glass; take a sailing lesson; tour the harbor; shop the quay and the antique mart—and this is just a beginning.

A Day at the Beaches   Stroll along the boardwalk, picnic in the adjacent parkland and gardens, and browse the stores one block from the beach.

An Afternoon at Kleinburg   A unique Canadian and Toronto experience—the Group of Seven landscape artists' work displayed in an idyllic setting.

Ontario Legislature, 111 Wellesley St. W., at University Ave.
☎ 325-7500.

East of the university, at the northern end of University Avenue, lies Queen's Park, surrounding the rose-tinted sandstone-and-granite Ontario Parliament Buildings, which are profusely carved, with stately domes, arches, and porte cocheres. Drop in around 2pm when the legislature is in session (fall through spring) for some pithy comments during the question period, or take one of the regular tours. It's best to call ahead to check times.

Admission: Free.

Open: From Victoria Day to Labor Day, tours given every half hour on weekends 9–11:30am and 1–4pm; call ahead at other times.
Subway: Queen's Park.

Royal Bank Plaza, Front and Bay sts.

Shimmering in the sun, Royal Bank Plaza looks like a pillar of gold—and in a way it is. More importantly, it's a masterpiece of design and architectural drama. Two triangular towers of bronze mirror glass flank a 130-foot-high glass-walled banking hall. The external walls of the towers are built in a serrated configuration so that they reflect a phenomenal mosaic of color from the skies and surrounding buildings.

In the banking hall, hundreds of aluminum cylinders hang from the ceiling, the work of Venezuelan sculptor Jesus Raphael Soto, while two levels below there's a waterfall and pine-tree setting naturally illuminated from the hall above.

Admission: Free.

Open: Year round. **Subway:** Union.

Did You Know...?

- Ernest Hemingway was hired by the *Toronto Star* at age 19 and was paid $150 per year.

- Babe Ruth hit the first of his 714 major-league home runs at Hanlan's Point Stadium on the Toronto Islands in 1914. He also managed to pitch a shutout.

- 2,500 ounces of gold were used as a coloring agent in the 14,000 windows of the Royal Bank building.

- The first injection of insulin was given at Toronto General Hospital in 1922.

- Standard time was invented by Torontonian Sir Sanford Fleming.

- Yonge Street is listed in the *Guinness Book of World Records* as the longest street in the world—1,178 miles.

- When Casa Loma was built between 1911 and 1914, it was the only castle in the world that had an electrically operated elevator and an indoor swimming pool. It also had solid-gold bathroom fixtures.

Cemeteries

Mount Pleasant Cemetery, 1643 Yonge St., or 375 Mount Pleasant Rd., north of St. Clair Ave. ☎ **485-9129.**

Home to one of the finest tree collections in North America, this cemetery is also the final resting place of many fascinating people. Of particular note are Glenn Gould, celebrated classical pianist; Drs. Banting and Best, codiscoverers of insulin; golfer George Knudson; and the Massey and Eaton families, whose mausoleums are impressive architectural monuments. Prime Minister William Lyon Mackenzie King; Canada's greatest war hero Lt. Col. William Barker; world king of the gypsies Zliticho Demitro; and 52 victims of Air Canada Flight 621, which crashed en route to Los Angeles in 1970 are also laid to rest here.

Admission: Free.

Open: Daily 8am–dusk.

Necropolis, 200 Winchester St., at Sumach St. ☎ **923-7911.**

This is one of the city's oldest cemeteries (1850). Many of the remains that are buried here, though, were originally buried in Potters Field, where Yorkville stands today, and were moved from there and reinterred here.

Before strolling through the cemetery, pick up a History Tour at the office. You'll find the graves of William Lyon Mackenzie, leader of the 1837 Rebellion, and his followers Samuel Lount and Peter Matthews—hanged for their part in the rebellion. Anderson Abbot, the first Canadian-born black surgeon; Joseph Tyrrell, who discovered dinosaurs in Alberta; Ned Hanlan, world-champion oarsman; Malcolm McEacheran, killed by the Fenians at the Battle of Ridgeway; George Brown, founder of the *Globe;* John Ross Robertson, founder of the *Toronto Telegram;* mayors, lawyers, architects . . . all these and more may be found in this 15-acre cemetery beyond the porte cochere and Gothic Revival chapel, designed by Henry Langley, who is also buried in the cemetery.

Admission: Free.

Open: Daily 8am–dusk.

IMPRESSIONS

It is impossible to give it anything but commendation. It is not squalid like Birmingham, or cramped like Canton, or hellish like New York or tiresome like Nice. It is all right. . . .
—Rupert Brooke, *Letters from America* (1913)

"One of the worst blue-devil haunts on the face of the earth," cried John Gaunt the Scottish immigrant poet in the days of the Family Compact. "The city has more grasping, greedy unctuous people in it than any other city in the world," shouts Ralph Maybank of Winnipeg, in the Parliament of Canada.
—Bruce Hutchinson, *The Unknown Country* (1943)

Uptown Toronto Attractions

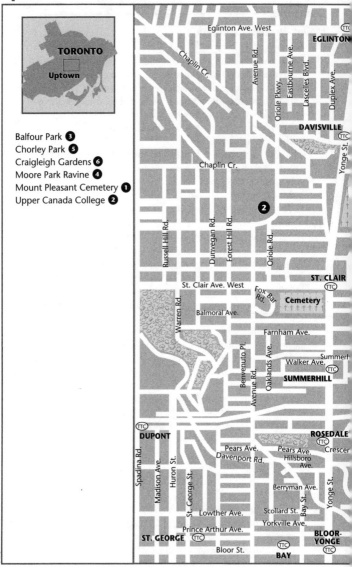

Balfour Park ❸
Chorley Park ❺
Craigleigh Gardens ❻
Moore Park Ravine ❹
Mount Pleasant Cemetery ❶
Upper Canada College ❷

Colleges & Universities ─────────

University of Toronto, 21 King's College Circle. ☎ **978-4111** or
978-5000 during summer.

Just south of the Royal Ontario Museum sprawls the main campus
of the University of Toronto, with its quiet wooded pathways,

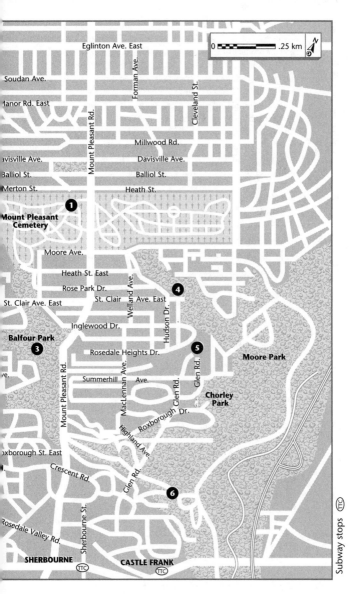

Subway stops ⓉⓉⒸ

ivy-covered buildings, and spreading lawns. Many scientific break-throughs have been made here. Insulin was discovered here, the first heart pacemaker was built here, and baby's pabulum was developed here.

Many famous Canadians have graduated from one or another of the colleges that make up the university, which was originally founded as King's College in 1849 and later refounded as the nonsectarian University of Toronto. Among the many Canadian notable graduates are several prime ministers, including Mackenzie King and Lester B. Pearson; politicians, such as former Ontario Premier William Davis and Sens. Keith Davey and Stephen Lewis; as well as such intellectual and literary lights as Dr. Norman Bethune, Robertson Davies, Morley Callaghan, Margaret Atwood, Northrop Frye, and Harold Innis.

Today the university has 52,000 students (36,000 full-time) and 6,200 faculty, spread over three campuses. Wander through the downtown St. George campus (see Walking Tour 4 in Chapter 7) and note the architecturally interesting buildings, such as the Gothic-inspired Hart House.

Admission: Free.

Open: June–Aug, tours leave from Hart House on Wellesley Street Mon–Fri at 10:30am and 1 and 2:30pm. Call **978-4111** at other times. **Subway:** Queen's Park or St. George.

Historic Buildings

Campbell House, 160 Queen St. W. ☎ 597-0227.

West of City Hall and just across the street from Osgoode Hall (see below), at the corner of University Avenue, sits the 1822 mansion of Loyalist and sixth chief justice of Upper Canada Sir William Campbell. In 1829 he retired to this mansion, where he resided with his pet alligator until he died in 1834 despite a diet of snipe prescribed by his physician.

Admission: $2.50 adults; $1.25 seniors, students, and children.

Open: Mid-Oct to late May Mon–Fri 9:30–11:30am and 2:30–4:30pm; late May to mid-Oct Mon–Fri 9:30–4:30pm, Sat–Sun noon–4:30pm. **Subway:** Osgoode.

Casa Loma, 1 Austin Terrace. ☎ 923-1171.

Every city has its folly, and Toronto has a charming one—complete with Elizabethan-style chimneys, Rhineland turrets, secret passageways, an 800-foot underground tunnel, and a mellifluous-sounding name: Casa Loma.

Sir Henry Pellatt, who built it between 1911 and 1914 at a cost of $3.5 million (plus $1.5 million for furnishings), had a lifelong and incurably romantic fascination with medieval castles—so he decided to build his own. He studied European medieval castles and gathered materials and furnishings, bringing marble, glass, and paneling from Europe, teak from Asia, and oak and walnut from prime areas of North America; and he imported Scottish stonemasons to build the massive walls that surround the six-acre site.

It's a fascinating place to explore. It has 98 rooms, including the majestic Great Hall, with its 60-foot-high hammerbeam ceiling; the Oak Room, where three artisans took three years to fashion the paneling; the Conservatory, with its elegant bronze doors, stained-glass dome, and pink-and-green marble; the battlements and tower; Peacock Alley, designed after Windsor Castle; Sir Henry's suite, containing a shower with an 18-inch-diameter shower head; the 1,700-bottle wine cellar; and the 800-foot tunnel to the stables (which alone cost $250,000), where horses were quartered amid the luxury of Spanish tile and mahogany. The house originally contained, by the way, 30 bathrooms, 25 fireplaces, 5,000 lights, and 3 bowling alleys. In 1923 when Pellatt was near bankruptcy, the house was auctioned for $131,600. How's that for real estate risk? The tour is self-guided; you'll be given an audio cassette on arrival.

Admission: $8 adults, $4.50 seniors and children 6–16.

Open: Daily 10am–4pm. **Subway:** Dupont; then walk two blocks north.

Colborne Lodge, High Park. ☎ 392-6916.

When John Howard, city surveyor and architect, had this house built in 1836 to 1837, it was way out in the country and difficult to travel to in the harsh winters. It's a charming English-style Regency cottage with a three-sided veranda that was built to take advantage of the view of Lake Ontario and the Humber River. In 1873 Howard donated the house and surrounding land to the city in return for an annual salary and so created High Park—a great recreational area.

Admission: $3.50 adults, $2.75 seniors and children 13–18, $2.50 children 12 and under.

Open: Jan 7–Mar 31, Sat–Sun and holidays noon–5pm; Apr 1–May 31 and Sept 1 to mid-Nov, Tues–Fri 9:30am–4pm, Sat–Sun and holidays noon–5pm; June 1–Aug 31, Tues–Sat 9:30am–5pm, Sun and holidays noon–5pm. Call ahead for hours in other months.

Fort York, Garrison Rd., off Fleet St. ☎ 392-6907.

Established by Lieutenant Governor Simcoe in 1793 to defend "little muddy York," as Toronto was then known, Fort York, between Bathurst Street and Strachan Avenue, was sacked by Americans in 1813. You can tour the soldiers' and officers' quarters and clamber over the ramparts, as well as view demonstrations and exhibits. The fort is two blocks east of Exhibition Place.

Admission: $5 adults, $3.25 teenagers 13–18 and seniors, $3 children 6–12.

Open: Summer (June–Oct) Tues–Sun 9:30am–5pm; winter Tues–Sun 10am–5pm. **Subway:** Bathurst; then streetcar no. 511 south.

The Grange, 317 Dundas St. W. ☎ 977-0414, ext. 237.

This is the oldest brick house in the city, and from 1910 to 1922 it was the first home of the Art Gallery. It was built in 1817 by D'Arcy Boulton, Jr., at the center of the Boulton estate, which extended from Queen Street to Bloor Street. The house passed first to D'Arcy's widow; then to her son; and then to his widow, who married Goldwin Smith, an English historian and professor at the University of Toronto, who made the Grange an intellectual and social center. He donated it to the Art Gallery. Today it has been restored to reflect the 1840s.

Admission: Included in admission fee to the Art Gallery.

Open: Wed 10am–10pm, Thurs–Mon 10am–5:30pm. **Closed:** Major holidays. **Subway:** St. Patrick or Dundas; then take a streetcar west.

Mackenzie House, 82 Bond St. ☎ 392-6915.

Friends and fund-raisers got together to purchase this house two blocks east of Yonge Street and south of Dundas Street for William Lyon Mackenzie, leader of the 1837 rebellion, who lived here from 1859 to 1861. This typical mid-19th-century brick row house gives you some idea of what Toronto must have looked like then, when the streets were lined with similar buildings. It's furnished in 1850s style, and in the back there's a print shop designed after Mackenzie's own.

Admission: $3.50 adults, $2.75 seniors and teenagers 13–18, $2.50 children under 12.

Open: Tues–Sat 9:30am–5pm, Sun and holidays noon–5pm. **Subway:** Dundas.

Osgoode Hall, 130 Queen St. W. ☎ 947-3300.

West of City Hall extends an impressive, elegant wrought-iron fence in front of an equally gracious building, Osgoode Hall, currently the home of the Law Society of Upper Canada and the superior courts of the province. (It is said that the fence was originally built to keep cows from trampling the flower beds.) Tours of the interior will show you the splendor of the grand staircase, the rotunda, the Great Library, and the fine portrait and sculpture collection. Building began in 1829 on this structure, troops were billeted here after the Rebellion of 1837, and the buildings now house the headquarters of Ontario's legal profession and several magnificent courtrooms—including one using materials from London's Old Bailey.

Admission: Free.

Open: Tours given Mon–Fri at 1 and 1:20pm in July–Aug only. Museum, year round Mon–Fri 10am–3:30pm. **Subway:** Osgoode.

Industrial Tours

Toronto Stock Exchange, Exchange Tower, 2 First Canadian Place, at the northeast corner of Adelaide and York sts. ☎ **947-4676.**

This is the largest public securities market in Canada, where almost $1 billion worth of stock is traded each day. Public presentations including a video and a computer demonstration are given at 2pm Tuesday through Friday.

Admission: Free.

Open: Mon–Fri 9am–4:30pm; public presentations are given Tues–Fri at 2pm.

Markets

Kensington Market, Kensington and Augusta aves. and Baldwin St.

In the early 20th century Kensington Market was a thriving market in the heart of what was then the Jewish community. Today the area is part Portuguese, part Caribbean, part Jewish, and part Asian. There is no central market building but rather a number of stalls and stores that stretch along several streets—Augusta and Kensington avenues and Baldwin Street. Again, get here early for the best scene.

Open: Daily. **Subway:** College or Dundas; then take the streetcar west.

St. Lawrence Market, 92 Front St. E. ☎ 392-7219.

This handsome food market is housed in a vast building that has been constructed around the facade of the second city hall that was built in 1850. Vendors sell fresh meat, fish, fruit, vegetables and dairy products as well as other foodstuffs. Best time to visit is early Saturday morning shortly after the farmers have brought their wares into town.

Open: Tues–Sat. **Subway:** King or Union.

Museums

The Bata Shoe Museum, 327 Bloor St. W. at the corner of St. George. ☎ 979-9199.

Imelda Marcos or anyone else interested in shoes and fashion history will love this museum housing the personal collection—9,000 items—of the Bata family. Now located in a brand-new building, scheduled to open in spring 1995, the three floors of galleries will display shoes from all over the world and from every time period. The main gallery, All About Shoes, is home to the plaster cast of the first human footprints discovered in Africa by anthropologist Mary Leakey, which date to 4 million B.C. It then traces the development of shoemaking, featuring shoes of all types—including moon boots and deep-sea diving boots as well as shoes of the rich and famous. In addition to the general historic exhibition, one display focuses on Canadian footwear fashioned by the Inuit, while another highlights 19th-century ladies' footwear. Another smaller gallery, which will house changing exhibits, currently contains shoe-related original art from children's literature.

Admission: $6 adults, $4 seniors/students, $2 children 5–14, $12 families.

Open: Tues–Wed and Fri–Sat 10am–5pm, Thurs 10am–8pm, Sun noon–5pm.

Hockey Hall of Fame, 30 Yonge St., at Front in BCE Place. ☎ 360-7735.

Ice hockey fans will thrill to see the original Stanley Cup (donated in 1893 by Lord Stanley of Preston), a replica of the Montréal Canadiens' locker room, Terry Sawchuck's goalie gear, Newsy Lalonde's skates, and the stick that Max Bentley used, along with photographs of the personalities and great moments in hockey history. Interactive displays and videos make it fun for all.

Admission: $8.50 adults, $5.50 seniors and children 3–13; children under 3 free.

Open: Summer Mon–Wed and Sat 9am–6pm, Thurs–Fri 9am–9pm, Sun 10am–6pm; winter Mon–Sat 9am–6pm, Sun 10am–6pm.

Black Creek Pioneer Village, 1000 Murray Ross Pkwy., Downsview, at Steeles Ave. and Jane St. ☎ **736-1733.**

Life here moves at the gentle pace of mid-19th-century rural Ontario. You can watch the authentically dressed villagers going about their chores—spinning, sewing, rail splitting, sheepshearing, and threshing. Enjoy their cooking, wander through the cozily furnished homesteads, visit the working mill, shop at the general store, and rumble past the farm animals in a horse-drawn wagon. There are over 30 restored buildings to explore in a beautifully landscaped village. The year is filled with special events from the great Easter egg hunt to Christmas by lamplight.

For your convenience, there's a dining room serving lunch and afternoon tea (open May to Thanksgiving and during December).

Admission: $7.50 adults, $5 seniors, $3.25 children and students; children under 4 free.

Open: May–Aug daily 10am–5pm; Sept Wed–Sun 10am–5pm; Oct–Nov Wed–Sun 10am–4:30pm; Dec daily 10am–4:30pm; Mar–Apr Wed–Sun 10am–4:30pm. **Closed:** Christmas Day and Jan to mid-Mar. **Subway:** Finch; then take bus no. 60 to Jane Street.

Canada Sports Hall of Fame, Exhibition Place. ☎ **260-6789.**

Located in the center of Exhibition Place, this three-floor sports hall is devoted to the country's greatest athletes in all major sports. It offers displays complemented by touch-screen computers that will tell you everything you could wish to know about particular sports personalities, famous race horses, and Canada's sport heritage.

Admission: Free.

Open: Daily 10am–4:30pm. **Subway:** Bathurst; then take streetcar no. 511 south to the end of the line.

Marine Museum, Exhibition Place. ☎ **392-1765.**

On the grounds of Exhibition Place stands the Marine Museum, which interprets the history of Toronto Harbour and its relation to the Great Lakes. In summer, visitors can also board the fully restored 1932 *Ned Hanlan,* the last steam tugboat to sail on Lake Ontario.

Admission: $3.50 adults, $2.75 teenagers 13–18 and seniors, $2.50 children under 12.

Open: Tues–Fri 9:30am–5pm, Sat–Sun noon–5pm. **Subway:** Bathurst; then take streetcar no. 511 south to the end of the line.

McLaughlin Planetarium, 100 Queen's Park Crescent. ☎ **586-5736.**

Located directly south of the Royal Ontario Museum, the McLaughlin Planetarium invites visitors to recline in the Theatre of the Stars under a 23-meter (75-foot) dome while a Zeiss Universal projector, and audiovisual system re-create the cosmos before their eyes. Laser-light concerts are also presented in the theater on a regular basis featuring brilliant multicolored three-dimensional laser light effects choreographed to rock and pop music. Complementing the Theatre of the Stars is the Astrocentre, a gallery displaying early astronomical instruments, a solar telescope, and a variety of interactive exhibits.

Admission: Star shows $5.50 adults, $3.50 student/senior, $2.75 children 14 years and under. Laser shows $8.50 all tickets, $6.50 children 14 and under at weekend matinees only.

Open: Call for show times. **Subway:** Museum or St. George.

The Museum for Textiles, 55 Centre Ave. ☎ **599-5321,** or **599-5515** for taped information.

This fascinating museum displays not only what you'd expect—fine Oriental rugs—but also tapestries from all over the world, including African storytelling cloth.

Admission: $5 adults, $4 students and seniors, $14 family.

Open: Tues–Fri 11am–5pm, Sat–Sun noon–5pm. **Subway:** Osgoode or St. Patrick.

Neighborhoods

The Beaches

This is one of the neighborhoods that makes Toronto a unique city. For here, near the terminus of the Queen Street East tram line, you can stroll or cycle along the lakefront boardwalk. Because of its natural assets it has become a much sought after residential neighborhood and there are plenty of well-stocked and eminently browsable stores along Queen Street. Just beyond Waverley Road, you can turn down through Kew Gardens to the boardwalk and walk all the way past the Olympic Pool (jam-packed in summer) to Ashbridge's Bay Park.

⭐ **Chinatown,** Dundas St. and Spadina Ave.

Stretching along Dundas Street west from Bay Street to Spadina Avenue and north and south along Spadina Avenue, Chinatown, home to many of Toronto's 350,000 Chinese citizens, is packed with fascinating shops and restaurants. Even the street signs are in Chinese here.

In **Dragon City,** a large shopping mall on Spadina that's staffed and patronized by Chinese, you'll find all kinds of stores, some selling exotic Chinese preserves like cuttlefish, lemon ginger, whole mango, ginseng, and antler, and others specializing in Asian books, tapes, and records, as well as fashions and foods. Downstairs, a fast-food court features Korean, Indonesian, Chinese, and Japanese cuisines.

As you stroll through Chinatown, stop at the **Kim Moon Bakery** on Dundas Street West (☎ **977-1933**) for Chinese pastries and a pork bun or go to one of the tea stores. A walk through Chinatown at night is especially exciting—the sidewalks are filled with people and neon lights shimmer everywhere. You'll pass windows where ducks hang gleaming, noodle houses, record stores selling the Top 10 in Chinese, and trading companies filled with all kinds of Asian produce. Another stopping place might be the **New Asia Supermarket,** around the corner from Dundas Street at 299 Spadina Ave.

For details see Walking Tour 3 in Chapter 7.

Greektown—The East End

Out along the Danforth stretches a Greek neighborhood where you can find some of the most crowded and frenetic restaurants in the city as well as traditional Greek merchants and stores—like Akropol, a Greek bakery that displays stunning multitiered wedding cakes in the window. It's an eclectic neighborhood. Along with the Greek food vendors and travel agents you'll also find stores like the Scandinavian Shoppe, which sells great glass and ceramics; Big Kids Hafta Play Too, which has some really cool T-shirts; and some New Age and alternative stores.

Mirvish Village

One of the city's most famous characters is Honest Ed Mirvish, who started his career in the 1950s with his no-frills store at the corner of Markham and Bloor streets (one block west of Bathurst), where the signs screaming bargains hit you from every direction. Among other things, Ed Mirvish rose to save the Royal Alexandra Theatre on King Street from demolition, established a whole row of adjacent restaurants for theater patrons, and finally developed this block-long area with art galleries, restaurants, and bookstores. His latest triumph was, of course, the purchase and renovation of London's Old Vic.

Stop by and browse, and don't forget to step into Honest Ed's on the corner.

Queen Street West Village

This street has over the years been known as the heart of Toronto's funky, avant-garde scene. Along this street are several clubs—Bamboo and the Rivoli, in particular—where some major Canadian artists/singers have launched their careers. The street is lined with an eclectic mix of stores and businesses. Although recent trends have brought such mainstream stores as the Gap to the street, it still retains a raw, authentic neighborhood edge. There's a broad selection of good-value bistro-style restaurants; a number of fine secondhand antiquarian bookstores; and a lot of funky fashion stores as well as outright junk shops, nostalgic record emporiums, kitchen supply stores, and discount fabric houses. East of Spadina the street is being slowly gentrified, but beyond Spadina it still retains its rough-and-ready energy.

For details see Walking Tour 2 in Chapter 7.

Yorkville

This is the name given to the area that stretches north of Bloor Street, between Avenue Road and Bay Street. Since its founding in 1853 as a village outside the city proper, Yorkville has experienced many transformations. In the 1960s it became Toronto's Haight-Ashbury, the mecca for young suburban runaways otherwise known as hippies. In the 1980s it became the shopping ground of the chic, who dropped their money liberally at such designer-name boutiques as Hermès, Courrèges, Gianni Versace, Cartier, and Turnbull & Asser and also at the neighborhood's many fine art galleries. In the early 1990s the recession left its mark on the area—a fact that became glaringly obvious when Creeds, a Toronto institution, shut its doors. The restored town houses began to look a little forlorn, but today the energy is back and Bloor Street and Hazelton Lanes continue to attract high-style stores, including most recently a branch of Tiffany's.

Stroll around and browse—or sit out and have an iced coffee in the sun at one of the cafés on Yorkville Avenue and watch the parade go by. Some good vantage points can be had at Hemingway's or any one of many cafés along Yorkville Avenue, all on the south side of the street. Most of these cafés have happy hours from 4 to 7 or 8pm.

Make sure you wander through the labyrinths of Hazelton Lanes between Avenue Road and Hazelton Avenue, where you'll find a maze of shops and offices clustered around an outdoor court in the center of a building that is topped with apartments—the most sought-after in the city. In the summer the courtyard is used for outdoor dining.

And while you're in the neighborhood (especially if you're an architecture buff), take a look at the red-brick building on Bloor Street at the end of Yorkville Avenue, which houses the Metro Library. If more libraries had been built like this one in the past, then perhaps study and learning would have come out of the dim and musty closets and into the world where they belong. Step inside—a pool and a waterfall gently screen out the street noise and pine fencelike partitions undulate through the area like those you find along the sand dunes. Step farther inside and the space opens dramatically to the sky. Every corner is flooded with light and air.

Parks & Gardens

Allan Gardens, stretching between Jarvis, Sherbourne, Dundas, and Gerrard sts. ☎ **392-7259.**

These gardens were given to the city by George William Allan, who was born in 1822 to wealthy merchant and banker William Allan. His father gave him a vast estate stretching from Carlton Street to Bloor Street between Jarvis and Sherbourne. George married into the Family Compact when he married John Beverley Robinson's daughter. A lawyer by training, he became a city councillor, mayor, senator, and philanthropist. The lovely old concert pavilion was demolished, but the glass-domed Palm House still stands in all its radiant Victorian glory.

Admission: Free.

Open: Daily. **Subway:** Dundas or Gerrard.

Edwards Garden, Lawrence Ave. and Leslie St. ☎ **397-1340.**

This quiet formal garden with a creek cutting through it is part of a series of parks. Gracious bridges arch over the creek, rock gardens abound, and rose and other seasonal flower beds add color and scent to the landscape. The garden is famous for its rhododendrons. The Civic Garden Centre operates a gift shop and gives walking tours on Tuesday and Thursday at 11am and 2pm.

Admission: Free.

Open: Daily dawn–dusk. **Subway:** Eglinton; then take the Leslie or Lawrence bus.

High Park, in the West End, extending south of Bloor Street to the Gardiner Expressway.

This 400-acre park was John G. Howard's great gift to the city. He lived in Colbourne Lodge, which still stands in the park. The park contains a large lake called Grenadier Pond; a small zoo; a swimming pool; tennis courts; sports fields; bowling greens; and vast expanses of green for baseball, jogging, picnicking, bicycling, and more.

Admission: Free.

Open: Daily dawn–dusk. **Subway:** High Park.

Tours

CITY TOURS A quick and easy way to orient yourself to the city is to take a two-hour bus tour that goes past such major sights as Eaton Centre, City Hall, the university, Yorkville, Casa Loma, Harbourfront, and the CN Tower. It usually operates between early May and the end of October and costs $22 adults, $20 seniors, and $16 for children. For information contact **Grayline Tours,** 184 Front St. E. (☎ **594-3310**).

A similar guided tour is also operated year round by **Toronto Tours,** 134 Jarvis St. (☎ **869-1372**).

HARBOR & ISLAND TOURS   Toronto Tours (☎ **869-1372**) operates one-hour tours of the port and the islands from May to September every hour on the hour between 10am and 5pm (until 8pm in July and August) for $11.95 adults, $9 seniors, and $5.95 for children 12 and under. If you pay a $2 premium you can enjoy the tour aboard a wooden-hulled launch. Tours leave from 145 Queen's Quay W. at the foot of York Street.

For a real thrill, board the schooner *The Challenge* for a one- or two-hour cruise weekdays at 2 and 4pm and weekends at noon, 2, 4, and 5pm.

The prices for one hour are $12.80 adults, $10.65 seniors, and $6.40 for children 4 to 14; for two hours $17.05, $13.80, and $10.65, respectively. For information call the **Great Lakes Schooner Company** at **601-0326.**

3 Especially for Kids

Top City Attractions

Look under "The Top Attractions" and "More Attractions," above, for the following Toronto-area attractions that have major appeal to kids of all ages. I've summarized them here in what I think is the most logical order, at least from a kid's point of view (the first five, though, really belong in a dead heat).

Ontario Science Centre (see p. 145) Kids race to be the first at this paradise of fun hands-on games, experiments, and push-button demonstrations—700 of 'em.

Canada's Wonderland (see p. 147) The kids love the rides in the theme park. But watch out for those video games, which they also love—an unanticipated extra cost.

Harbourfront (see p. 138) Kaleidoscope is an ongoing program of creative crafts, active games, and special events on weekends and holidays. There are also a summer pond, winter ice-skating, and a crafts studio.

Ontario Place (see p. 137) Waterslides, a huge Cinesphere, a futuristic pod, and other entertainments are the big hits at this recreational/cultural park on three artificial islands on the edge of Lake Ontario.

Metro Zoo (see p. 146) One of the best in the world, modeled after San Diego's—the animals in this 710-acre park really do live in a natural environment.

Toronto Islands–Centreville (see p. 139) Riding a ferry to this turn-of-the-century amusement park is part of the fun.

CN Tower (see p. 139) Especially for the "Tour of the Universe."

Royal Ontario Museum (see p. 144) The top hit is always the dinosaurs.

McLaughlin Planetarium (see p. 160) For special shows and stargazing.

Fort York (see p. 157) For its reenactments of battle drills, musket and cannon firing, and musical marches with fife and drum.

The Hockey Hall of Fame (see p. 159) Especially the interactive video displays.

Black Creek Pioneer Village (see p. 160) For craft and other demonstrations.

Casa Loma (see p. 156) For the stables and the fantasy rooms.

Art Gallery of Ontario (see p. 141) For its hands-on exhibit.

A Farm Park

Riverdale Farm, 201 Winchester St., east of Parliament, north of Gerrard. ☎ **392-6794.**

Idyllically situated on the edge of the Don Valley ravine, this early 20th-century farm is a favorite with small tots, who enjoy watching the cows and pigs and petting the other farm animals. Historic buildings, gardens, implement displays, and a large variety of livestock make for a surprising visit to the country in the heart of the city.

Admission: Free.

Open: Daily 9am–4, 5, or 6pm, depending on the season.

Out-of-Town Attractions

African Lion Safari, R. R. No. 1, Cambridge, ON.
☎ **519/623-2620.**

Kids enjoy driving through this 500-acre wildlife park, sighting lions and other game. The entrance fee entitles visitors to drive through the park, ride the *African Queen,* take the scenic railway, and see animal performances. There are playgrounds, too, for toddlers, as well as a water playground. Bring bathing suits.

Admission: $16.60 adults, $14.35 seniors and youths, $12.50 children 3–12.

Open: Mid-Apr to late Oct Mon–Fri 10am–4pm, Sat–Sun 10am–5pm. **Closed:** Nov–Apr. **Directions:** Take Hwy. 401 to Hwy. 6 south.

Chudleigh's, P.O. Box 176 (Hwy. 25 north of Hwy. 401), Milton, ON. ☎ **905/826-1252.**

A day here will introduce the kids to life on a farm. They'll enjoy the hay rides; pony rides; sleigh rides; and, in season, the apple picking and sugaring off of the maple trees. All of the produce is on sale, too, in the bake shop and fruit-and-vegetable markets.

Admission: Free.

Open: July 1–Oct daily 9am–7pm; Nov–June daily 9am–5pm.

Cullen Gardens and Miniature Village, 300 Taunton Rd. W., Whitby, ON. ☎ **905/668-6606** or **416/686-1600.**

The miniature village (made to one-half scale) has great appeal. The 25 acres of gardens and the shopping and live entertainment add to the fun.

Admission: $8.95 adults, $6.95 seniors, $3.95 children 3–12.

Open: Daily 9am–8pm. **Closed:** Mid-Jan to early Apr.

Wild Water Kingdom, Finch Ave., 1 mile west of Hwy. 427, Brampton, ON. ☎ **416/369-9453** or **905/794-0565.**

Kids love this huge water theme park complete with a 20,000-square-foot wave pool, tube slides, speed slides, giant hot tubs, and this year's thriller, the Cyclone water ride. In between they can use the batting cages or practice on the mini-golf circuit.

Admission: $16 adults, $13 children 4–9 and seniors.

Open: May to mid-June, Sat–Sun 10am–6:30pm; mid-June to Labor Day, daily 10am–11pm (water rides, to 8pm).

Entertainment

Ontario Centre for Puppetry Arts, 116 Cornelius Pkwy., Keele St. and Hwy. 401. ☎ **246-9222.**

The center presents performances occasionally at different locations. Call for information.

Admission: $4–$12.

Young People's Theatre, 165 Front St. E., at Sherbourne St. ☎ **862-2222** (box office) or **921-9842** (administration).

Devoted to the entertainment of young people. The season runs from November to May. Call for information. **Subway:** Union.

4   Special-Interest Sightseeing

For the Architecture Lover

For folks interested in the architectural development of Toronto there are certain highlights that should not be missed. Most are discussed either in the attractions sections, above, or in the various walking tours in Chapter 7. Therefore only their highlights are mentioned here. Those that have not been discussed elsewhere are treated in full here.

From the early period when the city was primarily a garrison, **Fort York** stands out.

Little else remains from the early 19th-century period, except, of course, the **Grange, Campbell House,** and **Colborne Lodge** in High Park.

The highlights of the mid-Victorian period include **St. Lawrence Market** and **St. Lawrence Hall, St. James Cathedral, University College,** and **Osgoode Hall.**

Buildings from the last three decades of the 19th century are numerous. Along Front Street in the old warehousing area there are many fine cast-iron buildings. See, in particular, the **Beardmore** and the **Gooderham Building** (the Flatiron). The **Bank of Montréal** at Yonge and Front streets is an ornate gem, while in domestic architecture many of the buildings along Jarvis and Sherbourne streets that were mansions still stand today in various states of repair. See also the **George Gooderham House** (the York Club) at 135 St. George St., at Bloor Street West. The **Ontario Legislative Buildings** in Queen's Park date from this High Victorian period, as does **Old City Hall** and two emporiums, one devoted to culture and the other to retailing—**Massey Hall** on Shuter Street and the **Bay** at Yonge and Richmond streets.

The Edwardian period is expressed in the homes of such magnates as **Joseph Flavelle** (Holwood) on Queen's Park Crescent and, most ostentatious of all, **Casa Loma.** The **Royal Alex** also dates from this period.

Some great skyscrapers from the 1920s and 1930s can be viewed if you stroll through the financial district down Bay Street from Old City Hall. **Sunnyside** and **Exhibition Place** date from the 1920s, when people flocked to the lakefront on their days off.

Highlights of the later 20th century must include the **New City Hall;** Mies van der Rohe's **Toronto Dominion Centre; Royal Bank Plaza** by Webb Zerafa Menker & Housden; **Ontario Place** by Craig, Zeidler & Strong; the **Metro Library** and **Scarborough Civic Centre,** both by Raymond Moriyama; the **Eaton Centre** by Bregman & Hamann and the Zeidler Partnership; **Roy Thomson Hall** by Arthur Erickson; **SkyDome;** and the **BCE building** on Front Street.

THE ANNEX This is a residential area containing marvelous Romanesque Revival, Queen Anne, Georgian Revival, and English

IMPRESSIONS

Toronto is New York . . . run by the Swiss.
—Peter Ustinov

Lord Bessborough, later Governor-General of Canada, once described Toronto as understanding two things perfectly—"The British Empire and a good horse."
—Jan Morris, *Travels* (1976)

Country specimens that any architecture lover will not want to miss. The area stretches west of Yorkville. Stroll down any of the streets in this neighborhood to get the flavor—Bedford, Admiral, St. George, Huron, and Madison.

On Madison, for example, stop and look at the house designed by E. J. Lennox, the **Lewis Lukes House** at no. 37, a marvelous solid Romanesque Revival residence featuring basket-weave brickwork. One of the first residences located in the Annex, which set the trend to move there, was the **Gooderham House** (1889–92), at 135 St. George St., at Bloor Street. It was designed by David Roberts for George Gooderham, president of the Gooderham & Worts Distillery. This massive Richardsonian building in stone, brick, and terra-cotta, with its towers and intricately patterned rounded arches, is today occupied by the York Club.

5 Outdoor Activities

Sports

Some wag once said that there's only one really religious place in Toronto, and that's **Maple Leaf Gardens,** 60 Carlton St. (☎ **977-1641**), where the city's ice-hockey team, the Maple Leafs, wield their sticks to the delight and screaming enthusiasm of fans. Tickets are nigh impossible to attain because they are sold by subscription. Your only hope is to find a scalper.

The **SkyDome,** on Front Street beside the CN Tower, is the home of the Blue Jays baseball team (World Series champs in 1992) and the Toronto Argonauts football team. For information, contact the Toronto Blue Jays, P.O. Box 7777, Adelaide St., Toronto, ON, M5C 2K7 (☎ **416/341-1000**). For Blue Jays tickets, call **341-1111;** for Argonauts tickets, call **872-5000.**

Racing takes place at **Woodbine Racetrack,** at Rexdale Boulevard and Hwy. 427, in Etobicoke (☎ **675-6110**), famous for the Queen's Plate (July) and the Rothman's International, a world classic turf race (October). Harness racing, too, in spring and fall.

Recreation

For additional information on golf courses, tennis, swimming pools, beaches, and picnic areas, call **Metro Parks** (☎ **392-1111** or **392-8186** Monday through Friday).

BEACHES The most popular beaches are found on the Toronto Islands—Centre Island and Wards Island—and, of course, at the Beaches at the east end of the city. The lake is severely polluted; these are *not* swimming beaches. Call Metro Parks for the locations of the best places to swim and also for the current state of lakefront beaches.

GOLF The following 18-hole municipal golf courses are open on a first-come, first-served basis. No membership or reservations are necessary. Clubs and caddy carts can be rented. Courses are open from dawn to dusk; the season begins around mid-April.

Dentonia Park Golf Course, Victoria Park Avenue (☎ 392-2558).

Don Valley Golf Course, 4200 Yonge St. (☎ **392-2465**).

Humber Valley Golf Course, Beattie Avenue, off Albion Road (☎ 392-2488).

Lakeview Golf Course, 1190 Dixie Rd., in Port Credit, 1km (.6 miles) south of the QEW (☎ **905/278-4411**).

Scarlett Woods Golf Course, Jane Street at Eglinton Avenue West (☎ 392-2484).

Tam O'Shanter Golf Course, Birchmount Road north of Sheppard Avenue East (☎ 392-2547).

SWIMMING   For **pool information,** call **392-1111.** There are many city indoor and outdoor pools.

The **University of Toronto Athletic Centre,** 55 Harbord St. at Spadina Avenue (☎ **978-4680**), opens the swimming pool free to the public on Sunday from 12:10 to 4pm.

TENNIS   The following outdoor courts are available free at any time:

Moss Park, at Sherbourne and Queen streets.

Riverdale Park, Broadview Avenue, south of Danforth.

Ryerson Community Park, Church Street, between Gerrard and Gould streets.

7

Strolling Around
Toronto

Toronto is almost a distant cousin of Los Angeles: it's a huge, sprawling city, and it's difficult to imagine walking everywhere. (Fortunately, Toronto, unlike Los Angeles, is blessed with a superefficient public transportation system.)

So the walking tours below aren't designed to give you an overview of the city; instead, they'll introduce you to the most colorful, exciting neighborhoods and areas that are packed with sights on almost every corner. We'll start with Harbourfront, which Torontonians have turned into a glorious playground opening onto the lake.

Walking Tour 1
Harbourfront

Start Union Station.

Finish Harbourfront Antiques Market.

Time Anywhere from three to eight hours, depending on how much time you spend shopping, eating, and daydreaming.

Best Time Sunday, when the Harbourfront Antiques Market is bustling.

As you start your tour, pause to look at the beaux arts interior of Union Station. From here, either take the LRT to York Quay or walk down York Street to Queen's Quay West. Directly ahead, across the street, is the:

1. **Queen's Quay Terminal,** a large complex that houses more than 100 shops and restaurants and, on the third floor, a theater specially designed for dance. Built in 1927 when lake and railroad trade flourished, this eight-story concrete warehouse has been attractively renovated and turned it to a light and airy marketplace with garden courts, skylights, and waterfalls.

    Although you'll find few bargains here, some of my favorite fun stores on the street level are **Rainmakers,** selling zillions of whimsical umbrellas plus terrific insulated rainwear; **Touch the Sky,** displaying colorful kites of all shapes and sizes; **Bree** for fine leather bags; **Crabtree & Evelyn** for soaps and other products to care for the body and appeal to the senses; **Suitables,** for reasonably priced silk fashions; and **Just Kidding,** for kids' fashions.

    On the upper level there's also plenty to choose from: **SciTech** for science games, clocks, globes, and all kinds of fun items associated with all the sciences; the **Nature Store,** which sells everything from bird feeders and coasters featuring birds, to carved loons, wilderness knives, compasses, and natural objects (even the T-shirts have paintings of birds on them); the classic Canadian **Tilley Endurables,** founded by Torontonian Alex Tilley

Walking Tour — Harbourfront

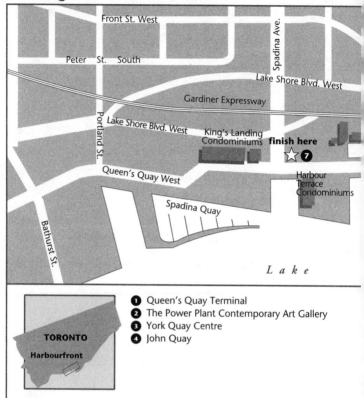

Front St. West

Peter St. South

Spadina Ave.

Lake Shore Blvd. West

Gardiner Expressway

Portland St.

Lake Shore Blvd. West

King's Landing Condominiums

finish here ☆ ❼

Queen's Quay West

Harbour Terrace Condominiums

Bathurst St.

Spadina Quay

Lake

TORONTO

Harbourfront

❶ Queen's Quay Terminal
❷ The Power Plant Contemporary Art Gallery
❸ York Quay Centre
❹ John Quay

(who invented the world's most endurable and adaptable hat as well as multipocketed jackets); and **Table of Contents,** selling all kinds of kitchen gear, napkins, tablecloths, and utensils.

Take a Break

If you want to sit out and watch the lakefront traffic—boat and human—go to **Spinnakers** or the **Boathouse Cafe** on the ground floor of Queen's Quay. Otherwise, go upstairs and dine at **Pink Pearl** (Chinese) or more casually at **La Bouchée.**

From Queen's Quay Terminal, walk along the water to:

2. The Power Plant Contemporary Art Gallery, a former power plant that has been converted to display modern art. The same building also houses the Du Maurier Theatre Centre, which presents works in French.

Behind this building, adjacent to Queen's Quay West, is the Tent in the Park, which shelters different events during the summer season. Walk west into the:

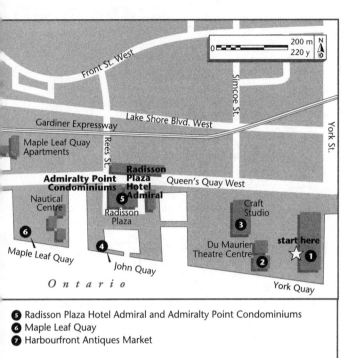

3. York Quay Centre, another interesting complex
containing a number of restaurants and galleries. Spend
some time in the Craft Studio watching the glassblowers,
potters, jewelry makers, and other artisans at work and
browse in the store that sells their work.

On the waterfront side in front of York Quay there's
a pond where kids operate model boats in summer; in
winter it turns into an ice-skating rink.

From York Quay, cross the Amsterdam Bridge above
Marina 4, checking out the wealth that's bobbing down
below. You'll arrive on:

4. John Quay. The first building you'll come to contains
four restaurants, beyond which you'll see the towers
of the:

**5. Radisson Plaza Hotel Admiral and Admiralty Point
Condominiums,** and across Queen's Quay West, the
HarbourPoint Condominiums. On the ground level
of the Admiralty Point Condos are a few interesting
stores: The Nautical Mind, which sells marine books,
photographs, navigational charts, and boating videos,

and the **Dock Shoppe,** filled with all kinds of sailing
gear and fashions.

Take a Break

Pop into the **Radisson Plaza Hotel Admiral,** which has
a couple of dining rooms, plus a pleasant poolside terrace
if it's a sunny day. Or try something fresh from
Wallymagoo's marine bar.

Continue west along Queen's Quay West past:

6. Maple Leaf Quay (unless you want to stop at the
Nautical Centre to sign up for sailing classes and the
like). Continue west and you'll see the Maple Leaf Quay
Apartments on your right and the Harbour Terrace
Condominiums farther along on your left on the
waterfront. Next door to the westernmost tower of the
Maple Leaf Quay Apartments is the:

7. Harbourfront Antiques Market, a terrific market in
which more than 100 dealers sell fine furniture, jewelry,
books, clocks, and art deco items. On Sunday there's
also an outdoor market featuring less established dealers.
Go on Sunday—few dealers are open during the week.

Take a Break

In the Harbourfront Antiques Market, **Dinah's Dinette**
has great fresh salads, sandwiches, quiches, and desserts.
Board the LRT and head back to Union Station.

Walking Tour 2
The Financial District & Queen Street Village

Start The CN Tower, near the corner of John and Front streets.
Finish At one of Queen Street West's watering holes.
Time Six to eight hours, depending on how long you take to
browse.
Best Time Anytime.

AROUND THE FINANCIAL DISTRICT Start by
going up the:

1. CN Tower, which is the tallest free-standing structure in
the world. Back down at the base, exit at the corner of
John and Front streets. From here, look east along Front
Street to see the glistening golden Royal Bank towers.
The new CBC Center stretches along the north side of
Front Street for a whole long block.

Walk north on John Street, cross Wellington,
and continue up to King Street. Turn right. On the
northeast corner of King Street sports fans will want
to stop in at **Legends of the Game.** Doors with
baseball-shaped handles open onto an emporium that

features the Wall of Fame and every conceivable sports collectible.

Continue walking along the north side of King Street to:

2. **The Princess of Wales Theatre,** which opened in 1993, the brainchild of son and father David and Ed Mirvish. If you can, go inside and get a look at the 10,000-square-foot artwork created by Frank Stella. Exit the theater and continue along King Street past a cluster of Ed Mirvish restaurant creations (drop into one just to check out the larger-than-life decor) and a wall of newspaper clippings about this gutsy, quintessential Torontonian who, with his great love and boostering of the city, seems a shier version of New York's Ed Koch. Next you'll come to:

3. **The Royal Alex.** This beloved theater, named after the king's consort, was built in 1906 and 1907 by John M. Lyle in a magnificent beaux arts style and was saved and refurbished by Ed Mirvish in 1963. Edwardian to a tee, it's loaded with gilt and velvet and sports an entrance foyer lined with green marble. On the south side of the street at the corner of King and Simcoe streets is:

4. **Roy Thomson Hall,** named after newspaper magnate Lord Thomson of Fleet. Built between 1972 and 1982 and designed by Arthur Erickson, the building's exterior looks very space age, and inside, the mirrored effects are dramatic. Tours are usually given of this fabulous concert hall at 12:30pm, but call ahead at **593-4828** to confirm if you really do want to see behind the scenes. If you don't want to take a tour, at least go in for a look.

Take a Break

Your best bet in this part of town is probably **Orso** or **Jump** for leisurely luncheons. For a quick-and-easy snack, seek out one of the casual dining spots in the concourse of First Canadian Place.

Continue walking east. You'll be walking through the heart of the financial district, surrounded by the many towers owned and operated by banks and brokerage, trust, and insurance companies. Cross Simcoe Street. On the northeast corner of King and Simcoe rises the Sun Life Centre; on the southeast corner stands:

5. **St. Andrew's Presbyterian Church,** a quietly inviting retreat from the city's pace and noise. Continue along the block to University Avenue. Opposite, on the northeast corner, is the:

6. **Sun Life Tower,** marked by a sculpture by Sorel Etrog. Farther along the block you'll find another sculpture, *Parent I* by Barbara Hepworth, in a courtyard setting

at the northwest corner of York Street. On the northeast corner stands the:

7. Exchange Tower, connected to the Toronto Stock Exchange at the corner of Adelaide and York streets.

Continue along King Street past:

8. First Canadian Place on the north side and the **Standard Life and Royal Trust Buildings** on the south, until you reach Bay Street. Again, there are views of the magnificent Royal Bank towers from here.

The intersection of Bay and King streets was once considered the precise geographical center of Toronto's financial power, and during the mining booms in the 1920s and 1950s, Bay Street was lined with offices that were filled with commission salesmen peddling stocks to the equivalent of the little ol' lady from Dubuque. This is the hub that gave Torontonians their reputation as a voracious band of money-grubbing folks that Hugh McLennan portrayed in his marvelous novel about Québec, *Two Solitudes.* Rising at King and Bay today is the:

9. Toronto Dominion Centre, built between 1963 and 1969 and designed by Mies van der Rohe in his sleek trademark style. The black steel and dark-bronze-tinted glass tower rises from its gray granite base launching pad.

Cross Bay Street. On the south side of King Street, architecture buffs will want to go into the:

10. Canadian Imperial Bank of Commerce (1929–31) just to see the massive banking hall—145 feet long, 85 feet wide, and 65 feet high—with its coffered ceiling, gilt moldings, and decorative sculpted friezes. The main entrance is decorated, for instance, with squirrels, roosters, bees, bears, and figures representing Industry, Commerce, and Mercury. For years this 34-story building dominated the Toronto skyline. In the early 1970s I. M. Pei was asked to design a new complex while preserving the old building. He set the new stainless-steel bank tower that glistens (thanks to its mercury lamination) back from King Street, creating Commerce Court.

Opposite, on the north side of King Street, note:

11. Scotia Tower, the red-tinted building.

Walk back to Bay Street and turn right going north. At no. 303 on the east side is the:

12. National Club Building. In 1874 the Canada First Movement, which had been started in Ottawa in 1868, became centered in Toronto. It established a weekly, *The Nation,* and entered politics as the Canadian National Association and founded the National Club. Eventually the movement's influence faded but its original ideas had

Walking Tour—
Financial District & Queen Street Village

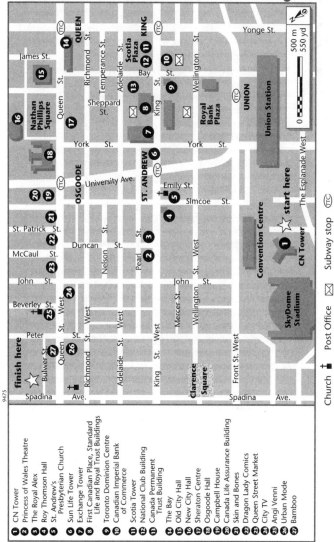

Key (map legend):

1. CN Tower
2. Princess of Wales Theatre
3. The Royal Alex
4. Roy Thomson Hall
5. St. Andrew's Presbyterian Church
6. Sun Life Tower
7. Exchange Tower
8. First Canadian Place, Standard Life and Royal Trust Buildings
9. Toronto Dominion Centre
10. Canadian Imperial Bank of Commerce
11. Scotia Tower
12. National Club Building
13. Canada Permanent Trust Building
14. The Bay
15. Old City Hall
16. New City Hall
17. Sheraton Centre
18. Osgoode Hall
19. Campbell House
20. Canada Life Assurance Building
21. Skin and Bones
22. Dragon Lady Comics
23. Queen Street Market
24. City TV
25. Angi Venni
26. Urban Mode
27. Bamboo

✝ Church ⊠ Post Office ☆ Subway stop

lasting influence. The club moved to these premises in 1907.

Across the street on the west side at the corner of Bay and Adelaide streets stands the:

13. Canada Permanent Trust Building (1928). Go in to view the beautifully worked art deco brass and bronze, particularly the elevator doors, which are chased and engraved with foliage and flowers.

Cross Adelaide Street. As you walk up Bay Street, the magnificently solid Old City Hall is clearly in view, but first, on the east side of Bay between Richmond and Queen, look at or, if you like, stop into:

14. The Bay, one of Canada's venerable retailers. The Bay (formerly Simpson's), along with arch rival Eaton's, has influenced the development of the downtown areas of most major Canadian cities.

Ahead looms the:

15. Old City Hall, reflected dramatically to the right in the Cadillac Fairview Office Tower at the corner of James and Queen streets. This solid, impressive building designed by Edward James Lennox is built out of Credit River Valley sandstone in a magnificent Romanesque Revival style that is obviously influenced by H. H. Richardson. Begun in 1885, it was opened in 1899, and for years its clock tower was a familiar skyline landmark. Today the building houses the provincial criminal courts. Go in to see the impressive staircase, columns with decorative capitals, mosaic floor, and stained-glass window (1898) by Robert McCausland depicting the union of Commerce and Industry watched over by Britannia. Pause on your way out to look down the canyon of Bay Street, the city's equivalent of New York's Wall Street. Bay Street curves around, and to your left there is suddenly the:

16. New City Hall, the city's fourth, built between 1958 and 1965; in modern sculptural style, it's the symbol of Toronto's new dynamism. Designed by Finnish architect Viljo Revell, who won the competition that was entered by 510 architects from 42 countries, including I. M. Pei, it has a great square in front with fountain and pool to which office workers flock in summer to relax and then in winter to skate. The square is named after Nathan Phillips, Toronto's first Jewish mayor, who helped push the project through. The Council Chamber, supported on a two-tier podium, looks like a flying saucer, but the glass walls make it seem open and accessible. Henry Moore's sculpture *The Archer* stands in front of the building—thanks to Mayor Phil Givens, who raised the money to buy it through public subscription after the city authorities refused to purchase it. This gesture encouraged Henry Moore to bestow a major collection of his works on the Art Gallery. The Council Chamber is flanked by two curved concrete towers that house the bureaucracy.

For the best view of City Hall, enter the:

17. **Sheraton Centre,** on the south side of Queen Street, and go up to the second-floor Long Bar, which overlooks the square.

Take a Break

For some light refreshment, stop in at one of several dining spots in the **Sheraton Centre.**

From City Hall, walk west along Queen Street. On your right behind an ornate wrought-iron fence that once kept out the cows you'll see:

18. **Osgoode Hall,** since the 1830s headquarters of the Law Society of Upper Canada, a kind of professional trade union. Named after the first chief justice of Upper Canada, the building was constructed in stages, starting with the East Wing in 1831 to 1832, the West Wing in 1844 to 1845, and the center block in 1856 to 1860. The last, with its Palladian portico, is the most impressive. Inside, the Great Library—112 feet long, 40 feet wide, and 40 feet high—with stucco decoration and coved domed ceiling is grand. The Ontario Supreme Court is across the street on the south side of Queen Street.

Keep walking west to University Avenue. On the northwest corner you can visit the:

19. **Campbell House,** the elegant Georgian residence of Sir William Campbell, a Scot who moved to York in 1811 and rose to become chief justice of Upper Canada. A handsome piece of Georgian architecture, it was moved to this location from a few miles farther east.

Behind Campbell House, on the northwest side of University Avenue, the:

20. **Canada Life Assurance Building** stretches northward. Atop the tower a neon sign provides weather reports— white flashes for snow, red flashes for rain, green beacon for clement weather, or red beacon for cloudy weather. If the flashes move upward the temperature is headed that way, and vice versa.

At University Avenue and Queen Street you can end the tour by boarding the subway at Osgoode to your next destination, or you can continue walking west along Queen Street to explore the many delights of this thoroughfare.

AROUND QUEEN STREET VILLAGE   This is one of the great "alternative" shopping and nightlife venues of the city and there are many stores that you'll want to browse in as you walk from University to Spadina and even beyond. Here are some likely ones along the route.

On the north side of the street, just west of Simcoe at no. 180, there's:

21. **Skin and Bones** for Native American arts, crafts, jewelry, lambskin fashions. At no. 200, west of St. Patricks, there's:

22. **Dragon Lady Comics** for collectors of old and new. Farther along, just west of McCaul Street, are a couple of places to take a break.

Take a Break

On the south side, just west of Simcoe, there's **Bayou Bistro,** a popular restaurant specializing in Cajun cuisine. On the north side on the same block you'll find another perennial dining favorite, the **Queen Mother Cafe,** serving Asian-accented bistro food.

23. Inside the: **Queen Street Market** you'll discover counters selling Chinese and barbecue food. There's also a juice bar and a Hillebrand wine outlet as well as fresh fruit and vegetable stands. At no. 256 you'll find **Pages,** a large, well-stocked bookstore selling hard- and softcovers and a very wide selection of magazines.
    Back on the south side:

24. **City TV's** screens can be watched and you can add your comments at **Speaker's Corner** at the corner of John Street. At no. 323A, **Black Market** (upstairs) features vintage clothing.
    Across the street, just west of Beverley, you'll find:

25. **Angi Venni,** a young Canadian designer, at no. 274. **Robin Kay's** store emphasizes environmental concerns, stocking natural-fabric fashions, duvets, and bed linens, recycled paper products, and such items as beeswax candles. **Du Verre** (no. 280) has a wide variety of glass vases, pitchers, and plates and proudly displays a sticker identifying it as an "alternative bridal registry." Next door at no. 282 the **Bakka Science Fiction Book Shoppe** amasses a vast selection in the genre. **The Snow Lion,** at no. 286, sells items from Tibet and the Himalayas—rugs, jackets, hats, gongs, tankas, and more. **ION Fashion,** at no. 290, as its name would suggest, displays cool, hip clothing, including children's fashions and accessories. **Zephyr,** at no. 292, appeals to the natural world for inspiration, proferring polished rocks and minerals, pyramids, crystals, butterflies, and other natural collectibles. Soho Street cuts in here on the north.
    On the south side beyond Peter Street are several browsable stores. Among them are these:

26. **Urban Mode,** at no. 387, for the latest Italian house-wares; **Aldo** for the latest foot fashions from Stone Ridge, Doc Martens, and others; funky fashion stores like outrageous **Fashion Crimes, Fix,** and **Fix 2;** and

John Fluevog with wild shoes for men and women at no. 399. At no. 403 **Club Monaco** offers more tailored sports fashions. Continue along to no. 415, **Steve's Music Store,** which features a vast array of musical instruments.

Back on the north side of the street, note:

27. Bamboo, a favorite city music club, with an au courant Caribbean flavor.

Take a Break

Several of the city's favorite bistros are located in this area. On the north side, the traditional French **Le Select** offers a pleasant outdoor dining area and skylit back room. The more avant-garde **Rivoli** has a billiard/snooker room upstairs. On the south side there's the classy celebrity favorite, **Bistingo,** as well as the more modest **Peter Pan** and the vegetarian **Earthtones.**

Also on the north side of the street you'll find **David Mason** upstairs at no. 342, featuring a well-cataloged stock of antique and general out-of-print and secondhand books. **Grafix** has well-priced art supplies; **Le Chateau,** a Montréal original, offers engaging fashions. At no. 356, **Edwards Books and Art** has some of the best prices on art books in the city and regularly advertises discounted titles in the local newspapers. Although it stocks the latest fiction and nonfiction, the store specializes in fine, illustrated books—cookbooks, gardening, art and architecture, and more.

Continue on to Spadina Avenue and board the streetcar back to the Osgoode or Queen subway stop. The unweary can continue along Queen Street beyond Spadina Avenue, discovering such wonderful rare-book dealers as **Steven Temple** and **Abelard,** along with other interesting stores.

Walking Tour 3
Chinatown & Kensington Market

Start   Osgoode subway station.

Finish   Toronto Public Reference Library.

Time   Six to eight hours, depending on whether or not you stop.

Best Time   Anytime except Monday (when the Art Gallery is closed).

AROUND CHINATOWN   From the Osgoode subway station, walk west on Queen Street. Turn right onto McCaul Street. On the west side of the street (left), if you're interested in crafts, you'll want to stop at:

1. Prime Gallery, at no. 52, which sells ceramics, jewelry, fabrics, and other art objects crafted by contemporary artisans.

On the right is:

2. **Village by the Grange,** an apartment/shopping complex
that's laid out in a series of courtyards (one even
contains a small ice-skating rink). Go into the complex
at the southern end and stroll through, emerging from
the food market. En route you'll come across many
inviting stores, like **Bellissimo Fashions,** featuring
appealing children's clothes, including Muppet-style
PVC jackets and Peruvian-style sweaters with appliquéd
numbers; and **18 Karat,** where the proprietors design
and craft jewelry behind the counter (show them what
you have in mind and they will craft it for you
beautifully).

Take a Break

Also in Village by the Grange is one of the city's oldest
and most popular Chinese restaurants—**Young Lok.**
The **Food Market** contains stalls selling everything—
12 varieties of freshly brewed coffee, schnitzels, satay,
Japanese noodles, salads, falafel, hot dogs, Chinese food,
kebabs, pizza, and fried chicken.

Continue north along McCaul, passing the Ontario
College of Art on the left side of the street, until you
reach Dundas Street, where on the left you'll encounter a
large Henry Moore sculpture entitled *Large Two Forms,*
which is precisely what it is.

Turn left. The entrance to the:

3. **Art Gallery of Ontario** is on the left. If you don't want
to go into the collections, you can browse the gallery
stores without paying admission.

Cross to the north side of Dundas, opposite the Art
Gallery. It's worth stopping in at the:

4. **Bau-Xi,** a gallery representing modern Canadian artists.
From here, walk west along Dundas, crossing Beverley
Street, into the heart of Chinatown, stopping in at the
grocery stores, bakeries, bookstalls, and other emporiums
selling exotic foods, handcrafts, and other items from
Asia.

What follows are some of my favorite browsing stops
along the stretch of Dundas Street between Beverley
Street and Spadina Avenue. On the south or left side as
you go west is:

5. **Tai Sun Co.,** at no. 407–09, a supermarket displaying
dozens of different mushrooms, all clearly labeled in
English, as well as all kinds of fresh Chinese vegetables,
meats, fish, and canned goods. **Melewa Bakery,** at no.
433, has a wide selection of pastries, like mung-bean and
lotus-paste buns. Outside **Kiu Shun Trading,** at no.
441, dried fish are displayed, while inside you'll find

numerous varieties of ginseng and such miracle remedies
as "Stop Smoking Tea" and delicacies as swallows nests.
   On the north side of the street:

6. **J & S Arts and Crafts,** at no. 430, is a good place to
pick up souvenirs, including kimonos and happy coats,
kung fu suits, address books, cushion covers, and
all-cotton Chinatown T-shirts for only $6. **New World
Book Store,** at no. 442, has a good selection of Chinese
and other Asian-language dictionaries as well as Chinese
cards.

   At the corner of Huron Street, on the north side of
Dundas:

7. **Ten Ren Tea,** no. 454, sells all kinds of teas—black,
oolong, and so forth—stored in large canisters in the
back of the store, as well as charming small ceramic tea
pots priced from $20 to $65. A large variety of gnarled
ginseng root is also displayed for sale. Next door, **W Y
Trading Co., Inc.,** has a great selection of records, CDs,
and tapes—everything from Chinese folk songs and
cantatas to current hit albums from Hong Kong and
Taiwan. This is one place a non-Chinese-speaking visitor
can read what the recording contains. **Furuya,** at no.
460, stocks Japanese specialties including some really
fine sushi oke, lacquer trays, bowls, boxes, and sake sets
as well as food and other specialties.

Take a Break

Right in Chinatown, **Champion House** is a good lunch
stop that offers comfortable, elegant surroundings (in
contrast to the strictly functional look that prevails in
Chinatown) and good Chinese cuisine. The specialty is
Peking duck, and a gong is sounded when it comes out
of the kitchen. They have other dishes, too, like beef
with ginger and green onions and also orange chicken,
priced from $9 to $13.

   At Spadina, turn left and walk to no. 251, the:

8. **Great China Herbs Center,** where the friendly store-
keeper welcomes curious visitors who come to look at
the exotic roots and fruits that are kept in large glass jars
and at other medicines like deer-tail extract and
liquid-gold ginseng or royal jelly. Best remedy of all
time is the "slimming tea." Watch them weigh each
item out on a hand-held weigh scale and total the bill
with a fast-clicking abacus.

   From here walk back up Spadina to Dundas and
cross Spadina to:

9. **Dragon City,** an Asian-style shopping complex on the
west side of Spadina at no. 280.

Spadina Avenue is the widest street in the city because the wealthy Baldwin family had a 132-foot swath cut through the forest from Queen Street to Bloor Street so that they could view the lake from their new home on the top of Spadina Hill. Later, in the early 20th century, it became Toronto's garment center, the equivalent of New York's Seventh Avenue and the focal point of the city's Jewish community.

Although it's still the garment center, with wholesale and discount fashion houses, and the fur district (farther south around Adelaide), today Spadina Avenue is more Asian than Jewish.

If you enjoy strolling through supermarkets filled with exotic Asian delights, including such fruits as durian in season, then go into the:

10. **New Asia Supermarket,** at no. 295–97, or cross the street and explore the:

11. **Tai Kong Supermarket.** Also on the west side of the street, the **WayKing Centre** contains a number of businesses—tailors; jewelers; trading companies; and Aquarium Fantasy, where you can watch the fierce-looking black moore, the piranha, and an all-time Asian favorite, the brilliant carp.

Take a Break

Here, why not join the Chinese at one of the food courts that serve all kinds of Asian cuisine. There's one downstairs at **Dragon City** and one upstairs at **WayKing Centre.** The stalls sell dim sum, noodles, curry, and all kinds of Asian fare. For the language-deficient, each of the dishes is pictured in color and assigned a number. Good food at low prices.

As the Asian community in Toronto has grown, different nationalities have opened their own specialty stores. Although many of the products are the same, there are also many products that are unique to a particular country. For example, there's the:

12. **Vientiane Trading Company,** at no. 334, where they label some vegetables in English, like lotus root, bamboo, and coriander.

Cross St. Andrews St. to no. 360, **Tap Phong Trading,** which has some terrific wicker baskets of all shapes and sizes: woks and ceramic cookware; heavy, attractive mortar and pestles; and other household items. Across the street:

13. **Rotman Hat Shop** at no. 345 has Panama hats that are as light as feathers and woven from the finest quality Ecuador plants. The store, which has been in business

Walking Tour—
Chinatown & Kensington Market

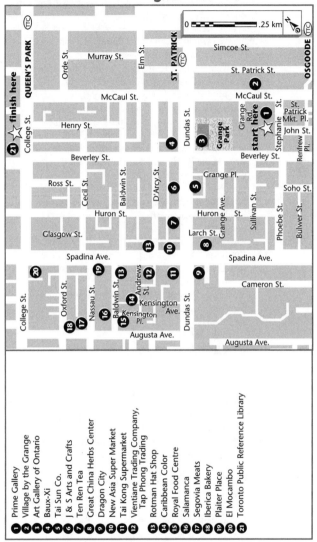

1. Prime Gallery
2. Village by the Grange
3. Art Gallery of Ontario
4. Baux-Xi
5. Tai Sun Co.
6. J & S Arts and Crafts
7. Ten Ren Tea
8. Great China Herbs Center
9. Dragon City
10. New Asia Super Market
11. Tai Kong Supermarket
12. Vientiane Trading Company, Tap Phong Trading
13. Rotman Hat Shop
14. Caribbean Color
15. Royal Food Centre
16. Salamanca
17. Segovia Meats
18. Iberica Bakery
19. Plaiter Place
20. El Mocambo
21. Toronto Public Reference Library

here for over 40 years, also stocks grouser hats and other fun headgear.

Continue shopping and browsing along Spadina and then double back to St. Andrews. Turn into St. Andrews and note the synagogue on the north side of the street.

AROUND KENSINGTON MARKET   Walk along St. Andrews to Kensington Avenue and turn right. Here you'll be in the heart of the Kensington Market area, which over the years has reflected the current ethnic scene that exists in the city. Once it was primarily a Jewish market; later it became more Portuguese; and today, it is a blend of Portuguese, Jewish, Caribbean, and Asian.

Walk north on Kensington Avenue. There are several West Indian groceries on this street, like:

14. **Caribbean Corner,** on the east side of the street, selling such items as plantains. On the west side, **Tropical Harvest** also displays Caribbean specialties, while next door **Mendel's Creamery** sells smoked fish, herring, cheeses, and fine dill pickles. Next door, **Cheese from Around the World** offers an enormous selection at good prices.

Continue along Kensington Avenue to Baldwin Street. If you look to the right you can see the bland buildings of **George Brown College,** named after the founder of the *Globe and Mail.* Turn left on Baldwin and check the produce at the:

15. **Royal Food Centre,** which sells a variety of Jamaican specialties including goat meat. On the same side of the street there are several fishmongers like Caribbean Seafood and Saigon, both displaying infinite varieties of fresh fish, including salted cod piled up in boxes out on the sidewalk.

Across the street:

16. **Salamanca,** at no. 204, has all kinds of grains, beans, nuts, and spices and Indian, Middle Eastern, and Mexican specialties.

At the end of Baldwin, turn right onto Augusta Avenue into the heart of the old Portuguese neighborhood. In addition to the discount clothing shops are several Latino stores. For example:

17. **Segovia Meats** stands alongside **Perola Super** at no. 247, which displays cassava and strings of peppers hung up to dry, and **Emporium Latino,** which sells cactus leaves and yucca among many other Latin American items.

Cross Nassau Street to the:

18. **Iberica Bakery,** at no. 279, the Sagres Fish Market, the Portuguese Meat Market, Agniar Grocery, and O'Cortador Meat Market, all on the east side of the street. They represent the few traces of the Portuguese presence at the Kensington Market area.

Turn right down Oxford Avenue and walk over to Spadina Avenue. Turn left to:

19. **Plaiter Place,** at no. 384, which has a huge selection of finely crafted wicker baskets, birdcages, woven blinds, bamboo steamers, hats, and other fun items. Stop, too, at **Fortune Housewares,** no. 388, to shop for kitchen and household items—including all the good brand names—for at least 20% off prices elsewhere in the city.

Turn around and continue north up Spadina to:

20. **El Mocambo,** the rock-and-roll landmark where the Rolling Stones played on March 4 and 5, 1977, in their heyday, and hop on the trolley traveling east along College Street to the subway. Along the route, you'll pass on the left (north) side of the street what used to be the:

21. **Toronto Public Reference Library,** an attractive classical revival building now occupied by the University of Toronto bookstore and Koffler Student Centre, and on the south corner of College Street and University Avenue, the weird-looking mirrored-glass Hydro Place.

Walking Tour 4
Queen's Park & the University

Start   Royal Ontario Museum.
Finish   Queen's Park.
Time   Three to four hours (more if you stop in at the museum).
Best Times   Anytime except Monday (when the museum's closed).

Take the subway to Museum to the:

1. **Royal Ontario Museum (ROM),** which is, of course, the great repository of the city's collections.

Walk south to Queen's Park and follow its curve to the right past:

2. **Holwood,** the residence of wealthy meatpacker Sir Joseph Flavelle, which is now used by the university's School of Law. The elegant and richly decorated house was nicknamed Porker's Palace. Inside, the grand hall has decorative art nouveau features and a ceiling painted in art nouveau style by Gustav Hahn.

Walk around to Hoskin Avenue. On the south side of the street stands:

3. **Wycliffe College,** founded in 1877 as a Low Church Anglican college and built in red brick in Romanesque Revival style. It stands across from:

4. **Trinity College,** the Anglican High Church college, founded as an independent university in 1851 by first Anglican bishop Strachan after King's College (the original university foundation) was declared nonsectarian in 1849. Trinity became part of the university in 1904. The Gothic buildings, the chapel, and the gardens are attractive sights.

At Devonshire Place, turn right and walk north to:

5. Massey College (1960–63), enclosed behind modern, concertina-folded screenlike walls. It has a cloistered yet inviting air, with fountains playing in the quadrangle. Designed by Ron Thom, it has a traditional, serene yet modern quality with Frank Lloyd Wright and Japanese elements.

Farther up Devonshire Place you'll come to:

6. St. Hilda's, a classic Georgian-style building housing the women's college that is part of Trinity.

Turn around and come back to Hoskin. Turn right and walk over to St. George past St. Thomas Aquinas Chapel to see the dreadnought of a building, the:

7. John P. Robarts Library, the building everyone loves to hate. This huge concrete hulk houses the research library and the rare-book library.

From here, turn back along Hoskin to Tower Road and turn right, walking toward the:

8. Soldier's Memorial Tower (1924), inspired by Magdalen's Big Tom, which stands between Gothic Hart House on the left and Romanesque University College on the right. Go into:

9. Hart House (1910–19), named after Hart Massey. It's consciously Oxford-like in style and atmosphere. Today, every U of T student belongs to Hart House, once an exclusive male domain. View the small chapel containing a memorial window created by Rosemary Kilbourn for Alice and Vincent Massey. Drift past the common rooms, where you'll probably observe a few students sleeping or lolling on couches, and proceed to the East Wing, which contains the Great Hall with its hammerbeam ceiling, stained-glass windows, and impressive fireplace. From the High Table, a stair-case leads to the Senior Common Room. Under the quadrangle, the Hart House Theatre is well known for its theatrical and other productions. The West Wing contains the Justina M. Barnicke Art Gallery, a fine collection of Canadian art.

Exit on the south side onto Hart House Circle. Proceed to your right around the circle. On the left is the:

10. Stewart Observatory, originally built in 1857 and reconstructed in 1908, and on the right stands:

11. University College, nicknamed the Godless College when it was founded in 1853 on nonsectarian lines. It was built from 1856 to 1859 by Cumberland and Storm in a fabulous Romanesque Revival style with fanciful towers and chimneys and intricately and heavily patterned round arches. Set around a quadrangle, the college has splendid East and West Halls in the south

Walking Tour—
Queen's Park & the University

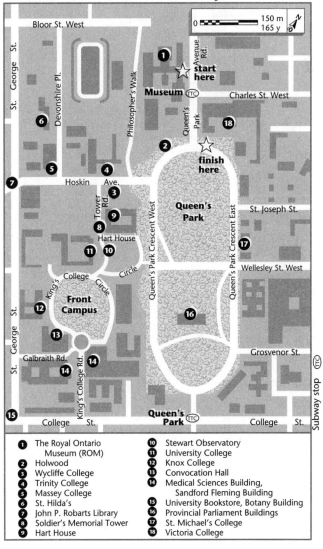

Map labels:

Bloor St. West
St. George St.
Devonshire Pl.
Philosopher's Walk
Avenue Rd.
1 start here
Museum (TTC)
Charles St. West
18
6
Queen's Park
5
2
7
Hoskin Ave.
4
3
finish here
Tower Rd.
9
8
11
10
Hart House
Queen's Park
St. Joseph St.
College Circle
Circle
King's College Circle
Queen's Park Crescent West
Queen's Park Crescent East
17
Wellesley St. West
12
Front Campus
St. George St.
13
16
Galbraith Rd.
14
King's College Rd.
14
Grosvenor St.
15
College St.
Queen's Park (TTC)
College St.
Subway stop (TTC)

0 — 150 m / 165 y

Legend:

1 The Royal Ontario Museum (ROM)
2 Holwood
3 Wycliffe College
4 Trinity College
5 Massey College
6 St. Hilda's
7 John P. Robarts Library
8 Soldier's Memorial Tower
9 Hart House
10 Stewart Observatory
11 University College
12 Knox College
13 Convocation Hall
14 Medical Sciences Building, Sandford Fleming Building
15 University Bookstore, Botany Building
16 Provincial Parliament Buildings
17 St. Michael's College
18 Victoria College

wing. The first women to enter the university were admitted to this college in 1884; there were nine at the end of that year. Go inside. The main staircase has a fantastic dragon newel post at the bottom.

Walk through into the quadrangle and around and out on the west side of the building. Turn left and walk south to King's College Circle. On your right will be:

12. **Knox College.** Go in to see the Gothic interior fan vaulting at the main entrance and the Caven Library with its hammerbeam ceiling.

Exit and continue around the circle to:

13. **Convocation Hall,** a monstrous Victorian bore. En route, you'll pass the far more elegant Simcoe Hall. Take some time to look back across the lawn at Hart House and the other university buildings across the circle.

Continue south to the:

14. **Medical Sciences Building** on the left, a concrete, brutalist building and the unimpressive classical revival **Sanford Fleming Building** on the right.

Exit onto College Avenue. If you want to, turn right to visit the:

15. **University bookstore,** at 214 College St., in the old city reference library, and then turn back and walk toward Queen's Park past the **Botany Building** and the lovely glass greenhouse that graces the rim of the park.

Walk into the park to the:

16. **Provincial Parliament buildings** (1886–92), an impressive example of Romanesque Revival created out of glorious pink sandstone. Beyond the entrance with its domed turrets is an impressive interior of carved wood, ornate cast and wrought iron, and a three-story legislative chamber with coved ceiling.

Exit at the northeastern rim of the circle to see:

17. **St. Michael's College,** which began in 1852 as a Roman Catholic boys' school, became affiliated with the university in 1881, and formally became a college in 1910. Nearby:

18. **Victoria College,** which was established in 1836 in Cobourg, Ontario, and moved here in 1892 when it became part of the University of Toronto. Originally a Methodist institution, it has been related to the United Church of Canada since 1925.

Note: Free tours of the university sponsored by the Alumni Association are given Monday through Friday at 10:30am and 1 and 2:30pm through the summer only. Call **978-5000.**

Walking Tour 5
St. Lawrence & Downtown East

Start   Union Station.

Finish   King subway station.

Time   Two to three hours, allowing for browsing time.

Best Time   Saturday (when the St. Lawrence Market is in full swing).

Worst Time   Sunday (when it's closed).

Begin at:

1. **Union Station** and check out its interior.

   Across the street, at the corner of York and Front streets, stands the:

2. **Royal York Hotel,** a venerable railroad hotel, longtime gathering place for Torontonians and home of the famous Imperial Room cabaret/nightclub (still there, but for dining and dancing only).

   Walk east on Front Street and, at the corner of Bay and Front, look up at the:

3. **Royal Bank Plaza,** two triangular gold-sheathed towers, one 41 floors, the other 26, joined by a 130-foot-high atrium.

   Cross Bay and continue east on Front Street. On the south side of the street is the impressive sweep of **One Front Street,** the main post office building, which for some reason reminds me of Buckingham Palace. On the north side of the street is the city's latest financial palace, Bell Canada Enterprises's:

4. **BCE Place,** Go inside. It's impressive and you can also enjoy the Movenpick Marche and the other stores in the concourse. The twin office towers are connected by a huge glass-covered galleria five stories high spanning the block between Bay and Yonge. Here, too, is the state-of-the-art **Hockey Hall of Fame.**

Take a Break

For a unique dining experience stop in **BCE Place's Marche,** which simulates a market dining experience. Across the courtyard, for fine dining, try the dramatically designed **Acqua.** Downstairs, there's also a food court with a variety of fast food and casual dining choices.

Back out on Front Street, continue to the northwest corner of Yonge and stop to admire the:

5. **Bank of Montréal** (1885–86), a suitably ornate building for the most powerful Canadian bank in the 19th century, banker to the colonial and federal governments. Inside, the banking hall rises to a beamed coffered ceiling with domed skylights of stained glass. The exterior, embellished with carvings, porthole windows, and a balustrade, is a sight in itself. From here, you can look along Front Street and see the weird mural by Derek M. Besant that adorns the famous and highly photogenic Flatiron or Gooderham Building (1892).

6. **The Gooderham Building** was built as the headquarters of George Gooderham, who had built upon his distilling business expanding into railroads, insurance, and philanthropy. It occupies a triangular site and the western tip of the five-story structure is beautifully curved—windows as well—and topped with a semicircular tower.

Continue along Front Street, crossing Yonge to stop in at the:

7. **O'Keefe Centre** and the **St. Lawrence Centre,** next door. In the former, the National Ballet of Canada and the Canadian Opera Company perform.

Continue along Front Street to:

8. **The Beardmore Building** (1872), at 35–39 Front St. E. This and the many other cast-iron buildings that line the street were the heart of the warehouse district in the late 19th century, close to the lakefront and rail heads. Now they're occupied by stores like **Frida Crafts,** which sells imports from Guatemala, India, and Bangladesh, as well as jewelry, bags, candles, and other knickknacks; and **Mountain Equipment Co-op,** stocked with everything an outdoor adventurer needs. At nos. 43–45, note the handsome cast-iron facades. Continue to Church Street, browsing in the stores.

Cross Church Street. More stores to browse in follow, like **Alf's Antiques** at no. 79, which is jammed with all kinds of Canadian pine and other furnishings—grandiose mirrors, lamps, paintings, and more. Next door **Ra** features a vast array of fashions, tablecloths, napkins, rugs, and other items mainly from India. At no. 83 **Kristina Appletree** is in total contrast featuring everything that is white and wonderful and Victorian—linens, lace, pillows—as well as china and glass.

Take a Break

The obvious and most fun place to stop is in the St. Lawrence Market at one of the stands offering fresh produce. Other choices, though, are **Le Papillon,** around the corner on Church Street, which features a raft of savory and dessert crepes, **Pizzeria Uno** on Front Street, or the **Victorian Tea Room** at 83 Front St.

Cross Market Street to the:

9. **St. Lawrence Market,** in the old market building on the right. Enter this great market hall, which was constructed around the city's second city hall (1844–45). The elegant pedimented facade that you see as you stand in the center of the hall was originally the center block of the city hall. Today the market is filled with all kinds of food vendors but is at its very best on Saturday, when the farmers bring in their fresh produce, starting at 5am.

Walking Tour—
St. Lawrence & Downtown East

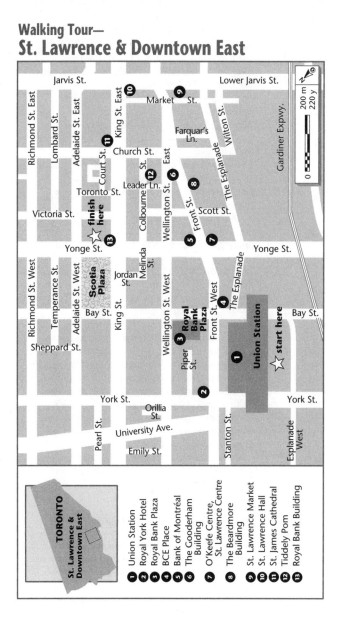

Jarvis St.

Lower Jarvis St.

Richmond St. East

Lombard St.

Adelaide St. East

King St. East

Market St.

Farquar's Ln.

Wilton St.

Gardiner Expwy.

200 m
220 y

Church St.

Court St.

Toronto St.

Colbourne St.

Leader Ln.

Wellington St. East

Front St.

Scott St.

The Esplanade

Victoria St.

finish here

Yonge St.

Yonge St.

Richmond St. West

Temperance St.

Adelaide St. West

Scotia Plaza

Melinda St.

Jordan St.

Wellington St. West

Royal Bank Plaza

The Esplanade

Bay St.

King St.

Front St. West

Bay St.

Sheppard St.

Piper St.

Union Station

start here

York St.

Orillia St.

Stanton St.

York St.

Pearl St.

University Ave.

Esplanade West

Emily St.

TORONTO
St. Lawrence & Downtown East

1. Union Station
2. Royal York Hotel
3. Royal Bank Plaza
4. BCE Place
5. Bank of Montréal
6. The Gooderham Building
7. O'Keefe Centre, St. Lawrence Centre
8. The Beardmore Building
9. St. Lawrence Market
10. St. Lawrence Hall
11. St. James Cathedral
12. Tiddely Pom
13. Royal Bank Building

Exit where you came in. Cross the street and cut through Market Lane Park and the shops at Market Square past the new market building. Turn right onto King Street to the:

10. **St. Lawrence Hall** (1850–51), the focal point of the community in the mid-19th century. This hall was

the site of grand city occasions, political rallies, balls, and entertainment. Frederick Douglass delivered an antislavery lecture here, Jenny Lind and Adelina Patti sang here in 1851 and 1860, respectively; Gen. Tom Thumb appeared here in 1862; and George Brown campaigned for Confederation here in this most elegant Palladian-style building with its domed cupola.

Cross the street and enter the 19th-century garden with a fountain and neatly trimmed flower beds that are filled with seasonal flowers. If you like, you can sit on a bench and rest while you admire the handsome proportions of St. Lawrence Hall and listen to the chimes of:

11. **St. James Cathedral,** which is adjacent to the garden on the north side of King Street. York's first church and first Anglican church was built here from 1803 to 1807. Originally a frame building, it was enlarged in 1818 and 1819 and replaced in 1831. The first incumbent was the Rev. George O'Kill Stuart, followed by John Strachan (pronounced Strawn), later the first bishop of Toronto, who conducted himself with great pomp from his mansion on Jarvis Street and wielded great temporal as well as spiritual power in the city. The second church was burned in 1839 and the first cathedral erected, but this, too, was destroyed by fire, in the great fire of 1849. The present building was begun in 1850 and finished in 1874. Inside, there's a Tiffany window in memory of William Jarvis at the northern end of the east aisle.

From here you can also view one of the early retail store buildings that were built when King Street was the main commercial street. Nos. 129–35 was originally built as an Army and Navy Store, using cast iron, plate glass, and arched windows so that the shopper could see what was available in the store.

Take a Break

From St. James, the venerable **King Edward Hotel** is only a block away if you need refreshment. Afternoon tea is served or you can stop for light fare or lunch in the **Café Victoria.** Both **La Maquette** and **Biagio** on King Street have very appealing outdoor dining courtyards.

From St. James, go south on Church Street and turn right into Colbourne Street. If you have kids, you might enjoy browsing at:

12. **Tiddely Pom,** which is devoted exclusively to children's books. Wine enthusiasts might want to check out **Wine Not,** an establishment that sells everything you need to make beer and wine—from corks and labels to glucose and vats.

From Colbourne, turn left down Leader Lane to Wellington, where you can enjoy a fine view of the mural on the Flatiron building and also of the rhythmic flow of mansard rooflines along the south side of Front Street.

Turn right and proceed to Yonge, then turn right and walk to King Street. Note the building on the northeast corner of Yonge and King before catching the subway. It's the:

13. **Royal Bank Building** (1913–15), designed by Carrere & Hastings.

Walking Tour 6
Bloor/Yorkville

Start   At the corner of Bloor and Yonge streets.

Finish   At the corner of Bloor and Yonge streets.

Time   As long as you want to make it—depends on how serious a shopper or collector you are. Just walking it will take an hour.

Best Times   Tuesday through Saturday (when everything is functioning).

Worst Time   Monday (when many of the galleries are closed).

Walk west along Bloor Street from Yonge Street on the north side of the street. The first complex you'll come to is the:

1. **Holt Renfrew Centre,** not to be confused with the Holt Renfrew store itself, which is the ultimate high-class Toronto emporium (the equivalent of Bloomingdale's or Bergdorf in New York).

Downstairs in the center you'll find several restaurants, including **Timothy's** for coffees from around the world. Also down here is one of my favorite fun stores, **Science City,** which is filled with books, games, puzzles, and models, all relating to the sciences—life, chemistry, physics, and astronomy—as well as serious stuff like telescopes, trilobites, and hologram watches.

Another intriguing browsing experience is **Geomania,** which features all kinds of rocks and polished minerals, some worked into attractive sculptures, others into vases, and still others into plain bookends and jewelry.

At street level you'll pass **Ashley China,** the premier shopping place for fine china, crystal, and silver; and **Eddie Bauer** for casual, good-looking sportswear.

Take a Break

On Holt Renfrew Centre's upper level, the **Bloor Street Diner** stays open from 11am to 3am daily and offers a

broad menu featuring everything from hot entrées to
sandwiches.

2. Holt Renfrew itself is a delight to shop. It's filled with
designer boutiques—Yves St. Laurent, Calvin Klein,
Donna Karan, Anne Klein, Moschino, Ralph Lauren,
and Victor Costa.

Continue west along Bloor to Bay Street. Cross Bay
Street, eyeing:

3. David's, at no. 66, for shoes; **Capezio** for shoes and
leotards; **Emporio Armani,** at no. 80, for the less
expensive Armani line; and **Harry Rosen** (no. 82),
one of Toronto's foremost men's designers.

Cross Bellair Street and continue past:

4. Boss, for quintessential men's fashions, the **Body Shop,**
and **Benetton,** at no. 102, to the **Irish Shop** (no. 110)
for women, which has fetching fashions, accessories, and
books, too. More stores follow—**Louis Vuitton;** the
Museum Collection, which stocks reproductions of
statues, models, Kosta Boda glass, ceramics, jewelry,
games, and art puzzles; and **Marc Laurent** for more
avant-garde designer clothes for men and women.

At Avenue Road you'll come to:

5. The Renaissance Shops, where you'll find **Secrett,** a
jewel-box-like jewelry store; **Giorgio Femme;** and the
Florentine Shop, crammed with all kinds of pretty
china and gift items from Florence.

This modern retail development is backdrop to the:

6. Church of the Redeemer (1879), a quiet enclave on
Bloor Street with inviting outdoor benches set against
the stone building with its slate roof and stolid belfry.

Cut through Renaissance Shops to Cumberland,
browsing as you go. Turn right onto Cumberland.

Take a Break

Il Posto is an attractive Yorkville restaurant tucked away
in a courtyard. In summer it's pleasant to lunch outside.
Fine Italian cuisine and desserts.

Start on the north side at:

7. Silverbridge, at no. 162, which sells beautifully crafted
modern jewelry. Move on to **Tascrew** for fine leathers;
Featherdown Quilts for bedroom comforts; and
Gianni Versace for the ultimate Italian shirts.

Backtrack slightly across the street to:

8. Nocean, at no. 161, featuring fun games and useful
gadgets, all sleekly designed, many from New York's
Museum of Modern Art.

Back on the north side, move on to:

Walking Tour—Bloor/Yorkville

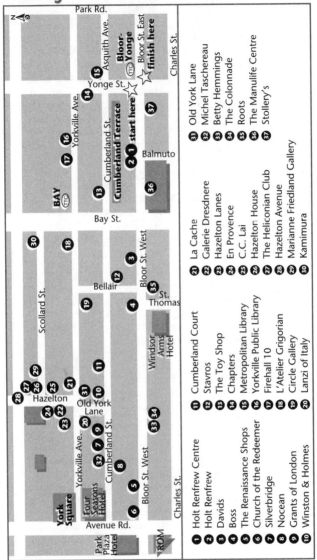

Park Rd.

Asquith Ave.

Charles St.

Bloor-Yonge TTC

Bloor St. East finish here ⭐

Yonge St.

⑮

⑭

Yorkville Ave.

⑯

⑰

Cumberland St.

Cumberland Terrace start here ⭐② ①

Balmuto

⑬

㊲

BAY TTC

⑬

㊱

Bay St.

㉚

⑱

Bloor St. West

③

⑫

Bellair

㉟

St. Thomas

Scollard St.

⑲

④

Windsor Arms Hotel

⑪

㉙

㉗ ㉖ ㉕ ㉑

㉛ ㉑ ⑩

㉘

Hazelton

㉔ ㉒

Old York Lane

㉓ ⑳

⑨

㉝ ㉞

Yorkville Ave.

㉜ ⑦

Cumberland St.

⑧

York Square

⑤

Four Seasons Hotel

Bloor St. West

Charles St.

⑥

Avenue Rd.

Park Plaza Hotel

ROM

① Holt Renfrew Centre
② Holt Renfrew
③ Davids
④ Boss
⑤ The Renaissance Shops
⑥ Church of the Redeemer
⑦ Silverbridge
⑧ Nocean
⑨ Grants of London
⑩ Winston & Holmes

⑪ Cumberland Court
⑫ Stavros
⑬ The Toy Shop
⑭ Chapters
⑮ Metropolitan Library
⑯ Yorkville Public Library
⑰ Firehall 10
⑱ L'Atelier Grigorian
⑲ Circle Gallery
⑳ Lanzi of Italy

㉑ La Cache
㉒ Galerie Dresdnere
㉓ Hazelton Lanes
㉔ En Provence
㉕ C.C. Lai
㉖ Hazelton House
㉗ The Heliconian Club
㉘ Hazelton Avenue
㉙ Marianne Friedland Gallery
㉚ Kamimura

㉛ Old York Lane
㉜ Michel Taschereau
㉝ Betty Hemmings
㉞ The Colonnade
㉟ Roots
㊱ The Manulife Centre
㊲ Stollery's

9. Grants of London for brilliantly colored avant-garde
ties, ultraluxurious robes, and spiffy suspenders.
Continue on to the **Guild Shop** (no. 140), the **Ontario
Crafts Council Store,** which sells very striking ceramics,
glass, baskets, jewelry, fabrics, and other craft items.
Upstairs, Inuit art is on display—sculpture and

paintings. You'll pay $1,500 for a soapstone bear, but it's worth coming here to see the work that is scouted and brought from the northern regions.

Also on the north side, at the corner of Old York Lane, stop in at the following shops:

10. **Winston & Holmes** (no. 138), a tobacco shop selling Dunhill Havana and La Gloria de Cubana, among many other cigars, plus shaving gear and Mont Blanc writing implements. They will mail order. Farther along there are a couple of fashion favorites—**Johanna's** and **Marilyn Brooks.** Continue on to no. 124, the **Papery,** which stocks stationery, photo albums, illustrated shopping bags, and cards.

Continue and turn left down a passageway to:

11. **Cumberland Court,** which shelters a number of shops. Before crossing Bellair note the park across the street. Financed by taxpayers' money, it's proved controversial. It's meant to show the natural development of Canada.

Take a Break

The **Bellair Café** is the place to see and be seen among the young professional up-and-comers, either in the back courtyard or out front. A glass of wine will cost $6.50; main courses range from $11 to $15. Go for a drink and a snack and to watch the street scene. The terrace out back is especially pleasant.

Stay on the south side of the street once you cross Bellair and you'll encounter:

12. **Stavros,** a tailor and shirtmaker, and **Kidding Awound,** stocking hundreds of music boxes, clockwork toys, and miniatures.

Cross Bay to:

13. **The Toy Shop,** on the north side—two floors filled with kids' games, toys, and books. On to **Dinah's Cupboard,** which has great salads and pâtés to go, gourmet teas, coffees, and vinegars, plus frozen items like vegetarian pasta to take home and pop in the oven.

Turn left onto Yonge. You'll pass:

14. **Chapters** for secondhand books; **Pottree and Pantree,** which stocks a full range of kitchenware and masses of glasses; **Cubita,** an inviting store selling Cuban coffee; and the **Cookbook Store,** an adventurous cook's dream come true.

Across Yonge Street stands:

15. **The Metropolitan Library** (1973–77), designed by Raymond Moriyama. It doesn't look that terrific from the outside, but go in and experience the interior. It'll make reading and studying seem a natural and wonderful part of life. Not everyone agrees, of course.

Turn left onto Yorkville Avenue and walk west. On the right stands:

16. **The Yorkville Public Library** (1906–07), at no. 22. It looks important with its porticoed entrance.

Just down the street on the same side stands:

17. **Firehall 10** (1876), at no. 34, an endearing Yorkville landmark that was rebuilt, except for the tower, from 1889 to 1890. The tower where the hoses are stored bears the coat of arms of the Town of Yorkville, saved from the town hall when it was demolished. The images—a beer barrel, jack plane, brick mold, anvil, and bull's head—represent the vocations of the town's early councillors.

Cross Bay Street to:

18. **L'Atelier Grigorian,** on the right, stocking a fantastic selection of classical and jazz CDs. Opposite is the **Omega Centre Bookstore,** filled with New Age titles. Whole sections are devoted to such subjects as shamanism, zen, graphology, Jung, and more.

Walk west and cross Bellair. On the left (south) side of the street you'll find the ultracommercial:

19. **Circle Gallery,** which has been selling the likes of Erté and others for many years. At no. 87, cooks will want to look over the offerings at the **Compleat Kitchen.** Upstairs at no. 87, **Primitives** has objects from Bali and Indonesia. **Paper Things** raises funds for the National Ballet by selling personalized stationery. Both the **Candle Emporium** and **Oh Yes, Toronto** have suitable gifts to bring home. **Ulysses Bookshop,** at no. 101, has a terrific selection of travel books.

Across the street, **Muti,** at no. 88, has stunning modern Italian majolica. **Namaste** (no. 112) features Himalayan imports, including some fine quality Tibetan jewelry. **Herat Carpets,** at the corner of Hazelton Avenue, offers a visual treat.

Take a Break

There are several possibilities for stops in this neighborhood. The best option, it seems to me, is **Hazelton Gourmet** in Hazelton Lanes where you can take advantage of the outdoor courtyard. **Movenpick Bistretto** is another good choice for great desserts or a good-value lunch, however. Good ethnic choices are **Zero** for Japanese, **Little Tibet,** and **Mandaloon** for Lebanese. A good popular café/bar, which is a favorite of mine, is **Hemingways.**

Back on the south side pass Old York Lane to:

20. **Lanzi of Italy** (no. 123), which has stylish items for the desk and an assortment of fine leather goods. At **Arctic,**

no. 125, there's an assortment of Inuit sculpture, jewelry, clothes, fur hats, and so on. You'll need to know how to sift out the quality items here.

Across the street:

21. **La Cache** displays a handsome mix of tablecloths, napkins, jewelry, and fashions. **L'Elegante** (no. 122) is a discount designer fashion house, while next door at no. 124, **Maison de la Presse** offers foreign newspapers and magazines, including all of the major U.S. papers.

Turn back from the Maison and go down Hazelton Avenue. First on the left you'll come to:

22. **Galerie Dresdnere**, and then **Kinsman Robinson, Nancy Poole's Studio,** and **Miriam Shiell**—all well-known galleries.

Beyond Laura Ashley, turn left into:

23. **Hazelton Lanes.** Hazelton Lanes is a difficult-to-negotiate collection of stylish boutiques and stores that is laid out on two levels around a central courtyard. The signs are poor and it's easy to get disoriented in this circular maze, where you'll find the sine qua non names of fashion and design. On the lower concourse there's **Chez Catherine,** a boutique that has dressed wealthy fashionable Toronto women for many years; **Gianni Versace, Krizia,** and **Valentino; Fogal** for fashionable hose and underwear in rainbow colors; the **General Store** at several locations, featuring kitchen/housewares in one location and gifts for the person who has everything (calculators, something called a fishing mate, Newtonian puzzles, and Filofax) at another; **Classical Record Shop; & Asser** for custom-made shirts; **Bart Leather and Suede** for men's leather fashions; **Brown's Shoes,** which besides its own label sells such well-known designers as Bruno Magli; **Timothy's Coffees of the World; Gianfranco Ferré** for dramatic feminine tailoring; and **Aquascutum** for the traditional look.

Take a Break

Both **Lox, Stock & Bagel** and **Hazelton Gourmet** have access to the outdoor courtyard and make good luncheon/snack spots.

On the upper level, the shopping feast continues with more great names, like **Rodier** and **Marc Lipman,** whose fun and artistic designs for kids' fashions include original T-shirts and many very appealing creations. **Mark McClaine** has good-looking Asian and Western antiques; **Joan & David**—names that need no description; plus, there are **Teuscher Chocolate of Switzerland** and **Roots,** a Canadian specialty store selling leather bags as well as T-shirts, sweaters, and shorts. **Alfred Sung** is another fashion name, and so are **Ralph Lauren** and **Giorgio Emporio.** Farther on there's **Wenger Chic,** featuring Austrian- and German-style fashions, and near the entrance to Avenue Road is **Giorgio Femme.**

You could spend the whole day shopping at Hazelton Lanes. Here I ask that you do a circular browse through and exit where you entered, returning in timely fashion to Hazelton Lane.

Back outside, turn left to:

24. En Provence, featuring fabulous country French tableclothes, napkins, placemats; Limoges china, featuring brilliantly colored designs and glazes by Laure Jady; and other decorative household items. Expensive and luxurious. Art lovers will want to stop into **Mira Godard,** a well-known city gallery that represents such famous Americans as Robert Motherwell, Larry Rivers, Frank Stella, Jacques Lipchitz, David Hockney, and Jasper Johns, plus many Canadians, such as Lawren Harris and Clark McDougall.

Backtrack a little and cross the street to relish the offerings at:

25. C.C. Lai, selling exquisite Asian art—furniture inlaid with mother of pearl, wonderful Oriental screens, Buddhas, jewelry, and more. Also check out the **Glass Art Gallery** at no. 21.

Continue north along Hazelton. On the right side you'll come to:

26. Hazelton House, at no. 33, originally part of the Olivet Congregational Church (1890), which now houses several galleries including **Sable-Castelli, Gallery 7,** and **Schieder.**

Next door, look at the facade of the church housing:

27. The Heliconian Club, which was founded in 1909 as a forum for women in the arts. Since 1921 the club has occupied this Carpenter Gothic Revival church built in 1876 as the Olivet Congregational. Note the triangular wooden lancet windows and filigree decoration. Next door in two town houses are jeweler **Sommer** and **Escada,** selling women's fashions.

Continue along:

28. Hazelton Avenue, observing the handsome Victorian homes on either side. Nos. 49–51 and 53–55 are particularly worth noting. No. 74 has an especially attractive fan window above the entrance and decorative window bays. No. 68 has a highly decorated gable.

Continue to Berryman; retrace your steps, turn left down Scollard, and stop at the:

29. Marianne Friedland Gallery, at no. 122, and **Elektra,** showing contemporary British art. (Gallery One is across the street.) Several stores down, **Ballenford Books,** at no. 98, has a superb selection of architecture books displayed in an exquisite town house that's part of a marvelous six-house row built in 1893. Look up at the fabulous gabling of these and other beauties along Scollard.

Continuing along Scollard Street, you reach the **Cygnet Gallery,** and at the corner of Bay Street:

30. **Kamimura,** exhibiting Japanese art.

From Scollard, cut through Village Stream, which connects to Yorkville Avenue. Turn right and walk along the south side to:

31. **Old York Lane,** and take it through to Cumberland. Turn right along Cumberland. On the north side, tucked downstairs, are stores that we missed earlier, like:

32. **Michel Taschereau** and **Ronald Windebanks,** both antiques dealers.

Take a Break

For an elegant stop, head into the **Four Seasons Studio Cafe** or stop in for the afternoon tea served in the lobby. In the Renaissance Plaza, you could also stop for a luncheon at **Enoteca.** The plaza has more casual dining spots, too.

Go through Renaissance Plaza back to Bloor Street. Cross the street and "do" the south side of Bloor, walking east, where:

33. **Betty Hemmings** has exquisite leather goods.

34. **The Colonnade,** at no. 131, was built from 1961 to 1964, one of the first buildings to combine residence, office, and retail space. It still does so, with the restaurants taking full advantage of the overhanging forecourt. Several stores are found at this address— their storefronts stretching along the street—**Max Mara, Lalique, Jaeger, Hermès, Chanel,** and **Town Shoes** among them. Continue walking along in front of the concourse, past such famous names as **Giorgio Couture** (no. 111), **Royal de Versailles, Cartier,** and **Cole Haan,** all at no. 101.

Cross St. Thomas Street to:

35. **Roots,** a quintessential Canadian store, and just down the street the first Canadian outpost of New York's very own **Tiffany & Co.** at no. 85.

Cross Bay Street to:

36. **The Manulife Centre** (no. 55), where you'll find **Birks,** a very traditional Canadian store that offers well-priced silver, crystal, and china, including Royal Doulton. **Calderone** specializes in shoes and leather goods. On the courtyard level there's a branch of Britain's **Marks**

and Spencer, well known for reasonably priced clothes and other goods.

Take a Break

There are several possibilities here—**Toby's Goodeats** for burgers and sandwiches; **Bemelmans** and the **Bloor Street Diner** for more elegant atmosphere and dining.

Cross Balmuto Street and walk to Yonge Street for a look at the merchandise at:

37. **Stollery's,** located in a 1929 building at the corner of Bloor and Yonge streets. A traditional Canadian store, it has good stocks of Dacks, Aquascutum, Burberry, and other British-inspired fashions for men and women.

8

Toronto Shopping
A to Z

Toronto's major shopping areas are the Bloor/Yorkville area for designer boutiques and top-name galleries; Queen Street West for a more funky mixture of fashion, antiques, and bookstores; and a number of shopping malls/centers like Queen's Quay down on the waterfront, the two-block-long Eaton Centre, and other smaller complexes like College Park, Royal Bank Plaza, and Village by the Grange.

The two great names in Toronto retailing are Eaton's and the Hudson's Bay Company (formerly Simpson's), both founded in the mid-19th century. They're still here and thriving. Canadian fashion names to look for are Alfred Sung, Cy Mann, and Norma.

The two major markets are Kensington Market and the St. Lawrence Market.

Store hours are generally Monday to Wednesday from 9:30 or 10am to 6pm and Saturday and Sunday from 10am to 5pm, with extended hours (8 to 9:30pm) on Thursday and usually Friday.

Provincial sales tax is 8%, but out-of-province visitors can reclaim it. Nonresidents can also reclaim the 7% **goods and services tax** (GST). See Chapter 3.

Best buys are mainly Canadian arts and crafts, which can be imported into the United States without duty.

Antiques

You'll find the greatest concentration of good-quality antiques at the Harbourfront Antiques Market, best visited Sunday when all the dealers are in residence (during the week many are at their stores). The finest antiques can be found in the Bloor/Yorkville area, with many shops a short walk from the Four Seasons Hotel, and in the Mount Pleasant/St. Clair area along the 500-, 600-, and 700-block of Mount Pleasant Road. The more funky and often more recent collectibles can be found at various stores along Queen Street West. Markham Village also has several antiques stores.

Abacus Antiques, 6 Ripley Ave. ☎ **760-9358.**

This store specializes in Canadian oak and pine furniture—rolltop desks, cabinets, tables, and chairs—and other nostalgia.

Also at Harbourfront Antiques Market.

Antiquers, 567 Mount Pleasant Rd. ☎ **481-4474.**

In this interesting shop, you will find antique and estate jewelry, rare Belleek pieces, silver, and other objets d'art.

Bernardi Antiques, 707 Mount Pleasant Rd., south of Eglinton Ave. ☎ **483-6471.**

Look here for discontinued Doulton figurines, art glass, paintings, carpets, silver, and furniture.

C. C. Lai, 9 Hazelton Ave. ☎ **928-0662.**

This cluttered store has fine Chinese antiques—exquisite inlaid furniture and screens, Buddhas, and jewelry—really beautiful pieces, both large and small.

Circa Antiques, 166 Davenport Rd. ☎ **961-3744.**

Circa is one of the best places to find formal and country French furniture, from Louis XIV and XV through Louis XVI and Second Empire. Buffets, tables, armoires, chairs, and desks are the main stock, along with sconces and chandeliers.

Fifty One Antiques Ltd., 21 Avenue Rd. ☎ **968-2416.**

A specialist in 17th- and 18th-century furniture, as well as Empire, Biedermeier, and other later styles, Fifty One Antiques also has lots of accessories, like lamps made from old bases, carvings, European paintings, and more.

★ **Harbourfront Antiques Market,** 390 Queen's Quay W. ☎ **260-2626.**

The 100-plus dealers here sell fine-quality antiques. On summer Sundays there's also a market outside featuring less established dealers. Although it's relatively quiet during the week, it's hopping on weekends, when more than 150 dealers open up; you'll have to get there early. Hours are Tuesday through Friday from 11am to 6pm, Saturday from 10am to 6pm, and Sunday from 8am to 6pm.

Journeys End, 612 Markham St. ☎ **536-2226.**

An appropriate name for the miscellaneous assortment of estate china, jewelry, silver, and furniture that winds up here in an amorphous display. Eminently browsable.

Mark McLaine, Hazelton Lanes. ☎ **927-7972.**

This marvelously eclectic store has unique items, like a pair of never-worn 1929 leather shoes, as well as pine furniture, French sconces, costume jewelry (especially deco), carved wood and stone

---

An Important Note on Prices

Unless stated otherwise, **the prices cited in this guide are given in Canadian dollars,** which is good news for U.S. travelers because the Canadian dollar is worth 26% less than the American dollar, but buys nearly as much. As we go to press, $1 Canadian is worth 74¢ U.S., which means that your $100-a-night hotel room will cost only U.S. $74, and your $6 breakfast costs only U.S. $4.44.

Here's a quick table of equivalents:

Canadian $	U.S.$
$1	$0.74
5	$3.70
10	$7.40
20	$14.80
50	$37.00
100	$74.00
200	$148.00

pieces, silver frames, perfume bottles, and blue-and-white Oriental ware. You'll find reproductions, too. A great place to browse. Prices range from $16 to $6,000.

★ **Michel Taschereau,** 176 Cumberland St. ☎ **923-3020.**

In this fine store you'll have to thread your way through the dense collection very carefully. You'll find 18th- and 19th-century English and French furniture, including large armoires, and French and English china, like Coalport, Derby, and Worcester. There's Lalique glass and Canadian folk art also.

Mostly Movables, 785 Queen St. W., west of Bathurst St.
☎ **865-9716.**

A large selection of furniture, mostly purchased at estate sales, is featured here, including wardrobes, dressers, couches, and dining-room sets (for as little as $950). Most of the pieces date from the 1920s on and cost $150 and up. Turn-of-the-century Canadian pine pieces are also available.

The Paisley Shop Limited, 889 Yonge St. ☎ **923-5830.**

A specialist in 18th- and 19th-century English furniture—dining tables, chairs, sideboards, mirrors, and desks—the Paisley Shop Limited also offers such accessories as porcelain, glass, and chandeliers. Upstairs is a selection of floral and other patterned cushions and lamps.

R. A. O'Neill Antiques, 100 Avenue Rd. ☎ **968-2806.**

This is the place for country furniture from around the world— French, German, English, American, Dutch, and Irish. Along with tables, chairs, chests, and cupboards, the stock includes samplers, baskets, lamps, decoys, and brass and tin objects.

Red Indian and Empire Antiques, 536 Queen St. W.
☎ **364-2706.**

The eclectic mixture of objects here spans the 1930s to the 1950s— fountain pens, Coke memorabilia, neon clocks, Bakelite jewelry, torchère lamps, wall sconces, mirrors, figurines, and other nostalgia. It's open Monday through Saturday from 11:30am to 6pm.

★ **Ronald Windebanks,** 21 Avenue Rd. ☎ **962-2862.**

This store is filled with treasures found by Mr. Windebank, who has a good eye for the unique object with character and whimsy. There's an eclectic array of furniture, porcelain, crystal, glass, botanical and ornithological prints, antique garden furniture, and grand urns, plus some charming carved animal folk art.

Stanley Wagman Antiques, 111 Avenue Rd. ☎ **964-1047.**

A major purveyor of French furniture, both country and formal, as well as art deco, Stanley Wagman also features marble fireplaces, chandeliers, and wall sconces.

Art

Most of these galleries are open Tuesday to Saturday from 10:30am to 5:30pm, so don't come around on Sunday or Monday.

Albert White, 80 Spadina Ave., at King St. ☎ **865-1021.**

This gallery for oils, sculpture, and prints has been open since 1966 and is one of the few places specializing in international art, representing such great names as Picasso, Henry Moore, Botero, Francis Bacon, and many others.

Bau-Xi, 340 Dundas St. W. ☎ **977-0600.**

This bi-level gallery exhibits paintings, sculpture, drawings, and prints by contemporary Canadian artists—Ted Godwin, Jack Shadbolt, Joseph Plaskett, Claude Breeze, Brian Kipping, Roly Fenwick, Robert Marchessault, and Hugh Mackenzie.

Circle Gallery, 83 Yorkville Ave. ☎ **961-5806.**

This is the place for the commercial and popular names in prints and lithography—Erté, Lebadang, Vasarely, and others.

Del Bello, 788 King St. W. ☎ **504-2422.**

This gallery specializes in showing international contemporary artists—European, Canadian, and American. It's well known for its annual miniature art show, held in November and December, which features works of 1,500 artists from 72 countries.

★ **Eskimo Art Gallery,** 12 Queen's Quay W. (opposite Westin Harbour Castle). ☎ **366-3000.**

This gallery carries about 500 small and large high-quality Inuit sculptures, most from Cape Dorset or Baffin Island. Prices range from $60 to $14,000. It's certainly one of the largest collections in the city.

★ **Feheley Fine Arts,** 45 Avenue Rd. (2nd floor). ☎ **323-1373.**

Inuit art is the specialty of this prestigious gallery. The Feheleys have collected, exhibited, and sold Inuit sculpture, prints, and drawings for over 30 years, and they personally select each artist and work of art. The gallery therefore offers a wide selection of the finest-quality sculpture and graphics from the Canadian Arctic; they range from small and primitive bone and ivory carvings to contemporary pieces.

Frame by Frame, 473A Church St., at Maitland St. ☎ **921-7149.**

This photography gallery specializes in work by contemporary Canadians only. Black-and-white and color works by as many as 10 photographers are on display.

Galerie Dresdnere, 12 Hazelton Ave. ☎ **923-4662.**

Another major gallery featuring contemporary Canadian artists, such as Peter Krausz (Montréal) and Stephen Lack (Montréal and New York), from coast to coast. Others include maritime realist Tom Forrestall, Bob Boyer (Regina), and Richard Overfield (Vancouver). Galerie Dresdnere has long been associated with artists from Montréal's Automatist School, such as Jean-Paul Riopelle and Borduas, and other important contemporary Canadian art movements.

Galerie Heritage, 137 Yorkville Ave. ☎ **967-1675.**

This gallery has operated in Toronto for 45 years. It specializes in international sculpture and also has several contemporary Gobelins tapestries commissioned from artists from 12 countries. It features four art showcases a year and six one-artist shows.

Gallery Moos, 622 Richmond St. W. ☎ 777-0707.

Another longtime Toronto gallery, in business for more than 30 years, this establishment represents international and Canadian contemporary artists, including Jean-Paul Riopelle.

Gallery One, 121 Scollard St. ☎ 929-3103.

A fixture on the Toronto art scene for 20 years, this gallery is associated with the abstract painters Jack Bush, Kenneth Lochhead, Joseph Drapell, Harold Feist, and Douglas Haynes, as well as with other Canadian artists like Anne Meredith Barry, David Blackwood, Christopher Broadhurst, Brian Burnett, William Goodrige Roberts, and sculptor Alan Reynolds. It also represents American artists Helen Frankenthaler, Kenneth Noland, Jules Olitski, and Stanley Boxer.

The Gallery Shop, in the Art Gallery of Toronto, 317 Dundas St. W. ☎ 979-6610.

Adjacent to the bookstore, this shop carries a great selection of reproductions of international and Canadian art, as well as posters and juvenile prints. Framing services are available.

Glass Art Gallery, 21 Hazelton Ave. ☎ 968-1823.

This gallery features the work of contemporary glass artists from all over the world. When I visited, the show featured the sculptural art of nine French artists. The exhibition changes every month, and the gallery also keeps on hand samples from artists they represent.

★ **Isaacs/Inuit Gallery of Eskimo Art,** 9 Prince Arthur Ave. ☎ 921-9985.

Inuit sculpture, prints, drawings, wall hangings, and antiquities from across the Arctic are featured here, in association with the Isaacs Gallery, the oldest contemporary gallery in the city. The pieces are museum quality. The gallery also specializes in early Native Canadian art and artifacts.

★ **Jane Corkin,** 179 John St. ☎ 979-1980.

This gallery specializes in historical and contemporary photographs by international and Canadian photographers. It represents 40 Canadians as well as the estates of André Kertesz, Irving Penn, and Horst.

Kamimura, 1300 Bay St., at Scollard. ☎ 923-7850.

This long, narrow downstairs gallery specializes in Japanese prints. It's open Tuesday through Saturday from 11am to 5pm.

Kaspar Gallery, 27 Prince Arthur Ave. ☎ 968-2536.

Specializing in Canadian art from the 19th century to the Group of Seven, the Kaspar Gallery features watercolors and contemporary artists, too.

Kinsman Robinson, 14 Hazelton Ave. ☎ 964-2374.

This bi-level gallery exhibits such contemporary Canadian artists as the color-drunk Norval Morrisseau, Henri Masson, Robert Katz,

John Newman, and Stanley Cosgrove, plus sculptors Esther Wertheimer, Maryon Kantaroff, Robert Davidson, and Joseph Jacobs.

Marianne Friedland Gallery, 122 Scollard St. ☎ 961-4900.

Since it opened in 1974, this gallery has shown contemporary Canadian and American artists, including Milton Avery, Philip Pearlstein, Al Held, Hans Hofmann, Margaret Priest, Karen Kulyk, Wolf Kahn, Ronald Boaks, Rafael Goldchain, and Suzanne Olivier.

Mira Godard, 22 Hazelton Ave. ☎ 964-8197.

Another major international player in Toronto, Mira Godard represents, among many others, such famous names as Botero, Robert Motherwell, Frank Stella, Larry Rivers, Jacques Lipchitz, David Hockney, and Jasper Johns, as well as Canadian greats Lawren Harris, Jean-Paul Riopelle, and Colville.

Nancy Poole's Studio, 16 Hazelton Ave. ☎ 964-9050.

For over 20 years this gallery has been exhibiting a roster of about 25 contemporary artists. Every two weeks the gallery mounts one-artist shows, except during the summer, when group shows take over.

Sable-Castelli, 33 Hazelton Ave. ☎ 961-0011.

A specialist in contemporary Canadian art, with names like David Craven, Paul Hutner, Eric Fischl, and others.

Books

★ Abelard Books, 519 Queen St. W. ☎ 366-0021.

This is one of my favorite rare-book stores in the city. It has a fabulous collection of early editions and other rare books, with every subject clearly cataloged. Armchairs invite leisurely browsing. A real book-lover's haven.

About Books, 83 Harbord St. ☎ 975-2668.

At this used-book store, the titles are all well cataloged and the selection is extensive—particularly strong in literature. Out-of-print and antiquarian volumes are available.

★ Albert Britnell Book Shop, 765 Yonge St., north of Bloor St. ☎ 924-3321.

A Toronto tradition, this wonderful store has a great selection of hard- and softcover books displayed handsomely on wooden shelves. The staff is very knowledgeable and helpful.

Another Man's Poison, 29 McCaul St. ☎ 593-6451.

This store is heaven for any aspiring architect, interior designer, or graphic artist because it's filled with a large worldwide stock of books on graphics, antiques, and collectibles—all aspects of design.

Atticus Books, 84 Harbord St. ☎ 922-6045.

The preeminent Toronto dealer in scholarly used books, it also stocks antiquarian books and illuminated manuscripts and has an art room in the back.

Bakka Science Fiction Book Shoppe, 282 Queen St. W.
☎ **596-8161.**

This store is the answer to a science-fiction buff's dreams. It stocks paperback and hardcover versions of both new and used science fiction and fantasy.

Ballenford Books, 98 Scollard St. ☎ **960-0055.**

Located in an architectural Victorian gem, this store sells architecture and design books only.

Bob Miller Book Room, 180 Bloor St. W. (Lower Concourse).
☎ **922-3557.**

This academic bookstore carries a wide selection of titles in the humanities and social sciences. Look for the fiction titles listed under "Recommended Books" in Chapter 1—you're likely to find them here.

Book Cellar Yorkville, 142 Yorkville Ave. ☎ **925-9955.**

This store is well stocked with art, travel, history, and fiction and also has a large selection of domestic and foreign magazines in the back room. It also stays open late—until 11pm during the week and until midnight on weekends.

Book City, 501 Bloor St. W. ☎ **961-4496.**

This store offers good discounts (10%) on new books as well as a large selection of remainders. It's a well-stocked general bookstore with large philosophy and religion sections. Open late daily.

There are other branches at 348 Danforth Ave. and 2350 Bloor St. W.

Children's Book Store, 2532 Yonge St., north of Eglinton.
☎ **480-0233.**

Here you'll find books, cassettes, and videos for kids from birth to age 14. A staff of librarians and teachers assist selection. The ultimate choice of book-loving kids. There are special events, too, on Sunday afternoons.

Coles The World's Biggest Bookstore, 20 Edward St.
☎ **977-7009.**

With 17 miles of bookshelves and more than a million books categorized into more than 50 specialty departments, Coles boasts that if you can't get it here, it doesn't exist. The store also stocks videos and cassettes. Coles also has locations at 726 Yonge St. (☎ **924-1707**); in Commerce Court Concourse (☎ **868-1782**); in the Eaton Centre (☎ **979-9348**); and at various other locations in the city and in the suburbs. Open late.

The Cookbook Store, 850 Yonge St., at Yorkville Ave.
☎ **920-2665.**

Everything's here for the cook and food lover, including international cookbooks organized by cuisine, wine books, professional books for restaurateurs, dessert books, health books, and also cooking and wine magazines.

⭐ **David Mason,** 342 Queen St. W. ☎ **598-1015.**

Another fine used-book store with plenty of first and collector's editions, the store has a huge selection on all subjects. Great bookish atmosphere.

⭐ **David Mirvish Books and Books on Art,** 596 Markham St. ☎ **531-9975.**

This is a fabulous large store specializing in current books on the visual arts—ceramics, sculpture, photography, art history, architecture, and other related subjects. Some out-of-print and rare titles are here, too. Good discounts are offered. Open Thursday and Friday until 9pm.

Dragon Lady Comic Shop, 200 Queen St. W., at University. ☎ **596-1602.**

Comic aficionados will find old and new comics here from 1950 to the present, as well as books related to comics. There are also posters and such collectibles as *Life* magazines (from 1915 on).

Edwards Books and Art, 356 Queen St. W. ☎ **593-0126.**

Edwards has a complete selection of quality art books, limited editions, imported books, and bargain books. The store lists its best deals for the week in the Saturday *Globe and Mail;* it has probably the best discounts on art books going.

Also at 170 Bloor St. W. (☎ **961-2428**), 2200 Yonge St. (☎ **487-5431**), and in the Beaches.

Gulliver's Travel Bookshop, 609 Bloor St. W., two blocks west of Bathurst St. ☎ **537-7700.**

The store carries a full range of travel guidebooks, as well as travel accessories like phrasebooks, maps, and background destination reading.

Longhouse Bookshop, 497 Bloor St. W., near Brunswick Ave. ☎ **921-9995.**

The Canadian specialist in Toronto, it carries a large selection of books on Native Canadian subjects, as well as a full range of Canadian literature, history, political science, poetry, and drama.

Old Favourites Book Shop, Hwy. 7, east of Markham. ☎ **294-3865.**

This is possibly the largest collection of used books in the country— about 300,000 to 400,000 paperbacks and hardbacks. Among the rare-book specialties are equestrian titles focusing on carriages, coaches, and horses.

Open Air Books & Maps, 25 Toronto St. ☎ **363-0719.**

The place to go for travel guidebooks, maps, and other books relating to the outdoors and ecology.

Pages, 256 Queen St. W. ☎ **598-1447.**

This large store is a fine, well-stocked general bookstore, with an extensive selection of foreign, literary, and other magazines.

Seekers Books, 509 Bloor St. W., at Borden. ☎ **925-1982.**

This store offers an eclectic assortment of new and used books, with an emphasis on Eastern religions, the occult, meditation, and other New Age titles, as well as literature and general books.

Smithbooks, Toronto Dominion Centre. ☎ **362-5967.**

This member of the famous Canadian chain is a well-stocked general bookstore, with plenty of titles on Toronto, along with best-sellers and a good selection of newspapers and magazines.

There are many locations in the metro area, including the Eaton Centre (☎ **979-9376**); Hudson's Bay Centre (☎ **967-7177**); Scotia Plaza (☎ **366-7536**); the Royal Bank Plaza (☎ **865-0090**); Queen's Quay (☎ **868-0928**); and most of the airport terminals.

Steven Temple Books, 489 Queen St. W., 2nd floor. ☎ **865-9908.**

This rare-book store specializes in 19th- and 20th-century literary first editions, with a large stock of Canadian literature. There's also a broad selection of good-condition used volumes in various fields.

Theatrebooks, 11 St. Thomas St. ☎ **922-7175.**

The ultimate theater bookstore has sections on opera, film, and dance. The vast number of plays is complemented by a large theater-criticism section and theater magazines.

This Ain't the Rosedale Library, 483 Church St. ☎ **929-9912.**

You could love it for its name alone, but it also has what has to be one of the largest collections of baseball books anywhere. It also carries fiction and books on media, film, art, and design. Some first editions.

Toronto Women's Bookstore, 73 Harbord St. ☎ **922-8744.**

This feminist bookstore has sections for lesbians, books by and about women of color, literary criticism, fiction, and titles that deal with violence against women and children.

Ulysses, 101 Yorkville Ave., between Bay St. and Avenue Rd. ☎ **323-3609.**

A travel-book specialist, the store is well stocked with travel guidebooks, maps, travel literature, and other travel accessories.

The University of Toronto Bookstore, 214 College St. ☎ **978-7908.**

With much more than just textbooks, this academic and general bookstore also features medical, computer, and children's books, plus U of T–crested gifts and clothes.

Writers & Co, 2005 Yonge St., South of Eglington (at Davisville). ☎ **481-8432.**

This store carries a broad selection of fiction and poetry titles as well as children's books and, strangely enough, books about baseball.

China, Silver & Glass

⭐ **Ashley China,** 50 Bloor St. W. ☎ 964-2900.

The ultimate store for china, silver, and glass, this beautiful establishment has elegant table displays of very expensive china, crystal, and flatware—all the top names at decent prices.

⭐ **Birks,** Manulife Centre. 55 Bloor St. W. ☎ 922-2266.

A quintessential, reliable Canadian store known for its jewelry, Birks also carries the top names in china, glass, silver, and other table accessories, like handsome cork tablemats. Prices are pretty good.

Also at the Eaton Centre (☎ 979-9311), First Canadian Place (☎ 363-5663), and other in-town and suburban locations.

Crafts

⭐ **The Algonquins Sweet Grass Gallery,** 668 Queen St. W., near Bathurst St. ☎ 368-1336.

This store, owned by an Ojibwa, has been in business for 20 years or so, specializing in Native Canadian arts and crafts—Iroquois masks, porcupine quill boxes, sculpture, antler carvings, prints, tamarack decoys, as well as moccasins and famous Cowichan hand-knits from British Columbia.

The Arctic Bear, 125 Yorkville Ave. ☎ 967-7885.

This store has an eclectic assortment of Inuit soapstone sculpture, fur and beaver hats, and some Native Canadian clothes and jewelry. You'll need to know precisely what you're looking for.

Art Zone, 592 Markham St., at Bloor and Bathurst sts. ☎ 534-1892.

Here you'll find a variety of glass art—stained glass, slumped glass (bent into marvelous shapes), fused glass, in which the colors have been melted together, as well as blown-glass vases and objects. Some glass jewelry sells for $10 to $15, but prices can rise into the thousands for custom work. The studio is adjacent.

⭐ **The Craft Gallery/Ontario Crafts Council,** 35 McCaul St. ☎ 977-3551.

A showcase for fine contemporary crafts from across Canada. Shows change every six to eight weeks and will feature everything from stained glass to ceramics and weaving. There's a library upstairs.

Frida Craft Stores, 39 Front St. E. ☎ 366-3169.

Canadian crafts plus items and artifacts from Africa, Asia, and Latin America are aesthetically displayed in a handsome high-ceilinged space. Everything from rugs and bags to costume jewelry, clothes, candles, and knickknacks is here. Open daily.

Five Potters Studio, 131A Pears Ave., between Avenue Rd. and Bedford Rd. ☎ 924-6992.

Located upstairs, this studio displays and sells the work of five women ceramists who have worked together for many years. Their work varies: Some pieces are functional, others sculptural; some are hand-worked, other pieces fashioned on the wheel. Feel free to observe the potters at work but call ahead for an appointment.

⭐ **Guild Shop,** 140 Cumberland St. ☎ 921-1721.

Famous for Native Canadian crafts. Wonderful selection of the best contemporary Canadian ceramics, glass, wickerwork, jewelry, textiles, and more. The upstairs gallery features Inuit sculpture and art gathered from the Northwest Territories.

Prime Gallery, 52 McCaul St. ☎ 593-5750.

This gallery displays contemporary crafts in all materials—ceramics, clay, fabric, and metal (jewelry). Prices range anywhere from $50 for a ceramic teapot to $8,000 for a brilliantly colored ceramic sculpture by Montréaler Paul Mathieu.

Snow Lion, 286 Queen St. W. ☎ 591-6858.

If you're looking for imported crafts you'll find many Tibetan and other Himalayan objects at this store. Jewelry, clothing, jackets, hats, gongs, and tankas are all available here, along with Buddhist books.

For screens, statues, howdahs, and other furnishings, including hand-knotted Tibetan rugs, go to **Snow Lion Interiors,** 575 Mount Pleasant Rd. (☎ 484-8859).

Department Stores

Eaton's, Eaton Centre, 290 Yonge St. ☎ 343-3528.

There are numerous Eaton's in metro Toronto. The flagship store is in the four-level Eaton Centre, which stretches two blocks from Dundas Street to Queen Street.

The Hudson's Bay Company, Queen and Yonge sts.
☎ 861-9111.

Arch rival to Eaton's, this downtown store (formerly Simpson's) still has a venerable feel.

Marks & Spencer, Manulife Centre, 55 Bloor St. W. ☎ 967-7772.

This is a branch of the famous British store that's known for good-quality goods and clothes at reasonable prices.

Discount

⭐ **Honest Ed's,** 581 Bloor St. W. ☎ 537-2111.

The original store that launched Ed Mirvish to fame and fortune has perhaps the biggest, most frenetic electric sign in Toronto. Check it out—as Ed says, it can't be beat, as long as you know what you're looking for. A Toronto experience.

Marilyn's, 130 Spadina Ave. ☎ 366-6777.

In the heart of the garment center, Marilyn has been in business for nearly 20 years, specializing in good-value discounted Canadian fashions. Each rack here carries 200 garments organized by color. The staff are trained to sift through the vast stock and create whole looks for women, dressing them from head to toe, including accessories. In this warehouse atmosphere you'll find discounts of 20% to 80%.

Fashions

CHILDREN'S

Bellissimo Fashions, 122 St. Patrick St., between Queen and Dundas sts. (in Village by the Grange). ☎ **340-6382.**

Bellissimo does indeed have beautiful, but fun, clothes for kids, including Peruvian-knit sweaters with appliquéd numbers or other pictures on them, as well as brilliantly colored Muppet-inspired PVC coats.

Crazy Mamas, 231 Carlton St., at Parliament. ☎ **969-9220.**

Started by two young mothers who know their business, this store has clothes for the newborn to size 10. It stocks Bravo, Deux Par Deux, Mouse Feathers, and Lemmi from Germany, among other name brands. It even sells a bright leopard-print receiving blanket, custom-made hats, and shoes. Not a bad way to start life.

Marci Lipman Graphics, Hazelton Lanes. ☎ **921-1998.**

This store stocks original, fun, "art" T-shirts and other kids' clothes with neat, unique designs.

Miniup Children's Boutique, 106 Yorkville Ave. ☎ **966-9337.**

A specialist in European imports—mainly French and Italian— from newborn to 12-year-olds. Miniup carries all the top names.

MEN'S

In addition to the listings below, Holt Renfrew carries men's clothing. See "Women's," below.

Alan Cherry, 33 Avenue Rd. ☎ **967-1115.**

Alan Cherry carries designer wear—Valentino, Giorgio Armani, and Emanuel Ungaro—as well as his own private-label clothes made in Italy. At the clearance center in the back of the store the old inventory winds up at discount—it's worth a look. There's some women's clothing, too.

Bulloch Tailors, 65 Front St. E., at Church St. ☎ **367-1084.**

A Toronto institution for more than 50 years, Bulloch has a reputation for outfitting the city's doctors, professionals, military men, and politicos. The emphasis is still on custom tailoring, with suits beginning at $700, but there's also a selection of ready-to-wear, most of which is made by Bulloch.

Cy Mann Clothiers, First Canadian Place ☎ **363-8599.**

A Canadian name for custom-made suits and shirts, Cy Mann has been in business for more than 40 years. Among the famous names the store has dressed are Raymond Burr, Dick Cavett, and Paul Anka. Prices are high, reflecting the quality of the workmanship, but they're still lower than you'd find in the United States. Suits are priced from $745, and they'll even custom-make one in three days.

George Bouridis, 193 Church St., between Dundas and Shuter sts. ☎ **363-4868.**

For almost 30 years this gentleman has been fashioning custom-made shirts and blouses as well as dressing gowns. He has 400 to 500 fabrics on hand from which to choose, from Switzerland, England, France, and Germany. Women's silk blouses cost $185 and up; men's 100%-cotton shirts, from $125. They'd retail for much more.

Harry Rosen, 82 Bloor St. W. ☎ **972-0556.**

Torontonians have been coming to this handsome traditional English-style store for years. The stock includes Valentino and Armani and more reasonably priced classics like Sedgwick. The upper-level Galleria features Barbera, Brioni, and D'Avenza. Accessories include a great selection of ties and shoes.

Also located at 11 Adelaide St. W. and the Eaton Centre.

Irish Shop for Men, 110 Bloor St. W. (in the mall). ☎ **922-9400.**

Best known for its jackets and linen shirts, the Irish Shop carries great sports jackets, including Donegal tweeds, plus shirts, trousers, caps, hats, and picnic blankets.

Stollery's, 1 Bloor St. W. ☎ **922-6173.**

This venerable store has been at this corner since 1901; it was originally a men's store, especially well known for its vast selection of shirts (with different sleeve lengths). Today it also stocks women's wear, with such English fashion names as Burberry and Aquascutum.

Thomas K. T. Chui, 754 Broadview Ave. ☎ **465-8538.**

For more than 20 years Mr. Chui has been dressing the wealthy and the famous, among them Joe Clark. The custom suits cost from $900; there are custom-made shirts, also.

Women's

Asylum, 42 Kensington Ave. ☎ **595-7199.**

Scour the racks for new and vintage clothing at this Kensington Market outlet. Dresses, reworked vintage jeans with patchwork and tattoos, men's Hawaiian shirts, belts, shoes, and skull-and-crossbone–design items—they're all here.

Benetton, 102 Bloor St. W. ☎ **968-1611.**

Stylish, colorful, well-fashioned clothes at bearable prices are available for everyone. There's another outlet in the Eaton Centre.

Chanel, 131 Bloor St. W. ☎ **925-2577.**

The name says it all—classic all the way. This boutique, one of two in Canada, carries the designer's full line.

Chez Catherine, 55 Avenue Rd. ☎ **967-5666.**

A long-established doyenne of the Canadian fashion scene, this store consists of four designer boutiques—Valentino, Versace, Gianfranco Ferré, and Krizia—plus a showcase of other European designers. It's known for personalized service. There's a full line of accessories, including shoes.

⭐ **Club Monaco,** 403 Queen St. W. ☎ **979-5633.**

If you're looking for casual wear and sportswear, this is a very pleasant shopping experience. There are other locations at the Eaton Centre; Hazelton Lanes; 1950 Queen St. E., in the Beaches; and the Yorkdale Shopping Centre.

Gianni Versace, 55 Avenue Rd. ☎ 922-1900.

Fine Italian design is the hallmark of Gianni Versace's clothing and accessories.

★ **Holt Renfrew,** 50 Bloor St. W. ☎ 922-2333.

This beautiful, well-laid-out store has several boutiques, including Giorgio Armani, Donna Karan, Anne Klein, Yves St. Laurent, and more. Of course, you'll find top-quality fashions and accessories.

★ **Irish Shop,** 110 Bloor St. W. ☎ 922-9400.

This is a lovely store, well-stocked with Irish fashions, lace, shawls, and accessories. Books, too.

Jaeger, 131 Bloor St. W. (in the Colonnade). ☎ 966-3544.

The classic British name for fashions, Jaeger has another branch in Eaton Centre.

Krizia Boutique, 55 Avenue Rd. (in Hazelton Lanes). ☎ 929-0222.

Upbeat and creative as ever, this boutique stocks the full line from Milan—jackets, pants, sweaters, and dresses, as well as belts and jewelry.

Norma, 116 Cumberland St. ☎ 923-5514.

Famous for her very expensive hand-knit jackets decorated with beads, sequins, and more, Norma makes Toronto her home base Although the prices are still high, you'll save a little on these exquisite treasures here. She has branched out to leathers, coats, and rainwear.

Suitables, Queen's Quay, 207 Queen's Quay W. ☎ 203-0655.

Among the many silk blouses, skirts, and suits is a full range of hand-washable silk shirts that sell three for $150. Needless to say, some folks come from far and wide every year to pick up a supply.

Valentino, 55 Avenue Rd. ☎ 922-5666.

The name says it all. This is Italian design at its best—dresses, blouses, and evening gowns—as well as belts and jewelry.

Food

Arlequin Restaurant, 134 Avenue Rd. ☎ 928-9521.

The display up front is mouthwatering—salads, pâtés, melt-in-the-mouth croissants, pastries, and more.

Daniel et Daniel, 248 Carlton St. ☎ 968-9275.

You'll find a full display of all kinds of foods and gourmet items—breakfast pastries, hot and cold hors d'oeuvres, salads, sandwiches, quiches, minipizzas, and desserts.

David Wood Food Shop, 1110 Yonge St., at Roxborough St.
☎ 968-2960.

This store that serves the Rosedale set stocks an array of jams and chutneys, including the Silver Palate brands and local Catherine's antipasto, as well as cheeses, deli items, coffees, and a variety of take-out—poached salmon, vegetarian and seafood salads, soups—50 to 60 items in all.

Dinah's Cupboard, 50 Cumberland St. ☎ **921-8112.**

This small, cluttered store has a fine selection of gourmet items to go, as well as frozen dishes to take home and microwave. Great salads, pâtés, vegetarian pasta, and croissants, as well as teas, coffees, vinegars, oils, and herbs.

⭐**Dufflet Pastries,** 787 Queen St. W., near Bathurst St.
☎ **368-1812.**

This specialty baker supplies many restaurants with their pastries and desserts. The special Dufflet cakes include a white- and dark-chocolate mousse, almond meringue, and many other singular creations. Fine coffees and teas are served, too.

Global Cheese Shoppe, 76 Kensington Ave. ☎ **593-9251.**

More than 150 varieties of cheese are discounted here. It's worth the trip to Kensington Market.

Sweet Temptations, 207 Queen's Quay Terminal. ☎ **203-0512.**

This store is famous for offering every kind of candy available — chocolate-covered almonds and peanuts, gummy bears, and a broad selection of Canadian and imported chocolates, including handmade Belgian chocolates that sell for $1 or $1.50 apiece. Frozen yogurt and ice cream, too.

⭐**Ten Ren Tea,** 454 Dundas St. W., at Huron St. ☎ **598-7872.**

At this fascinating Chinatown store, you can pick up some fine Chinese tea, which is stored in large canisters at the back of the store. The tiny ceramic teapots also make nice gifts in the $20-to-$30 price range. Many people are beginning to collect them.

Teuscher of Switzerland, 55 Avenue Rd. (in Hazelton Lanes).
☎ **961-1303.**

Truffles (12 kinds) are the specialty here—the favorite being champagne. Other kinds of chocolates are also sold—containing various nuts, nougat, marzipan, and fruit. All are handmade in Zurich and flown in once a week.

Furs

Fur sales take place twice a year—in summer when business is slow (the best time to negotiate a deal) and every January right after Christmas when the dealers are anxious to get rid of their inventory.

The wholesale fur warehouse is the **Balfour Building,** at 119 Spadina Ave.; it's worth starting here and shopping all the showrooms you can find in the building.

A la Mode Furs, 686 Bathurst St. ☎ **539-9999.**

This name includes several long-time local fur wholesalers—Sable Bay Furs, Leader Furs (established 1873), Stanley Walker, S. Kuretzky (an original), and Norcan Furs. On the premises you'll find 13,000 square feet of space divided into several showrooms. Mink is the number-one item, followed by beaver, raccoon, fox, sable, and lynx. The prices are wholesale, but in summer, when business is slow, they're even better.

Imperial Fur Company, 509 Rogers Rd., south of Eglinton (at Keele). ☎ **653-6688.**

Check out the factory showroom for mink, fox, raccoon, and coyote. If you don't find a design you like, they'll custom-make a coat for you.

Norman Rogul Fur Company, 480 Adelaide St. W. ☎ **862-7577.**

Reputed furrier to Her Majesty the Queen and other royals and celebrities.

Gifts & Miscellaneous

E. K. R. Zephyr, 292 Queen St. W. ☎ **593-0795.**

Wind chimes, jewelry, and wooden toys and rocking animals are the stock-in-trade of this appealing cooperative for Canadian crafts.

The Gallery Shop, in the Art Gallery of Toronto, 317 Dundas St. W. ☎ **979-6610.**

Books, gifts, jewelry, reproductions, and rental art are all featured in this new complex in the lobby of the museum.

⭐ **General Store,** 55 Avenue Rd. (in Hazelton Lanes). ☎ **323-1527.**

These are three stores under the same name in Hazelton Lanes. The first carries gifts for the person who has everything—gimmicky and sophisticated calculators, Newtonian puzzles, Filofaxes, and games. The adjacent branches carry house- and kitchenwares and fun paper items.

⭐ **Geomania,** 50 Bloor St. W. ☎ **920-1420.**

Geomania is filled with highly polished, brilliantly colored pieces of minerals and stones, some fashioned into elegant jewelry, others crafted into vases, bookends, and other decorative pieces. A vision.

J & S Arts & Crafts, 430 Dundas St. W. ☎ **977-2562.**

In the heart of Chinatown, this store has a variety of good reasonably priced gifts and souvenirs—kimonos and happy coats, kung-fu suits, cushion covers, address books and diaries with handsome silk-embroidered covers, and all-cotton Chinatown T-shirts for only $6.

Legends of the Game, 322 King St. W. ☎ **971-8848.**

Anyone looking for a gift for a sports lover ought to find something at this temple to sports, complete with Wall of Fame and baseball-handled entrance doors. Memorabilia of all sports are on sale, including autographed photos, old and new baseball and hockey cards, old and new comics, and jerseys that have been worn by players.

Oh Yes, Toronto, 101 Yorkville Ave. ☎ **924-7198.**

The ultimate souvenir store—everything in it features the Toronto name. Sweats, T-shirts, oven mitts, bags, buttons, and mugs range in price from $2 to $30.

There are also branches at Queen's Quay West (☎ **203-0607**), Eaton Centre (☎ **593-6749**), and Terminal 3 (☎ **905/672-8594**).

Rotman Hat Shop, 345 Spadina Ave. ☎ **977-2806.**
This store has been in business here for over 40 years, and it retains the flavor of yesterday, when the area was more Jewish than it is today. Here you'll find the finest, light-as-a-feather Panama hats, as well as other fun headgear, like grouser hats.

⭐ **Science City,** 50 Bloor St. W., in the Holt Renfrew Centre. ☎ **968-2627.**
A favorite of kids and adults alike, this store has an assortment of games, models, kits, and books relating to science—physics, chemistry, and biology—as well as very expensive telescopes and optics, hologram watches, trilobites, and other fossil specimens. All kinds of fun, mind-expanding stuff.

Touch the Sky, 207 Queen's Quay W. ☎ **203-0578.**
Kites and windsocks are the specialty here, plus wind chimes, mobiles, Frisbees, and balloons—great inexpensive gifts.

Housewares & Kitchenware

⭐ **En Provence,** 20 Hazelton Ave. ☎ **975-9400.**
This store has a beautiful selection of French decorative items for the home—ceramics, table accessories, wrought-iron and wood furniture, and, on the second floor, the most luxurious fabrics by Les Olivades for household use. This is French country style at its best.

Fortune Housewares, 388 Spadina Ave. ☎ **593-6999.**
This well-stocked store has a great selection of utensils and other household/kitchen items—chopping boards, aprons, Copco pots, and other brand-name items—at 20% or more off the regular prices around town.

Plaiter Place, 384 Spadina Ave. ☎ **593-9734.**
This must be the city's premier wicker emporium, bar none. Every conceivable use is made of wicker: You'll find all kinds of objects made from wicker and bamboo here—birdcages, blinds, steamers, hats, and baskets galore in all shapes, sizes, and styles.

Tap Phong Trading, 360 Spadina Ave. ☎ **977-6364.**
All kinds of utensils, woks, bamboo steamers, ceramic and stainless-steel cookware, mortar and pestles, and terrific baskets are jammed into this small space. Fun shopping.

Jewelry

Birks Jewelers, 220 Yonge St., in the Eaton Centre. ☎ **979-9311.**
A well-known Canadian retailer with stores in towns across Canada, Birks stocks fine silver and jewelry at fair prices. Also at the Manulife Centre (☎ **922-2266**), First Canadian Place (☎ **363-5663**), and at other in-town and suburban locations.

⭐ **18 Karat,** 71 McCaul St. ☎ **593-1648.**
The owners of this store will craft jewelry on the premises according to your design. They will also do repairs and redesigns of antique settings. Show them what you have in mind and they will execute it.

First Toronto Jewellery Exchange, 215 Yonge St. ☎ **340-0008.**
Thirty stores under one roof.

Silverbridge, 162 Cumberland St. ☎ **923-2591.**
The sterling-silver jewelry here is designed by Costin Lazar and manufactured in Toronto. It's modern and reflects the talents of Mr. Lazar, who is also a sculptor. Necklaces, bracelets, and earrings, as well as cuff links, money clips, and key holders are priced from $60 to $1,400.

Yonge Dundas Jewellery Exchange, 295 Yonge St.
☎ **340-0008.**
A complex containing more than 20 stores.

Magazines, International Newspapers & Books ———

Lichtman's News & Books, Yonge and Richmond sts.
☎ **368-7390.**
Local and international newspapers and magazines, as well as hard- and softcover books, are sold here and also at the Atrium on Bay, at Yonge and Bloor streets, at Yonge and Eglinton, and in the BCE building.

Great Canadian News Company, BCE Place. ☎ **363-2242.**
More than 2,000 magazines and 60 newspapers all displayed under one roof—a print-media buff's dream.

Maison de la Presse Internationale, 124 Yorkville Ave.
☎ **928-0418.**
This large store has foreign magazines and newspapers galore. It's a convenient place to pick up the *New York Times, Wall Street Journal, Financial Times,* and the like.

Malls & Shopping Centers ————————

Atrium on Bay, Bay and Dundas sts. ☎ **980-2801.**
Sixty stores on two floors sell fashions, shoes, jewelry, and more.

College Park Shops, 444 Yonge St. ☎ **597-1221.**
More than 100 stores spread out on two floors, this is a more intimate and less harried version of the Eaton Centre.

⭐ **Eaton Centre**, 220 Yonge St. ☎ **979-3300.**
This glass-domed galleria has more than 360 shops and restaurants on four levels, with plenty of places to rest and eat lunch, too. This is where the real people shop.

⭐ **Hazelton Lanes**, 55 Avenue Rd. ☎ **968-0853.**
This complex is for the wealthy and those who wish to appear so, with all the great designer fashion names and more on two levels. And it has some fine rest stops.

Holt Renfrew Centre, Bloor St. W. No phone.
Not to be confused with the store of the same name, which is far more upscale, the center is much more down to earth. You wouldn't find Teas 'n' Tarts in Holt Renfrew. My favorite stores on the downstairs level are Science City and Geomania.

⭐ **Queen's Quay Terminal,** 207 Queen's Quay. ☎ **203-0510.**
More than 100 shops and restaurants, including fashion and gift boutiques, are housed here in a converted waterfront warehouse. Remember, the rents are high. Open daily from 10am to 9pm.

Royal Bank Plaza, Bay and Front sts. ☎ **974-2880.**
More than 60 shops are directly accessible from Union Station and the subway. Don't miss the building above.

Village by the Grange, 122 St. Patrick St., between Queen and Dundas sts. ☎ **598-1414.**
More than 70 shops are complemented by several major restaurants. The International Food Market is good for budget dining.

Markets

⭐ **Kensington Market,** along Baldwin, Kensington, and Augusta aves.
Originally a Jewish market, then a Portuguese market area, today it offers all kinds of ethnic foods from Middle Eastern to West Indian. A Toronto experience.

⭐ **St. Lawrence Market,** 92 Front St. E. ☎ **392-7219.**
This historic market is still favored by Torontonians for its fresh produce—from figs to fish. Best day is Saturday when the farmers come into town and the market opens at 5am. Hours are Tuesday through Thursday from 8am to 6pm, Friday from 8am to 7pm, and Saturday from 5am to 5pm.

Music

CD Bar, 325A Yonge St. (north of Dundas). ☎ **977-6863.**
Remember the good old days when you could listen to the *records* in the store? Well, you can still do so here. Thousands of titles are in stock for your listening pleasure.

Classical Record Shop, 55 Avenue Rd. (in Hazelton Lanes).
☎ **961-8999.**
Listen to the melodies emanating from this store. It stocks a large selection of CDs, audio tapes, and videos for the classical-music lover.

HMV, 333 Yonge St. ☎ **596-0333.**
One of the city's largest music emporiums, HMV also offers an added bonus: the opportunity to listen before you buy. Several other locations, too.

L'Atelier Grigorian, 70 Yorkville Ave. ☎ **922-6477.**
This store has a fantastic selection of CDs—jazz and classical only.

Record Peddler, 621 Yonge St. ☎ **975-4848.**
This specialty store stocks British imports, LPs, and CDs in rock, blues, jazz, and reggae. No classical or country.

Sam the Record Man, 347 Yonge St.
This famous Toronto record outlet is so vast and busy that the telephone number is unlisted. It has the largest laser-disc selection in the city.

Tobacco

Winston & Holmes, 138 Cumberland St. ☎ **968-1290.**

Although it's not old, this store has all the appearance of tradition and age. A large selection of well-made pipes is on display behind glass; there's a broad selection of Cuban and other cigars, and all the other smoking requisites. Fine fountain pens are stocked, too, along with men's shaving accoutrements and toiletries. Mail order available.

Also at Queen's Quay (☎ **203-0344**) and 2 First Canadian Place (☎ **363-7575**).

Toys

Carriage Trade Dolls, 584 Mount Pleasant Rd. ☎ **481-1639.**

A real specialty doll store, Carriage Trade carries modern vinyl and porcelain dolls, including some that are anatomically correct, dolls that you can wash, and so on. It also stocks a full range of carriages, cribs, bassinets, socks, bibs, and more—all for dolls. Also has some serious modern collector pieces.

Kidding Awound, 91 Cumberland St. ☎ **926-8996.**

Windup toys—music boxes and clockwork toys—antique toys, and other interesting items are available here. Great therapy for adults.

Kidstuff, 738 Bathurst St., one block south of Bloor St. ☎ **535-2212.**

This store does not stock video and computer games, but concentrates instead on cooperative games, Lego, Playmobile, puppets, art supplies, and other imported and educational toys.

Little Dollhouse Company, 617 Mount Pleasant Rd.
☎ **489-7180.**

This charming store makes all-wood handcrafted dollhouse kits in about 12 different styles, many Victorian, complete with shingles, siding, doors, and windows. They also sell dollhouse furniture, lighting, wallpaper, and building supplies—wood, metal, and plastic—and display 100 room settings. Dollhouse kits range from $100 to $600, while finished dollhouses are about twice the price.

Science City Jr., 50 Bloor St. W. ☎ **986-2627.**

A great store, it's full of games, puzzles, models, and books about science, and serious stuff like telescopes, trilobites, and hologram watches.

Top Banana, 639 Mount Pleasant Rd. ☎ **440-0111.**

A traditional toy store featuring educational and imported toys, like Brio wooden trains from Sweden, Ravensburger puzzles and games, Eduframe toys, art supplies, and plenty of products from Playmobil, Playskool, and Little Tikes. Audio cassettes and books, too.

The Toy Shop, 62 Cumberland St., at Bay St. ☎ **961-4870.**

The two floors of creative toys, books, and games here include videos from around the world.

Wines

You'll have to shop the LCBO outlets. Look them up in the *Yellow Pages* under "Liquor Control Board of Ontario." The most convenient downtown locations are College Park (☎ **977-3277**); 2 Bloor St. E. (☎ **925-6965**); 87 Front St. E. (☎ **368-0521**); Manulife Centre, 55 Bloor St. W. (☎ **925-5266**); the Eaton Centre (☎ **979-9978**); and Union Station (☎ **368-9644**). More extensive selections are found at the **Vintages** stores, like the one in Hazelton Lanes on the concourse.

9

Toronto Nights

Toronto has the National Ballet of Canada, the Canadian Opera Company, the Toronto Symphony, two large arts centers, two concert halls, a special dance theater, and theaters galore (with a reputation second only to those on Broadway), plus enough bars—plush, pub, wine, jazz, casual, and otherwise—clubs, cabarets, and other entertainments to keep anyone spinning. For local happenings, check *Where Toronto* and *Toronto Life,* as well as the *Globe and Mail,* the *Toronto Star,* and the *Toronto Sun.* For the hipper scene get hold of a copy of *Eye* or *Now,* both free and available at Maison de la Presse and outside many other bookstores and stores around the city.

DISCOUNT TICKETS   For day-of-performance half-price tickets, go to the **Five Star Ticket Booths** at Yonge and Dundas streets outside the Eaton Centre on the southwest corner. Cash and credit cards are taken. It's open Tuesday through Saturday from noon to 7:30pm and Sunday from 11am to 3pm. For information call **596-8211.**

---

1   The Performing Arts

Major Performing-Arts Companies

In addition to the following major performing-arts companies, Toronto has many local, homegrown companies offering all sorts of concerts and performances. Check the newspapers for details.

OPERA & CLASSICAL MUSIC

Canadian Opera Company, 227 Front St. E. ☎ **872-2262** for tickets at the O'Keefe Centre box office, or **363-6671** for administration.

The Canadian Opera Company began its life in 1950 with 10 performances of three operas. It now stages eight different operas at the O'Keefe Centre, spread over the nine months from September to April.

   Prices: Tickets $27–$85.

Tafelmusik Baroque Orchestra, 427 Bloor St. W. ☎ **964-6337** for tickets, or **964-9562** for administration.

This group plays baroque music on authentic period instruments, giving a series of concerts at Trinity/St. Paul's United Church at 47 Bloor St. W. Other performances are given in Massey Hall.

Toronto Mendelssohn Choir, 60 Simcoe St. ☎ **598-0422.**

A world-renowned choir, this group first performed in Massey Hall in 1895. Its repertoire ranges from Verdi's *Requiem,* Bach's *St. Matthew Passion,* and Handel's *Messiah* to the soundtrack of *Schindler's List.*

Toronto Symphony Orchestra, 60 Simcoe St. ☎ **598-3375** for tickets, **593-7769** for administrative offices.

The symphony performs at Roy Thomson Hall from September through June. The repertoire ranges from classics to pop and new Canadian works. In June and July, concerts are given at outdoor venues throughout the city.

Theater Companies

Canadian Stage Company, 26 Berkeley St. ☎ **368-3110** for tickets, or **367-8243** for administration.

The Canadian Stage Company performs comedy, drama, and musicals in the St. Lawrence Centre and also presents free summer Shakespeare performances in High Park. Call for dates and programs.

Prices: Tickets $18–$75; discount tickets for seniors and students sometimes available 30 minutes before the performance.

★ **Young People's Theatre,** 165 Front St. E. ☎ **862-2222.**

In Toronto you'll have no problem finding kids' entertainment, for the city has taken its children's theater very seriously with the Young People's Theatre. Here, in a theater seating 468, they put on such whimsical, fun productions as *Pinocchio, The Secret Garden,* and *The Oracle,* plus enchanting productions of such classics as *A Midsummer Night's Dream* and *A Christmas Carol.* There might be one problem: kids have been known to weep when the show ends.

Prices: Tickets, from $25 adults, $15 seniors and children under 18.

DANCE COMPANIES

★ **National Ballet of Canada,** 157 King St. E. ☎ **362-1041** or **366-4846** for information on programs and prices.

Most famous of all Toronto's cultural contributions is perhaps the National Ballet of Canada, the nation's largest classical and modern dance company. It was launched at Eaton Auditorium in Toronto on November 12, 1951, by English ballerina Celia Franca, who served

---

The Major Concert & Performance Hall Box Offices

For Ticketmaster's telecharge service, call **872-1111.**

Elgin and Winter Garden Theatres, 189–191 Yonge St. (near Queen Street; ☎ **872-5555**).

Massey Hall, 178 Victoria St. (at Shuter Street; ☎ **593-4828** or **872-4255**).

O'Keefe Centre, 1 Front St. E. (☎ **872-2262**).

Pantages Theatre, 244 Victoria St. (near Shuter Street; ☎ **872-2222**).

Premiere Dance Theatre, in the York Quay Centre, 235 Queen's Quay W. (☎ **973-4000**).

Royal Alexandra Theatre, 260 King St. W. (☎ **872-3333**).

Roy Thomson Hall, 60 Simcoe St. (☎ **872-4255**).

SkyDome, 300 The Esplanade W. (☎ **341-3663**).

St. Lawrence Centre for the Arts, 27 Front St. E. (☎ **366-7723**).

Young People's Theatre, 165 Front St. E. (☎ **862-2222**).

initially as director, principal dancer, choreographer, and teacher. Over the years the company and stars like Karen Kain have achieved great renown. Among the highlights of its history have been the invitation to perform at Expo '70 in Osaka, Japan; its 1973 New York debut (which featured Nureyev's full-length *Sleeping Beauty*); and Baryshnikov's appearance with the company soon after his defection in 1974.

Besides its tours of Canada and other countries, the company performs its regular seasons in Toronto at the O'Keefe Centre in the fall, at Christmas, and in the spring, as well as making summer appearances before enormous crowds at the open-air theater at Ontario Place. Included in the repertoire are such classics as *Swan Lake, The Nutcracker,* and *The Taming of the Shrew;* and a variety of modern works, including William Forsythe's highly acclaimed *the second detail,* Glen Tetley's *Alice,* and resident choreographer John Alleyne's *Interrogating Slam.*

Prices: Tickets $14–$69.

Toronto Dance Theatre, 80 Winchester St. ☎ **967-1365** for administrative offices, **973-4000** (at the Premiere Dance Theatre) for tickets.

The leading contemporary dance company in Toronto performs two seasonal programs per year at the Premiere Dance Theatre.

Prices: Tickets $19–$31.

Major Multipurpose Performance & Concert Halls

Massey Hall, 178 Victoria St. ☎ **363-7301** or **872-4255** for tickets and program information.

A Canadian musical landmark, this 2,757-seat auditorium hosts a variety of programming, including classical, rock, ethnic, and theatrical presentations.

Prices: Vary with the performance.

O'Keefe Centre, 1 Front St. E. ☎ **393-7469,** or **872-2262** for the box office.

With its 60- by 130-foot stage and 3,223-seat auditorium, the O'Keefe Centre is home to the Canadian Opera Company and the National Ballet of Canada. It also presents the very best in live entertainment—hit Broadway musicals like *Cats* and *Grand Hotel,* variety and family shows, diverse international superstars such as Johnny Mathis and Céline Dion, comedians, and dance companies. Tickets may be purchased at the box office or by phone (there's a service charge for phone orders).

The O'Keefe Centre restaurant is available for pretheater dining. Call **393-7478** for reservations. **Subway:** Union.

Prices: Opera and ballet tickets $14–$85; other shows $15–$55, depending on the performance.

Premiere Dance Theatre, in the Queen's Quay Terminal Building, Queen's Quay W. ☎ **973-4000.**

Toronto boasts a theater specifically designed for dance. For information on productions and the dance series, phone the Harbourfront box office from 1 to 8:30pm daily. Toronto's leading contemporary dance companies, the Toronto Dance Theatre, Desrosiers Dance Theatre, and the Danny Grossman Dance Company, perform their seasons here.

Prices: Tickets $22–$35.

Roy Thomson Hall, 60 Simcoe St. ☎ **593-4822** for administration; **872-4255** or **593-4828** for tickets and program information.

Toronto's premier concert hall presents top international performers of classical music, jazz, big-band music, and comedy. It is also home to both the Toronto Symphony Orchestra and the Toronto Mendelssohn Choir.

The hall was designed to give the audience a feeling of extraordinary intimacy with every performer—none of the 2,812 seats is more than 107 feet from the stage. The exterior of the building itself is spectacular—dove-colored, petal-shaped, and enveloped in a huge glass canopy that's reflective by day and transparent by night. **Subway:** St. Andrews.

Prices: Vary with the performance.

St. Lawrence Centre for the Arts, 27 Front St. E. ☎ **366-7723.**

The prime tenant is the Canadian Stage Company, which presents a season at the St. Lawrence Centre. In addition, many classical music concerts, recitals, and chamber-music concerts featuring internationally famous artists are given here, most in the Jane Mallet Theatre.

Prices: Tickets $20–$50 for theater productions, $20–$60 for other performances; discount tickets for seniors and students sometimes available 30 minutes before the performance.

Theaters

As the section that follows demonstrates, Toronto has become a very active theater city, with many small theater groups producing exciting offbeat drama—a slowly burgeoning Toronto equivalent of Off-Broadway. Since there are a great many of these smaller companies, I have picked out only the few whose reputations have been established. If you'd like to do some talent-scouting of your own, pick up the local newspaper or a local magazine, scan the myriad productions, and find the next Sir Laurence Olivier.

THE TOP VENUES

In addition to **O'Keefe Centre** and the **St. Lawrence Centre for the Arts** (see "Major Multipurpose Performance & Concert Halls," above), the city's big theaters include the Royal Alexandra Theatre, fondly referred to as the Royal Alex.

The Elgin and Winter Garden Theatres, 189–191 Yonge St. ☎ **363-5353,** or **872-5555** for the box office.

Two theater gems have been dusted off for the 1990s. This double-stacked theater opened in 1913 and cost $500,000—no mean sum in those days. Today it cost $29 million to refurbish it, restoring the stucco-and-gilt interior to its former beauty. The 1,500-seat Elgin has a domed ceiling; the upstairs Winter Garden seats 1,000 and is designed to re-create a bosky copse with real beech leaves and lanterns covering the ceiling. Both theaters offer everything from Broadway musicals to dramas, concerts, and opera.

Guided tours are given at 5pm Thursday and 11am Saturday (Sunday, too, during July and August). The tour costs $4 adults, $3 students and seniors.

Prices: Tickets $25–$80, depending on the performance.

Pantages Theatre, 244 Victoria St. ☎ **872-2222** for tickets, **362-3218** for administration.

This magnificent old theater has been restored to host splashy Broadway shows like *The Phantom of the Opera,* which reopened the theater. It originally opened in 1920 showing silent films and hosting vaudeville performances.

Prices: Tickets $40–$91; discount seats available two hours before the performance.

Royal Alexandra Theatre, 260 King St. W. ☎ **593-0351,** or **872-3333** for tickets.

Shows from Broadway migrate north to the Royal Alex. Tickets are often snapped up by subscription buyers, so your best bet is to write ahead to the theater (260 King St. W., Toronto, ON, M5V 1H9).

The theater itself is quite a spectacle. Constructed in 1907, it owes its current lease on life to owner Ed Mirvish, who refurbished it (as well as the surrounding area) in the 1960s. Inside it's a riot of plush, reds, gold brocade, and baroque ornamentation, with a seating capacity of 1,493. Apparently, you're wise to avoid the second balcony and also the seats under the circle. **Subway:** St. Andrews.

Prices: Tickets $35–$91, depending on the show.

ADDITIONAL OFFERINGS

Factory Theatre, 125 Bathurst St. ☎ **864-9971.**

Since 1970, the Factory Theatre has been presenting new Canadian plays on its two stages. Here, promising new authors get the chance to develop and showcase their works. In the past productions have toured successfully to London and New York. The Bathurst streetcar runs nearby.

Prices: Tickets $7.50–$23.

Tarragon Theatre, 30 Bridgman Ave. ☎ **536-5018,** or **531-1827** for tickets.

The Tarragon Theatre, near Dupont and Bathurst, opened in the early 1970s and continues to produce original works by Canadian playwrights—Michel Tremblay, David French, John Murrell, Mavis Gallant, and Judith Thompson, for example—and an occasional classic or Off-Broadway play. It's a small, intimate theater where you can get coffee and apple juice in the foyer.

Prices: Tickets $14–$23; on Sun, pay what you can afford.

Theatre Passe Muraille, 16 Ryerson Ave. ☎ **363-2416** for tickets, **363-8988** for administration.

Theatre Passe Muraille started in the late 1960s when a group of actors began experimenting and improvising original Canadian material.

There are two stages, the main one seating 220 and "The Backspace" seating 70. **Subway:** Queen; then streetcar west to Bathurst.
    Prices: Tickets $15–$22.

Toronto Truck Theatre, 94 Belmont St. ☎ 922-0084.

The Toronto Truck Theatre is the home of Agatha Christie's *The Mousetrap,* now in its 18th year. It's Canada's longest-running show.
    Prices: Tickets $14–$20.

ESPECIALLY FOR KIDS

For enthralling theater productions designed especially for kids, check out the **Young People's Theatre** (see "Theater Companies" under "Major Performing-Arts Companies," above).

Dinner Theater & Comedy Shows ─────────────

The Laugh Resort, 26 Lombard St. ☎ 364-5233.

If you want to share some laughter with the likes of Gilbert Gottfried, Paula Poundstone, and other up-and-comers, then this is the place.
    Prices: Varying cover charges Tues–Wed $5, Thurs $7, Fri $12, Sat $15.

Limelight Supper Club, 2026 Yonge St. ☎ 482-5200.

Musical revues and comedy are the specialty at the Limelight, where you can have dinner while enjoying the entertainment.
    Prices: Dinner and show, $31; Show only, Sat $15.

★ The Second City, 110 Lombard St. ☎ 863-1111.

One of Toronto's wittiest theater groups, Second City specializes in improvisational comedy. This is the company that nurtured John Candy, Dan Aykroyd, and Bill Murray and continues to turn out talented young actors. The skits are always funny and topical. Its home is an old fire hall that now houses a theater seating 200 and a restaurant.

Second City has had a marked impact on North American entertainment with its various workshops, touring company, seasoned resident company, and internationally syndicated TV series.

Reservations are required.
    Prices: Show only, Mon–Thurs $13, Fri $16, Sat $20, Sun $11. Dinner is available, with menu entrees from $10–$18.

Ukrainian Caravan, 5245 Dundas St. W. ☎ 231-7447.

For an evening of Cossack dance, song, and comic repartee, head for the Ukrainian Caravan at Kipling Street. There are shows on Saturdays only; dinner begins at 7:30pm, the show at 9pm. **Subway:** Dundas; then a streetcar west.
    Prices: Dinner and show, $22–$35 per person.

Yuk-Yuk's Komedy Kabaret, 1280 Bay St. ☎ 967-6425.

Situated in the heart of Yorkville, Yuk-Yuk's is Canada's original home of stand-up comedy. Comic Mark Breslin founded the place, inspired by New York's Catch a Rising Star and Los Angeles's the

Comedy Store. It has launched such stars as Howie Mandel, Jim Carrey, and Norm McDonald. Besides the comics, other bizarre and hilariously grotesque troupes find their way to this spotlight. Monday is the night for New Talent Improv. Reservations are needed on Saturday. **Subway:** Bay.

Prices: Tickets, Mon $4, Tues–Thurs and Sun $5, Fri $8, Sat $10.

2   The Club & Music Scene

Country, Folk, Rock & Reggae

★ **Bamboo,** 312 Queen St. W. ☎ **593-5771.** Call 10am–5pm.

Bamboo, decked out in Caribbean style and colors, offers an exciting assortment of reggae, calypso, salsa, and world-beat sounds. The club takes up one side of the space, while a small restaurant decorated with masks from New Guinea occupies a small side area.

The menu mixes Caribbean, Indonesian, and Thai specialties. Thai spicy noodles are really popular, blending shrimp, chicken, tofu, and egg. Lamb and potato roti and Caribbean curry chicken served with gado gado, banana, and steamed rice are other examples. Music starts at 10pm. Drinks run $4 to $5. **Subway:** Osgoode or Queen; then a streetcar west.

Admission: Mon–Thurs $5, Fri–Sat $10.

Birchmount Tavern, 462 Birchmount. ☎ **698-4115.**

This is the city's longtime country venue, attracting a broad range of Canadian and American artists, including Lynn Anderson, Johnny Paycheck, and many more. The music goes on Wednesday to Sunday from 9pm to 1am.

Admission: Fri–Sat $5.

El Mocambo, 464 Spadina Ave. ☎ **928-3566.**

A rock-and-roll landmark where the Stones chose to take their gig in the 1970s. Today international blues and rock artists perform upstairs while the downstairs room features rockabilly sounds and also folk one night a week.

Admission: Varies.

Free Times Cafe, 320 College St. ☎ **967-1078.**

The back room is one of the city's regular folk and acoustic music venues. Monday night is open house.

Admission: $4–$6, depending on the group.

Horseshoe Tavern, 368 Queen St. W. ☎ **598-4753.**

An old traditional Toronto venue that attracts a cross section of people from age 20 to 60. Live music on Thursday to Saturday attracts a hard-driving crowd; it's country on Monday to Wednesday. Bands go on at 10pm.

Admission: Thurs–Sat $7.

Lee's Palace, 529 Bloor St. W. ☎ **532-7383.**

With raucous, loud rock featuring local bands downstairs every night, Lee's Palace is for the young who have poor hearing. There's a DJ dance bar upstairs Thursday to Saturday.

Admission: Varies, depending on the group.

⭐ **The Rivoli,** 332 Queen St. W. ☎ **597-0794.**

Currently this is the club for an eclectic mix of performances, including blues, rock, hard rock, and R & B. On Sunday and Monday it's jazz. Shows begin at 9:30pm and continue to 1am. People dance if so inspired. Upstairs there's a billiard room and espresso bar.

Admission: $2–$8.

Jazz & Rhythm & Blues

Toronto is a big jazz town—especially on Saturday afternoon, when many a hotel lounge or restaurant lays on an afternoon of rip-roaring rhythm.

In addition to the clubs listed below, **Bamboo,** listed under "Country, Folk, Rock & Reggae," above, also offered some of the hottest jazz in town when I last visited.

⭐ **Albert's Hall,** upstairs at the Brunswick House, 481 Bloor St. W. ☎ **964-2242.**

At Albert's you'll find the funkiest blues in the city—Bo Diddley, Biscuit Boy, Eddy Shaw, and the like from 9pm on Monday to Saturday.

Admission: Mon–Wed free, Thurs–Sat $5–$10.

Ben Wick's, 424 Parliament St. ☎ **961-9425.**

There's jazz, usually on Saturday night only, at this comfortable English-style pub named after local cartoonist Ben Wick. The music begins at 8:30pm.

Admission: Free.

The Chelsea Bun, at the Chelsea Inn, 33 Gerrard St. ☎ **595-1975.**

The Chelsea Bun is another of my favorite Saturday-afternoon jazz spots, where the crowd gathers at 3pm and listens until 7pm. Six days a week there's also a piano player and a live band playing Top 40 tunes from 9pm to 1am.

Admission: Free.

Clinton Tavern, 693 Bloor St. W. ☎ **535-9541.**

This typical down-home bar with log-cabin walls features blues and rock.

Admission: $5 and up, depending on performance. Closed Sunday.

⭐ **George's Spaghetti House,** 290 Dundas St. E. ☎ **923-9887.**

George's, at Sherbourne Street, is an old Toronto favorite, featuring local jazz groups, including Moe Koffman and his quintet. The music goes from 8:30pm to 12:30am Monday to Thursday and 9pm to 1am on Friday and Saturday.

Admission: Wed–Thurs $4, Fri–Sat $5; no cover for last set or at the bar.

★ **Montreal Bistro Jazz Club,** 65 Sherbourne St. ☎ **363-0179.**

A cool atmosphere for an array of jazz artists—Tommy Flanagan, Oliver Jones, Marion McPartland. Great, too, because the bistro is next door.

Admission: Varies.

★ **Top O' the Senator,** 249 Victoria St. ☎ **364-7517.**

Toronto's most atmospheric jazz club is a long, narrow room with a bar down one side and a distinct 1930s look. It's a great place to hear fine jazz by international artists like Harry Connick, Jr. and Betty Carter. The atmosphere is only added to by the funky old movie theater seats set around tables, the couches alongside the performance area, and portraits of band leaders and artists on the walls. Open Tuesday to Sunday. On the third floor Senator Cabaret features a variety of musical, cabaret, comedy, and theatrical performances in an intimate space seating 80.

Admission: Fri–Sat $10, Thurs $8; may vary depending on the artist.

Dance Clubs

Dance clubs come and go—the hottest spot can turn into the coldest potato almost overnight—so bear with me if some of those listed below have disappeared or changed. Meanwhile, here are some of the currently crowded spots on the Toronto scene.

First, let me just remind you of **Misty's,** at the Toronto Airport Hilton International, 5875 Airport Rd. (☎ **677-9900**).

Horizons, in the CN Tower, converts from a cocktail bar into a dance club at 9 or 10pm. See Section 3, "The Bar Scene," later in this chapter.

Berlin, 2335 Yonge St. ☎ **489-7777.**

This is one of the more sophisticated clubs, attracting a well-heeled crowd ranging from 25 to 55. Currently it's indulging in a Latin craze, with salsa on Tuesday night. Wednesday is Greek night and on Thursday there's dancing to a DJ; and on weekends there's more dancing to the house band and a DJ, too. Berlin is open Tuesday and Thursday until 2am, Friday and Saturday until 3am; it's closed other days.

Admission: Tues $8, Thurs $3, Fri–Sat $10.

Brandy's, 70 the Esplanade. ☎ **364-6674.**

Brandy's is a singles spot that packs them in in droves. It's decorated with oak furniture, hanging plants, and lots of Tiffany-style lamps. On Friday and Saturday there's dancing to a DJ's Top 40 sounds. Expect to spend $4 for a beer, $4.75 for a shot.

Admission: Free.

Chick 'n' Deli, 744 Mount Pleasant Rd. ☎ **489-3363.**

At Chick 'n' Deli, south of Eglinton Avenue, Tiffany-style lamps and oak set the background for Top 40 or rhythm and blues every night. The dance floor is always packed.

Chicken wings and barbecue are the specialties, along with nachos, salads, and a selection of sandwiches—club, corned beef, and so on.

On Saturday afternoon the sounds are Dixieland. Entertainment begins at 9pm on Monday to Friday (from 4pm on Sunday and from 3:45 to 7pm on Saturday).

Admission: Free.

Hard Rock Cafe, Gate 1, SkyDome. ☎ **341-2388.**

A branch of the famous chain. There's DJ entertainment Thursday to Saturday, plus food and rock-and-roll memorabilia.

Admission: Free.

Loose Moose, 220 Adelaide St. W. (between Simcoe and Duncan sts.). ☎ **971-5252.**

This is a crowd pleaser for a younger set, who like the multilevel dance floors, the DJ, and the booze and schmooze. Starts every night at 9pm.

Admission: Free.

Phoenix Concert Theatre, 410 Sherbourne St. ☎ **323-1251.**

Rock and roll, blues, and pop get the crowds dancing.

Admission: Varies; Fri–Sat $5–$8.

RPM, 132 Queen's Quay E. at Jarvis. ☎ **869-1462.**

This large disco attracts a young crowd for the singles scene.

Admission: Varies.

Rockit, 120 Church St. (south of Richmond). ☎ **947-9555.**

In this pizzeria, bar, and dance club, different nights feature different sounds and attract different crowds. On Friday and Saturday a DJ spins the dance tunes. The proceedings begin at 9pm and go to 2am.

Admission: Fri–Sat $5–$10.

Sneaky Dees, 431 College St. ☎ **368-5090.**

The pool tables and Mexican food complement the alternative rock sounds that go on in the club upstairs until 1:30am. Downstairs the bar is open weekdays until 3am, 5am on weekends.

Admission: $4–$6.

Studebakers, 150 Pearl St. ☎ **591-7287.**

Drop in here if you want to hear the old sounds from the 1950s, 1960s, and 1970s. It's nostalgia time.

Admission: Free.

Whiskey Saigon, 250 Richmond St. W. ☎ **593-4646.**

In two large rooms—one black, one white—the crowds frolic to their heart's content in Euro-disco style. Open Thursday to Saturday.

Admission: Varies.

A Gay Country Bar

Badlands and Neighbors, 9 Isabella St. ☎ **960-1200.**

Toronto's only gay and lesbian country and western dance club has free instruction in line dancing and two-step every Monday, Tuesday, and Wednesday evening. Downstairs is a neighborhood bar and restaurant with live entertainment, karaoke, and talent contests.

Admission: Free.

3 The Bar Scene

The current night scene has spawned a flock of attractive bar-bistros that also have billiard/pool tables. You can enjoy cocktails, a reasonably priced bistro meal, and a game of billiards in a comfortable, aesthetically pleasing decor.

Note: Bars and pubs that serve drinks only are open Monday through Saturday from 11am to 1am. Establishments that also serve food are open Sunday, too.

Pubs & Bars

First, let me list some of my favorite hotel bars. For a really comfortable bar where you can really settle into some conversation, go to the rooftop bar atop the ⭐ **Park Plaza** at 4 Avenue Rd. (☎ **924-5471**). An old literary haunt, it's comfortable and the view and outdoor terrace are also splendid. The fairly formal **Chartroom,** at the Westin Harbour Castle, 1 Harbour Square (☎ **869-1600**), has a good view of the lake and the island ferry. The **Consort Bar** at the King Edward Hotel, 37 King St. E. (☎ **863-9700**), is also comfortable, as is **La Serre,** at the Four Seasons, 21 Avenue Rd. (☎ **964-0411**). The **Chelsea Bun,** at the Chelsea Inn, 33 Gerrard St. W. (☎ **595-1975**), has a fine selection of single-malt whiskeys and good musical entertainment. If you prefer a pubby atmosphere, there's the **Good Queen Bess,** in the Sheraton Centre, 123 Queen St. W. (☎ **361-1000**). At the airport, check out the **Banyan Tree** at the Regal Constellation, 900 Dixon Rd. (☎ **675-1500**), a comfortable piano bar.

And now for the independents.

Alice Fazooli's, 294 Adelaide St. W. ☎ 979-1910.

Baseball art and memorabilia, including a full-scale model of an outfielder making a wall catch, fills this large bar and dining room. It's always jam-packed with an older business crowd either quaffing in the bar or feasting in the back on crabs cooked in many different styles, pizza, pasta, and raw-bar specialties.

Bellair Café, 100 Cumberland St. ☎ 964-2222.

The midtown Bellair Café has a sleek suede ambience attracting a fashion-conscious and celebrity crowd. It gets really jammed every night and on weekends, both inside at the square bar and outside on the terrace. Drinks cost from $5 to $8.

⭐ Bemelman's, 83 Bloor St. W. ☎ 960-0306.

With its mirrors, marble, gleaming brass rails, and plants, Bemelman's has a certain Manhattan air about it, and the characters who inhabit it are dramatic and trendy. A long stand-up marble-top bar is the focus for the action; in the back you can get a decent meal, choosing from a large menu offering soups, salads, sandwiches, pastas, and egg dishes as well as fish, chicken, pork, and beef. Weather permitting, there's an outdoor patio open from April to October. The bar is well known for its huge martini list. This is also a popular place for brunch from 11:30am to 4pm on Sunday. Open from noon to 3am Monday through Friday, 11am to 3am Saturday, and 11am to midnight Sunday, (The restaurant closes three or four hours earlier.) Drinks cost anywhere from $5 to $8.

The Brunswick House, 481 Bloor St. W. ☎ 964-2242.

For a truly unique experience, go to the Brunswick House, a cross between a German beer hall and an English north-country workingmen's club. Waiters move between the Formica tables in this cavernous room carrying high trays of frothy suds to a largely student clientele. Impromptu dancing breaks out to the background music that drowns out the sound at least of the two large-screen TVs. And while everyone's quaffing or playing bar shuffleboard and billiards, they're entertained by the famous Rockin' Irene who has been here years belting out three rollicking sets at the piano on Friday and Saturday nights. An inexpensive place to down some beer. Upstairs, there's a good jazz, blues, and rhythm-and-blues spot called Albert's Hall (see "Jazz & Rhythm & Blues," above).

Centro, 2472 Yonge St. ☎ 483-2211.

Downstairs at the restaurant, this comfortable, well-patronized bar is a relaxing place to listen to the pianist and get to know the sophisticated mid-30s-and-up crowd. Closed Sunday.

C'Est What?, 67 Front St. E. ☎ 867-9499.

Downstairs in one of the historic warehouse buildings. The rough-hewn walls and cellarlike atmosphere are reminiscent of a Paris *cave.* On one side it's casual and comfortable, attracting a young, politically conscious crowd (board games are available), while on the other, live jazz, rock, or folk is featured. There's a cover charge, depending on the group.

The Duke of Westminster, First Canadian Place. ☎ 368-1555.

Designed in England and shipped and assembled here, this pub offers 16 beers and ales on tap (usually about $4 a half pint, $6 a pint, for imported premium beers). The Duke of Westminster offers a classy English atmosphere that seems to attract those very English types for a good frothy English pint.

The Duke of York, 39 Prince Arthur Ave. ☎ 964-2441.

The Duke of York offers plush surroundings and snacks such as steak-and-kidney pie and bangers and mash in an English country-pub atmosphere. Snacks available.

The Gem, 1159 Davenport Rd. ☎ 654-1182.

A small down-to-earth, retro-style spot, the Gem attracts an artist/musician crowd. The music is 1950s and 1960s, and the decor nostalgic kitsch—black, red, and vinyl in a tacky-trendy style.

Hemingway's, 142 Cumberland St. ☎ 968-2828.

A Yorkville watering hole with a definite Aussie-Kiwi flavor, Hemingway's features piano or other entertainment Thursday to Saturday. A pint of beer is $4.80. The rooftop patio is great in summer.

Jack Russell Pub, 27 Wellesley St. E. ☎ 967-9442.

A comfortable local that attracts a mixed crowd—families, professionals, and students—it's located in an old heritage house. The main pub, complete with dart board, is warmed in winter by a fire and offers a patio in summer. Upstairs on the third floor there's a large tavern with games room. In between there's the Henley room, decked out with rowing regalia. Friendly place to go and chat. It sells 12 types of draft.

Madison, 14 Madison Ave. ☎ 927-1722.

Madison has to be one of the city's most popular gathering places, with people jamming every floor and terrace of this town house. Everyone seems to know everyone else.

Milano, 325 King St. W. ☎ 599-9909.

Up front there's a bar and beyond it lie several billiard tables. The dining area is off to the side and in summer French doors open to the street, making for a pleasant Parisian atmosphere. The bistro-style food consists of burgers, sandwiches, and such items as tiger shrimp.

Pepinello, 180 Pearl St. (between Duncan and John sts.).
  ☎ 599-6699.

Pepinello is currently attracting crowds to the downstairs bar, which features vino bianco and vino rosso, and the upstairs dining area, which offers separate serving counters for pizza, pasta, and risotto.

⭐ **Queen's Head,** 263 Gerrard St. E. at Parliament. ☎ 929-0940.

A friendly, freewheeling bar, the Queen's Head is the kind of place where you can meet the locals, make friends, and join in the ribald discussions at the bar.

⭐ **The Real Jerk,** 709 Queen St. E. ☎ 463-6906.

The original was out east and small, but it became so popular that it moved to a larger space. The hip crowd digs the moderately priced superspiced Caribbean food—jerk chicken, curries, shrimp Creole, rotis, and patties—and the lively crowd and hot music background. No reservations. Open Tuesday through Saturday from 4:30pm to 1am and Sunday from 2 to 11pm.

⭐ **Rotterdam,** 600 King St. W. (at Portland St.). ☎ 868-6882.

This brew pub is a beer-drinker's heaven, serving more than 200 different labels as well as 40 different types on draft. It's not an after-work crowd that gathers here, but by 8pm the tables in the back are filled and the long bar is jammed. In summer the patio is fun, too.

Scotland Yard, 56 The Esplanade. ☎ 364-6572.

With its Victorian bric-a-brac and heavy bar with phony beer pumps, Scotland Yard has the flavor of a casual English local where you can stand around the bar or play a game of darts or shuffleboard in between pints. There's a mixed crowd. At night there's a small dance floor and the place has a DJ from Thursday to Sunday. Domestic beer is $3.75.

Squeeze Club, 817 Queen St. W. ☎ **365-9020.**

This laid-back bar/restaurant and pool hall attracts a mixed crowd ranging from 18 to 50. Weekends, it's the place to go on Queen for R & B. Pop sounds take over during the week. A frequently chosen venue for rock-celebrity and other private parties.

Wheatsheaf Tavern, 667 King St. W. ☎ **364-3996.**

Designated a historic landmark, this is the city's oldest tavern, having been in operation since 1841. Classy it ain't, but for sports mavens, it's home, with five screens showing great moments in sports. The jukebox features 1,200 choices, and there's also a pool table and an outdoor patio.

Wine Bars

The Hop and Grape, 14 College St. ☎ **923-2715.**

The Hop and Grape provides, not surprisingly, beer on one level and wine on another, and it's one of the most popular wine bars in the city. On the ground floor the pub offers 58 types of beer with 12 varieties on draft. Upstairs, the wine bar offers a selection of 100 wines, some by the glass and some by the bottle. Imported beers are $4.50 and up, a 5-ounce glass of wine $4.25 and up. The wine bar is closed on Sunday.

Raclette, 361 Queen St. W. ☎ **593-0934.**

Raclette stocks more than 150 wines, including 28 that are available by the glass; the bar also offers raclette (a round of melted cheese). Wines start at $4 a glass. Open Sunday to Wednesday from 11:30am to 11pm; Thursday to Saturday from 11:30am to 1am.

⭐ **Vines,** 38 Wellington St. E. ☎ **869-0744.**

Vines provides a pleasant atmosphere in which to sample a glass of champagne or any one of 60 wines, priced between $4 and $10 for a 4-ounce glass. Salads, cheeses, and light meals, served with fresh french sticks, are available. **Subway:** King.

Cocktails with a View

⭐ **Aquarius 51 Lounge,** 55 Bloor St. W. ☎ **967-5225.**

A comfortable cocktail bar on the 51st floor of the Manulife Centre. Go for the lit skyline.

Horizons, 301 Front St. W. ☎ **360-8500.**

For obvious reasons, Horizons, perched on the CN Tower, can be difficult to get into because of the crowds. But it's worth the wait to sip that drink and gaze at the panoply of Toronto's lights. It's open from 11am to 2am Monday through Saturday and from noon to 11pm on Sunday. No jeans are allowed on Friday and Saturday nights. At 9 or 10pm, it converts from a cocktail bar to a dance club. **Admission:** $12 charge for the elevator.

Gay Bars

The Rose Cafe, 547 Parliament St. ☎ **928-1495.**

> This is the most popular lesbian bar, with a pool table and games room downstairs, a restaurant and dance area upstairs.

Woody's, 467 Church St. (south of Wellesley). ☎ **972-0887.**

> A friendly and popular local bar, Woody's is frequented mainly by men but welcomes women. It's considered a good meeting place.

4   More Entertainment

Film

Cineplex, in the Eaton Centre. ☎ **593-4535.**

> Although it's easy enough to find a movie theater in the *Yellow Pages* or the local daily newspapers, you should know about Toronto's exceptional film buffs' heaven. Always wary of describing anything as the biggest, let me just say that the film complex houses 17 theaters with seating capacities ranging from 57 to 137.
>
> Exterior screens over the Cineplex entrance in the Eaton Centre, display ongoing slide presentations and an annunciator board in the lobby lists all movies and starting times. Recent releases are the staples. **Subway:** Dundas.
>
> There's also a Cineplex Market Square at 80 Front St. E. (☎ **364-2300**).
>
> **Prices:** Tickets $8.

Cinematheque Ontario, 70 Carlton. ☎ **967-7371** or **923-3456** (box office).

> This organization shows the best in contemporary cinema. The programs include directors' retrospectives, plus new films not available for commercial release from France, Germany, Japan, Bulgaria, and other countries. The films are shown at the Art Gallery of Ontario.
>
> **Prices:** Tickets $7.50 adults, $3.75 seniors.

10

Excursions from Toronto

FOR INFORMATION ABOUT THE AREA SURROUNDING TORONTO, CONTACT THE **Ontario Ministry of Tourism and Recreation,** 77 Bloor St. W., Toronto, ON, M7A 2R9 (☎ **416/314-0944,** or toll free **800/ONTARIO**). The offices are open from Monday through Friday from 8:30am to 5pm (daily from mid-May to mid-September). Or write to **Ontario Travel,** Queen's Park, Toronto, ON, M7A 2E5.

---

1   Niagara-on-the-Lake

Only 80 miles from Toronto, Niagara-on-the-Lake is one of the best-preserved and prettiest 19th-century villages in North America, with its lakeside location and tree-lined streets bordered by handsome clapboard and brick period houses. Such is the setting for one of Canada's most famous events, the Shaw Festival.

INFORMATION   The **Niagara-on-the-Lake Chamber of Commerce,** 153 King St. (P.O. Box 1043), Niagara-on-the-Lake, ON, L0S 1J0 (☎ **905/468-4263**), will provide information and help you find accommodations at one of 55 local bed-and-breakfasts. Open Monday to Friday from 9am to 5pm, Saturday and Sunday from 10am to 5pm.

SPECIAL EVENTS   Devoted to the works of George Bernard Shaw and his contemporaries, the ✪ **Shaw Festival** plays in three theaters: the historic Court House, the exquisite Festival Theatre, and the Royal George Theatre. Ticket prices for all three theaters range from $10 (for lunchtime performances) to $50 on weekends.

The Shaw Festival opens in early May and runs to mid-October, offering nine plays. Some recent performances have included Shaw's *Arms and the Man, Pygmalion,* and *The Doctor's Dilemma,* and *Lulu* by Frank Wedekind.

An added attraction is the free lunchtime conversations (on Saturdays in July and August).

For more information, write or phone Shaw Festival, P.O. Box 774, Niagara-on-the-Lake, ON, L0S 1J0 (☎ **416/468-2172**). Or from New York, Pennsylvania, Ohio, and Michigan, call toll free **800/267-4759.**

What to See & Do ———————————————

Niagara Historical Society Museum, 43 Castlereagh St., at Davy. ☎ **905/468-3912.**

The Niagara Historical Museum houses over 20,000 artifacts pertaining to local history, including many possessions of United Empire Loyalists who first settled the area at the end of the American Revolution. The museum also offers guided walking tours of the area for $2.50, but they must be booked in advance.

Admission: $2.50 adults, $1 teenagers 12–18, 50¢ children.

Open: Jan–Feb weekends 1–5pm; Mar, April, Nov, Dec daily 1–5pm; May–Oct daily 10–5pm.

⭐ **Fort George National Historic Park,** Niagara Parkway. ☎ 905/468-3938.

South along the Niagara Parkway at the Fort George National Historic Park, it's easy to imagine taking shelter behind the stockade fence and watching for the enemy from across the river, even though today there are only condominiums on the opposite riverbank. The fort played a key role in the War of 1812, when the Americans invaded and destroyed it in May 1813. Although rebuilt by 1815, it was abandoned in 1828 and not reconstructed until the 1930s. View the guard room with its hard plank beds, the officers' quarters, the enlisted men's quarters, and the sentry posts. The self-guided tour includes interpretive films and, occasionally, performances by the Fort George Fife and Drum Corps.

Admission: $2.75 adults, $1.25 youths 6–18; free for seniors and children under 5; family rate, $7.

Open: Mid-May to June, daily 9:30am–4:30pm; July–Labor Day, daily 10:30am–5:30pm; Labor Day–Oct, daily 9:30am–4:30pm; Nov to mid-May, Mon–Fri by appointment only.

A SHOPPING & NOSTALGIA STROLL   A stroll along Queen Street will take you to some entertaining shopping stops. At the 1866 **Niagara Apothecary Shop,** 5 Queen St. (☎ 905/468-3845), with its original black-walnut counters and the contents of the drawers marked in gold-leaf script, the original glass and ceramic apothecary ware is on display. **Maple Leaf Fudge,** 14 Queen St. (☎ 905/468-2211), offers 35 varieties that you can watch being made on marble slabs. **Greaves Jam** is run by fourth-generation jam makers. **Loyalist Village,** at no. 12 (☎ 905/468-7331), has distinctively Canadian clothes and crafts, including Inuit art, Native Canadian decoys, and sheepskins. The **Shaw Shop,** next to the Royal George, has GBS memorabilia and more. There's also a Dansk outlet and several galleries selling contemporary Canadian and other ethnic crafts, and a charming toy store, the **Owl and the Pussy Cat,** at 16 Queen St. (☎ 905/468-3081).

NIAGARA-ON-THE-LAKE WINERIES   If you take Highway 55 (Niagara Stone Road) out of Niagara-on-the-Lake, you'll come to **Hillebrand Estates Winery** (☎ 905/468-7123), just outside Virgil. It's open year round; tours are given daily at 11am and 1, 3, and 4pm; the wine shop is open 10am to 6pm daily.

If you turn off Highway 55 and go down York Road, you'll reach **Château des Charmes,** west of St. Davids (☎ 905/262-5202). Tours are given daily. Open 10am to 6pm.

The **Konzelmann Winery,** Lakeshore Road (☎ 905/935-2866), can be reached by driving out Mary Street. Tours are given June to late August Wednesday to Saturday at 2pm; in winter, on Saturday only.

For other wineries in the region, see "Winery Tours" in the Niagara Falls section of this chapter.

Excursions from Toronto

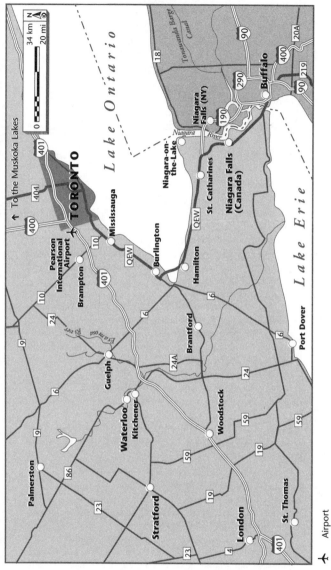

Where to Stay

In summer, don't despair if you're having trouble nailing down a room somewhere. Contact the Chamber of Commerce (see above), which provides an accommodations-reservations service. Best bets are bed-and-breakfast accommodations.

VERY EXPENSIVE

Gate House Hotel, 142 Queen St. (P.O. Box 1364), Niagara-on-the-Lake, ON, L0S 1J0. ☎ **905/468-3263.** 9 rms. A/C MINIBAR TV TEL

Rates: $135–$155 double. **Closed:** Jan to mid-Mar.

Instead of being done in country Canadian, the rooms here are decorated in cool, up-to-the-minute Milan style. Guest rooms have a turquoise marbleized look accented with ultramodern basic black lamps, block marble tables, leatherette couches, and bathrooms with sleek Italian fixtures.

Pillar & Post Inn, 48 John St. (at King St.), Niagara-on-the-Lake, ON, L0S 1J0. ☎ **905/468-2123.** 91 rms. A/C MINIBAR TV TEL

Rates: $140–$200 double; $160 fireplace room. Extra person $20.

Rustic to every last inch of barn board, the Pillar & Post has 48 rooms with wood-burning fireplaces. Although all are slightly different, each room will certainly contain early Canadian-style furniture, Windsor-style chairs, a color TV tucked into a pine cabinet, and historical engravings, plus modern conveniences. In the back there's a secluded pool (some rooms facing the pool on the ground level have bay windows and window boxes).

   Dining/Entertainment: The dining room occupies a former canning factory and basket-manufacturing plant that was converted to a restaurant in 1970. An adjoining craft shop sells country quilts, kitchenware, pine furniture, dolls, toys, and more. The menu features continental cuisine—roasted lamb with kiwi, mint, and garlic sauce, for example. Prices range from $13 to $23. There's also a comfortable lounge.

   Facilities: Outdoor pool, sauna, whirlpool.

Prince of Wales Hotel, 6 Picton St., Niagara-on-the-Lake, ON, L0S 1J0. ☎ **905/468-3246.** 105 rms. A/C TV TEL

Rates: May–Oct, $115–$190 single, $120–$200 double, from $240 suite; Nov–Apr, $100 single, $115 double. Extra person $12. Special packages available.

For a lively atmosphere that retains the elegance and charm of a Victorian inn, the Prince of Wales has it all: full recreational facilities; lounges, bars, and restaurants; and 105 rooms, some with colonial-style furniture and others with brass bedsteads—all beautifully decorated with antiques or reproductions and color-coordinated carpeting, drapes, and spreads. Most rooms have minibars.

   The original section of the hotel was built in 1864. In the Prince of Wales Court, rooms are larger, huge wardrobes house TVs, and botanical prints on the walls set the tone. The newer wing has been well designed to match the original red-brick and cream exterior with its slate dormer roof.

   Dining/Entertainment: An impressive old oak bar from Pennsylvania dominates the quiet bar off the lobby. Royals, the elegant main dining room, serves breakfast, lunch, and dinner, offering a

Niagara-on-the-Lake

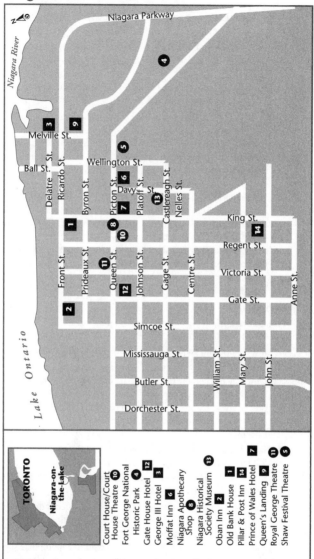

dozen dinner entrées, from grilled tiger prawns with lime and cilantro to beef tenderloin with a peppercorn sauce. Prices range from $18 to $24. At lunch, light dishes are featured, like ham-and-leek quiche and cold poached salmon with dill sauce ($9 to $12). Three Feathers Café is light and airy for breakfast, lunch, or tea. The Queen's Royal lounge is a pleasant drinking spot.

Facilities: Indoor pool, sauna, whirlpool, sun and exercise room, platform tennis court.

Queen's Landing, P.O. Box 1180, at the corner of Byron and Melville sts., Niagara-on-the Lake, ON, L0S 1J0. ☎ **905/468-2195.** 137 rms.

Rates: $165 room without fireplace; $175 room with fireplace; $215 room with fireplace and Jacuzzi.

Overlooking the river but also within walking distance of the theater, the Queen's Landing is a fine establishment where 70 rooms have fireplaces and some 32 have Jacuzzis. Each room is spacious and comfortably furnished with pine furnishings, a half-canopied or brass bed, wingback chairs, and a large desk; each is also equipped with a push-button phone, a color cable TV, and a clock-radio.

Dining/Entertainment: The lounge, with its fieldstone fireplace, is cozy; and the dining room looks out over the yacht-filled dock. At dinner about a dozen or so fish and meat dishes are offered, priced from $17 to $25 for such dishes as roasted pork tenderloin with spicy red-pepper sauce or grilled halibut with lime-butter glaze. Breakfast, lunch, and Sunday brunch are served here, too.

Facilities: Indoor pool, whirlpool, sauna, exercise room, lap pool, bicycle rentals.

EXPENSIVE

The George III, 61 Melville St., Niagara-on-the-Lake, ON, L0S 1J0. ☎ **416/468-4207.** 8 rms. A/C TV

Rates (including continental breakfast): $90–$110 standard double; $115 double with balcony.

Down by the harbor, the George III offers attractive rooms with pretty wallpaper and quilts and flounce pillows on the beds. Amenities include clock-radios, TVs, hairdryers, and coffeemakers. A continental breakfast is delivered to your door. Room 8 has a large balcony.

Moffat Inn, 60 Picton St., Niagara-on-the-Lake, ON, L0S 1J0. ☎ **905/468-4116.** 22 rms. A/C TV TEL

Rates: May to mid-Oct and Christmas/New Year's holidays, $85–$110 double; mid–Oct to late Apr, $65–$110 double.

Niagara-on-the-Lake has another fine accommodation at the Moffat. There are 22 comfortable rooms available (7 with fireplaces). Most are furnished with brass beds and wicker and bamboo pieces, TVs, and hairdryers. A nice touch is the tea kettle and appropriate supplies in every room. Free coffee is available in the lobby. Restaurant and bar on premises.

★ **Oban Inn,** 160 Front St. (at Gate St.), Niagara-on-the-Lake, ON, L0S 1J0. ☎ **905/468-2165.** 21 rms. A/C TV TEL

Rates: $95 single; $135 standard double, $160 double with lake view. Winter midweek and weekend packages available.

With a prime location overlooking the lake, the Oban Inn is probably *the* place to stay. It's located in a charming white Victorian house with a green dormer-style roof and windows, plus a large veranda. The gardens are a joy to behold and a source of the bouquets on each table in the dining room and throughout the house.

Each of the comfortable rooms is unique. Some have a chintz decor, but all have TVs, antique chests, and early Canadian-style headboards. Each is likely to have a candlewick spread on the bed, a small sofa, dressing table, and old prints on the walls—it's all very homey and comfortably old-fashioned. One or two rooms have showers only, so if you want a bath, be sure to request it.

Dining/Entertainment: Bar snacks and light lunches and dinners are available downstairs in the pubby piano bar, with its leather Windsor-style chairs and hunting prints over the blazing fireplace. The dining room serves a menu priced from $18 to $21. A similar luncheon is available for $7 to $10. Meals are usually served only in sittings.

★ **The Old Bank House,** 10 Front St. (P.O. Box 1708), Niagara-on-the-Lake, ON, L0S 1J0. ☎ **905/468-7136.** 2 rms (without bath), 5 rms (with bath), 1 suite (with bath). A/C

Rates (including breakfast): $90 double without bath, $110–$115 double with bath; $130 one-bedroom suite; $225 Rose Suite.

The Georgian Old Bank House, beautifully situated by the river, was built in 1817 as the first branch of the Bank of Canada. The inn is operated by Marjorie Ironmonger. It has four rooms, each with a washbasin and sharing a full bathroom plus an extra toilet. In addition, there are three suites with private baths and separate entrances and a two-bedroom suite with a sitting room and bathroom. All rooms are tastefully decorated and have air-conditioning; all but one have a refrigerator and coffee or tea supplies. The sitting room, with a fireplace, is very comfortable and furnished with Sheraton and Hepplewhite pieces. The Garden Room is very appealing, with a private entrance and a trellised deck.

A SPORTS ENTHUSIAST'S PARADISE

White Oaks Inn and Racquet Club, Taylor Rd.,
Niagara-on-the-Lake, ON, L0S 1J0. ☎ **905/688-2550.** 90 rms, 17 suites. A/C TV TEL

Rates: $100–$125 single or double; $160 Executive Suite.

Not far from Niagara-on-the-Lake, the White Oaks is a fantastic facility for the fitness freak. Anyone can come here, spend the whole weekend, and not stir outside the resort. Take a break and enjoy the lounge area, the outdoor terrace café, a formal restaurant, and a pleasantly furnished café/coffee shop, or schedule a massage.

The rooms are as good as the facilities, each featuring oak furniture, gray-blue or blue-rose decor, vanity sinks, and additional niceties like a phone in the bathroom and complimentary shampoo, cologne, and toothbrush. The Executive Suites also have brick fireplaces, marble-top desks, Jacuzzis (some heart-shaped), and bidets. Deluxe suites also have sitting rooms and the ultimate in furnishings.

Facilities: Four outdoor tennis courts, eight air-conditioned indoor tennis courts, six squash courts, three racquetball courts, Nautilus room, jogging trails, sauna, suntan beds, day-care center with fully qualified staff.

Where to Dine

MODERATE

The Buttery, 19 Queen St. ☎ 468-2564.

Cuisine: CANADIAN/ENGLISH/CONTINENTAL. **Reservations:** Recommended (required for Henry VIII feast).

Prices: Henry VIII dinner $42.75; tavern menu main courses $6–$14; dinner main courses $7–$16. MC, V.

Open: Summer, daily 11am–midnight; other months, daily noon–8pm. Henry VIII feast, Fri at 9pm and Sat at 9:30pm; tea, daily 2–5pm.

The Buttery has been a main-street dining landmark for years, known for its weekend Henry VIII feasts, when "serving wenches" will "cosset" you with food and wine while jongleurs and musickers entertain you. You'll get broth, chicken, roast lamb, roast pig, sherry trifle, syllabub, and cheese to be washed down with a goodly amount of wine, ale, and mead.

A full tavern menu is served from 11am to 5:30pm, featuring spareribs, filet mignon, shrimp in garlic sauce, and English specialties. The dinner menu lists breast of chicken with chardonnay sauce and leg of lamb served with a real garden-mint sauce. Finish with key lime pie or mud pie. Take home some of the fresh baked goods— pies, strudels, dumplings, cream puffs, or scones. An after-theater menu is served from 10pm to 12:30am.

Fans, 135 Queen St. ☎ 468-4511.

Cuisine: CHINESE.

Prices: Main courses $8–$18 at dinner, $5–$8 at lunch. AE, MC, V.

Open: Daily noon–10pm. **Closed:** Mon in off-season.

Some of the best food in town can be found in this comfortable Chinese spot, decorated with fans, cushioned bamboo chairs, and round tables spread with golden tablecloths. In summer, the courtyard also has tables for outdoor dining. The cuisine ranges from Cantonese to Szechuan. Singapore beef, moo shu pork, Szechuan scallops, and lemon chicken are just a few of the dishes available. If you wish, you can order Peking duck 24 hours in advance.

The Old Bakery Restaurant, 59 Queen St. ☎ 468-7217.

Cuisine: CONTINENTAL.

Prices: Main courses $13–$23. MC, V.

Open: Summer, daily 10am–8pm; fall, daily 11am–3pm. **Closed:** Jan–Apr 1.

The Old Bakery Restaurant features veal parmigiana, duck à l'orange, filet mignon, and filet of sole. Breakfast and lunch are served, too. The decor is plain and homey.

Ristorante Giardino, 142 Queen St. ☎ 468-3263.

Cuisine: ITALIAN.
Prices: Main courses $19–$30 at dinner. AE, MC, V.
Open: Summer, lunch daily noon–2pm; dinner daily 5:30–9pm. Winter, dinner only, daily 5:30–9pm.

On the ground floor of the Gate House Hotel is this sleek, ultra-modern Italian restaurant with gleaming marble-top bar and brass accents throughout. The food is northern Italian with Asian and other accents, with a dozen or so main courses—steamed salmon with balsamic vinegar and olive oil, veal loin chop napped with vodka, and breast of chicken with orange-ginger sauce. Desserts include amaretto tiramisu—lady fingers soaked in amaretto and espresso, buried in sweet cream cheese, and topped with cocoa—or an innovative fresh strawberry peppercorn surprise.

BUDGET

The George III, 61 Melville St. ☎ 468-4207.

Cuisine: CANADIAN.
Prices: Main courses $8–$13. MC, V.
Open: Daily 11:30am–10pm. **Closed:** Mid-Nov to Apr 15.

Down by the harbor, the George III is a good budget dining choice for chicken wings, burgers, sandwiches, and stir-fries. There's a publike atmosphere and a pleasant outdoor patio.

SPECIALTY DINING

The **Niagara Home Bakery,** 66 Queen St. (☎ 468-3431), is the place to stop for chocolate-date squares, cherry squares, croissants, cookies, and individual quiches.

For breakfast, go to the **Stagecoach Family Restaurant,** 45 Queen St. (☎ 468-3133), for a down-home budget-priced meal. No credit cards are accepted.

---

2 Niagara Falls

Niagara Falls, with its gimmicks, amusement parks, wax museums, daredevil feats, and a million motels (each with a honeymoon suite complete with a heart-shaped bed), may seem rather tacky and commercial, but somehow the falls still steal the show; on the Canadian side, with its parks and gardens, nature manages to survive with grace.

ORIENTATION Park at Rapid View, several kilometers from the falls, or in Preferred Parking (overlooking the falls—it costs more), and take the **People Mover** (☎ 357-9340), an attraction in itself, making 20 stops from Rapid View to the Spanish Aero Car. Shuttles to the falls also operate from downtown and Lundy's Lane; an all-day pass costs $4 for adults and $2 for children 12 and under in-season only.

INFORMATION Contact the **Niagara Falls Canada Visitor and Convention Bureau,** 5433 Victoria Ave., Niagara Falls, ON, L2G 3L1 (☎ 905/356-6061), or the **Niagara Parks Commission,** Box 150, 7400 Portage Rd. S., Niagara Falls, ON, L2E 6T2 (☎ 905/356-2241).

Summer information centers are open at Table Rock House, the *Maid of the Mist,* and Rapids View.

What to See & Do

VIEWING THE FALLS   Aboard the ⭐ *Maid of the Mist,* 5920 River Rd. (☎ 905/358-5781), you'll make your way through the turbulent waters around the American Falls; past the Rock of Ages; and to the foot of the Horseshoe Falls, where 34.5 million gallons fall per minute over the 176-foot-high cataract. Your sunglasses will mist, but that won't detract from the thrill of the experience. Fares are $9.55 for adults and $5.90 for children 6 to 12; children 5 and under are free.

Boats leave from the dock on the parkway just down from the Rainbow Bridge. Trips operate daily from mid-May through October 24.

Take the elevator at Table Rock House, which drops you 125 feet through solid rock to the Journey Behind the Falls (☎ 905/354-1551) and viewing portals. Open all year. Admission is $5.25 for adults and $2.65 for children 6 to 12; children under 6 are free. Take a nine-minute spin in a chopper over the whole Niagara area. Helicopters leave from the heliport, adjacent to the whirlpool at the junction of Victoria Avenue and Niagara Parkway, daily from 9am to dusk, weather permitting, except in January. Contact Niagara Helicopters, 3731 Victoria Ave. (☎ 905/357-5672).

Or ride up in the external glass-fronted elevators 520 feet to the top of the Skylon Tower Observation Deck at 5200 Robinson St. (☎ 905/356-2651). The observation deck is open daily from 10am to 9pm (from 8am to 1am June through Labor Day). There's also a basement amusement park. Adults pay $6; seniors, $5; and children 12 and under, $3.50.

There's another fabulous view from the 325-foot Minolta Tower Centre, 6732 Oakes Dr. (☎ 905/356-1501). On-site attractions include the *Waltzing Waters* (a computerized music, light, and water show, shown nightly from May to October for free) and a family entertainment center featuring rides. The tower is open daily year round from 9am to 11pm (closed December 24 and 25). The Entertainment Centre is open April to November daily from 9am to 9pm. Admission to the tower is $5.95 for adults and $4.95 for students and seniors.

For a thrilling introduction to Niagara Falls, stop by the IMAX Theater and view the raging swirling waters in *Niagara: Miracles, Myths, and Magic,* shown on a six-story-high screen. It's at 6170 Buchanan Ave. (☎ 905/374-IMAX).

The Falls By Night   Don't miss seeing the falls lit by 22 xenon gas spotlights (each producing 250 million candlepower of light), in shades of rose pink, red magenta, amber, blue, and green. Schedules are as follows: November to February, 7 to 9:30pm; March, 7 to 10pm; April, 7:30 to 10:30pm; May, 9pm to midnight; June, 9:15pm to midnight; July, 9:15pm to 12:30am; August, 9pm to 12:30am;

Niagara Falls

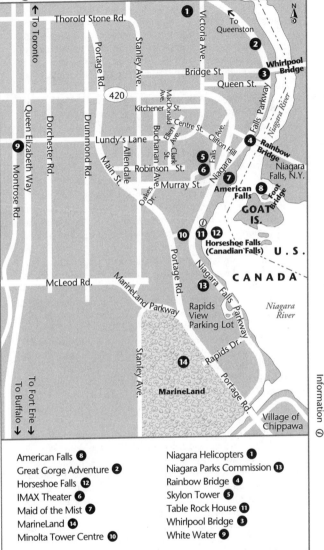

September 1 to Labor Day, 8pm to 12:30am; Labor Day to October, 8 to 11pm.

⭐ **ATTRACTIONS ALONG THE NIAGARA PARKWAY** The Niagara Parkway provides a delightful 35-mile stretch of parkland and gardens.

Half a mile north of Niagara Falls, you'll reach the **Spanish Aero Car** (☎ **356-2241**), a cable car that will whisk you on a 3,600-foot jaunt between two points in Canada, high above the whirlpool, providing excellent views of the surrounding landscape. Open daily from May through the third Sunday in October: from 9am to 6pm in May, 9am to 8pm in June, 9am to 9pm in July and August, 10am to 7:30pm in September, and 9am to 5pm in October. Admission is $4.75 for adults and $2.40 for children 6 to 12; children under 6 are free.

From here you'll pass the **Whirlpool Golf Club** (☎ **905/356-1140**), an outstanding public course. Greens fees are $32 for 18 holes; from October 1 to the second Sunday in November, it costs $22 for 9 or 18 holes.

Next stop is the **School of Horticulture.** Stop for a free view of the vast gardens there before going on to look at the **Floral Clock,** containing 25,000 plants in its 40-foot-diameter face.

From here you can drive to **Queenston Heights Park,** site of a major battle during the War of 1812. On October 13, 1812, an American force invaded Canada here. Although the British forces won the Battle of Queenston Heights, General Brock was killed. You can take a walking tour of the battlefield.

Picnic or play tennis (for $5 an hour) in this shaded arbor before visiting the **Laura Secord Homestead,** on Partition Street in Queenston (☎ **905/262-4851**), home of this redoubtable woman. It contains a fine collection of Upper Canadian furniture from the 1812 period as well as artifacts recovered from an archaeological dig. It's open from Victoria Day weekend (late May) to Labor Day, daily 10am to 6pm. Tours are given every half hour, and admission is $1.

Next stop is the Georgian-style **McFarland House** (☎ **905/468-3322** or **356-2241**), built in 1800 and home to John McFarland, "His Majesty's [George III] Boat Builder." It's open daily: Victoria Day to June 30, from 1 to 4pm; July until Labor Day, from 11am to 5pm. Admission is $1.25 for adults and 75¢ for children. The last tour is at 4:30pm.

From here the parkway continues toward Niagara-on-the-Lake, lined with fruit farms and wineries, notably the **Inniskillin Winery,** Line 3, Service Road 56 (☎ **905/468-3554** or **468-2187**), **Reif Winery** (☎ **905/468-7738**), and **Kurtz Orchards** (☎ **905/468-2937**). The first is especially famous for its icewine and is open Monday through Saturday from 10am to 6pm from May to October and 10am to 5pm November to April. The self-guided tour is detailed and informative and features such sidebars as the history of the cork, as well as the wine-making process. They are given daily at 10:30am and 2:30pm from June to October (Saturday only from November to May). At Reif Winery, tours are given on Saturdays only.

A trip along the parkway will take you by the Table Rock complex to the **Park Greenhouse,** a year-round free attraction (open daily from 9:30am to 7pm during July and August, until 4:15pm in other months).

Farther along, visit the **Dufferin Islands,** where the children can swim, rent a paddle boat, and explore the surrounding woodland areas, while you play a round of golf on the illuminated nine-hole par-three course. Open from the second Sunday in April to the last Sunday in October.

A little farther on, stop for a picnic in **King's Bridge Park** and stroll along the beaches before driving on to **Fort Erie** (☎ **905/871-0540**), a reconstruction of the fort that was seized by the Americans in July 1814, besieged later by the British, and finally blown up as the Americans retreated across the river to Buffalo. Guards in period costume stand sentry duty, fire the cannons, and demonstrate drill and musket practice. Open from the first Saturday in May to Canadian Thanksgiving (U.S. Columbus Day) from 10am to 5:30pm daily. Admission is $3.75 for adults, $3.50 for seniors, and $2.25 for children 6 to 16; kids under 6 are free.

MORE ATTRACTIONS   Everyone loves **White Water,** 7430 Lundy's Lane (☎ **905/357-3380**), for its five water slides, wave pool, and hot tub. Take a picnic and spend the day (there's also a snack bar). Open spring through fall, daily from 10am to dusk. Admission is $14 per day ($11 for children aged 3 to 7), which entitles you to come back at night (or anytime) when the lights go on. The kids can also ride three small slides designed specially for them.

At **MarineLand,** 7657 Portage Rd. (☎ **905/356-8250**), King Waldorf, MarineLand's sea lion mascot, presides over the performances of killer whales, dolphins, and sea lions. The indoor aquarium features a display of freshwater fish and a marine multispecies show with harbor seals as the main attraction. Visit the animal display areas where you can pet and feed the deer and see buffalo, elk, rhea, and more. There are three restaurants or you can spread your picnic lunch on one of the many tables provided.

MarineLand and also has theme-park rides: The big thriller is Dragon Mountain®, a roller coaster that loops, double-loops, and spirals its way through 1,000 feet of tunnels.

Open July and August daily 9am to 6pm; other months, 10am to 4pm. The park closes at dusk and is closed from October to late May. Admission in summer is $20 for adults and $17 for children 9 and under and seniors; children under 4 enter free. Check ahead for prices in other seasons. For taped information, call **905/356-9565.** To get there, drive south on Stanley Street and follow the signs or from QEW take the McLeod Road exit and follow the signs.

The **Niagara Falls Museum,** 5651 River Rd. (☎ **905/356-2151**), displays everything from Egyptian mummies to shells, fossils, and minerals, and the "Freaks of Nature" display. Open daily in summer from 8:30am to 11pm; in winter hours are irregular, usually weekends only, from 10am to 5pm. Admission is $5.75 for adults, $3.95 for students 12 to 18, $5.25 for seniors, and $2.95 for children under 11; children under 5 are free.

There's a whole slew of sideshows on **Clifton Hill**—Ripley's Believe It or Not, Castle Dracula, the Houdini Museum, Movieland

Wax Museum, and Louis Tussaud's Wax Museum—all of them charging about $5 for adults and $2.50 for children.

WINERY TOURS Niagara is set in the fruit- and wine-producing area of the Niagara escarpment. The Niagara peninsula has over 25,000 acres of select vineyards cultivating some 45 varieties of wine grapes. There are a number of wineries in the region: Barnes, Château Gai, Inniskillin House, Andrés, and Brights. At **Brights,** 4887 Dorchester Rd. (☎ **905/357-2400**), the largest winery in Canada, you can see champagne processed in the European way by fermenting the wine in the bottle, and at any of the wineries you can view the wine-making process from the moment the grapes enter the crush house to the fermentation, bottling, and packaging stages. And then comes the fun part—the wine tasting.

Probably the best time to visit is during vendange or harvest season, from the first week in September to the end of October. At Brights, free one-hour tours are offered year round Monday through Friday at 10:30am and 2 and 3:30pm; and 2 and 3:30pm Saturday and Sunday. Call **905/357-2400**, or write: Brights Winery Tours, P.O. Box 510, Niagara Falls, ON, L2E 6V4. For other winery tours and tastings, write to: Andrés Wines, P.O. Box 10550, Winona, ON, L8E 5S4 (☎ **905/643-TOUR,** or toll free **800/263-2170**).

Where to Stay

In Niagara Falls it seems as though every other sign advertises a motel. In summer rates fluctuate according to what the market will bear—some proprietors won't even quote rates ahead of time. You can secure a reasonably priced room if you're lucky enough to arrive on a "down night." For example, at a very fine hotel, I was offered a room for $55 when the official rates were $89 and up. So push a little. Keep requesting a lower rate. Don't take no for an answer.

VERY EXPENSIVE

Niagara Falls Renaissance Fallsview, 6455 Buchanan Ave., Niagara Falls, ON, L2G 3V9. ☎ **905/357-5200.** 262 rms. A/C MINIBAR TV TEL

Rates: $155–$210 single or double; $190–$230 whirlpool rooms.

The Ramada Renaissance features tastefully furnished rooms with oak furniture and TVs tucked away in cabinets. Bathrooms have double sinks and all the modern accoutrements.

Dining/Entertainment: There are a coffee shop and a cocktail lounge on the 19th floor.

Facilities: Indoor pool; whirlpool; health club featuring saunas, squash and racquetball courts, and fitness and weight room.

Skyline Brock, 5685 Falls Ave., Niagara Falls, ON, L2E 6W7. ☎ **905/374-4444,** or toll free **800/648-7200.** 233 rms. A/C TV TEL

Rates: Mid-June to Sept, $109–$200 double; Oct–Dec and Apr to mid-June, $89–$140 double; winter, $70–$109 double. Children under 18 stay free in parents' room. Extra person $10. Special packages available.

For an unblemished view of the falls, try the Skyline Brock or the Skyline Foxhead. The Brock has been hosting honeymooners and falls visitors since 1929. It still has a certain air of splendor, with a huge chandelier and marble walls in the lobby. About 150 of the rooms face the falls. City-view rooms are slightly smaller and less expensive. There are minibars in rooms on the 11th floor and up.

Dining/Entertainment: The 10th-floor Rainbow Room, with a lovely view, serves a popular menu that includes half a roast chicken with cranberry sauce, salmon hollandaise, and prime rib, priced from $16 to $25. Isaac's Bar is available for drinks.

Skyline Foxhead, 5875 Falls Ave., Niagara Falls, ON, L2E 6W7. ☎ **905/357-3090,** or toll free **800/648-7200.** 399 rms. A/C TV TEL

Rates: Mid-June to Sept, $145–$210 double, Oct–Dec and Apr to mid-June, $115–$165 double; winter, $80–$110 double. Extra person $10. Children under 18 stay free in parents' room. Special packages available.

Built over 20 years ago, the Foxhead has 399 rooms (about half with balconies) spread over 14 floors, and it has recently undergone an extensive renovation. Each room has a private bath or shower, a color TV with in-room movies, and climate control.

Dining/Entertainment: The 14th-floor penthouse dining room takes fair advantage of the view with its large glass windows and serves a daily buffet for breakfast, lunch, and dinner, with nightly dancing to a live band (in season). Or there's the Steak and Burger for reasonably priced fare.

Facilities: Outdoor rooftop pool.

EXPENSIVE

Holiday Inn by the Falls, 5339 Murray St. (at Buchanan), Niagara Falls, ON, L2G 2J3. ☎ **905/356-1333.** 122 rms. A/C TV TEL

Rates: Mid-June to Labor Day, $100–$150 single or double; Memorial Day to mid-June and Labor Day to mid-Oct, $75–$105 single or double; Apr to Memorial Day, $60–$95 single or double; winter, $55–$85 single or double. Extra person $6–$9; rollaway bed $10; crib $5.

The Holiday Inn by the Falls has a prime location right behind the Skylon Tower, only minutes from the falls. It's not part of the international hotel chain (the owner had the name first and still refuses to sell it). Each room is large, with ample closet space, an additional vanity sink, color-coordinated modern furnishings, a telephone, and a color TV. Most of the rooms have balconies. Dining facilities, a gift shop, and an indoor and an outdoor heated pool and patio are available.

The Village Inn, 5685 Falls Ave., Niagara Falls, ON, L2E 6W7. ☎ **905/374-4444,** or toll free **800/648-7200.** 205 rms. A/C TV TEL

Rates: Mid-June to Oct, $190 double; Apr to mid-June, $70 double. Special packages available. **Closed:** Jan–Mar.

Behind the two Skylines, the Village Inn is ideal for families—all its rooms are large. Some family suites have 700 square feet, which includes a bedroom with two double beds and a living room. There are an outdoor heated swimming pool and a restaurant.

MODERATE

The Americana, 8444 Lundy's Lane, Niagara Falls, ON, L2H 1H4.
☎ **905/356-8444.** 82 rms, 29 suites. A/C TV TEL

Rates: Late June to late Aug, $70–$110 single or double; Sept–June, $40–$80 single or double. Extra person $5.

The Americana is one of the nicer moderately priced motels on this strip, set in 25 acres of grounds with a pleasant shady picnic area, two tennis courts, indoor and outdoor swimming pools, whirlpool, sauna, and a squash court. The large rooms are fully equipped with telephones, color TVs, vanity sinks, and full bathrooms. Some suites have whirlpool tubs and fireplaces. A dining room, lounge, and coffee shop are on the premises.

Michael's Inn, 5599 River Rd., Niagara Falls, ON, L2E 3H3.
☎ **905/354-2727.** 130 rms. A/C TV TEL

Rates: June–Sept 15, $65–$150 double; $200–$400 bridal suite. Oct–May, $50–$140 double; $150–$300 bridal suite.

At this four-story white building overlooking the Niagara River gorge, the large rooms are nicely decorated, with modern conveniences. Many are whirlpool theme rooms like the Garden of Paradise or Scarlett O'Hara rooms. There's a solarium pool out back. The Ember's Open Hearth Dining Room is just that: The charcoal pit is enclosed behind glass so you can see all the cooking action. There's a lounge, too.

Red Carpet Inn, 4943 Clifton Hill, Niagara Falls, ON, L2G 3N5.
☎ **905/357-4330.** 77 rms, 6 suites. A/C TV TEL

Rates: Mid-May to June, $76.50 single or double; July–Sept, $96.50 single or double; Oct–Dec, $68.50 single or double; Jan to mid-May, $54.50 single or double.

Just up Clifton Hill, around the corner from the Foxhead, window boxes with geraniums draw the eye to the Red Carpet Inn. Two floors of rooms sit around a courtyard with an outdoor heated pool; the honeymoon suites have canopied beds and extraplush decor, while the other rooms have colonial-style furniture and pink walls, clock-radios, full bathrooms, and color TVs. Rooms 54 through 58 have a direct view of the falls; 12 rooms have private balconies. Convenient facilities include a washer-dryer, a gift shop, two restaurants, and a beer garden.

Nelson Motel, 10655 Niagara River Pkwy., Niagara Falls, ON, L2E 6S6. ☎ **905/295-4754.** 25 rms. A/C TV TEL

Rates: June 16–Sept 12, $55–$90 single or double; Sept 13 to mid-Nov and mid-Mar to June 15, $35–$55 single or double. Rollaways and cribs extra. MC, V. **Parking:** Free. **Closed:** Mid-Nov to mid-Mar.

For budget accommodations try the Nelson Motel, run by John and Dawn Pavlakovich, who live in the large house adjacent to the motel units. The units have character, especially the family units with a double bedroom adjoined by a twin-bedded room for the kids. Regular units have modern furniture, some with color and some with black-and-white TV. Singles have shower only. All units face the fenced-in pool and neatly trimmed lawn with umbrellaed tables and shrubs (none has a telephone). It's located a short drive from the falls overlooking the Niagara River, away from the hustle and bustle of Niagara itself.

A NEARBY PLACE TO STAY IN QUEENSTON

★ **South Landing Inn,** at the corner of Kent and Front sts. (P.O. Box 269), Queenston, ON, L0S 1L0. ☎ **905/262-4634.** 23 rms. A/ C TV

Rates: Mid-Apr to end of Oct, $90–$110 double; Nov to mid-Apr, $60–$70 double. AE, MC, V. **Parking:** Free.

In the nearby village of Queenston, the South Landing Inn has rooms with bath and color TV. Five units are in the old original inn built in the early 1800s and their early Canadian furnishings, including poster beds, reflect this era. The rest are in the modern annex. There's a distant view of the river from the inn's balcony. In the original inn you'll also find a cozy dining room with red gingham covered tables, where breakfast is served for $4.

CAMPING

There's a **Niagara Falls KOA** at 8625 Lundy's Lane, Niagara Falls, ON, L2H 1H5 (☎ **905/354-6472**), which has 365 sites (some with electricity, water, and sewage) plus three dumping stations. Facilities include water, flush toilets, showers, fireplaces, store, ice, three pools (one indoor), sauna, and games room. Fees are $23 minimum for two; each additional adult, $5; each additional child 4 to 17, $3; hookups range from $3 for electricity, $4 for water and electricity, and $6 for water, electricity, and sewage. Open April 1 to November 1.

Where to Dine

EXPENSIVE

Casa D'Oro, 5875 Victoria Ave. ☎ **356-5646.**
Cuisine: ITALIAN. **Reservations:** Recommended.
Prices: Main courses $12–$18. AE, DC, DISC, ER, MC, V.
Open: Lunch Mon–Fri noon–3pm; dinner Mon–Fri 4–11pm, Sat 4pm–1am, Sun 4–10pm.

For fine dining amid opulent surroundings one goes to Casa d'Oro to savor Italian delights amid an overwhelming array of gilt busts of Caesar, Venetian-style lamps, statues of Roman gladiators, Roman columns, and murals of Roman and Venetian scenes. Taste the splendors of clams casino or the brodetto Antonio (a giant crouton topped with poached eggs and floated on savory broth garnished with parsley and accompanied by grated cheese). Follow with specialties like saltimbocca alla romana, pollo cacciatore, or sole basilica (flavored with lime juice, paprika, and basil). Then, if you can bear it, choose from the dessert wagon or really spoil yourself with cherries jubilee or bananas flambé and an espresso.

At the back of the Casa d'Oro, stroll over the Bridge of Sighs and onto the disco floor of the Rialto Room, where you can dance from 9pm to the wee hours to Top 40 music, except on Sunday and Monday. Wednesday and Thursday are karaoke and DJ nights respectively.

Hungarian Village Restaurant, 5329 Ferry St. ☎ 356-2429.

Cuisine: HUNGARIAN/CONTINENTAL. **Reservations:** Recommended, especially on weekends.
Prices: Main courses $10–$18. AE, MC, V.
Open: Tues–Fri 4pm–1am, Sat noon–1am, Sun noon–midnight.

Authentic Hungarian specialties are the attractions here: chicken paprikas, veal goulash, and the Transylvanian wooden platter (beef tenderloin, pork chop, veal cutlet, cabbage roll, and sausage, piled high on a bed of rice and served with french fries and sweet-and-sour cabbage; $30 for two). For dessert, there's palacsinta or Viennese pastries. Continental dishes are also available.

Happy Wanderer, 6405 Stanley Ave. ☎ 354-9825.

Cuisine: GERMAN. **Reservations:** Not accepted.
Prices: Main courses $10–$26. AE, MC, V.
Open: Daily 8am–11pm.

Real gemütlichkeit greets you at the chalet-style Happy Wanderer, where you can lay your knapsack down and tuck into a host of schnitzels, wursts, and other German specialties. Transport yourself back to the Black Forest among the beer steins and the game trophies on the walls. The several rooms include the Black Forest Room, with a huge, intricately carved sideboard and cuckoo clock, and the Jage Stube, with solid wood benches and woven tablecloths. At lunch there are omelets, cold platters, sandwiches, and burgers. Dinner might start with goulash soup, proceed with bratwurst, knockwurst, rauchwurst (served with sauerkraut and potato salad) or a schnitzel—wiener, Holstein, or jaeger. All entrées include potatoes, salad, and rye bread. Desserts include, naturally, Black Forest cake and apple strudel (under $5).

Queenston Heights, 14276 Niagara Pkwy. ☎ 262-4274.

Cuisine: CANADIAN/CONTINENTAL.
Prices: Main courses $16–$19. AE, DISC, MC, V.
Open: Lunch Mon–Fri noon–3pm; dinner Mon–Fri 5–9pm; Sat noon–10pm, Sun noon–9pm. **Closed:** Mon in winter.

The star of the Niagara Parkway Commission's eateries stands dramatically atop Queenston Heights. Set in the park among fir, cypress, silver birch, and maple, the open-air balcony affords a magnificent view of the lower Niagara River and the rich fruitland through which it flows. Or you can sit under the cathedral ceiling with its heavy crossbeams where the flue of the stone fireplace reaches to the roof.

At lunchtime, light entrées, seafood, pizza, pasta, salads, and lamb burgers (from $9 to $12) are offered. At dinner, among the selections might be filet of Atlantic salmon with strawberry champagne hollandaise, roast pork with an apricot peppercorn glaze, and prime rib. Afternoon tea is also served from 3 to 5pm in summer season.

Go for a drink on the deck. There's a terrific view.

Victoria Park Restaurant, 6345 Niagara Pkwy. ☎ **356-2217.**

Cuisine: CANADIAN/CONTINENTAL.
Prices: Main courses $12–$19. AE, MC, V.
Open: Early May to mid-Oct, daily 11:30am–10pm. **Closed:** Late Oct to early May.

Within a stone's throw of both the Canadian and the American falls, the Victoria Park offers a terrace for outdoor dining, a comfortable inside dining room warmed by its globe lights, a cafeteria, and a fast-food outlet pushing hot dogs and ice cream. In the dining room and terrace, you'll find an elaborate menu with a whole range of appetizers (bruschetta and tiger shrimp with spicy salsa and Dijon mayonnaise) and main courses that include prime rib, lemon chicken breast, and fettucine with shrimp and okra. The main dish prices include vegetable, potato, and fresh-baked rolls. There's a children's menu featuring burgers and lasagne.

BUDGET

Betty's Restaurant & Tavern, 8921 Sodom Rd. ☎ **295-4436.**

Cuisine: CANADIAN.
Prices: Main courses $6–$15; burgers and sandwiches under $6. AE, MC, V.
Open: Mon–Sat 7am–10pm, Sun 9am–9pm.

Betty's is a local favorite for honest food at fair prices. It's a family dining room where the art and generosity surface in the food—massive platters of fish-and-chips, roast beef, and seafood platters, all including soup or juice, vegetable, and potato. There are burgers and sandwiches, too, all under $6. If you can, save room for enormous portions of home-baked pies. Breakfast and lunch also offer good low-budget eating.

Table Rock Restaurant, Niagara Pkwy. ☎ **354-3631.**

Cuisine: CANADIAN/INTERNATIONAL. **Reservations:** Recommended.
Prices: Main courses $16–$20. AE, DISC, MC, V.
Open: Summer Sun–Thurs 9am–10pm, Fri–Sat 9am–11pm; winter, lunch and dinner only.

Located only a few yards from the Canadian Horseshoe Falls, the Table Rock Restaurant offers such dinner choices as prime rib; grilled tiger shrimp marinated with tomato, onion, garlic, olive oil, and rum; or chicken schnitzel with mushrooms and cheese sauce. Pizza, pasta, ribs, and light entrées are the luncheon choices. Breakfast is also a good bet here.

DINING WITH A VIEW

Besides the view from atop the 520-foot tower at the **Skylon Tower Restaurants** (☎ **356-2651, ext. 274**), you can enjoy breakfast, lunch, or dinner buffets ($10, $16, or $27, respectively) in the Summit Suite dining room, or lunch or dinner in the Revolving Restaurant, where typical favorites like chicken cordon bleu, veal Oscar, and surf and turf are priced from $27 to $40 at dinner, $15 to $18 at lunch. It's open daily from 11:30am to 2:30pm for lunch and from 5 to 10:30pm for dinner (summer only—in other months, hours vary).

You can also dine atop the **Minolta Tower,** 6732 Oakes Dr. (☎ **356-1501**), in the Pinnacle on typical North American favorites—steak, salmon, grilled chicken. At lunch prices range from $8 to $15; at dinner, from $15 to $30.

3 Stratford

Home of the world-famous Stratford Festival, this town manages to capture the prime elements of the Bard's birthplace, from the swans on the Avon River to the grass banks that sweep down to it where you can picnic under a weeping willow before attending a Shakespearean play.

INFORMATION For the first-rate visitor information, go to the **information booth** by the river on York Street at Erie. It's open from May to early November, Sunday through Wednesday from 10am to 5pm and Thursday through Saturday from 10am to 8pm. At other times, contact **Tourism Stratford,** 88 Wellington St., Stratford, ON, N5A 6W1 (☎ **519/271-5140**).

The Stratford Festival

★ Since its modest beginnings on July 13, 1953, when *Richard III,* starring Sir Alec Guinness, was staged in a huge tent, Stratford's artistic directors have all built on the radical but faithfully classic base originally provided by Tyrone Guthrie to create a repertory theater with a glowing international reputation.

Stratford has three theaters: the **Festival Theatre,** 55 Queen St. in Queen's Park, with its dynamic thrust stage; the **Avon Theatre,** 99 Downie St., with a classic proscenium; and the **Tom Patterson Theatre,** an intimate 500-seat theater on Lakeside Drive.

World famous for its Shakespearean productions, the festival also offers both classic and modern theatrical masterpieces. Recent productions have included Gilbert and Sullivan's *Mikado* (which went on to great success on Broadway), Thornton Wilder's *Our Town,* Chekhov's *Uncle Vanya, Timon of Athens* and *Measure for Measure* (both by Shakespeare), and *Les Belles Soeurs* by Michel Tremblay. Among the company's alumnae are such famous names as Maggie Smith, Sir Alec Guinness, Alan Bates, Christopher Plummer, Irene Worth, Julie Harris, and Gordon Thompson. Present stars include Nicholas Pennell, Brian Bedford, Pat Galloway, Goldie Semple, and Colm Feore.

Tom Patterson Theatre productions in particular are loved for their creative risk-taking and the excitement generated by the intimate space.

In addition to attending plays, visitors may enjoy "Meet the Festival," a series of informal discussions with members of the acting company, production, or administrative staff; "Post Performance Discussions" that follow Tuesday- and Thursday-evening performances; and backstage tours, offered every Sunday morning from mid-June to the end of October. The last cost $5 for adults, $2.50 for seniors and students (advance reservations recommended).

The season usually begins early in May and continues until mid-November. For tickets, call **519/273-1600;** or write to the Stratford Festival, P.O. Box 520, Stratford, ON, N5A 6V2. Tickets are also available in the U.S. and Canada at Ticketron outlets. Telephone orders taken beginning in late February.

What to See & Do

Are there summer pleasures in Stratford beside the theater? Within sight of the Festival Theatre, **Queen's Park** has picnic spots beneath tall shade trees or down by the water's edge where the swans and ducks gather. To the east and west of the theater, footpaths follow the Avon River and Lake Victoria.

Past the Orr Dam and the 90-year-old stone bridge, through a rustic gate, lies a very special park, the **Shakespearean Garden.**

If you turn right onto Romeo Street North from Highways 7 and 8 as you come into Stratford, you'll find the **Gallery/Stratford,** 54 Romeo St. (☎ **519/271-5271**), which mounts varied shows. Open Sunday and Tuesday through Friday from 1 to 5pm and Saturday from 10am to 5pm from September through May; June through the first week of September, open Tuesday through Sunday from 9am to 6pm. Admission is $3.50 for adults and $2.50 for students 12 and up and seniors.

Stratford is a historic town, and $1^1/_2$-hour **guided tours of early Stratford** are given Monday through Saturday July to Labor Day, leaving at 9:30am from the visitor's booth by the river.

Boat and canoe rentals are available at the Boathouse, located behind and below the information booth. Open daily from 9am until dark in summer. Contact **Avon Boat Rentals,** 40 York St. (☎ **519/271-7739**).

Where to Stay

When you book your theater tickets, you can also, at no extra charge, book your accommodations. The festival can book you into the type of accommodation and price category you prefer, from guest homes with $45 rates to first-class hotels charging over $125. Call or write the **Festival Theatre Box Office,** P.O. Box 520, Stratford, ON, N5A 6V2 (☎ toll free **800/567-1600,** or **519/273-1600**).

EXPENSIVE

Bentleys, 107 Ontario St., Stratford, ON, N5A 3H1.
　　☎ **519/271-1121.** 13 suites. A/C TV TEL

Rates: July–Oct, $150 double, (50% off Sun and Mon). Nov–June, $90 double. Extra person $20.

The soundproof rooms here are in fact luxurious duplex suites, each with a bathroom, telephone, air-conditioning, a color TV, and an efficiency kitchen. Period English furnishings and attractive drawings, paintings, and costume designs on the walls make for a pleasant ambience. Five of the suites have skylights.

Festival Motor Inn, 1144 Ontario St. (P.O. Box 811), Stratford, ON, N5A 6W1. ☎ **519/273-1150.** Fax 519/273-2111. 151 rms. A/C TV TEL

Rates: Main building, $88 single, $89 double, $105 twin. Outside units (with no inside access and no refrigerator), $80 single, $85 double. New deluxe rooms $130–$160 double. Extra person $8; cot $6. Winter rates about 30% lower.

With its black-and-white motel-style units, the Festival Motor Inn is set back off Highways 7 and 8 in 10 acres of nicely kept landscaped grounds. The place has an old English air with its stucco walls, Tudor-style beams, and high-back red settles in the lobby. The Tudor style is maintained throughout the large modern rooms, all with wall-to-wall carpeting, matching bedspreads and floor-to-ceiling drapes, reproductions of old masters on the walls, and full bathroom. Some of the bedrooms have charming bay windows with sheer curtains, and all rooms in the main building have refrigerators. Other facilities include two tennis courts, shuffleboard, dining room, coffee shop, and an indoor pool with outdoor patio.

The Queen's Inn, 161 Ontario St., Stratford, ON, N5A 3H3. ☎ **519/271-1400.** 31 rms. A/C TV TEL

Rates: May–Oct, $90 small double, $120 queen, $125 bedsitting room, from $150 suite. Nov 1–May 1, $64 small double, $69 queen, $95 bedsitting room, from $115 suite.

Conveniently located in the town center, the Queen's Inn has been recently restored. The rooms, all with private bath, air-conditioning, push-button phones, and TVs, have been pleasantly decorated in pastels and pine.

Facilities include the Boar's Head Pub and two restaurants—the Queen Victoria room and the Queen's Table—both serving traditional Canadian/continental food.

MODERATE

23 Albert Place, 23 Albert St., Stratford, ON, N5A 3K2. ☎ **519/273-5800.** 34 rms. A/C TV TEL

Rates: $80–$90 double; $104 minisuite; from $115 suite.

Right across from the Avon Theatre, the Albert Place sports large rooms with high ceilings. Furnishings are simple and modern. Rooms have TVs, air-conditioning, and push-button phones; some have separate sitting rooms. A complimentary continental-style breakfast is available in the lobby for guests.

Stratford

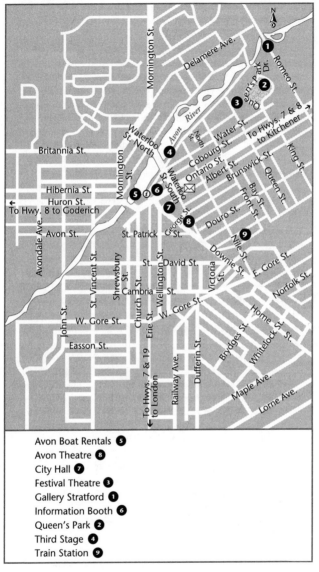

Avon Boat Rentals ❺
Avon Theatre ❽
City Hall ❼
Festival Theatre ❸
Gallery Stratford ❶
Information Booth ❻
Queen's Park ❷
Third Stage ❹
Train Station ❾

A PICK OF THE B&BS

For more information on the Stratford bed-and-breakfast scene, write to **Tourism Stratford,** 88 Wellington St., Stratford, ON, N5A 6W1 (☎ **519/271-5140**). It's open 8:30am to 5pm Monday to Friday.

Acrylic Dreams, 66 Bay St., Stratford, ON, N5A 4K6.
☎ **519/271-7874.** 4 rms (3 with bath). A/C

Rates (including breakfast): $85 double; $100 suite. Two-night minimum on weekends. No credit cards.

Acrylic Dreams has a funky, modern, artsy atmosphere thanks to its artist-owners. The house is furnished with cottage-style antiques except for the living room, which is furnished in New Wave with transparent acrylic furniture. Upstairs there's a suite with private bath and living room. On the ground floor there are two doubles with bath plus a double with an antique iron-and-brass bed that shares a bathroom. The full breakfast will vary from day to day. It might bring, for example, orange juice and coffee, peaches and peach yogurt, scrambled eggs, and bagels (but no meat since the owners are vegetarians). There's a phone for guests' use and the suite has a TV.

Ambercroft, 29 Brunswick St., Stratford, ON, N5A 3L9.
☎ **519/271-5644.** 5 rms (1 with bath). A/C
Rates (including continental breakfast): $50 single; $65 double; $85 twin with private bath.

Ambercroft has four rooms sharing two baths (two doubles, a queen, and a twin), plus a twin with private bath. There's a comfy sitting room with plenty of slipcovered chairs and sofas, a small TV room, and a patio out back. An extended continental breakfast is served—fresh fruit, cereal, muffins, and croissants.

Avonview Manor, 63 Avon St., Stratford, ON, N5A 5N5.
☎ **519/273-4603.** 4 rms (none with bath).
Rates (including breakfast): $65 double. No credit cards.

Located on a quiet street in an Edwardian house, Avonview Manor has four rooms with fans, all attractively and individually furnished. One room has a brass bed covered with a floral-pattern quilt and flouncy pillows and is large enough for a couch and oak rocker. Another room has a cherry acorn bed, cherry dresser, and love seat. Mennonite quilts cover the beds. The rooms share two bathrooms.

A full breakfast is served in a bright dining room overlooking the garden, and a kitchen equipped with an ironing board is available on the first floor. The living room is very comfortable, particularly in winter in front of the stone fireplace. Smoking is allowed only on the porch.

Brunswick House, 109 Brunswick St., Stratford, ON, N5A 3L9.
☎ **519/271-4546.** 6 rms (none with bath).
Rates (including breakfast): $60 and up. No credit cards.

If you stay here you'll enjoy the very literate surroundings created by owners Geoff Hancock and Gay Allison—portraits of Canadian authors and poetry on the walls, books everywhere, and the chance to run into a literary personality. There are six rooms, sharing two baths, all nicely decorated and with ceiling fans. One is a family room with a double and two single beds. Each room has a personal decorative touch—a Mennonite quilt, posters by an artist friend, or a parasol atop a wardrobe. A full breakfast is served. Smoking is restricted to the veranda.

⭐ **Deacon House**, 101 Brunswick St., Stratford, ON, N5A 3L9.
☎ **519/273-2052.** 6 rms.

Rates (including continental breakfast): $80–$86 double. Extra person $20. A/C

Deacon House, a shingle-style structure built in 1907, has been restored by Diane Hrysko and Mary Allen. They have six rooms, all with bath, all decorated in country style with iron-and-brass beds, quilts, pine hutches, oak rockers, and rope-style rugs. My favorite rooms are on the top floor. The living room with fireplace, TV, wingbacks, and sofa, is comfortable. The guest kitchen is a welcome convenience; so too is the second-floor sitting/reading room. A continental breakfast is served.

Flint's Inn, 220 Mornington St., Stratford, ON, N5A 5G5.
☎ **519/271-9579.** 2 rms (none with bath), 1 suite (with bath). A/C
Rates (including breakfast): $65 double; $85 suite.

This steep-mansard-roofed house, built in 1862, has three air-conditioned units. One is a large suite with a sun porch, a balcony, a private bath, and a refrigerator. The iron-and-brass bed sports an old quilt, and among the decorative features are an old butter churn and a bottle collection. The other two rooms share a bathroom. The living room, with its marble fireplace and pine furnishings, is inviting. At breakfast, homemade muffins, juice, and coffee are accompanied by eggs Benedict or something similar. The garden is well kept and filled with the wonderful scent of lilac in season.

The Maples, 220 Church St., Stratford, ON, N5A 2R6.
☎ **519/273-0810.** 5 rms (1 with bath). A/C
Rates (including breakfast): $50 single; $65 double.

The Maples is owned and run by Maureen Doneathy and Mary Taylor, who keep five nice rooms—four doubles and one single—and serves juice, fruit, and homemade breads and muffins at breakfast. The house is a red-brick Victorian with a balcony.

Shrewsbury Manor, 30 Shrewsbury St., Stratford, ON, N5A 2V5.
☎ **519/271-8520.** 3 rms (none with bath). A/C
Rates: $55–$60 double.

At Shrewsbury Manor, an old Victorian built in 1872, there's a twin room and a master bedroom with a bed complete with Turkish-style canopy. Another room's bed sports a colorful log-cabin quilt made by owner Beryl Morningstar herself. The shared bathroom is large and the whole place is very comfortable.

Woods Villa, 62 John St. N., Stratford, ON, N5A 6K7.
☎ **519/271-4576.** 5 rms (none with bath). A/C TV
Rates (including breakfast): $85 double for the first night ($75 additional nights).

This late 18th-century house is home to Ken Vinen, who has a passion for collecting and restoring Wurlitzers, Victrolas, and player pianos, which are found throughout the house. There are five rooms sharing two bathrooms. Four have fireplaces, and all have color TVs and air-conditioning. Rooms are large and a good value. Guests are welcome to use the pool, lounges, and the TV in the living room.

Ken has other talents—at breakfast he may choose to make some doughnuts or muffins, served along with a full meal, while Barney and Fred, the macaws, add their comments. No indoor smoking. Pets and children not permitted.

A NEARBY PLACE TO STAY & DINE

⭐ **Langdon Hall,** RR 3, Cambridge, ON, N3H 4R8.
☎ **519/740-2100,** or toll free **800/268-1898.** Fax 519/740-8161.
36 rms, 7 suites. A/C TEL TV

Rates (including continental breakfast): $195–$230 single or double; from $320 suite. AE, DC, ER, MC, V.

The elegant house that stands at the head of the curving, tree-lined drive was completed in 1902 by Eugene Langdon Wilks, youngest son of Matthew and Eliza Astor Langdon, a granddaughter of John Jacob Astor. It remained in the family until 1987, when its transformation into a small country house hotel was begun. Today its 200 acres of lawns, gardens, and woodlands make for an ideal retreat. The main house, of red brick with classical pediment and Palladian-style windows, has a beautiful symmetry. Inside, a similar harmony is achieved. Throughout, the emphasis is on comfort rather than grandiosity, whether in the conservatory, the veranda where tea is served, or the lounge with its comfortable club chairs and Oriental rugs.

The majority of the rooms are set around the cloister garden. Each room is individually decorated; most have fireplaces. The furnishings consist of handsome antique reproductions, mahogany wardrobes, ginger-jar porcelain lamps, wingchairs and armchairs upholstered with luxurious fabrics, fine Oriental rugs, gilt-framed pictures, and such nice touches as fresh flowers and terry bathrobes. The light and airy dining room overlooking the lily pond offers fine continental cuisine. Beyond the cloister, down a trellis arcade, and through a latch gate lies the herb and vegetable garden and beyond that the swimming pool (with an attractive poolhouse), tennis court, and croquet lawn. Other facilities include a whirlpool, sauna, exercise room, billiard room, and cross-country ski trails.

Where to Dine

EXPENSIVE

⭐ **The Church,** Brunswick and Waterloo sts. ☎ 273-3424.
Cuisine: CONTINENTAL. **Reservations:** Required well in advance.
Prices: Summer fixed-price dinner $38.50–$45.50. AE, MC, V.
Open: Tues–Sat 11:30am–1am, Sun 11:30am–11pm. **Closed:** Mon, unless there's a special concert or play.

The Church must be one of the few restaurants in Canada where you have to reserve three weeks in advance. Still, it's a unique privilege because the food is so good and the decor is incredible. The organ pipes and the altar are still intact, along with the vaulted roof, carved woodwork, and stained-glass windows—you can sit in the nave or the side aisles and dine to the sounds of Bach. Fresh flowers and elegant table settings further enhance the experience.

In summer, there's a special five-course fixed-price dinner and an à la carte luncheon and after-theater menu. Appetizers might include Szechuan chicken salad with mango and Oriental dressing or salmon mousse with saffron-yogurt sauce and salmon caviar. Among the entrées might be loin of lamb en croute with an orange and rosemary pesto in natural jus; caribou in a juniper-thyme-seaweed sauce; or roast five-spice duck with ginger mango. There's also a short vegetarian menu. The pièce de résistance among the desserts might be chocolate praline pâté in hazelnut sauce and Cointreau or a trio of ices like chocolate Tía Maria and raisin, mango and coconut, and white peach sorbet. This is a very special dining experience.

The upstairs Belfry Bar is a popular pre- and post-theater gathering place for cocktails, snacks, and full lunch, dinner, and after-theater dinner menus.

★ **The Old Prune,** 151 Albert St. ☎ **271-5052.**
Cuisine: CONTINENTAL. **Reservations:** Recommended.
Prices: Fixed-price dinner $36–$45; main courses $9–$12 at lunch or after theater. AE, MC, V.
Open: Lunch Wed–Sun 11:30am–2pm; dinner Tues–Sun 5–9pm; after-theater supper Fri–Sat 9pm–midnight.

Another of my Stratford favorites, the Old Prune is run by two charming, witty women—Marion Isherwood and Eleanor Kane. Set in a lovely Edwardian home, it has three dining rooms and a garden patio. The proprietors have given the place a Québec flair, which is reflected in both the decor and the menu.

At dinner the price of your entrée will determine the prix fixe price for your appetizer, main course, and a dessert. The chef uses organically grown meats and vegetables in an imaginative way that creates strong flavorsome dishes, like the medallions of rabbit with apple slices and cider-glazed onions or the warm duck confit with a mélange of organic greens topped with walnut oil and black-currant vinegar. The late-supper menu features lighter entrées, like risotto with grilled sea scallops, goat-cheese salad, or Arctic char. For dessert there are mouth watering combinations such as rhubarb compote with fresh strawberries and Grand Marnier ice cream or chocolate cake with coffee ice cream.

★ **Rundles,** 9 Cobourg St. ☎ **271-6442.**
Cuisine: INTERNATIONAL. **Reservations:** Required.
Prices: Three-course table d'hôte $42.50–$50. AE, ER, MC, V.
Open: Lunch Wed and Sat–Sun noon–2:30pm; dinner Tues–Sun. On Fri–Sat an after-theater menu is available. **Closed:** During the winter the restaurant closes and functions occasionally as a cooking school until theater season comes again.

Rundles' large windows take advantage of its beautiful setting overlooking Lake Victoria. Its owner, Jim Morris, eats, sleeps, thinks, and dreams food, and chef Neil Baxter delivers exquisite cuisine to the table. The three-course table d'hôte, including appetizer, main course, dessert, and coffee, will always offer some palate-pleasing combinations of flavors like the clear shrimp bouillon flavored with hot peppers and lemongrass and garnished with shiitake mushrooms and shrimp dumplings, or the barbecue skewered bay scallops and vegetables with sweet fries and salsa. Among the eight or so main dishes there might be grilled Atlantic salmon with lentils and caramelized onions, cumin, and fenugreek sauce; or crisp confit of duck, Japanese eggplant, and zucchini. As for dessert my choice would be the zesty lemon tarts, but the sherry trifle is also a dream. The dining area is very contemporary with its gray spotlighted tables, good cutlery and crystal, and contemporary art (including some bizarre sculpture by Victor Tinkl). The restaurant follows the theater schedule.

Wolfy's, 127 Downie St. ☎ 271-2991.

Cuisine: ECLECTIC. **Reservations:** Recommended.
Prices: Pretheater prix fixe $18.50–$26; à la carte main courses $12–$20. AE, MC, V.
Open: Lunch Tues–Sun 11:30am–2pm; dinner Tues–Sat 5–8:30pm.

Wolfy's has won a loyal local and visitor following with its well-prepared, flavorful cuisine. It's located in a former fish-and-chips shop and the original decor is still evident—the booths, the counter and stools, and the old fish fryer serving as a display cabinet in one corner. Yet it has a New Wave flavor. The walls are decorated with vibrant art by Kato. On the limited menu might be found a rice-and-vegetable stir-fry with peanut-butter sauce, Caribbean pepper chicken, salmon with rhubarb relish, shrimp with coconut-milk lemongrass broth, and rack of lamb with a salad of different lettuces. Desserts are equally appealing. Caramelized walnut tart, peach-nectarine fruit tart or the brownie with orange caramel sauce—a perennial favorite on the menu.

MODERATE

Bentley's, 107 Ontario St. ☎ 271-1121.

Cuisine: CANADIAN/ENGLISH. **Reservations:** Not accepted.
Prices: Light fare $6–$8; main courses $12–$15. AE, DC, ER, MC, V.
Open: Daily 11:30am–1am.

For budget dining and fun to boot, go to Bentley's, the local watering hole. In summer you can sit on the garden terrace.

In this atmosphere you can savor some light fare—deep-fried calamari, grilled shrimp, vegetarian wontons, chicken fingers—along with sandwiches and salads, which are served all day. Dinner items are more substantial, like roast chicken, baked sole, sirloin, or prime rib.

Keystone Alley Café, 34 Brunswick St. ☎ **271-5645.**

Cuisine: CONTINENTAL. **Reservations:** Recommended.
Prices: Main courses under $7 at lunch, $12–$18 at dinner. AE, MC, V.
Open: Lunch Mon–Sat 11am–4pm; dinner Tues–Sat 5–9pm.

Actors often stop in for lunch at the Keystone Alley Café. There are butcher-block tables as well as a counter where you can order a light lunch—soups, salads, burgers, sandwiches, New York cheesecake, and a daily selection of muffins.

At night the atmosphere changes, and there's a full dinner menu featuring eight or so items, such as calves' liver with apple-and-shallot compote and pink-peppercorn sauce; pork loin in sauce of honey, lime, ginger, and Calvados with caramelized apricots and water chestnuts; and grain-fed chicken with mango, ginger, and coriander cream sauce. Wine and beer are available.

Olde English Parlour, 101 Wellington St. ☎ **271-2772.**

Cuisine: ENGLISH. **Reservations:** Recommended during theater season.
Prices: Snacks under $8; main courses $10–$20. AE, MC, V.
Open: Mon 11:30am–11pm. Tues–Sat 11:30am–1am, Sun 11:30am–9pm.

For medium-priced fare, head for the Olde English Parlour. In this pubby atmosphere, you can select sandwiches, steak-and-kidney pie, fish-and-chips, and other British fare, along with burgers, seafood, and steaks.

Café Mediterranean, in the Festival Square Building. ☎ **271-9590.**

Cuisine: LIGHT FARE. **Reservations:** Not accepted.
Prices: Most items under $6. No credit cards.
Open: Summer. Mon–Tues 8am–6pm, Wed–Sat 8am–7pm, Sun 10am–2pm; winter, Mon–Sat 9am–5pm.

In the Festival Square Building, the Café Mediterranean is great for made-to-order sandwiches, fruit flans, croissants (cheese, almond, and chocolate), quiches, salads, pastries, and crepes. You can take them out or dine there while seated on director's chairs.

Let Them Eat Cake, 82 Wellington St. ☎ **273-4774.**

Cuisine: DESSERTS. **Reservations:** Not accepted.
Prices: Breakfast and lunch items under $5; desserts $1–$4. MC, V.
Open: Summer Mon 7:30am–6pm, Tues–Fri 7:30am–12:30pm, Sat 9am–12:30pm, Sun 11am–6pm; winter Mon–Sat 7:30am–5pm, Sun 8:30am–2:30pm.

Let Them Eat Cake is great for breakfast (bagels, scones, and croissants), and lunch (soups, salads, sandwiches, quiche, and chicken pot pie), but best of all for dessert. There are about 30 items to choose from—pecan pie, orange Bavarian cream, lemon bars, carrot cake, Black Forest cake, and chocolate cheesecake among them.

PICNIC FARE & WHERE TO EAT IT

Stratford is really a picnicking place. Take a hamper down to the banks of the river or into the parks: Plenty of places cater to this business. **Rundles** will make you a super sophisticated hamper; **Café Mediterranean** has salads, quiches, crepes, and flaky meat pies and pastries. Or go to **Lindsay's,** 40 Wellington St. (☎ **273-6000**), which offers all kinds of salads—pasta, grains, and vegetables—pâtés; fish, chicken, and meat dishes; soups; and breads and pastries. The shop also sells imported specialty foods. Open in summer Tuesday through Saturday from 10am to 6pm, and Sunday from 11am to 2pm (June through September only).

Appendix

Metric Conversions

Length

1 millimeter	=	0.04 inches (*or* less than $1/16$ inch)
1 centimeter	=	0.39 inches (*or* just under $1/2$ inch)
1 meter	=	1.09 yards (*or* about 39 inches)
1 kilometer	=	0.62 mile (*or* about $2/3$ mile)

To convert **kilometers to miles,** take the number of kilometers and multiply by .62 (for example, 25km × .62 = 15.5 miles). To convert **miles to kilometers,** take the number of miles and multiply by 1.61 (for example, 50 miles × 1.61 = 80.5 km).

Capacity

1 liter	=	33.92 ounces
	=	1.06 quarts
	=	0.26 gallons

To convert **liters to gallons,** take the number of liters and multiply by .26 (for example, 50 l × .26 = 13 gal). To convert **gallons to liters,** take the number of gallons and multiply by 3.79 (for example, 10 gal × 3.79 = 37.9 l).

Weight

1 gram	=	0.04 ounce (*or* about a paperclip's weight)
1 kilogram	=	2.2 pounds

To convert **kilograms to pounds,** take the number of kilos and multiply by 2.2 (for example, 75kg × 2.2 = 165 lbs). To convert **pounds to kilograms,** take the number of pounds and multiply by .45 (for example, 90 lb × .45 = 40.5kg).

Temperature

°C –18°   –10   0   10   20   30   40
°F   0°   10   20   32   40   50   60   70   80   90   100

To convert **degrees C to degrees F,** multiply degrees C by 9, divide by 5, and add 32 (for example $^9/_5 \times 20°C + 32 = 68°F$). To convert **degrees F to degrees C,** subtract 32 from degrees F, multiply by 5, and divide by 9 (for example: $85°F - 32 \times ^5/_9 = 29°C$).

INDEX

GENERAL INFORMATION

SIGHTS & ATTRACTIONS

TORONTO & ENVIRONS

Note: * Indicates an author's favorite

EXCURSION AREAS

ACCOMMODATIONS

TORONTO & ENVIRONS

AT THE AIRPORT

DOWNTOWN

METRO EAST

METRO WEST

MIDTOWN

UPTOWN

EXCURSION AREAS

Key to Abbreviations: B = Budget; M = Moderate; E = Expensive; VE = Very Expensive; B&B = Bed & Breakfast; * = Author's Favorite; Hs = Hostel

RESTAURANTS

TORONTO & ENVIRONS

BY CUISINE

Key to Abbreviations: IE = Inexpensive; M = Moderate; E = Expensive; VE = Very Expensive; B&B = Bed & Breakfast; * = Author's Favorite; HS = Hostel

BY LOCATION

Now Save Money On All Your Travels By Joining FROMMER'S™ TRAVEL BOOK CLUB The World's Best Travel Guides At Membership Prices!

Frommer's Travel Book Club is your ticket to successful travel! Open up a world of travel information and simplify your travel planning when you join ranks with thousands of value-conscious travelers who are members of the Frommer's *Travel Book Club*. Join today and you'll be entitled to all the privileges that come from belonging to the club that offers you travel guides for less to more than 100 destinations worldwide. **Annual membership is only $25.00 (U.S.) or $35.00 (Canada/Foreign).**

The Advantages of Membership:

1. Your choice of **three free** books (any **two** Frommer's Comprehensive Guides, Frommer's $-A-Day Guides, Frommer's Walking Tours or Frommer's Family Guides—plus **one** Frommer's City Guide, Frommer's City $-A-Day Guide or Frommer's Touring Guide).

2. Your own subscription to the **TRIPS & TRAVEL** quarterly newsletter.

3. You're entitled to a **30% discount** on your order of any additional books offered by the club.

4. You're offered (at a small additional fee) our **Domestic Trip-Routing Kits.**

Our **Trips & Travel** quarterly newsletter offers practical information on the best buys in travel, the "hottest" vacation spots, the latest travel trends, world-class events and much, much more.

Our **Domestic Trip-Routing Kits** are available for any North American destination. We'll send you a detailed map highlighting the best route to take to your destination—you can request direct or scenic routes.

Here's all you have to do to join:

Send in your membership fee of $25.00 ($35.00 Canada/Foreign) with your name and address on the form below along with your selections as part of your membership package to the address listed below. Remember to check off your three free books.

If you would like to order additional books, please select the books you would like and send a check for the total amount (please add sales tax in the states noted below), plus $2.00 per book for shipping and handling ($3.00 Canada/Foreign) to the address listed below.

FROMMER'S TRAVEL BOOK CLUB
P.O. Box 473
Mt. Morris, IL 61054-0473
(815) 734-1104

[ ] **YES!** I want to take advantage of this opportunity to join Frommer's Travel Book Club.

[ ] My check is enclosed. Dollar amount enclosed_____*

(all payments in U.S. funds only)

Name _____

Address _____

City _____ State _____ Zip _____

Phone ( ) _____(In case we have a question regarding your order).

All orders must be prepaid.

To ensure that all orders are processed efficiently, please apply sales tax in the following areas: CA, CT, FL, IL, IN, NJ, NY, PA, TN, WA and CANADA.

*With membership, shipping & handling will be paid by Frommer's Travel Book Club for the three FREE books you select as part of your membership. Please add $2.00 per book for shipping & handling for any additional books purchased ($3.00 Canada/Foreign).

Allow 4-6 weeks for delivery for all items. Prices of books, membership fee, and publication dates are subject to change without notice. All orders are subject to acceptance and availability.

Please send me the books checked below:

FROMMER'S COMPREHENSIVE GUIDES

*(Guides listing facilities from budget to deluxe,
with emphasis on the medium-priced)*

	Retail Price	Code		Retail Price	Code
☐ Acapulco/Ixtapa/Taxco, 2nd Edition	$13.95	C157	☐ Jamaica/Barbados, 2nd Edition	$15.00	C149
☐ Alaska '94-'95	$17.00	C131	☐ Japan '94-'95	$19.00	C144
☐ Arizona '95 (Avail. 3/95)	$14.95	C166	☐ Maui, 1st Edition	$14.00	C153
☐ Australia '94-'95	$18.00	C147	☐ Nepal, 2nd Edition	$18.00	C126
☐ Austria, 6th Edition	$16.95	C162	☐ New England '95	$16.95	C165
☐ Bahamas '94-'95	$17.00	C121	☐ New Mexico, 3rd Edition (Avail. 3/95)	$14.95	C167
☐ Belgium/Holland/ Luxembourg '93-'94	$18.00	C106	☐ New York State '94-'95	$19.00	C133
☐ Bermuda '94-'95	$15.00	C122	☐ Northwest, 5th Edition	$17.00	C140
☐ Brazil, 3rd Edition	$20.00	C111	☐ Portugal '94-'95	$17.00	C141
☐ California '95	$16.95	C164	☐ Puerto Rico '95-'96	$14.00	C151
☐ Canada '94-'95	$19.00	C145	☐ Puerto Vallarta/ Manzanillo/Guadalajara '94-'95	$14.00	C135
☐ Caribbean '95	$18.00	C148			
☐ Carolinas/Georgia, 2nd Edition	$17.00	C128	☐ Scandinavia, 16th Edition (Avail. 3/95)	$19.95	C169
☐ Colorado, 2nd Edition	$16.00	C143	☐ Scotland '94-'95	$17.00	C146
☐ Costa Rica '95	$13.95	C161	☐ South Pacific '94-'95	$20.00	C138
☐ Cruises '95-'96	$19.00	C150	☐ Spain, 16th Edition	$16.95	C163
☐ Delaware/Maryland '94-'95	$15.00	C136	☐ Switzerland/ Liechtenstein '94-'95	$19.00	C139
☐ England '95	$17.95	C159	☐ Thailand, 2nd Edition	$17.95	C154
☐ Florida '95	$18.00	C152	☐ U.S.A., 4th Edition	$18.95	C156
☐ France '94-'95	$20.00	C132	☐ Virgin Islands '94-'95	$13.00	C127
☐ Germany '95	$18.95	C158	☐ Virginia '94-'95	$14.00	C142
☐ Ireland, 1st Edition (Avail. 3/95)	$16.95	C168	☐ Yucatan, 2nd Edition	$13.95	C155
☐ Italy '95	$18.95	C160			

FROMMER'S $-A-DAY GUIDES

(Guides to low-cost tourist accommodations and facilities)

	Retail Price	Code		Retail Price	Code
☐ Australia on $45 '95-'96	$18.00	D122	☐ Israel on $45, 15th Edition	$16.95	D130
☐ Costa Rica/Guatemala/ Belize on $35, 3rd Edition	$15.95	D126	☐ Mexico on $45 '95	$16.95	D125
☐ Eastern Europe on $30, 5th Edition	$16.95	D129	☐ New York on $70 '94-'95	$16.00	D121
☐ England on $60 '95	$17.95	D128	☐ New Zealand on $45 '93-'94	$18.00	D103
☐ Europe on $50 '95	$17.95	D127	☐ South America on $40, 16th Edition	$18.95	D123
☐ Greece on $45 '93-'94	$19.00	D100	☐ Washington, D.C. on $50 '94-'95	$17.00	D120
☐ Hawaii on $75 '95	$16.95	D124			
☐ Ireland on $45 '94-'95	$17.00	D118			

FROMMER'S CITY $-A-DAY GUIDES

	Retail Price	Code		Retail Price	Code
☐ Berlin on $40 '94-'95	$12.00	D111	☐ Madrid on $50 '94-'95	$13.00	D119
☐ London on $45 '94-'95	$12.00	D114	☐ Paris on $50 '94-'95	$12.00	D117

FROMMER'S FAMILY GUIDES

(Guides listing information on kid-friendly hotels, restaurants, activities and attractions)

	Retail Price	Code		Retail Price	Code
☐ California with Kids	$18.00	F100	☐ San Francisco with Kids	$17.00	F104
☐ Los Angeles with Kids	$17.00	F103	☐ Washington, D.C. with Kids	$17.00	F102
☐ New York City with Kids	$18.00	F101			

FROMMER'S CITY GUIDES

(Pocket-size guides to sightseeing and tourist accommodations and facilities in all price ranges)

	Retail Price	Code		Retail Price	Code
☐ Amsterdam '93-'94	$13.00	S110	☐ Montreal/Quebec City '95	$11.95	S166
☐ Athens, 10th Edition (Avail. 3/95)	$12.95	S174	☐ Nashville/Memphis, 1st Edition	$13.00	S141
☐ Atlanta '95	$12.95	S161	☐ New Orleans '95	$12.95	S148
☐ Atlantic City/Cape May, 5th Edition	$13.00	S130	☐ New York '95	$12.95	S152
☐ Bangkok, 2nd Edition	$12.95	S147	☐ Orlando '95	$13.00	S145
☐ Barcelona '93-'94	$13.00	S115	☐ Paris '95	$12.95	S150
☐ Berlin, 3rd Edition	$12.95	S162	☐ Philadelphia, 8th Edition	$12.95	S167
☐ Boston '95	$12.95	S160	☐ Prague '94-'95	$13.00	S143
☐ Budapest, 1st Edition	$13.00	S139	☐ Rome, 10th Edition	$12.95	S168
☐ Chicago '95	$12.95	S169	☐ St. Louis/Kansas City, 2nd Edition	$13.00	S127
☐ Denver/Boulder/Colorado Springs, 3rd Edition	$12.95	S154	☐ San Diego '95	$12.95	S158
☐ Dublin, 2nd Edition	$12.95	S157	☐ San Francisco '95	$12.95	S155
☐ Hong Kong '94-'95	$13.00	S140	☐ Santa Fe/Taos/ Albuquerque '95 (Avail. 2/95)	$12.95	S172
☐ Honolulu/Oahu '95	$12.95	S151			
☐ Las Vegas '95	$12.95	S163	☐ Seattle/Portland '94-'95	$13.00	S137
☐ London '95	$12.95	S156	☐ Sydney, 4th Edition	$12.95	S171
☐ Los Angeles '95	$12.95	S164	☐ Tampa/St. Petersburg, 3rd Edition	$13.00	S146
☐ Madrid/Costa del Sol, 2nd Edition	$12.95	S165	☐ Tokyo '94-'95	$13.00	S144
☐ Mexico City, 1st Edition	$12.95	S170	☐ Toronto '95 (Avail. 3/95)	$12.95	S173
☐ Miami '95-'96	$12.95	S149	☐ Vancouver/Victoria '94-'95	$13.00	S142
☐ Minneapolis/St. Paul, 4th Edition	$12.95	S159	☐ Washington, D.C. '95	$12.95	S153

FROMMER'S WALKING TOURS

*(Companion guides that point out the places
and pleasures that make a city unique)*

	Retail Price	Code		Retail Price	Code
☐ Berlin	$12.00	W100	☐ New York	$12.00	W102
☐ Chicago	$12.00	W107	☐ Paris	$12.00	W103
☐ England's Favorite Cities	$12.00	W108	☐ San Francisco	$12.00	W104
☐ London	$12.00	W101	☐ Washington, D.C.	$12.00	W105
☐ Montreal/Quebec City	$12.00	W106			

SPECIAL EDITIONS

	Retail Price	Code		Retail Price	Code
☐ Bed & Breakfast Southwest	$16.00	P100	☐ National Park Guide, 29th Edition	$17.00	P106
☐ Bed & Breakfast Great American Cities	$16.00	P104	☐ Where to Stay U.S.A., 11th Edition	$15.00	P102
☐ Caribbean Hideaways	$16.00	P103			

FROMMER'S TOURING GUIDES

*(Color-illustrated guides that include walking tours,
cultural and historic sites, and practical information)*

	Retail Price	Code		Retail Price	Code
☐ Amsterdam	$11.00	T001	☐ New York	$11.00	T008
☐ Barcelona	$14.00	T015	☐ Rome	$11.00	T010
☐ Brazil	$11.00	T003	☐ Tokyo	$15.00	T016
☐ Hong Kong/Singapore/ Macau	$11.00	T006	☐ Turkey	$11.00	T013
☐ London	$13.00	T007	☐ Venice	$9.00	T014

*Please note: If the availability of a book is several months away, we may
have back issues of guides to that particular destination.
Call customer service at (815) 734-1104.*